Official Autodesk Training Guide

Learning
Autodesk® Maya®
2008

Foundation

D1378412

Autodesk

Acknowledgments

Art Direction:
Michiel Schriever

Sr. Graphic Designer:
Luke Pauw

Cover Image:
© 2007 Sony Pictures Animation, Inc.
All Rights Reserved.

Copy Editor:
Claire Tacon

Technical Editor:
Julio Lopez

DVD Production:
Roark Andrade, Peter Verboom

Project Manager:
Lenni Rodrigues

Content Marketing Manager:
Carmela Bourassa

Director – Products, Planning and Tools
Michael Stamler

Special thanks go out to:

Mariann Barsolo, Tonya Holder, Robert Lin, Katriona Lord-Levins, Heather McDiarmid and Mary Ruijs.

This book would not have been possible without the generous support of Sony Pictures Animation Inc. We would like to extend a special thank you to Rebecca Aghakhan-Mooshiabad, Erik Borzi, Rachel Falikoff, Melissa Sturm, David Hail, Andrea Pace, Jerry Schmitz, Sande Scoredos and Kristen Tarnol.

Primary Author

Marc-André Guindon, NeoReel

Marc-André Guindon is the founder of NeoReel Inc. (*www.NeoReel.com*), a Montreal based production facility. He is an Autodesk® Maya® Master and an advanced user of Autodesk® MotionBuilder™ software. Marc-André and NeoReel have partnered with Autodesk Inc. on several projects, including *The Art of Maya* and the *Learning Maya* series from version 6.0 to present. NeoReel was also a driving force behind the Maya Techniques™ DVDs, such as *How to Integrate Quadrupeds into a Production Pipeline* and *Maya and Alias MotionBuilder*.

www.NeoReel.com

Marc-André has established complex pipelines and developed numerous plug-ins and tools, such as *Animation Layers* for Maya, for a variety of projects in both the film and game industries. His latest film projects include pre-visualisation on *Journey 3-D* (Walden Media), as well as *Unearthed* (Ambush Entertainment), *XXX: State of the Union* (Revolution Studios), *Scooby-Doo™ 2* (Warner Bros. Pictures) and *Dawn of the Dead* (Universal Pictures). He also served in the game industry to integrate motion capture for *Prey* (2K Games) for the Xbox 360™, *Arena Football™: Road to Glory* (EA Sports) and the *Outlaw Game Series: Outlaw Volleyball™, Outlaw Golf™* and *Outlaw Tennis™* (Hypnotix).

Marc-André continues to seek challenges for himself, NeoReel and his talented crew.

Contributing Author

Cathy McGinnis

Cathy McGinnis is an Autodesk Certified Instructor who worked as a lighting TD at Weta Digital in Wellington, New Zealand. Prior to moving down under, Cathy was a technical product specialist for Autodesk, specializing in rendering in both Maya and mental ray for Maya. Cathy has been a Maya trainer since the birth of the software and has been a contributor to several Autodesk publications including *Learning Maya 8| Foundation, Learning Maya 7 | The Modeling & Animation Handbook* and *Learning Maya 7|The Special Effects Handbook*.

About *Surf's Up*

A few minutes into Surf's Up and it is clear this is not your typical animated movie—the characters interact with the camera, there is a retro film clip straight out of the 1970s and the water looks so good that you just want to dive in.

The film follows Cody Maverick, a penguin who leaves his hometown of Shiverpool, Antarctica to follow in the footsteps of his idol, surfing legend "Big Z." Surf's Up is the second feature length animated picture from Sony Pictures Animation, and stars Jeff Bridges and Shia LaBeouf, with cameos from professional surfers Kelly Slater and Rob Machado. The movie was produced by Christopher Jenkins and directed by Ash Brannon (Toy Story 2™) and Chris Buck (Tarzan™) and uses a documentary style, drawing from the traditions of both the great surf films and Christopher Guest mockumentaries.

"This was a really fun movie to get to do research for," Rob Bredow, Visual Effect Supervisor explains, "because it was penguins and surfing, which are two fun things." To prepare for such an ambitious project, the team at Sony Pictures Imageworks went on some unusual field trips. "We took our entire crew surfing," Bredow says, "We got a group to give us surf lessons—mostly I think we learned what it felt like to wipe out."

To help capture the look of the penguins, many of the character animators, modelers and riggers also went to SeaWorld to collect reference images. Mike Ford, Character Set-up Supervisor, explains "They really opened up their doors and showed us the behind-the-scenes of the penguin encounter. We got to go in and be really close to Emperor penguins; see how dense the feathers are. That inspired us to take it where we went."

The characters and sets were designed to look quite natural, in keeping with the documentary feel, but they still have the heightened look possible with animation. For instance, while the texturing on the feathers is almost photo-realistic, the characters have stylized markings on their sides. David Schaub, Animation Director at Sony Imageworks, describes how, "All the lead penguins have different patterns—unique lines for Cody and Lani, Big Z has the hibiscus edge and Tank has his bad boy tattoos."

One of the things that make Surf's Up unique is the documentary style, which incorporates archival images such as paintings, magazine articles, vintage postcards, film clips and even hieroglyphics. "One of the great things about the movie," Bredow says, "was getting to create all the history behind the movie." To make the archival material look authentic, the team paid close attention to detail. Bredow reveals that, "We got some old stock footage with real scratches that had really been aged over the years and then extracted all those scratches and recomposited them over our work."

It can be argued that the water plays as big a role in Surf's Up as the penguins. From the inky waters in Antarctica to the turquoise waves on Pen Gu Island, the water reflects the mood of the scene and acts as a physical and emotional obstacle. It is the first movie to tackle so much animated water, with characters moving through, over, and under the surface. "The biggest challenge in this movie was the waves," Bredow says. "Water is always a challenge, but especially breaking waves—that's kind of the holy grail of water simulation. We wanted the audience to feel that they had ridden the waves themselves when they walked out of the theatre."

"The directors had always talked about the wave being a character," Ford says, "So we took that to heart and said let's make it a character as part of our character pipeline."

"We animated them like a character," Bredow explains, "but of course waves don't have bones, so you don't animate them the traditional way—we used a series of blend shapes to control the movement of the waves."

To make the surfing look more natural, various details were added to the water during animation, including wake trails and splash. To create the effect of the sea foam around the board, Schaub says that "a particle system was built, so that when the lip comes crashing over the top of the wave and hits the water, it triggers an explosion of white water that we can see interactively in the animator's file. This gave us a pretty accurate representation of the ultimate shape and volume of the white water before it gets rendered in effects."

While the team used a combination of software to create the final water animation, much of it was done in Autodesk® Maya® software. "Maya is the core of the front-end pipeline at Sony Imageworks," Ford explains, "It is used for modeling, layout, animation, and some effects work." By leveraging the power of Maya Embedded Language (MEL) Python® and the Maya's API, the team customized the software to overcome many of the film's challenges. Schaub comments that, "We never have the question, 'well can the software do that?' Because if it doesn't, the way the program is built allows us to create a tool that will do that."

Although the movie has a lot of action, one of the strongest scenes in the film is a quieter moment, where Cody and his hero, Big Z, carve a surfboard together. At over 1800 frames, it is a much longer sequence than is typical in an animated movie, where clips rarely run longer than a few hundred frames. "There was concern that it wouldn't hold up as a performance in the movie because it's so long," Schaub admits, "but we really wanted to prove that we could do this. You rarely get to do these long bits of performance, and it was great to have these extended moments where you could really let the characters perform."

"Whenever you get a scene that is that long," Ford says, "you get an animator working on it for months." To overcome this production obstacle, they had to find ways to break up the sequence so that the animation could keep moving down the pipeline. Schaub explains that, "We found convenient break points by acting the scene out ahead of time. Layout would set up a session with four or five different cameras placed the way they would be if they were filming it on set." Once the sequence was performed and filmed, the directors reviewed the footage and decided where the cuts could logically go.

Of course, animation is only half of the performance and the scene also succeeds because of the remarkable voice talent. In traditional animation, actors typically record their lines individually in separate voiceover sessions, which can create a canned feel. Surf's Up breaks new ground because the actors were in the same room, which allowed them to improvise. Ford says that, "A lot of people have commented that the dialogue felt like the characters were really there, actually interacting with each other, and that's because they actually were."

Since its release, the critical feedback for Surf's Up has been glowing, as Bredow can attest. "People who have seen the movie have really appreciated the attention to detail that has gone into it. The question that I've loved getting from various people is 'How did you paint out the surfers and put the penguins in?'"

Table of Contents

Project 03

Project 04

Project 05

How to use this book

How you use *Learning Autodesk Maya 2008 | Foundation* will depend on your experience with computer graphics and 3D animation. This book moves at a fast pace and is designed to help you develop your 3D skills. If this is your first experience with 3D software, we suggested that you read through each lesson and watch the accompanying demo files on the DVD, which may help clarify the steps for you before you begin to work through the tutorial projects. If you are already familiar with Maya software or another 3D package, you might choose to look through the book's index to focus on those areas you'd like to improve.

Updates to this book

In an effort to ensure your continued success with the lessons in this book, please visit our web site for the latest available updates: *www.autodesk.com/learningtools-updates*

Windows and Macintosh

This book is written to cover Windows® and Macintosh® platforms. Graphics and text have been modified where applicable. You may notice that your screen varies slightly from the illustrations, depending on the platform you are using.

Things to watch for:

Window focus may differ. For example, if you are on Windows, you have to click on the panel with your middle mouse button to make it active.

To select multiple attributes in Windows, use the **Ctrl** key. On Macintosh, use the **Command** key. To modify pivot position in Windows, use the **Insert** key. On Macintosh, use the **Home** key.

Autodesk packaging

This book can be used with either **Autodesk® Maya® Complete 2008, Autodesk® Maya® Unlimited 2008**, or the corresponding version of **Autodesk® Maya® Personal Learning Edition** software, as the lessons included here focus on functionality shared among all three software packages.

As a bonus feature, this hands-on book will also introduce you to compositing in Autodesk® Combustion®.

Learning Autodesk Maya DVD-ROM

The Learning Autodesk Maya DVD-ROM contains several resources to accelerate your learning experience including:

- Learning Maya support files
- Instructor-led podcasts to guide you through the projects in the book
- A link to a trial version of Autodesk® Combustion® software
- Autodesk Maya reference guides

Installing support files

Before beginning the lessons in this book, you will need to install the support files. Copy the *project* directories found in the *support_files* folder on the DVD disc to the *Maya\projects* directory on your computer. Launch Maya and set the project by going to **File** → **Project** → **Set...** and selecting the appropriate project.

Windows: C:\Documents and Settings\username\My Documents\maya\projects

Macintosh: Macintosh HD:Users:username:Documents:maya:projects

Understanding Maya

To understand Autodesk® Maya® software, it helps to understand how it works at a conceptual level. This introduction is designed to give you the *story* about Maya. In other words, the focus of this introduction will be on how different Maya concepts are woven together to create an integrated workspace.

While this book teaches you how to model, animate and render, these concepts are taught with a particular focus on how the underlying architecture in Maya supports the creation of animated sequences.

You will soon learn that the Maya architecture can be explained by a single line—*nodes with attributes that are connected*. As you work through the book, the meaning of this statement will become clearer and you will learn to appreciate how the Maya interface lets you focus on the act of creation, while giving you access to the power inherent in the underlying architecture.

The user interface (UI)

The Maya user interface (UI) includes a number of tools, editors and controls. You can access these using the main menus or special context-sensitive marking menus. You can also use *shelves* to store important icons or hotkeys to speed up workflow. Maya is designed to let you configure the UI as you see fit.

To work with objects, you can enter values using coordinate entry or you can use more interactive 3D manipulators. Manipulator handles let you edit your objects with a simple click+drag.

The Maya UI supports multiple levels of *undo* and *redo* and includes a drag-and-drop paradigm for accessing many parts of the workspace.

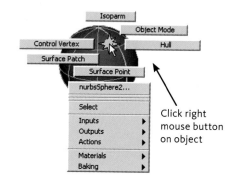

Click right mouse button on object

Marking menu

Working in 3D

In Maya, you will build and animate objects in three dimensions. These dimensions are defined by the cardinal axes that are labeled as X, Y and Z. These represent the length (X), height (Y) and depth (Z) of your scene. These axes are represented by colors—red for X, green for Y and blue for Z.

The Maya default has the Y-axis pointing up (also referred to as *Y-up*).

As you position, scale and rotate your objects, these three axes will serve as your main points of reference. The center of this coordinate system is called the origin and has a value of 0, 0, 0.

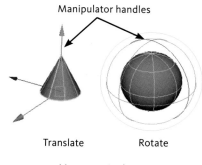

Manipulator handles

Translate   Rotate

Maya manipulators

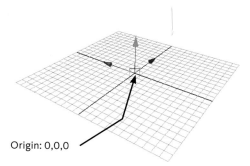

Origin: 0,0,0

The cardinal axes

UV coordinate space

As you build surfaces in Maya, they are created with their own coordinate space that is defined by U in one direction and V in another. You can use these coordinates when you are working with *curve-on-surface* objects or when you are positioning textures on a surface.

One corner of the surface acts as the origin of the system and all coordinates lie directly on the surface.

You can make surfaces *live* in order to work directly in the UV coordinate space. You will also encounter U and V attributes when you place textures onto surfaces.

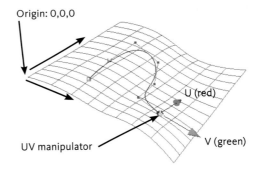

UV coordinates on a live surface

Views

In Maya, you visualize your scenes using view panels that let you see into the 3D world.

Perspective views let you see your scene as if you were looking at it with your own eyes or through the lens of a camera.

Orthographic views are parallel to the scene and offer a more objective view. They focus on two axes at a time and are referred to as the *top*, *side* and *front* views.

In many cases, you will require several views to help you define the proper location of your objects. An object's position that looks good in the top view may not make sense in a side view. Maya lets you view multiple views at one time to help coordinate what you see.

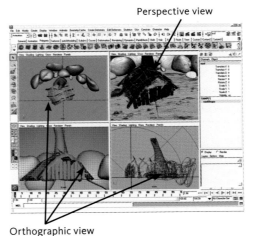

Orthographic and Perspective views

Cameras

To achieve a particular view, you look through a digital camera. An Orthographic camera defines the view using a parallel plane and a direction, while a Perspective camera uses an *eye point*, a *look at point* and a *focal length*.

Perspective and Orthographic cameras

Image planes

When you work with cameras, it is possible to attach special backdrop objects called *image planes* to the camera. An image plane can be placed onto the camera so that as the camera moves, the plane stays aligned.

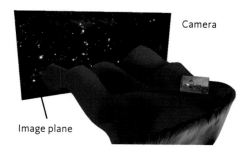

Camera

Image plane

Image plane attached to a camera

Image plane seen looking through the camera

The image plane has several attributes that allow you to track and scale the image. These attributes can be animated to give the appearance that the plane is moving.

THE DEPENDENCY GRAPH

The Maya system architecture uses a procedural paradigm that lets you integrate traditional keyframe animation, inverse kinematics, dynamics and scripting into a node-based architecture that is called the **Dependency Graph**. As mentioned on the first page of this introduction, the Dependency Graph could be described as *nodes with attributes that are connected*. This node-based architecture gives Maya its flexible procedural qualities.

Below is a diagram showing a primitive sphere's Dependency Graph. A procedural input node defines the shape of the sphere by connecting attributes on each node.

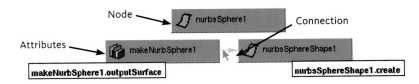

The Dependency Graph

Nodes

Every element, whether it is a curve, surface, deformer, light, texture, expression, modeling operation or animation curve, is described by either a single node or a series of connected nodes.

A *node* is a generic object type. Different nodes are designed with specific attributes so that the node can accomplish a specific task. Nodes define all object types including geometry, shading and lighting.

Shown below are three typical node types as they appear on a primitive sphere:

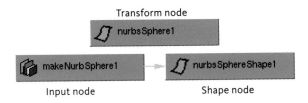

Node types on a sphere

Transform nodes contain positioning information for your objects. When you move, rotate or scale, this is the node you are affecting.

Shape nodes contain all the component information that represents the actual look of the sphere.

Input nodes represent options that drive the creation of your sphere's shape such as radius or endsweep.

The Maya UI presents these nodes to you in many ways. On the right is an image of the Channel Box where you can edit and animate node attributes.

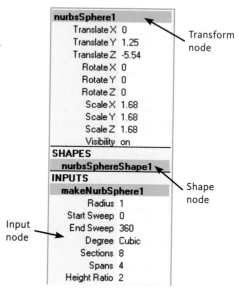

Channel Box

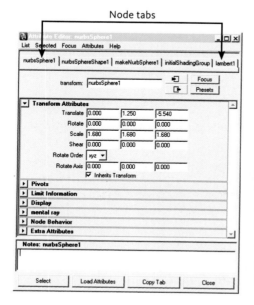

Attribute Editor

Attributes

Each node is defined by a series of attributes that relate to what the node is designed to accomplish. In the case of a transform node, *X Translate* is an attribute. In the case of a shader node, *Color Red* is an attribute. It is possible for you to assign values to the attributes. You can work with attributes in a number of UI windows including the *Attribute Editor*, the *Channel Box* and the *Spread Sheet Editor*.

One important feature is that you can animate virtually every attribute on any node.

This helps give Maya its animation power. You should note that attributes are also referred to as *channels*.

Connections

Nodes don't exist in isolation. A finished animation results when you begin making connections between attributes on different nodes. These connections are also known as *dependencies*. In modeling, these connections are sometimes referred to as *construction history*.

Most of these connections are created automatically by the Maya UI as a result of using commands or tools. If you desire, you can also build and edit these connections explicitly using the *Connection Editor*, by entering *MEL* (Maya Embedded Language) commands, or by writing MEL-based expressions.

Pivots

Transform nodes are all built with a special component known as the pivot point. Just like your arm pivots around your elbow, the pivot helps you rotate a transform node. By changing the location of the pivot point, you get different results.

Pivots are basically the stationary point from which you rotate or scale objects. When animating, you sometimes need to build hierarchies where one transform node rotates the object and a second transform node scales. Each node can have its own pivot location to help you get the effect you want.

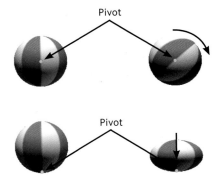

Rotation and scaling pivots

Hierarchies

When you are building scenes, you have learned that you can build dependency connections to link node attributes. When working with transform nodes or joint nodes, you can also build hierarchies, which create a different kind of relationship between your objects.

In a hierarchy, one transform node is *parented* to another. When Maya works with these nodes, it looks first at the top node, or *root* node, then down the hierarchy. Therefore, motion from the upper nodes is transferred down into the lower nodes. In the diagram below, if the *group1* node is rotated, then the two lower nodes will rotate with it.
If the *nurbsCone* node is rotated, the upper nodes are not affected.

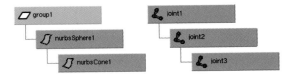

Object and joint hierarchy nodes

Joint hierarchies are used when you are building characters. When you create joints, the joint pivots act as limb joints while bones are drawn between them to help visualize the joint chain. By default, these hierarchies work just like object hierarchies. Rotating one node rotates all of the lower nodes at the same time.

You will learn more about joint hierarchies later in this introduction (see "Skeletons and Joints"), where you will also learn how *inverse kinematics* can reverse the flow of the hierarchy.

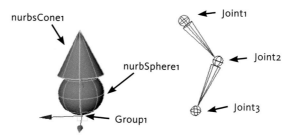

Object and joint hierarchies

MEL & Python scripting

MEL™ stands for Maya Embedded Language. In Maya, every time you use a tool or open a window, you are using MEL. MEL can be used to execute simple commands, write expressions or build scripts that will extend the Maya software's existing functionality of the software. The Script Editor displays commands and feedback generated by scripts and tools. Simple MEL commands can be typed in the Command Line, while more complex MEL scripts can be typed in the Script Editor.

Python™ scripting is for programmers who would like to implement their tools using an alternate and popular scripting language. The implementation of Python scripting in Maya provides the same access to native Maya commands as is provided through MEL. Note that only the built-in Maya commands are accessible through Python programming language.

Scripting is the perfect tool for technical directors who are looking to customize Maya to suit the needs of a particular production environment. Animators can also use scripting to create simple macros that will help speed up more difficult or tedious workflows.

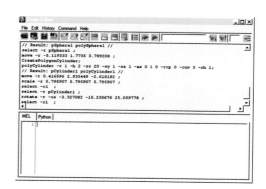

The Script Editor

ANIMATION

When you animate, you bring objects to life. There are several different ways in which you can animate your scenes and the characters who inhabit them.

Animation is generally measured using frames that mimic the frames you would find on a film reel. You can play these frames at different speeds to achieve an animated effect. By default, Maya plays at 24 frames per second, or 24FPS.

Keyframe animation

The most familiar method of animating is called *keyframe animation*. Using this technique, you determine how you want the parts of your objects to look at a particular frame, then you save the important attributes as keys. After you set several keys, the animation can be played back with Maya filling motion in between the keys.

When keys are set on a particular attribute, the keyed values are stored in special nodes called *animation curve* nodes.

These curves are defined by the keys that map the value of the attribute against time. The following is an example of several animation curve nodes connected to a transformation node. One node is created for every attribute that is animated.

Once you have a curve, you can begin to control the tangency at each key to tweak the motion in between the main keys. You can make your objects speed up or slow down by editing the shape of these animation curves.

Generally, the slope of the graph curve tells you the speed of the motion. A steep slope in the curve means fast motion, while a flat curve equals no motion. Think of a skier going down a hill. Steep slopes increase speed while flatter sections slow things down.

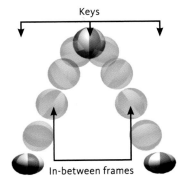

Keys and in between frames

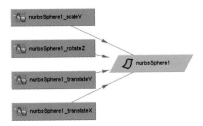

Dependency Graph showing curve nodes

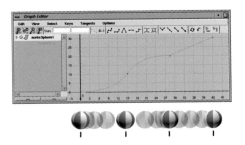

Graph Editor

Path animation

Path animation is already defined by its name. You can assign one or more objects so that they move along a path that has been drawn as a curve in 3D space. You can then use the shape of the curve and special path markers to edit and tweak the resulting motion.

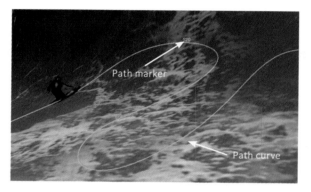

Path animation

Non-linear animation

Non-linear animation is a way to layer and mix character animation sequences independently of time. You can layer and blend any type of keyed animation, including motion capture and path animation. This is accomplished through the Trax Editor.

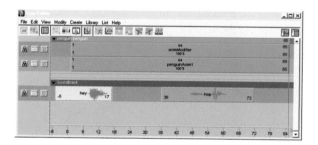

Trax Editor

Reactive animation

Reactive animation is a term used to describe animation in which one object's animation is based on the animation of another object.

An example of this technique would be moving gears when the rotation of one gear is linked to the rotation of other gears. You can set keys on the first gear and all the others will animate automatically. Later, when you want to edit or tweak the keys, only one object needs to be worked on and the others update reactively.

Diagram of animated gears

You can set up reactive animation using a number of tools including those outlined below:

Set Driven Key

This tool lets you interactively set up an attribute on one object to drive one or more attributes on another.

Expressions

Expressions are scripts that let you connect different attributes on different nodes.

Constraints

Constraints let you set-up an object to *point at*, *orient to* or *look at* another object.

Connections

Attributes can be directly linked to another attribute using dependency node connections. You can create this kind of direct connection using the Connection Editor.

DYNAMICS

Another animation technique is *dynamics*. You can set up objects in your scene that animate based on physical effects such as collisions, gravity and wind. Different variables are *bounciness*, *friction* or *initial velocity*. When you play back the scene, you run a simulation to see how all the parts react to the variables.

This technique gives you natural motion that would be difficult to keyframe. You can use dynamics with rigid body objects, particles or soft body objects.

Rigid body objects are objects that don't deform. You can further edit the rigid body by setting it as either *active* or *passive*. Active bodies react to the dynamics, whereas passive bodies don't.

To simulate effects such as wind or gravity, you add *fields* to your dynamic objects.

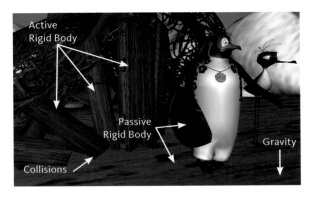

Rigid body simulation of surfboard and house colliding

Particles are tiny points that can be used to create effects such as smoke, fire or explosions. These points are emitted into the scene where they are also affected by the dynamic fields.

Particles   *Soft bodies*

Soft bodies are surfaces that you deform during a simulation. To create a soft body, create an object and turn its points into particles. The particles react to the dynamic forces, which in turn deform the surface.

MODELING

The objects you want to animate are usually built using either NURBS surfaces or polygonal meshes. Complementary to these two basic geometry types, subdivision surfaces (SubDs), mix the best features of both NURBS and polygons. Maya offers you both of these geometry types so that you can choose the method best suited to your work.

NURBS curves

NURBS stands for *non-uniform rational b-spline* which is a technical term for a spline curve. By modeling with NURBS curves, you lay down control points and smooth geometry will be created using the points as guides.

Shown below is a typical NURBS curve with important parts labeled:

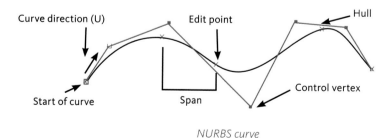

NURBS curve

These key components define important aspects of how a curve works. The flexibility and power of NURBS geometry comes from your ability to edit the shape of the geometry using these controls.

As your geometry becomes more complex, you may need more of these controls. For this reason, it is usually better to start out with simpler geometry so that you can more easily control the shape. If you need more complex geometry, then controls can be inserted later.

NURBS surfaces

Surfaces are defined using the same mathematics as curves, except now they're in two dimensions—U and V. You learned about this earlier when you learned about UV coordinate space.

Below are some of the component elements of a typical NURBS surface:

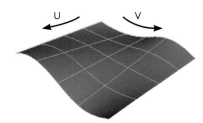

NURBS surface

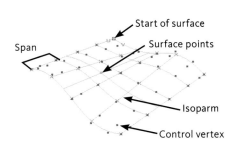

NURBS components

Completed NURBS model

Complex shapes can be, in essence, sculpted using this surface type as you push and pull the controls to shape the surface.

Polygons

Polygons are the most basic geometry type available. Whereas NURBS surfaces interpolate the shape of the geometry interactively, polygonal meshes draw the geometry directly to the control vertices.

Below are some of the components found on a polygonal mesh:

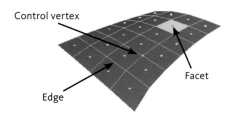

Polygon components

You can build up polymeshes by extruding, scaling and positioning polygonal facets to build shapes. You can then smooth the shape to get a more organic look for your model.

Polygonal model before and after smoothing

Subdivision surfaces

Subdivision surfaces exhibit characteristics of both polygon and NURBS surfaces, allowing you to model smooth forms using comparatively few control vertices. They enable you to create levels of detail exactly where you want.

Construction history

When you create models, the various steps are recorded as dependency nodes that remain connected to your surface.

In the example below, a curve has been used to create a revolved surface. Maya keeps the history by creating dependencies between the curve, a revolve node and the shape node. Edits made to the curve or the revolve node will update the final shape.

Many of these nodes come with special manipulators that make it easier to update the node attributes. In the case of the revolve, manipulators are available for the axis line and for the revolve's sweep angle.

It is possible to later delete history so that you are only working with the shape node. Don't forget though, that the dependency nodes have attributes that can be animated. Therefore, you lose some power if you delete history.

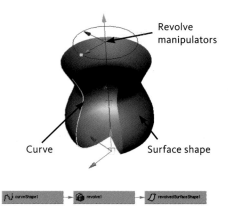

Revolve surface with dependencies

DEFORMATIONS

Deformers are special object types that can be used to reshape other objects. By using deformers, you can model different shapes, or give animations more of a squash and stretch quality.

Deformers are a powerful Maya feature—they can even be layered for more subtle effects. You can also bind deformers into skeletons or affect them with soft body dynamics.

The following shows some basic deformer types that are available:

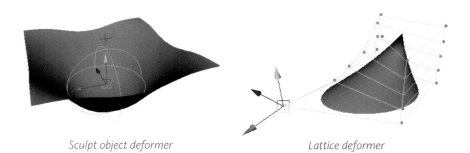

Sculpt object deformer   *Lattice deformer*

Sculpt objects

Sculpt objects lets you deform a surface by pushing it with the object. By animating the position of the sculpt object, you can achieve animated surface deformations.

Lattices

Lattices are external frames that can be applied to your objects. If you then reshape the frame the object is deformed in response.

Clusters

Clusters are groups of CVs or lattice points that are built into a single set. The cluster is given its own pivot point and can be used to manipulate the clustered points. You can weight the CVs in a cluster for more control over a deformation.

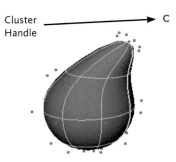

Cluster deformer

CHARACTER ANIMATION

Character animation typically involves the animation of surfaces using skeleton joint chains and inverse kinematic handles to help drive the motion.

Skeletons and joints

As you have already learned, skeleton joint chains are actually hierarchies. A skeleton is made of joint nodes that are connected visually by bone icons. Binding geometry to these hierarchies lets you create surface deformations when the joints are rotated.

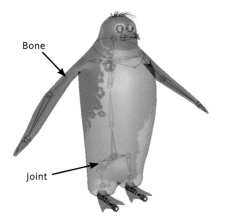

Joints and bones

Inverse kinematics

By default, joint hierarchies work like any other hierarchy—the rotation of one joint is transferred to the lower joint nodes. This is known as *forward kinematics*. While this method is powerful, it makes it hard to plant a character's feet or move a hand to control the arm.

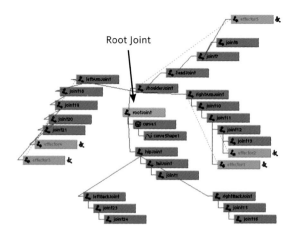

Root Joint

Character joint hierarchy

Inverse kinematics lets you work with the hierarchy in the opposite direction. By placing an IK handle at the end of the joint chain, Maya will solve all rotations within that joint chain. This is a lot quicker than animating every single joint in the hierarchy. There are three kinds of inverse kinematic solvers—the IK spline, the IK single chain and the IK rotate plane.

Each of these solvers is designed to help you control the joint rotations with the use of an IK handle. As the IK handle is moved, the solver solves joint rotations that allow the end joint to properly move to the IK handle position.

The individual solvers have their own unique controls. Some of these are outlined below:

Single chain solver

The *single chain solver* provides a straightforward mechanism for posing and animating a chain.

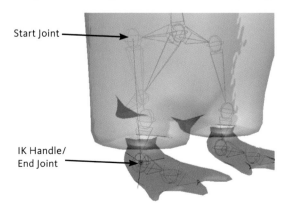

Start Joint

IK Handle/
End Joint

IK single chain solver

Rotate plane solver

The *rotate plane solver* gives you more control. With this solver, the plane that acts as the goal for all the joints can be moved by rotating the plane using a *twist attribute* or by moving the *pole vector handle*.

IK spline solver

The IK spline solver lets you control the chain using a spline curve. You can edit the CVs on the spline to influence the rotation of the joints in the chain.

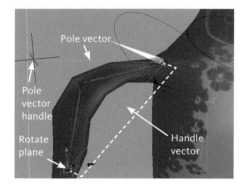

IK spline solver

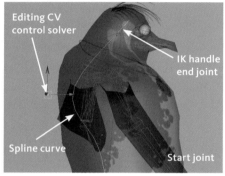

IK rotate plane solver

Skinning your characters

Once you have a skeleton built, you can bind skin to the surfaces of your character so that they deform with the rotation of the joints. You can use either soft skinning or hard skinning. Smooth skinning uses weighted clusters while rigid skinning does not.

Surface deformations

Flexors

In some cases, skinning a character does not yield realistic deformations in the character's joint areas. You can use *flexors* to add this secondary level of deformations to help control the tucking and bulging of your character.

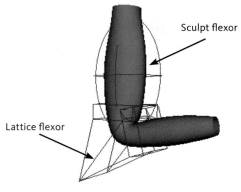

Flexors

RENDERING

Once your characters are set up, you can apply color and texture, then render with realistic lighting.

Shading networks

Adding texture maps and other rendering nodes create shading networks. At the end of every shading network is a shading group node. This node has specific attributes such as displacement maps and mental ray® software for Maya ports, but more importantly, it contains a list of objects that are to be shaded by that network at render time. Without this node at the end of the network, the shader won't render.

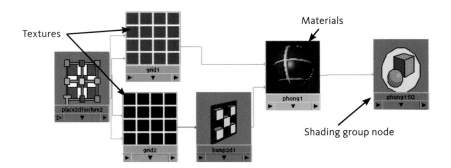

Shading group dependencies

You can think of a shading network as a bucket into which you place all the color, texture and material qualities that you want for your surface. Add a light or two and your effect is achieved.

Texture maps

To add detail to your shading groups, you can *texture map* different attributes. Some of these include bump, transparency and color.

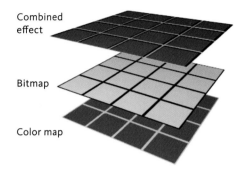

Combined effect

Bitmap

Color map

Texture map layers

Lighting

You can add light to your scenes using any number of lights. These lights let you add mood and atmosphere to a scene in much the same way as lighting is used by a photographer. You can preview your lights interactively as you model, or you can render to see the final effect.

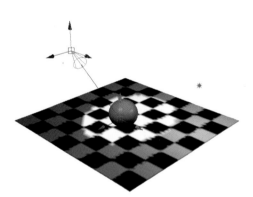

Light manipulator

Motion blur

When a real-life camera takes a shot of a moving object the final image is often blurred. This *motion blur* adds to the animated look of a scene and can be simulated in Maya. There are two types of motion blur—a 2 1/2 D solution and a 3D solution.

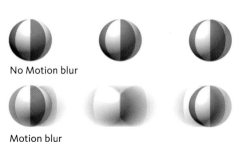

No Motion blur

Motion blur

Motion blur

Hardware rendering

Hardware rendering uses the power of your graphics card to render an image. This is a quick way to render as the quality can be very good or it can be used to preview animations. You will need to use the hardware renderer to render most particle effects. These effects can be composited in later with software rendered images of your geometry.

Hardware rendering

A-buffer rendering

The Maya rendering architecture is a hybrid renderer. It uses an EAS (Exact Area Sampling) or A-buffer algorithm for primary visibility from the eye (camera), and then raytraces any secondary rays.

A-buffer rendering

Raytrace rendering

Raytracing lets you include reflections, refractions and raytrace shadows into your scenes. Only objects that have their raytrace options turned on will use this renderer. Raytracing is slower than the A-buffer algorithm and should only be used when necessary.

Raytrace rendering

Note: *Objects have raytracing turned On by default, but the renderer's raytracing is turned Off by default.*

How the renderer works

The Maya renderer works by looking through the camera at the scene. It then takes a section or tile and analyzes whether or not it can render that section. If it can, it will combine the information found in the shading group (geometry, lights and shading network) with the Render Settings information, and the whole tile is rendered.

As the renderer moves on to the next section, it again analyzes the situation. If it hits a tile where there is more information than it wants to handle at one time, it breaks down the tile into a smaller tile and renders.

Rendering of A-buffer tiles in progress

When you use raytracing, each tile is first rendered with the A-buffer, then the renderer looks for items that require raytracing. If it finds any, it layers in the raytraced sections. When it finishes, you have your finished image, or if you are rendering an animation, a sequence of images.

IPR

The Interactive Photorealistic Renderer gives you fast feedback for texturing and lighting updates without needing to re-render.

IPR rendering in progress

Conclusion

Now that you have a basic understanding of what Maya is designed to do, it is time for you to start working with the software directly. The concepts outlined in this introduction will be clearer when you experience them firsthand.

Project 01

In Project One, you are going to learn the basics of object creation, along with the fundamentals of animation, shaders and textures. This will give you the chance to explore the Autodesk® Maya® workspace while building your scene.

You will start by creating a house similar to the one from the Sony Pictures Animation Inc. *Surf's Up* movie. You will then fill it with simple models in order to learn about create, move and modify objects. Then, you will explore the rudiments of hierarchies and animation by creating a simple door. After that, you will experiment with shaders and textures, which will allow you to render your scene.

These lessons offer you a good look at some of the key concepts and workflows that drive Maya. Once this project is finalized, you will have a better understanding of the Maya user interface and its

Lesson 01
Primitives

This lesson teaches you how to build and transform primitives in 3D space in order to create a rudimentary environment and house, which you will use to setup all your animations. You will explore the Maya user interface (UI) as you learn how to build and develop your scene.

In this lesson you will learn the following:

- How to set a new Maya project
- How to create primitive objects
- How to move objects in 3D space
- How to duplicate objects
- How to change the shape of objects
- How to use the Maya view tools
- How to change the display of your objects
- How to name your objects
- How to save your scene

Setting up Maya

The first step is to install the Autodesk® Maya® software. Once that is done, you should copy the Learning Maya support files to your Maya *projects* directory. The support files are found in the *support_files* directory on the DVD-ROM included with this book.

In order to find your *projects* directory, you need to launch Maya at least once so that it creates your user directory structure. Here is where the *projects* directory is typically located on your machine:

> **Windows**: *Drive:\Documents and Settings\[username]\My Documents\maya\projects*
>
> **Mac OS X**: *Users/[username]/Documents/maya/projects*

> **Note:** *To avoid the Cannot Save Workspace error, ensure that the support files are not read-only after you copy them from the DVD-ROM.*

When Maya is launched for the first time and you have other Maya versions installed, you will be asked if you want to copy your preferences or use the default preferences. In order to follow the course, you should be using default preferences. If you have been working with Maya and have changed any of your user interface settings, you may want to delete or back-up your preferences in order to start with the default Maya configuration.

Creating a new project

Maya uses a project directory to store and organize all of the files (scenes, images, materials, textures, etc.) related to a particular scene. When building a scene, you create and work with a variety of file types and formats. The project directory allows you to keep these different file types in their unique sub-directory locations within the project directory.

1 Launch Maya

2 Set the project

To manage your files, you can set a project directory that contains sub-directories for different types of files that relate to your project.

- Go to the **File** menu and select **Project → Set...**

   A window opens that directs you to the Maya projects directory.

- **Open** the folder *support_files*.

- Click on the folder named *project1* to select it.

- Click on the **OK** button.

  This sets project1 as your current project.

- Go to the **File** menu and select **Project** → **Edit Current...**

  Make sure that the project directories are set up as shown below. This ensures that Maya is looking into the proper sub-directories when it opens up scene files.

Edit Project window

- Click the **Accept** button when done.

3 Make a new scene

- Select **File** → **New Scene**.

  This will create a new scene in the current directory when you save it.

Build the environment

Every scene you create in Maya will most likely contain objects such as surfaces, deformers, skeleton joints or particle emitters. For this scene, you will build a house using planks and boxes, but first, you will need a large outdoor environment.

To start, you will build a ground plane surrounded by a large sky dome. These first objects will be a primitive polygonal plane and a primitive NURBS sphere. You can view the finished scene to get an idea of what you are about to create by opening the file called *01-house_01.ma*.

1 Change menu sets

There are five main menu sets in Maya: *Animation, Polygons, Surfaces, Dynamics* and *Rendering*. These menu sets are used to access related tool sets.

- From the drop-down menu at the left edge of the Status Line (Toolbar), select **Polygons**.

  As you change menu sets, the first six menu items and the Help menu item along the top of the viewport remain the same while the remaining menu items change to reflect the chosen menu set.

Menu set pop-up menu

2 Create a polygonal plane

A primitive plane will be used as a large ground plane on which you will build the house. It will be built using polygonal geometry. Throughout this lesson and in the next project, you will learn more about this geometry type.

- **Disable** the interactive creation mode of models by selecting **Create** → **Polygon Primitives** → **Interactive Creation**.
- From the **Create** menu, select **Polygon Primitives** → **Plane**.

  A small plane is created at the origin.

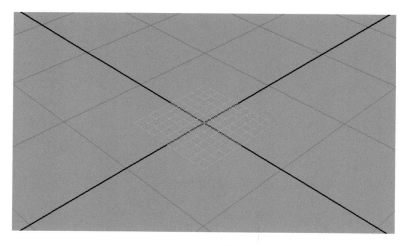

Perspective view of pPlane1

3 Change the plane's dimensions

The plane is a procedural model. This means that it is broken down into parts called *nodes*. One node contains its positioning information, one contains its shape information and another contains input information that defines the plane's construction history using attributes such as width, height and subdivisions. You can edit this input node's attributes in the Channel Box in order to edit the plane's basic shape.

The Channel Box is found at the right side of the screen and lets you make changes to key attributes very easily.

> **Note:** *If your Channel Box is not along the right side of the screen, you can access it by selecting* **Display** → **UI Elements** → **Channel Box/Layer Editor.**

- From the Channel Box's **Inputs** section, click on *polyPlane1*.

  This will make several new attributes available for editing.

- Type **100** in the **Width** entry field and press the **Enter** key.

- Type **100** in the **Height** entry field and press the **Enter** key.

  Now the plane is very large in the Perspective view, but this is intended since you don't want to see any ground plane edges as you are working.

pPlane1	
Translate X	0
Translate Y	0
Translate Z	0
Rotate X	0
Rotate Y	0
Rotate Z	0
Scale X	1
Scale Y	1
Scale Z	1
Visibility	on

SHAPES
pPlaneShape1

INPUTS
polyPlane1

Width	100
Height	100
Subdivisions Width	10
Subdivisions Height	10
Create UVs	Normalize a

Channel Box

> **Note:** *Another method for increasing the size of the plane would be to scale it. In Maya, you can often achieve the same visual results using many different methods. Over time, you will begin to choose the techniques that best suit a particular situation.*

4   Rename the plane node

You should rename the existing transform node to make it easier to find later.

- Click on the *pPlane1* name at the top of the Channel Box to highlight it.

- **Type** the name *ground*, then press the **Enter** key.

Channels Object	
ground	
Translate X	0
Translate Y	0
Translate Z	0

Renaming the node in the Channel Box

5   Create the sky

You will now create another object to be used as a large sky dome.

- **Disable** the interactive creation mode of models by selecting **Create → NURBS Primitives → Interactive Creation**.

- Select **Create → NURBS Primitives → Sphere.**

6   Modify the sphere

- With the *pSphere1* still selected, set the **Scale X**, **Y** and **Z** in the Channel Box to **50**.

  The sphere should now be as big as the ground plane.

Note: *You can zoom out in the perspective view to see the entire scene by holding the Alt key and click+dragging the RMB.*

- Click on the *makeNurbSphere1* input node in the Channel Box.

- Set the following:

    End Sweep to **180**;

    Sections to **4**.

  By changing the sphere's input, the sphere automatically updates. The sphere is now half a sphere with fewer sections.

7   Rotate the sphere

- With the *pSphere1* still selected, set **Rotate X** and **Y** in the Channel Box to **-90** degrees.

  Doing this rotates the sphere so it covers the ground plane. You now have a closed environment in which you will create the rest of the scene.

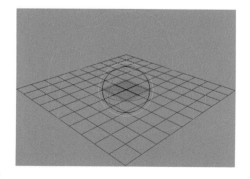

The ground plane with a sky dome

8 Rename the sphere

- **Rename** the *pSphere1* to *skydome*.

Viewing the scene

When you work in 3D space, it is important to see your work from different angles. The different view panels let you see your work from the front, top, side and Perspective angles.

You can also use the view tools to change the views in order to reposition how you see your scene. In some cases, a view change is like panning a camera around a room, while in other cases a view change might be like rotating an object around in your hand to see all the sides. These view tools can be accessed using the **Alt** key in combination with various mouse buttons.

1 Edit the Perspective view

You can use the **Alt** key with your mouse buttons to tumble, track and dolly in your Perspective view.

- Change your view using the following key combinations:

  Alt + LMB to tumble;

  Alt + MMB to track;

  Alt + LMB + MMB or **Alt + RMB** to dolly.

  *You can also combine these with the **Ctrl** key to create a bounding box dolly where the view adjusts based on a bounding box. This is useful when you want to dolly on a precise section of the view or quickly dolly out to get the general look of the scene.*

  Ctrl + Alt + LMB to box dolly.

  Click+drag from left to right to dolly in, and from right to left to dolly out.

  You can also undo and redo view changes using the following keys:

  To **undo** views use [;

  To **redo** views use] .

- Alter your Perspective window until it appears as shown here:

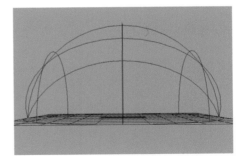

New Perspective view

2   Four view panels

By default, a single Perspective window is shown in the workspace. To see other views of the scene, you can change your panel layout.

- At the top of the Perspective view panel, go to the **Panels** menu and select **Saved Layouts → Four View**.

You can now see the environment using three Orthographic views—top, side and front—that show you the models from a projected view. You can also see them in a Perspective view that is more like the everyday 3D world. This multiple view set-up is very useful when positioning objects in 3D space.

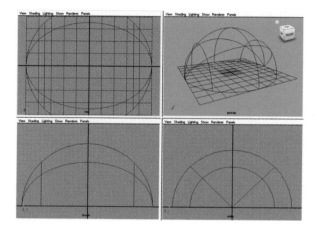

Four view panels

Tip: *Tapping the keyboard **spacebar** will switch from a single view panel to a four view panel.*

3   Edit the view in the side view

Orthographic views use similar hotkeys—except that you cannot tumble by default in an Orthographic view.

- In the side view, change your view using the following key combinations:

    Alt + MMB to track;

    Alt + LMB + MMB or **Alt + RMB** to dolly.

• Keep working with the *Orthographic* views until they are set up as shown:

New orthographic views

4   Frame Selected and Frame All

Another quick way to navigate in the different views is to use the Frame Selected or Frame All hotkeys for the active view.

• Select the *ground* plane.

• While in the four view panels, move your mouse over a view.

• Press the **f** hotkey to frame the selected geometry in the view under your mouse.

• Press the **a** hotkey to frame everything visible in the view under your mouse cursor.

• Press **Shift+a** hotkey to frame everything in all views at once.

Setting display options

The view panels let you interactively view your scene. By default, this means viewing your scene as a wireframe model. To better evaluate the form of your objects, you can activate hardware shading.

1   Turn on hardware shading

To help visualize your objects, you can use hardware shading to display a shaded view within any panel.

• From the Perspective view's **Shading** menu, select **Smooth Shade All**.

This setting affects all of the objects within the current view panel.

Smooth shaded view

> **Tip:** *You can also turn on Smooth Shading by moving your cursor over the desired panel, clicking with your middle mouse button and pressing the 5 key. The 4 key can be used to return the panel to a wireframe view.*

2   Hide the grid

You can hide the world grid to simplify your view using one of two óptions:

- From the *any* view panel's **Show** menu, select **Grid** to hide the grid for that view only.

   OR

- From the **Display** menu, deselect **Grid** to hide the grid for all views.

Moving inside the environment

In order to have the feeling of being inside the environment in the Perspective view, you need to move the Perspective camera inside the sky dome geometry. You will soon realize that even if you can see inside the sky dome, sometimes its geometry will appear in front of the camera while moving, thus hiding the interior. The following steps will prevent this from happening.

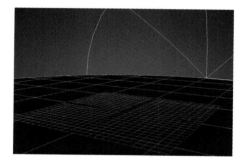

Perspective inside the environment

1   Change the sky's display

To simplify your scene interaction, there is a way of seeing inside the sky dome even when the camera is outside of it. To do so, you will have to change the way the geometry is displayed. The following actions are somewhat more advanced than what you will undertake in this project, but they will allow you to see inside the environment more easily.

- Select the *skydome*.

- Select **Window → Attribute Editor**.

   The Attribute Editor is similar to the Channel Box but with many more accessible attributes.

- **Expand** the **Render Stats** section by clicking the small arrow button.

   This section controls how the models are displayed in the viewports and render time.

- **Disable** the **Double Sided** attribute.

   This tells Maya to hide the sides of the geometry facing away from the camera.

- **Enable** the **Opposite** attribute.

   This tells Maya that you want the geometry to be displayed inside out.

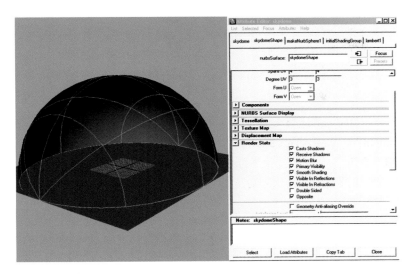

Seeing inside the environment

Create rocks

In order to establish a proper environment set, you should hide the horizon line with objects. In this example, you will create large rocks to place between the sky dome and the upcoming house. To create a rock, you will start from a primitive NURBS sphere, tweak its shape and then place several of them around the set.

1   Create a NURBS sphere

Here, you will use the hotbox as an alternative method for accessing tools.

- Press and hold the **spacebar** anywhere over the interface to display the hotbox.

Hotbox access to menu items

- In the hotbox, select **Create** → **NURBS Primitives** → **Sphere**.

  Another sphere is placed at the origin.

> **Tip:** *You can access all functions in Maya using either the main menus or the hotbox. As you become more familiar with the hotbox, you can use the UI options found in the **Display** menu to turn off the panel menus and therefore reduce screen clutter.*

2 Rename the sphere

- Click on the *pSphere1* node's name at the top of the Channel Box and type the name *rock*.

3 Position the rock

You can now use the **Move Tool** to reposition the rock in the scene.

- Select the **Move Tool** in the Toolbox on the left of the interface, or press **w**.

Manipulator handle

> **Tip:** *The transform manipulator has three handles that let you constrain your motion along the X, Y and Z-axes. These are labeled using red for the X-axis, green for the Y-axis and blue for the Z-axis. The Y-axis points up by default, which means that Maya is "Y-up."*

- **Click+drag** on the green manipulator handle to move the rock along the **Y-axis** until the bottom of the rock is flush with the ground plane.

  You will notice that the manipulator handle turns yellow to indicate that it is active.

4 Reposition the rock

When moving in an Orthographic view, you can work in two axes at once by dragging on the center of the manipulator or constraining the motion along a single axis using the handles.

- In the front view, **click+drag** on the square center of the manipulator to move the sphere along both the X and Y-axes.

- Use the manipulator to position the rock in the background of the scene.

  By convention, a 3D scene is always facing the positive Z-axis. This means that objects with greater Z-axis values will be closer to the foreground of the scene and objects with smaller Z-axis values will be further in the background.

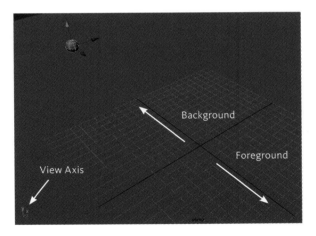

The sphere placed in the background

5 Transform the rock

Instead of using the sphere's input node to change its size, try using the scale manipulator. You can also experiment by translating and rotating the sphere into a proper position on the ground surface.

- Select the **Scale Tool** in the Toolbox on the left side of the interface.

- Using the different axes of the **Scale Tool**, change the shape of the sphere so it looks like a big rock.

- Switch to the **Translate Tool** by pressing the **w** hotkey to translate the object.

- Switch to the **Rotate Tool** by pressing the **e** hotkey to rotate the object.

- You can switch back to the **Scale Tool** by pressing the **r** hokey.

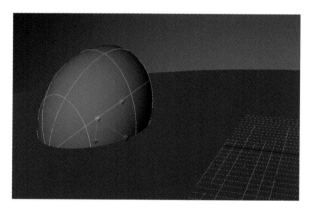

The large rock's position

Toolbox

Tip: *Each cube at the end of the Scale manipulator represents a different axis except for the central one which controls all three axes at the same time. You can also hold down Ctrl and click+drag on an axes to proportionally scale the two other axes.*

6 Change the shape of the rock

At this time, the rock is very round and does not represent a rock very well. So now that you are familiar with transforming an object, you will learn how to modify the shape of an object.

- With the *rock* selected, press the **f** hotkey to frame it in the view.

- In the **Status Line** located at the top of the interface, click the **Component Mode** button.

The Component Mode button

*Working in this mode will display the components of the currently selected geometry. You can then select and transform the points defining a surface's shape. Polygon points are called **vertex/vertices** and NURBS points are called **control vertices** or **CVs**.*

- **Click+drag** around CVs in the viewport to select them.

Tip: *When selecting components, hold down **Shift** to toggle the new selection, hold down **Ctrl** to deselect the new selection and hold down **Ctrl +Shift** to add the new selection to the currently selected group of components.*

- Randomly **move**, **rotate** and **scale** the components to model the shape of the sphere so it looks more like a sooth rock.

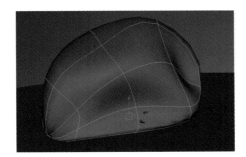

Randomly shaped rock

- Click on the **Object Mode** button in the Status Line to exit the comonent mode.

Object mode

7 Make more rocks

Instead of always starting from a default primitive object, you can duplicate an existing one, preserving its position and shape.

- Select your *rock* and select **Edit → Duplicate**.

When using the duplicate function, the new objects will be renamed to rock1. Subsequent duplicates will be named rock2, rock3...

Tip: *You can use the **Ctrl+d** hotkey to duplicate the selected geometry without going into the menu each time.*

- **Create** a stack of rocks forming a rocky crescent in the back of the environment.

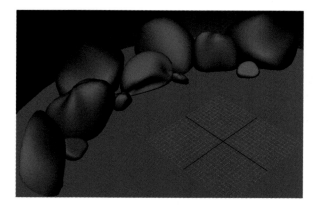

Stack of rocks

> **Tip:** *If the skydome gets in the way when you select and modify objects, you can temporarily hide it. To do so, select the geometry to hide, then select* **Display →** **Hide → Hide Selection**. *To show the last hidden objects, select* **Display → Show →** **Show Last Hidden**. *To show all hidden objects, select* **Display → Show → All**.

8   Move the rocks

- If your stack of rocks is not located at the correct position in the environment, click on one rock, then hold down the **Shift** key and click the remaining rocks one by one to select them all.

- Press **Ctrl+g** to group them together so you can move them all at once.

- **Move** the new group as needed.

9   Adjust NURBS smoothness

The display of NURBS surfaces in a viewport can be adjusted by increasing/decreasing its smoothness.

- Select the *rocks*.

- From the main **Display** menu, select **NURBS**.

- Select any of the menu items between **Hull**, **Rough**, **Medium**, **Fine** or **Custom NURBS Smoothness**.

  These settings will affect how selected NURBS objects are displayed in all view panels.

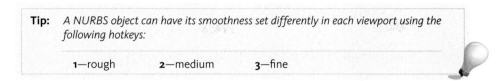

Tip: *A NURBS object can have its smoothness set differently in each viewport using the following hotkeys:*

1—rough   **2**—medium   **3**—fine

10   Save your work

- From the **File** menu, select **Save Scene As...**

- Enter the name *01-house01.ma*.

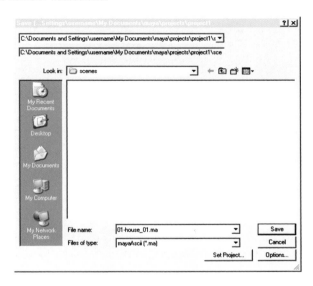

Windows Save As dialog box

- Click the **Save** button or press the **Enter** key.

Building the house

Now that you know how to place objects and interact with the Perspective view, you can start building the house itself. You will start by creating the front walls of the house with planks, then you will create a simple rooftop, and you will finish by creating a large tree trunk to be used as a chimney.

1 Making planks

The duplicate tool has options that allow you to duplicate multiple copies of the same object, separated by a fixed translation or rotation value. For example, if you make one plank, you can make many other copies separated by five units, all in one easy step.

- **Create** a polygonal cube and **scale** it so it looks like a vertica plank.

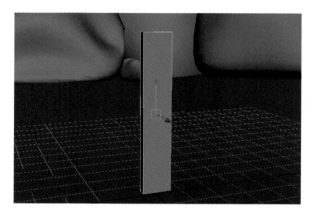

Placement of one plank

- **Rename** the cube *plank*.
- Select **Edit → Duplicate Special → ❑**.
- Set the **Number of Copies** to **10**.

In order to determine the proper translation axis, look at the view axis located at the bottom left corner of each view. If you want the copies to be created along the positive X-axis, enter a positive value in the first field of the translation vector.

Axis letter points toward its positive values

- Set the appropriate **Translate** value to **1.5** and leave the others to **0**.
- Click the **Duplicate Special** button.
- Select Edit → Undo or press **z** to undo the action and try again if the plank was not duplicated as expected.

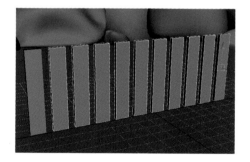

The duplicated shelves

2   Tweak the shape of the wall

- Select all the *planks*.

- Go into **Component Mode** to display the polygonal vertices.

- Change the shape of the wall so it looks similar to the following:

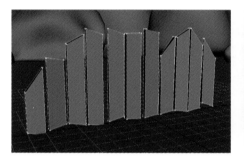
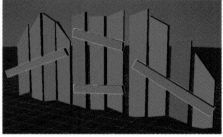

The front wall of the house

The planks used to create wall sections and a door

- Place horizontal planks behind the wall to create wall sections. The central planks will be used as a door.

> **Tip:**   When scaling an object, you can hold down the control key and **click+drag** one of the axes to proportionally scale the other two axes.

3   Rooftop

In this step, you will create the structure to hold the roof. Here, the house will be shaped more like a hut, but feel free to experiment with the shape that you would like.

- Select **Create → Polygon Primitives → Cone**.

- Highlight the cone's **Inputs** in the Channel Box.

- Set the following:

>   **Radius** to **0.5**;
>
>   **Height** to **15**;
>
>   **Subdivisions Axis** to **5**;
>
>   **Subdivisions Height** to **3**;
>
>   **Subdivisions Cap** to **0**.

- **Move** the *pCone1* towards the back of the house and **rotate** it as follows:

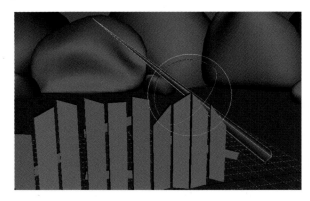

Modified cone primitive

- **Rename** the cone to *roofBranch*.
- **RMB** on the *roofBranch* to pop up its contextual radial menu, and select **Vertex**.

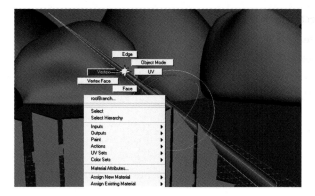

Polygon context menu

- Edit the vertices to get a branch-like shape.

Tip: *You might want to go into wireframe mode (hotkey **4**), in order to select components more easily.*

- **Duplicate** more *roofBranches* and modify them to finish the roof structure.

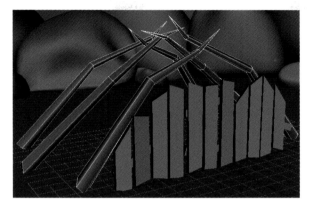

The beams in place

4   Roof cover

The roof of the house should technically be made of thousands of smaller branches, but in this example, you will only cover the roof with a large plane and you will use a texture later in this project to simulate the roof material.

- Select **Create → Polygon Primitives → Plane**.

  A plane will appear at the origin.

- Make sure the **Subdivisions Width** and **Height** are set to **10** in the **Inputs** section of the **Channel Box.**

- **Move** the plane closer to the top of the roof so that the spikes of the *roofBranches* interpenetrate with the plane.

- Go into **Component Mode** and **tweak** the shape of theroof as shown.

The shape the roof plane

- **Rename** the plane to *roof.*

5   Tree trunk

As a last addition to the house, you will add a large tree trunk in the back of the house which will come out like a chimney.

- Select **Create → Polygon Primitives → Cone**.
- Highlight the cone's **Inputs** in the Channel Box.

- Set the following:

    Radius to **4**;

    Height to **30**;

    Subdivisions Axis to **10**;

    Subdivisions Height to **10**;

    Subdivisions Cap to **0**.

- **Move** the *pCone1* towards the back of the house and up so it stands on the ground.

- Go into **Component Mode** and **tweak** the shape of the cone as follows:

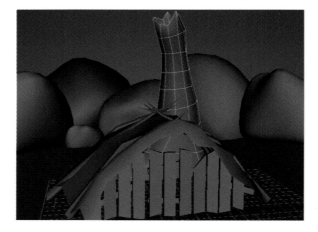

The chimney model

- **Rename** the cone to *chimney*.

6 Save your work

- From the **File** menu, select **Save Scene As...**

- Enter the name *01-house_02.ma* and click the **Save** button.

    Make sure you save this file since you will be continuing with it in the next lesson.

> **Note:** *Throughout this book, you will be using the final saved file from one lesson as the start file for the next, unless specified otherwise. Save your work at the end of each lesson to make sure that you have the start file ready. Othewise, you can use the scene files from the support files found on the DVD that accompanies this book.*

Conclusion

Congratulations! You have completed your first exercise using Maya. You should now be able to easily navigate the different views and change the basic hardware display settings. You should also be confident in creating, duplicating, transforming and renaming objects, along with using the translation, rotation and scale manipulators. At this point you should also understand the difference between Component mode and Object mode. As well, be careful to save scene files.

In the next lesson, you will explore in greater depth how to model objects and details.

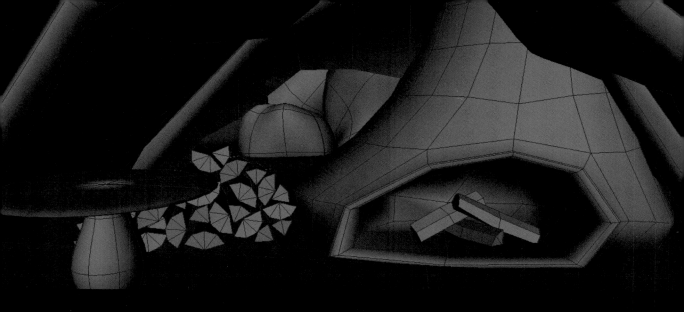

Lesson 02
Adding Details

In this lesson you will modify existing models to enhance the richness of the scene. You will first change the shape of the chimney to have a fireplace at its base. You will then add a table using a different modeling technique. This is a good time to experiment with basic modeling tools and concepts.

In this lesson you will learn the following:

- How to open a scene
- How to extrude and move polygonal faces
- How to smooth polygonal objects
- How to delete polygonal faces
- How to fill holes in polygonal geometry
- How to combine polygonal objects
- How to move the pivot of an object
- How to draw and revolve a curve
- How to snap to grid
- About construction history
- How to delete construction history

Working with a good file

Use the scene that you saved in the previous lesson or use the one provided in your scenes directory, *01-house_02.ma*.

1   Open a scene

There are several ways to open a scene in Maya. The following are three easy options:

- From the **File** menu, select **Open Scene**.

  OR

- Press **Ctrl+o**.

  OR

- Click on the **Open** button located in the top menu bar.

File Open button

2   Find your scene

In the **File Open** dialog box, if you cannot immediately locate *01-house_02.ma*, it might be because your project is not correctly set or that Maya did not direct you into the *scenes* directory.

- At the top of the dialog box, if the path is not pointing to the project created in the last lesson, click the **Set Project...** button at the bottom of the window and browse to find the correct project directory. When you find it, click **OK**.

  When you open a scene, it should now automatically take you to your current project's scenes directory. If it doesn't, open the combo box located at the top of the dialog in Windows and near the bottom of the dialog in Mac OS X and select **Current scenes***.*

- Select *01-house_02.ma* and click **Open**.

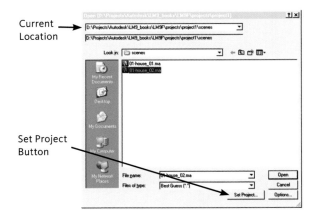

File Open dialog

3   Save Scene As

Since you will be modifying this scene, it is a good idea to save this file under a new name right away. Doing so will allow you to keep a copy of the previous lesson in case you would like to start this lesson over.

- Select **File → Save Scene As...**.
- Type *02-addingDetails_01* in the **File name** field.
- Select *MayaASCII (*.ma)* in the **Files of type** field.

  Maya can save its files in two different types of formats:

    Maya ASCII (.ma) saves your scene into a text file which is editable in a Text Editor. Though this format takes up more space on your drive, it is possible to review and modify its content without opening it in Maya. Experienced users find this very useful.

    Maya Binary (.mb) saves your scene into a binary file which is compiled into computer language. This format is faster to save and load, and takes up less space on your drive.

Create a fireplace

In this example, you will use the existing tree trunk geometry to create a fireplace. By extruding polygonal faces, you will add polygonal geometry to what is already there, thus increasing the detail of the object.

1   Extrude polygon faces

Extruding polygons is a very common action. To do an extrusion, you first need to pick polygonal face components, and then execute the tool that will display a useful all-in-one manipulator to move around the new polygons.

- With the *chimney* selected, press the **f** hotkey to frame it in the view.
- **Move** the Perspective view inside the house to see the base of the chimney properly.
- With the *chimney* geometry still selected, press the **F11** hotkey to go into Component mode with the polygonal faces enabled.

Tip: *There are several hotkeys for going into Component and Object modes. The more you use Maya, the better you will know the difference between these modes. The polygon-related hotkeys are listed here:*
> **F8** – *Toggle between Object mode and the last Component mode*
> **F9**   – *Display vertices*
> **F10** – *Display edges*
> **F11** – *Display faces*
> **F12** – *Display UVs*

- Select a polygon face by clicking with your **LMB** on the dot located at the center of the face to extrude.

  The face will be highlighted in orange to show that it is currently selected.

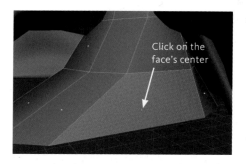

Click on the face's center

The face to be used to extrude the fireplace

Tip: *You can also **click+drag** around face centers to select faces. Combine this action with the **Shift** key to toggle, the **Ctrl** key to deselect or the **Shift+Ctrl** keys to add faces to the current selection.*

- Select **Edit Mesh → Extrude**.

  A manipulator is displayed at the selection. This manipulator has all translation, rotation and scale manipulators integrated.

  Single click on an arrow to display the translation manipulator.

  Single click on the outer circle to display the rotation manipulator.

  Single click on a square to display the scale manipulator.

  Toggle between local and global transformation by clicking on the round icon.

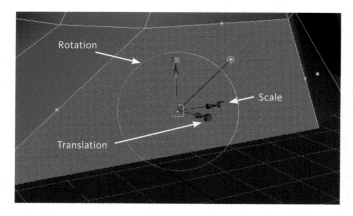

The all-in-one manipulator

- **Click+drag** the blue arrow manipulator to translate the face slightly outward to create a small border.

- Select **Edit Mesh → Extrude** again.

> **Tip:** *You can invoke the last command used (Extrude) by pressing the g hotkey rather than always going back into the menus.*

- **LMB** on a square of the manipulator to enable its scale function.

- **LMB+drag** on the central square to scale down the extruded face.

- **LMB** on an arrow of the manipulator to use the translate function.

- **LMB** translate the face so the bottom border is above the ground plane.

- Select **Edit Mesh → Extrude** again.

- **LMB** translate the new faces toward the inside of the chimney to create the inside of the fireplace.

- Press **F8** to return to Object mode.

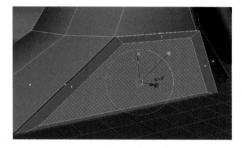

Manipulate the face to make a border

2 Mesh smooth

The look of the chimney is quite rough and boxy at this time. This can be changed using the polygon **Smooth** command.

- Select the *chimney* geometry.

- Select **Mesh → Smooth.**

  Doing so will smooth out the geometry.

- **Tweak** the resulting geometry in Component mode to suit your liking.

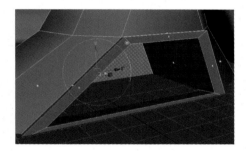

Final shape of the fireplace

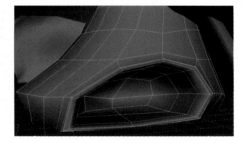

The smoothed chimney geometry

3   A wood log

You will now take some time to add a small pile of wood to go with the fireplace.

- **Create** a primitive polygonal cylinder.
- Highlight the *polyCylinder1* node in the Channel Box.
- Highlight the attribute name *Radius* in the Channel Box.
- In any viewport, **MMB+drag** to the left to decrease the attribute's value.

Tip: *When attributes are highlighted in the Channel Box, middle mouse dragging in a viewport invokes a virtual slider that changes the attributes' values. Drag left to decrease the value and right to increase the value.*

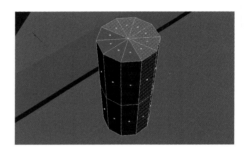

- Set the following:

  Radius to **0.4**;

  Subdivision Axis to **10**;

  Subdivision Height to **2**;

  Subdivision Cap to **1**.

- **Rename** the cylinder to *woodLog*.
- **Move** the *woodLog* closer to the fireplace.

The faces to be deleted

4   Delete faces

In order to give the impression that the wood log was cut into smaller pieces, you will now delete polygonal faces on one side of the geometry.

- With the *woodLog* still selected, press the **F11** hotkey to go in Component mode.
- Select the polygonal faces on the top, side and bottom of the *woodLog* to be removed.

Tip: *It might be easier to select faces while displaying the wireframes by pressing the 4 hotkey.*

- Press the **Delete** key on your keyboard to delete the faces.

5 Fill the wood log

The last step has created a hollow looking wood log which is not what you want. You will now close the opening of the wood log with the **Fill Hole** command.

- Press **F8** to go into Object mode.

- Select **Mesh → Fill Hole.**

    Notice how the wood log now looks more like an object rather than an empty shell.

- Press **F9** to go in Component mode with the vertices displayed.

- **Tweak** the shape of the wood log as wanted.

Take some time to create and duplicate more wood logs and stack them beside the chimney. Also, place some of them in the fireplace.

6 Combine polygonal objects

You might come across situations where you would like multiple polygonal objects to be treated as one single object. The **Combine** command will do that for you. You will use this feature to combine the stacked wood logs together.

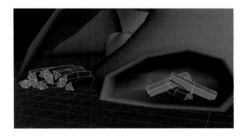

The wood logs in place

> **Note:** *Keep in mind that combined objects can no longer be individually moved. If individual objects need to move, group the objects instead.*

- Select all the *woodLogs* stacked beside the fireplace.

- Select **Mesh → Combine.**

    The logs are now combined into a single object.

- **Rename** the combined geometry to *woodStack.*

7 Center pivot

Notice that when objects are combined together, the pivot of the new object is placed at the center of the world. There are different ways of placing the object's pivot in a better location.

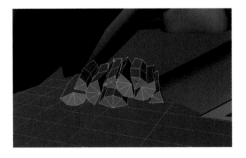

The combined wood stack

- With the *woodStack* selected, select the **Move Tool** by pressing **w**.
- Zoom out and notice where the object's pivot is located.
- Press the **Insert** key on your keyboard (**Home** on Macintosh).

  Doing so changes the current manipulator to the **Move Pivot Tool***.*
- Using the different axes on the manipulator, place the pivot at the desired location.
- Press the **Insert** key again to recover the default manipulator.

  OR
- Select **Modify** → **Center Pivot**.

  Using this command automatically places the pivot at the center of its object.
- **Move**, **rotate** and **scale** the *woodStack* at the desired location.

Tip: *If you would like more wood logs in your wood stack, you can duplicated the combined object and place it on top of the existing wood stack.*

8   Save your scene
- **Save** your scene as *02-addingDetails_01.ma*.

Create a table

In this exercise, you will use a different approach to create geometry that will introduce several new tools. Instead of starting from a primitive to create a table, you will draw a profile curve, which will then be revolved to create a round table.

1   Draw a curve

The first step for modeling your table is to draw the table's profile curve.

- Tap the **spacebar** to go into the *four view* panel, and then tap it again with the mouse cursor placed over the *front* view.
- Select **Show** → **None** from the view's menu, then select **Show** → **NURBS Curves**.

  Doing so will clean the viewport so you can concentrate on your curve modeling.
- Select **Create** → **EP Curve Tool**.
- Hold down **x** to **Snap to Grid** and **draw** your first point at the origin.
- **Draw** the following curve and make sure to snap your last curve point on the origin vertical axis grid line.

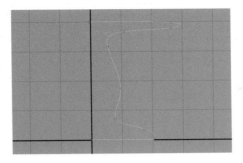

The table profile curve

Tip: *You can press the Delete key to delete the last drawn curve point.*

- Hit **Enter** to complete the curve.
- Press **F11** to go into Component mode and fine tune the curve's shape.
- Press **F8** to go into Object mode.

2   Revolve the table

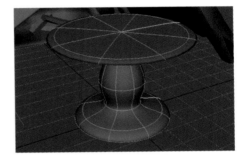

- Go back into the Perspective view.
- Press **F4** to select the **Surfaces** menu set.
- With the profile curve selected, select **Surfaces → Revolve.**
- **Rename** the new geometry to *table*.

The revolved table

3   Construction history

All the different tools used thus far are still present in the scene. For instance, because of the construction history, you can still tweak the shape of the table by modifying the profile curve. Construction history nodes are also accessible through the Inputs section of the Channel Box. Changing nodes involved in the construction history will allow you to tweak action taken, without undoing and losing all of your work.

Note: *Construction history will be discussed in greater depth in Lesson 6.*

- With the *table* selected, highlight the *revolve1* nodes in the **Inputs** section of the Channel Box.
- Try changing attribute values to see its effect on the geometry.
- Try to change the shape of the original curve to see its effect on the geometry.

> **Note:** *Construction history can be very handy, but it can also lead to unexpected results, especially with object topology changes.*

4 Delete construction history

Construction history is always kept when doing certain operations. This history is sometimes not wanted as it increases file size and loading time. You will now delete the construction history from your scene.

- Select the *table* geometry.
- To delete the construction history from the selected models, select **Edit** → **Delete by type** → **History**.

  The construction history is now gone from the Inputs section of the Channel Box.

- To delete all the history in the scene, select **Edit** → **Delete All by type** → **History**.

> **Tip:** *Be careful when deleting an entire scene's history since history is sometimes required. For instance, character deformations are done via history. To delete only construction history, use* **Edit** → **Delete All by type** → **Non-Deformer History**.

5 Place the table

- **Move** and **scale** the table to place it in the house.

The scaled table

6 Save your work

- Save the scene as *02-addingDetails_02.ma*.

Conclusion

You have begun to develop skills that you will use throughout your work with Maya. Both polygonal and NURBS modeling are entire subjects on their own. You will get to do more in-depth modeling in the next projects, but for now, you will continue experiencing different general Maya topics.

In the next lesson, you will bring colors into your scene by assigning shaders and textures to your objects.

Lesson 03
Shaders and Textures

Now that you have created an environment, you are ready to add colors and render your scene. The rendering process involves the preparation of materials and textures for objects.

In this lesson you will learn the following:

- How to work with a menu-less UI
- How to work with the Hypershade
- How to create shading groups
- What are procedural textures
- How to import and assign file textures
- What is an alpha channel
- How to render a single frame

Hiding the general UI

In the last two lessons, you used menus, numeric input fields and other UI elements to work with your scene. In this lesson, you will hide most of the user interface and rely more on the hotbox and other hotkeys to access the UI without actually seeing it onscreen.

1 Scene file

- Continue using the file you created from the last lesson or open *02-addingDetails_02.ma* from the *support_files/scenes* directory.

2 Turn off all menus

- If you are in *Four View* panel layout, position your cursor over the *perspective* view panel, then press the **spacebar** quickly to pop up to a full screen.

- Press and hold down the **spacebar** to open the hotbox.

> **Tip:** *Tapping the spacebar can be used to toggle between window panes and holding down the spacebar can bring up the hotbox.*

- Click on **Hotbox Controls**.

- From the marking menu, go down to **Window Options** and set the following:

  Show Main Menubar to **Off** (Windows only);

  Show Pane Menubars to **Off**.

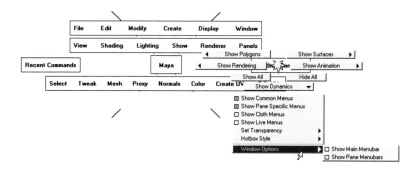

Marking menu

Now the various menus are hidden and you must rely on the hotbox to access tools.

3 Turn off all the workspace options

- From the hotbox, select **Display** → **UI Elements** → **Hide All UI Elements**.

Simplified UI

You now have a much larger working area that will let you focus more on your work.

4 Change the panel organization

- Press and hold down the **spacebar** to evoke the hotbox.

- Click in the area above all the menus to apply the north marking menu.

- Select **Hypershade/Render/Persp** from this marking menu.

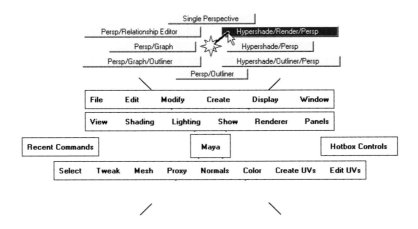

Hypershade/Render/Persp layout

Tip: *Each of the four quadrants surrounding the hotbox and the hotbox's center all contain their own marking menu sets. You can edit the contents of these menus using* **Window → Settings/Preferences → Marking Menus Editor**.

This saved layout puts a Hypershade panel above a Perspective panel and a Render View panel.

The Hypershade is where you will build shading networks and the Render View is where you will test the results in your scene.

Tip: **Click+drag** *the pane divisions to change the width/height of the different windows in the layout.*

5 Open the Attribute Editor

- From the hotbox, select **Display → UI Elements → Attribute Editor**.

Now you also have an Attribute Editor panel on the right side of the workspace. This will make it easy to update shading network attributes.

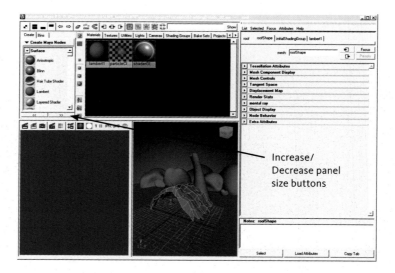

New UI layout

Hotkeys

When working with a minimal UI, you will rely on the hotbox and hotkeys for your work. The following is a list of relevant hotkeys that you may need to use as you work:

spacebar	Hotbox/window popping
Ctrl + a	Show/hide Attribute Editor
f	Frame selected
a	Frame all
q	Pick Tool
w	Move Tool
e	Rotate Tool
r	Scale Tool
t	Show Manipulator Tool
y	Invoke last tool
g	Repeat last command
Alt + v	Start/stop playback
Alt + Shift + v	Go to first frame

Note: *For a complete listing of available hotkeys, go to* **Window → Settings/Preferences → Hotkey Editor**

Shading networks

To prepare the environment, house and objects for rendering, you need to add color and texture. This is accomplished using *shading networks* that bring together material qualities, textures, lights and geometry to define the desired look.

The Hypershade

The Hypershade panel is made up of three sections—the Create bar, the Hypershade tabs and the work area. The Create bar allows you to create any rendering nodes required for your scene. The Hypershade tabs list all nodes that make up the current scene, while the work area allows you to look more closely and alter any part of the shading network's graph.

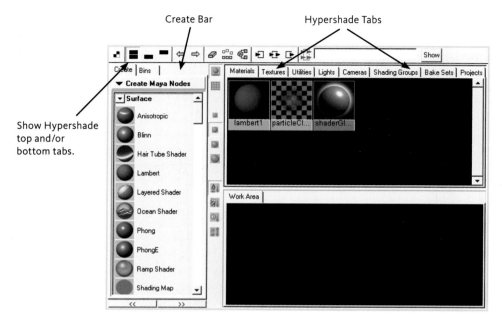

Close-up of Hypershade

> **Note:** *The same mouse and key combinations that you use in the orthographic viewports can be used for maneuvering in the Hypershade work area.*

Creating shading networks

A shading network consists of a series of nodes that input into a *shading group*. A shading group is a node which defines the various rendering attributes of its related objects, such as surface shading, volumetric shading, displacement shading, etc.

In the following examples, you will create several nodes that define the material qualities of the garage, boxes, shelves and door.

1   Build sky material

To build a material for the sky, you will use the Hypershade and Attribute Editor.

- Click on the **Show top and bottom tabs** button located at the top left of the Hypershade.

- At the top of the Create bar section, click on the tab **Create**.

- Click on the **down arrow** just below the **Create** tab, and make sure **Create Maya Nodes** is selected from the pop-up.

  This offers you a series of icons that represent new Maya nodes, such as surface materials.

- Click on **Lambert**.

  This adds a new Lambert material under the materials' Hypershade tab and in the work area. You will also see the Attribute Editor update to show the new node information.

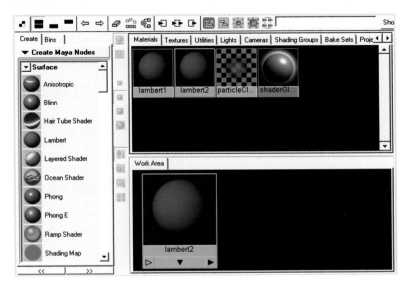

New node in Hypershade

Lambert is a particular type of shader which gives you control over the look of flat materials without shiny highlights.

2   Rename the material node

- In the Attribute Editor, change the name of the material node to *skyM*.

  The M designation is to remind you that this node is a material node.

Tip: *You can also hold down the Ctrl key and double-click on the node in the Hypershade to rename it.*

3 Edit the material's color

To define how the material will render, you will need to set color attribute.

- In the Attribute Editor, click on the color swatch next to the **Color** attribute.

This opens the Color Chooser. This window lets you set color by clicking in a color wheel and editing HSV (Hue, Saturation, Value) or RGB (Red, Green, Blue) values.

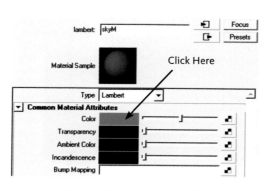

Color swatch in the Attribute Editor

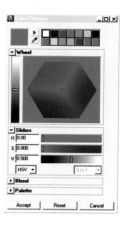

Color Chooser

- Choose a light blue color and click the **Accept** button.

4 Assign the material

- With your **MMB**, **click+drag** on the *skyM* node, drag it from the Hypershade panel into the Perspective view and drop it on the *skyDome* object.

This assigns the material to the object.

Tip: *It is a good idea to be in Hardware Shading mode to ensure that the assignment is correct. The hotkey is **5** on your keyboard.*

Creating a procedural texture map

To give the rocks a grainy look, a fractal procedural texture will be added to the *rock's* material color. A procedural texture means the look of the texture is driven by attributes and drawn by mathematical functions. You will also experiment with the drag and drop capabilities of the Hypershade.

Assigned shader

1   Rock material

- In the Hypershade, clear the work area by holding down the right mouse button and selecting **Graph** → **Clear Graph** or press the **Clear Graph** button at the top of the Hypershade.

The Clear Graph button

  This clears the workspace so that you can begin working on a new shading network.

- From the Create bar section, create a **Blinn** material.

  Blinn shaders give you control over the shininess of your material.

- In the Attribute Editor, change the name of the material node to *rockM*.

- Select every *rock* in the scene then **RMB** on your material *rockM* and select **Assign Material to Selection**.

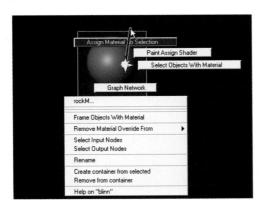

Assign material to selection

> **Tip:** *This method of assigning materials works better than the* **click+drag** *method when you want to assign a material to multiple objects.*

- With *rockM* selected, locate the **Specular Shading** section in the attribute editor, then set the following:

    Eccentricity to **0.8**;

    Specular Roll Off to **0.3**;

    Specular Color to **Brown**;

    Reflectivity to **0**.

2   Fractal texture

If you look at the rocks in shaded mode, you will notice that they look quite flat. This is because they do not have a grainy texture assigned. Adding a fractal procedural texture will greatly help to enhance the look of the rocks.

- In the Create bar section of the Hypershade, scroll down to the **2D Textures** section.

    This section allows you to create new textures.

- **MMB** drag a **Fractal** from the Create bar anywhere into the work area.

- In the work area of the Hypershade, click with your **MMB** on the **Grid** icon and drag it onto the *rockM* material node.

    When you release the mouse button, a pop-up menu appears offering you a number of attributes that can be mapped by the fractal texture.

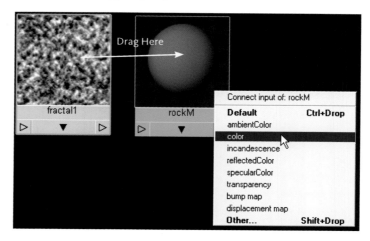

MMB+drag from the fractal onto the material

- Select **color** from the menu to map the *fractal* to the material node's *color* attribute.
- Click on the **Rearrange Graph** button at the top of the Hypergraph panel.

The Rearrange Graph button

> **Tip:** Rearranging the work area will organize the view so connections appear from left to right. This is very useful for following the flow of connections.

3   View the texture

In order to see the texture in the viewport, you will need to enable hardware texturing.

- Over the Perspective window, click with your **MMB** to make it the active window.
- Open the hotbox and select **Shading** → **Hardware Texturing**.

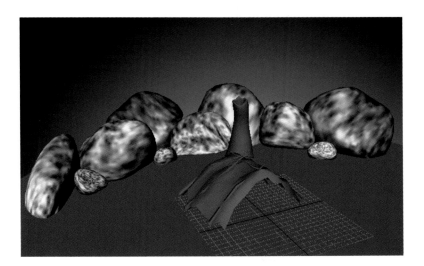

Hardware texturing

> **Tip:** You can also turn on hardware texturing by making the desired panel active and pressing the **6** key.

4 Edit the fractal attributes

- In the Hypershade, click on the *fractal* node.
- In the Attribute Editor (**Ctrl+a** to show it if hidden), open the **Color Balance** section.
- Click on the color swatch next to the **Color Gain** attribute.
- Choose any color you want and click the **Accept** button.
- Click on the color swatch next to the **Color Offset** attribute.
- Choose any color you want and click the **Accept** button.
- Under the **Fractal Attributes** section, tweak the attributes to your liking.

  The attributes found in this section control the way the fractal is being evaluated.

- At the top of the Attribute Editor, select the *place2dTexture* tab.

  This tab shows different placement options for the fractal texture.

- Change the fractal's placement attributes as shown below:

  Repeat U to **2**;

  Repeat V to **1**.

  The Attribute Editor allows you to easily update the look of a procedural texture to your liking.

Rock texture

Note: *The viewport texture shading is a representation of what your textures looks like, but it might not reflect perfectly how your scene will render.*

5   Display the whole shading group

- With the *rockM* texture selected in the Hypershade, click on **Input and Output Connections**.

Input and Output Connections button

This displays some other nodes that help define this shading group.

- Press the **Alt** key and **click+drag** with your left and middle mouse buttons to zoom out.

- Press the **a** hotkey to frame everything in the view.

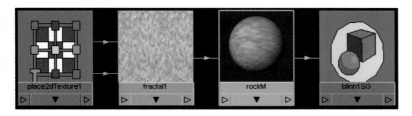

Complete shading network

Map a file texture

You will create a material for the ground plane using a file texture instead of a procedural texture. Many digital artists like to create textures in a 2D paint package. For the ground surface, you will use a beach texture.

1   Create a material for the ground

- From the Hypershade panel's work area **RMB** and select **Graph** → **Clear Graph**.

- Scroll to the **Surface** section in the Create bar and select **Lambert**.

- **Rename** this node *groundM*.

Sand texture

2   Create a file texture node

To load an external texture, you need to start with a file texture node.

- **Double-click** on the *groundM* material to display its Attribute Editor (if hidden).
- In the Attribute Editor, click on the **Map** button next to **Color**. The map button is shown with a small checkered icon.

This opens the Create Render Node window.

Map button

- Click on the **Textures** tab.
- In the **2D Textures** section, click on **File**.

A file node is added to the Lambert material. The appropriate connections have already been made.

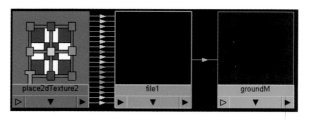

New file texture node

3   Import the file texture

- In the Attribute Editor for the file node, click on the **File folder** icon next to **Image name**.
- Select the file named *sand.tif* from your project *sourceimages* directory, then click on the **Open** button.

The file texture is now loaded into the shading network.

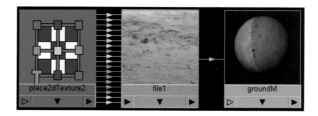

File texture node

Note: *This file will be available only if you set up your project correctly from the support_files and if it is set to current.*

> **Note:** *The file texture does not import the image into Maya. Instead, it keeps a path to the specified file and loads it on request from your drive.*

4 Apply the textured material to the ground

- Select the *ground* surface in the *Perspective* view.

- In the Hypershade, click on the *groundM* node with your **RMB** and choose **Assign Material to Selection** from the pop-up menu.

    The texture is assigned to the ground surface.

Ground with texture applied

5 Roof texture

For the roof texture, you will use a texture with an *alpha channel*. This means that the texture contains the regular color channels, plus an alpha channel, which stores the transparency of the texture. This is perfect for the roof since the branches composing it will not be entirely opaque.

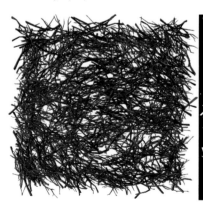 

Roof texture, color and alpha channel displayed

- **Repeat** the last exercise to create a **Lambert** shader with a mapped **File texture**.

- **Rename** the Lambert shader to *roofM*.

- Open the Attribute Editor for the new file texture, and then click on the **Browse** button.

- Select the file named *roof.tif* from your project *sourceimages* directory, then click on the **Open** button.

  Maya will automatically detect and connect the alpha channel to the **transparency** *attribute of the Lambert.*

Roof with transparent texture

6 Complete the scene

Before continuing with the next lesson, it is a good idea to assign materials to the remaining objects in your scene. Experiment with 2D procedural texture nodes such as *Noise*, *Ramp* and *Cloth*. The following is an example of the completed scene:

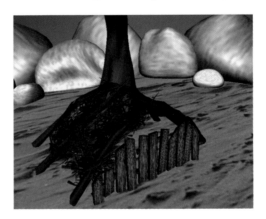

The completed house

Note: *A wood texture can be found in the support_files's sourceimages directory.*

Tip: *You can assign textures to polygonal faces by first selecting the faces and then assigning a shader to them.*

Test render

Now that you have materials and textures assigned, it is a good time to do a test render.

1   Display Resolution Gate

Your current view panel may not be displaying the actual proportions that will be rendered. You can display the camera's resolution gate to see how the scene will actually render.

- Make the Perspective view the active panel.

- Use the hotbox to select **View** → **Camera Settings** → **Resolution Gate**.

The view is adjusted to show a bounding box that defines how the default render resolution of 640x480 pixels relates to the current view.

- Dolly into the view so that it is well composed within the resolution gate. Try to set up a view where you see every object.

Keep in mind that only objects within the green surrounding line will be rendered.

2   Your first render

- In the Render View panel, click with your **RMB** and select **Render** → **Render** → **persp** from the pop-up menu.

The resolution gate displayed

Render View panel

You can now see a rendered image of your scene. However, because you have not created any lights, the image renders using a default light.

- Try adding lighting to your scene by creating lights from the **Create** → **Lights** menu.

Note: *Lights are going to be covered later in this book.*

- **Render** your scene again.

3   Zoom into the rendering

You can zoom in and out of the rendered image using the **Alt** key and the dolly and track hotkeys.

- Use the **Alt** key and the **LMB** and **RMB** to zoom in and out of the view.

Now you can evaluate in more detail how your rendering looks at the pixel level.

Close-up of rendering

- In the Render View panel, click with your **RMB** and choose **View** → **Real Size**.

4   Save your work

- Through the hotbox, select **Save Scene As** from the **File** menu.
- Enter the name *03-textures_01.ma*, then press the **Save** button.

Conclusion

You have now been introduced to some of the basic concepts for texturing and rendering a 3D scene. The Maya shading networks offer a lot of depth for creating the look of your objects. You have learned how to create materials, procedural textures and file textures, and rendered a single frame to preview the look of your shaders with default lighting.

In the next lesson, you will add light and shader effects that will only be visible at render time.

Lesson 04
Animation Basics

You have built a simple house using various primitive objects and then textured them. You will now learn about the basics of hierarchies and animate the door so that it opens up.

In this lesson you will learn the following:

· How to change and save preferences

· How to group and parent objects

· How to understand parent inheritance

· How to set keyframes

· How to use the Time Slider

· How to use the Graph Editor

· How to select animation curves and keyframes

· How to change keyframe tangents

· How to traverse a hierarchy

Project 01

Preferences

You can now reset the interface to its default settings. Also, be sure to set your preferences to have an infinite undo queue.

1 Turn on all menus

- From the hotbox, click on Hotbox Controls.
- From the marking menu, go down to **Window Options** and set the following:

  Show Main Menubar to **On** (Windows only);

  Show Pane Menubars to **On**.

  The menu bars are back to normal.

2 Turn on all of the workspace options

- Select **Display** → **UI Elements** → **Show All UI Elements**.

  You are now back to the default Maya interface.

3 Change the Attribute Editor settings

You might want the Attribute Editor to open in its own window rather than in the Maya interface. The following will show you how to set your preference accordingly.

- Select **Window** → **Settings/Preferences** → **Preferences**.
- In the left **Categories** list, make sure **Interface** is highlighted.
- Set **Open Attribute Editor** to **In separate window**.
- You can do the same for **Open tool settings** and the **Open Layer Editor** if wanted.

  The different editors will now open in their own separate windows rather than cluttering the main interface.

4 Infinite undo option

By default, Maya has a limited amount of undo in order to reduce the memory usage of your computer. You will specify here if you want to keep an undo queue larger than the default setting.

- In the **Categories** list, highlight **Undo**.
- Make sure **Undo** is set to **On**.
- Set the **Queue size** to what you think is an appropriate value, such as **50**.

  OR

- Set the **Queue** to **Infinite**.

  The amount of undo is now defined to your liking.

5 Save your preferences

- In order to save these preferences, you must click the **Save** button.

  The next time you open Maya, these settings will be used.

Note: *You can also save your preference by selecting* **File** → **Save Preferences.**

Organize your scene

Before animating objects, you need to make sure that the task will be as simple as possible. You will need to easily find the objects in your scene and animate them as intended. Placing objects logically into hierarchy is going to do just that. To do so, you will learn how to group and parent objects together as well as learn how to use the Outliner.

You can think of scene organization as having groups and sub-groups. For instance, you can have an *environment* group that contains everything in the scene. Then you can have a *house* group, which will contain everything related to the house and in the house group, you can have a *woodLogs* group.

Thus far you have modeled a bunch of objects, but you haven't looked at how they were organized behind what you saw in the viewports.

1 Hierarchy

It is very important to understand the concept of a hierarchy. A hierarchy consists of the grouping of child nodes under parent nodes. When transforming a parent node, all of its children will inherit its transformation. The following steps explain how to create a hierarchy of objects:

- To better visualize what you are about to do, open the Outliner by selecting **Window** → **Outliner...**

  The Outliner lists all the nodes in your scene along with their hierarchies. Currently, in your scene, you can see the default Maya cameras, all of the prior lesson objects, every component of your environment and, at the very bottom, two default sets.

- Scroll in the Outliner to see the current organization of the scene.

  The first four nodes in the Outliner are always the default cameras. Following that are your scene contents, and then the different default object sets.

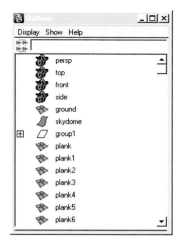

The Outliner

2   Groups

- Holding down the **Shift** key, **select** all your scene's content from the Outliner starting from the *ground* down to *table*.

  Doing so selects the geometry just like when selecting in a viewport.

- Select **Edit → Group**.

  The selected geometry is now all grouped under a group node.

- **Double-click** on the newly created *group* to enable the rename function directly in the Outliner.

- Enter the name *environmentGroup*, then hit **Enter** to confirm the name change.

- **Expand** the group to see its content by clicking on the **plus** (+) sign next to *environmentGroup*.

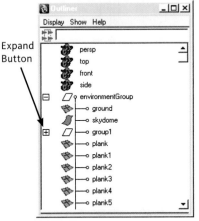

Expand Button

Hierarchy expanded

Note: *A new default group has its pivot at the origin and all of its attributes are set to their default values.*

3   Organizing the hierarchy

You will now create a group for the house within the environment group.

- Select the all the objects called *plank*.

- Press **Ctrl+g** to group them.

  A new group is created within the environmentGroup, containing only the plank objects.

- **Rename** *group* to *houseGroup*.

- Select all the remaining house objects that are not already in *houseGroup*.

- Press and hold the **MMB** over the selection and drag them over the *houseGroup*.

  As you can see in the following images, dragging and dropping nodes onto another one will set them as the child of the object they were dragged onto.

> **Note:** *Notice the green highlight on the houseGroup, which shows one or more of its children is currently selected.*

- Select *houseGroup*.
- **MMB+drag** it in the Outliner just under the *environmentGroup* geometry and **drop** it when you see only a single black border highlight.

  Doing so reorders the scene hierarchy.

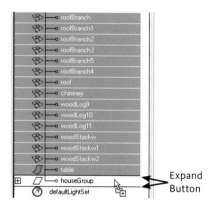

Drag

Drop

> **Tip:** *Notice that when dragging objects in the Outliner, one black line shows that it will be placed in-between two nodes, while two black lines show that the objects will be parented.*

4   Parenting

- In the viewport, select the wood logs located in the fireplace.
- In the Outliner, hold **Ctrl** then select the *chimney*.

  Make sure the chimney is selected last.

- From the **Edit** menu, select **Parent**.

  OR

- Press **p** on your keyboard.

  Doing so will parent the woodLog objects to the chimney object.

Tip: *Use Shift+p to unparent.*

5 Completing the hierarchy

- Organize the hierarchy so that it looks like the following:

hierarchy

Tip: *To expand a hierarchy along with all the children, hold down the Shift key before clicking the Expand button in the Outliner.*

Understanding inheritance

Hierarchies are useful to organize your scene, but they also play a role with animation. For instance, if you transform a parent object, all of its children and grandchildren will follow that transformation. Thus, it is essential to freeze transformations of objects to reset their transformation attributes to their default, without moving the object. You must also make sure that all objects' pivots are appropriately placed for your needs.

1 Freezing transformations

At this time, most of your objects have some values in their translate, rotate and scale attributes. When you animate your objects, those values will come into play and make your task more difficult. To make it easier, you can freeze an object's transformations.

- Select the *environmentGroup*.
- Select **Edit → Select Hierarchy**.
- Select **Modify → Freeze Transformations**.

Doing so resets all the selected objects' attributes to their default values.

> **Tip:** If you do not want to freeze all the attributes of an object, you can open the command's option box to specify which attributes need freezing.

2   Center pivots

Since the groups and objects might not have their pivots at a centered location, it is a good idea to place all the pivots in one easy step.

- Select the *environmentGroup*.

- Select **Edit → Select Hierarchy**.

- Select **Modify → Center Pivot**.

  Every pivot is now located at the best centered location. When an object has children, the command takes into account the entire sub-hierarchy to position the pivot.

3   Child values

When you transform a parent object, none of its children's values change.

- Select the *houseGroup*.

- **Rotate** and **translate** it in to modify its positioning.

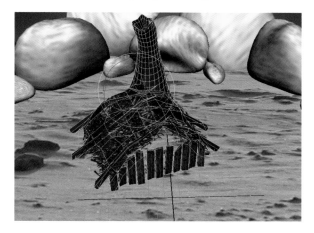

Rotate and translate the house

- Select any of its children, and notice that all of their values are still zero.

- Select *chimney* and **move** it.

- Notice the *woodLogs* rotation values did not change.

4   Pivot placement

You will now see how the pivot of an object, when well placed, can simplify your task when it comes to moving an object.

- Select the *houseGroup*, set its **scale X**, **Y** and **Z** to **1.5**.

  All of the group's children follow the parent scaling, but the floor of the house is going down through the ground.

- **Undo** the previous action.

- Still with the *houseGroup* selected, press the **Insert** key on your keyboard to bring up the **Move Pivot Tool**.

- From the *front* or *side* orthographic view, place the pivot on the ground plane.

 Tip: *You can snap it to the grid by holding down the x hotkey.*

- Press **Insert** again to exit the tool.

- Set the *houseGroup* **scale X**, **Y** and **Z** to **1.5**.

  Notice how you do not have to compensate for the scaling by moving the house up on the Y-axis.

Animating the door

You now have enough knowledge of scene hierarchy and object inheritance to create your first simple animation.

1   Door group

Before animating the door, you must consider your needs in animation and make sure that you can achieve such animation with your scene setup. At this time, you require a group containing only the door. Furthermore, you need the pivot of that door to be located around the hinge area; otherwise, your door would rotate from its center, which is not ideal.

- Select all the *planks* that are part of the door.

- **Group** the planks together.

- **Rename** the group to *doorGroup*.

- Select **Modify → Center Pivot**.

- Use the **insert key** to move the pivot to where you think the hinges should be.

- Test your door setup by rotating the *doorGroup* on its Y-axis.

Rotating the door open

- **Undo** the last move to reset the door to its default position.

2   The timeline

The first step with animation is to determine how long you would like your animation to be. By default, Maya plays animation at a rate of 24 frames per seconds (FPS), which is a standard rate used for film. So if you want your animation to last one second, you need to animate 24 frames.

- In the Time Slider and Range Slider portion of the interface, change **Playback End Time** to **100**.

The frames in the Time Slider now go from 1 to 100. One hundred frames is just above four seconds of animation in 24FPS.

Start Time

End Time

Playback Start Time

Playback End Time

Time Slider and Range Slider

3   Setting keyframes

Luckily, you do not need to animate every single frame in your animation. When you set keyframes, Maya will interpolate the values between the keyframes.

- Press the **First Frame** button from the playback controls to make the current frame **1**.

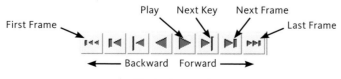

Play   Next Key   Next Frame

First Frame

Last Frame

Backward   Forward

Playback controls

- Select the *doorGroup*.
- Make sure all of its rotation and translation values are set to **0**.
- At the top of the interface, change the current menu sets for **Animation**.

Tip: *The Animation menu set hotkey is* **F2**.

- With the *doorGroup* still selected, select **Animate → Set Key**.

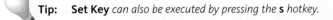

Tip: **Set Key** *can also be executed by pressing the* **s** *hotkey.*

- In the current frame field on the left of the rewind button, type **25** and hit **Enter**.
  Notice the position of the current frame mark in the Time Slider.

The current frame mark

- Type **125** in the **Rotate Y** field of the *doorGroup* and hit **Enter**.
- Press the **Alt** key over the viewport in order to remove focus from the Y-axis field, then hit the **s** hotkey to **Set Key** at frame **25**.

4   Playback preferences

Before you play your animation, you need to set the Maya playback properly.

- Click the **Animation Preferences** button found at the far right side of the Range Slider.

The animation preferences button

This opens the preferences window directly on the animation and playback options.

- In the **Timeline** category, under the **Playback** section, make sure that **Playback Speed** is set to **Real-time (24FPS)**.
- Click the **Save** button.

- Press the **Rewind** button, then press the **Play** button in the playback controls area to see your animation.
- To stop the playback of the animation, press the **Play** button again or hit **Esc**.
- You can also drag the current frame by **click+dragging** in the Time Slider area.

Dragging in the Time Slider

Notice the red ticks at frame 1 and frame 25, specifying keyframes on the currently selected objects.

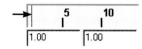

A keyframe tick in the Time Slider

5   Tweak the animation

You now have a partially animated door, but it is still missing refinement. Maybe you think the animation is too slow or too fast. In order to change the timing of the animation, you can drag keyframes directly in the Time Slider.

- With the *doorGroup* still selected, hold down the **Shift** key, then click on frame **25** in the Time Slider.

Doing so highlights frame 25 with a red zone. This zone is actually a manipulator that allows you to translate keyframes in the Time Slider.

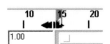

The keyframe manipulator

- **Click+drag** the red zone to frame **15**.

The door animation now starts at frame 1 and stops at frame 15.

- Click anywhere in the Time Slider to remove the keyframe selection.
- Go to frame **35**.
- With the *doorGroup* still selected, set the **Rotate Y** attribute to **140**.
- Click on the **Rotate Y** attribute name in the Channel Box.

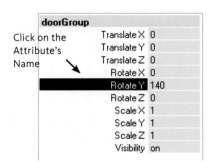

Select only the Rotate Y attribute

- Click and hold the **RMB** over that same attribute.

  This will pop up the attribute context menu.

- Select **Key Selected**.

  Doing so will set a keyframe on that attribute for every selected object.

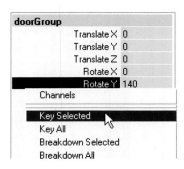

Select Key Selected from the attribute menu

Tip: You can use Shift+w, Shift+e and Shift+r to keyframe only the translation, rotation and scale attributes respectively.

- **Playback** your animation.

  You will notice that the door is opening fast for the first 15 frames and then slows down as it approaches frame 35.

Note: To delete keyframes in the Time Slider, simply set the current time marker on a keyframe, then RMB and select Delete. To delete multiple keyframes at the same time, select the keyframes using the keyframe manipulator (using the Shift key), then RMB and select Delete.

6 The Graph Editor

The Graph Editor is the place where you can look at all the keyframes on an object and see their interpolations as curves (function curves or fcurves).

- Select the *doorGroup*.

- Select **Window → Animation Editors → Graph Editor**.

- Select **View → Frame All** to frame the entire curve, or press the **a** hotkey.

- Press the **Alt** key and **click+drag** with the **LMB** and **MMB** to dolly in and out of the graph.

- Press the **Shift+Alt** keys and **click+drag** with the **LMB** and **MMB** to constrain the dolly along the dragged axis.

- Press the **Shift+Alt** keys and **click+drag** left and right with the **MMB** to constrain track along the dragged axis.

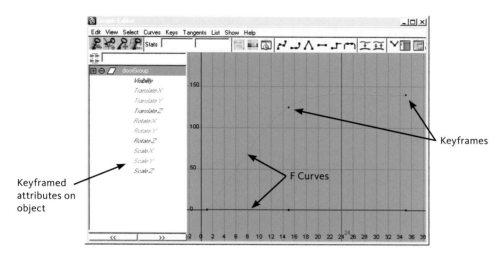

Keyframes

F Curves

Keyframed
attributes on
object

The fcurves on the doorGroup

The keyframes you have set are represented by black dots. Animation curves are always color coded red, green and blue for X, Y and Z axes. The animation curve going up is yellow because you have changed only the rotate Y attribute on the door. All other keyframes were set at 0.

7   Selecting keyframes

- Experiment selecting animation curves and keyframes in the Graph Editor.

Note: *You can select an entire animation curve by clicking on the curve itself. You can select keyframes by clicking on them. You can also modify the selection using the **Ctrl** and **Shift** hotkeys.*

- With the **Move Tool** selected, **MMB+drag** keys around in the Graph Editor.

Tip: *Use **Shift+MMB** dragging to constrain the axis of translation of the keyframe.*

8   Modifying keyframes

In order to modify only the Rotate Y keyframes without affecting other animation curves, you can display only the desired curve in the Graph Editor. You will now modify the animation so the door progressively gains speed when it is opening and loses speed once opened.

- In the Outliner section located on the left of the Graph Editor, highlight the **Rotate Y** attribute.

  Only this animation curve is now visible.

- Select the first and last keyframes of the animation curve.

- Select **Tangents → Flat**.

  This sets the keyframes to be flat, which causes a gradual acceleration and deceleration of the animation.

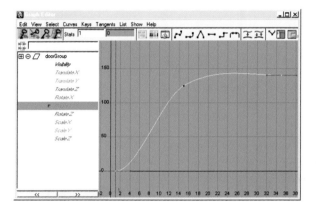

Flat tangents

> **Note:** *Notice how the animation curve goes slightly above 140 around frame 25. This will cause the door to overshoot its animation and rotate a bit further than what was keyed. While this effect is desired in this example, you might want to correct the situation by moving down the keyframe at frame 15 or simply edit its tangent.*

- **Playback** your animation.

- Continue experimenting. Once you like your animation, **close** the Graph Editor.

> **Note:** *To delete keyframes, select them in the Graph Editor then press the Delete key.*

9   Traversing a hierarchy

You can traverse hierarchies using the arrows on your keyboard. Traversing a hierarchy is useful for selecting objects without manually picking the object in the viewport or through the Outliner.

- Select any door *plank*.

- Open the Outliner to see the effect of the upcoming steps.

- Press the **Up arrow** to change the selection to the parent of the current selection (*doorGroup*).

- Press the **Up arrow** again to select the *wallGroup*.

- Press the **Up arrow** again to select the *houseGroup*.

- Press the **Up arrow** again to select the *environmentGroup*.

Tip: *You can use the following hotkeys to traverse a hierarchy:*

Up arrow—*Parent*	**Down arrow**—*First child*
Right arrow—*Next child*	**Left arrow**—*Previous child*

---

10   Save your work

- **Save** your scene as *04-animationBasics_01.ma*.

Conclusion

You have now touched upon some of the basic concepts of hierarchies and animation. Maya utilizes more powerful tools than described here to help you bring your scenes to life, but these basic principles represent a great step forward. As well as learning how to group and parent objects together, you also learned about inheritance of transformation and animation and worked with two of the most useful editors—the Outliner and the Graph Editor.

The next lesson is a more in-depth look at most of the tools that you have been using since the beginning of this project. Once you have read this lesson, you will be able to make your own decisions about how to reach the different windows, menu items and hotkeys.

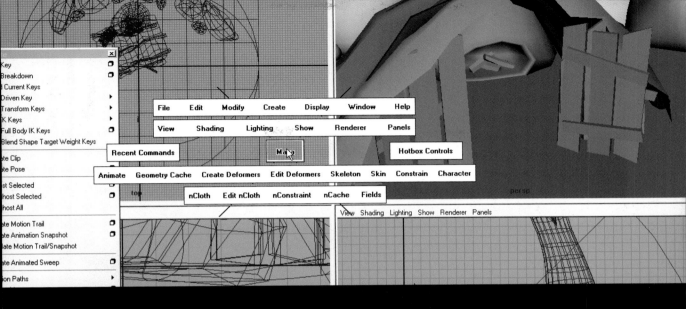

Lesson 05
Working with Maya

If you completed the first four lessons, you have worked with Maya from modeling and animation to shading and rendering. Now is a good time to review some of the UI concepts that you worked with and introduce new concepts in order to provide a more complete overview of how Maya works.

It is recommended that you work through this lesson before proceeding with the subsequent lessons in the book. This lesson explores the basic UI actions that you will use in your day-to-day work.

In this lesson you will learn the following:

- About the Maya interface
- About the different UI parts

The workspace

You have learned how to build and animate scenes using different view panels and UI tools. The panels offer various points of view for evaluating your work—such as Perspective views, Orthographic views, graphs and Outliners—while the tools offer you different methods for interacting with the objects in your scene. Shown below is the workspace and its key elements:

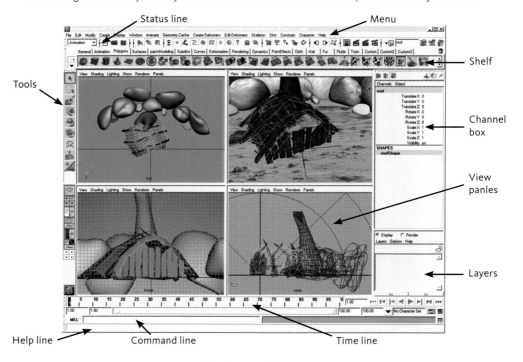

The Maya workspace

Layouts

When Maya is first launched, you are presented with a single Perspective view panel. As you work, you may want to change to other view layouts.

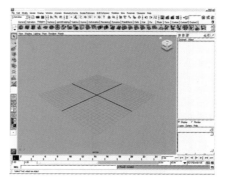

The default layout

1 Change your view layouts

- Go to the view panel's **Panels** menu and select a new layout option from the **Layouts** pop-up menu.

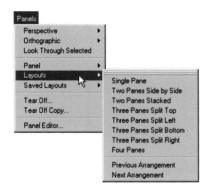

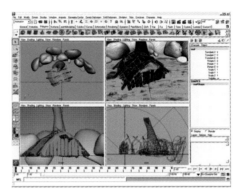

The Layouts pop-up menu   *A four-view layout*

You can set up various types of layouts ranging from two to four panels.

Tip: *If you are looking at several view panels simultaneously and want to focus on one of them, put your cursor in that view and tap the spacebar. The view will become full-screen. Tap the spacebar again and the panels will return to the previous layout.*

View panels

As you begin to build and animate objects, you will want to view the results from various points of view. It is possible to place either Perspective or Orthographic views in each panel.

1 Change the content of a view panel

- Go to the view panel's **Panels** menu and select a view type from either the **Perspective** or **Orthographic** pop-ups.

View tools

When you are working with Perspective and Orthographic views, you can change your view-point by using hotkey view tools. The following view tools allow you to quickly work in 3D space using simple hotkeys:

1 Tumble in a Perspective view

- Press the **Alt** key and **click+drag** with the **LMB**.

> **Tip:** *The ability to tumble an Orthographic view is locked by default. To unlock this feature, you need to select the desired Orthographic view and under* **View**, *go to* **Camera Tools** *and unlock it in the* **Tumble Tool → □.**

2 Track in any view panel

- Press the **Alt** key and **click+drag** with the **MMB**.

3 Dolly in or out of any view panel

- Press the **Alt** key and **click+drag** with both the **LMB** and **MMB** or only with the **RMB**.

> **Tip:** *You can also track and dolly in other view panels, such as the Hypergraph, the Graph Editor, Visor, Hypershade and even the Render View window. The same view tools work for most panel types.*

View Cube

The View Cube appears in the top right corner of the scene's Perspective view and shows your current camera view.

You can move between views by clicking parts of the View Cube. Clicking any of the cube sections will rotate the current camera view to selected view. Clicking the home icon will move the camera back to the default Perspective view.

The View Cube

1 Turn the View Cube on and off

- Select **Show → Manipulators**

2 Turn the View Cube on and off

- Select **Window → Settings/Preferences → Preferences.**
- In the **Categories** section, select **ViewCube** and choose your favourite settings.

Other panel types

As well, you can change the content of the view panel to display other types of information, such as the Hypershade or Graph Editor.

1   Change the content of a view panel

- Go to the view panel's **Panels** menu and select a panel type from the **Panel** pop-up menu.

In the workspace below, you can see a Hypergraph panel for helping select nodes, a Graph Editor for working with animation curves and a Perspective view to see the results.

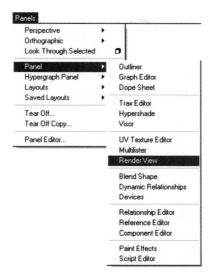

The Panels pop-up menu

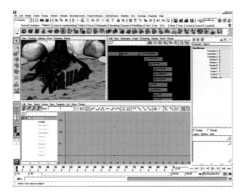

The workspace with various panel types

Saved layouts

As you become more familiar with Maya, you may want to set up an arrangement of panels to suit a particular workflow. For example, you may want a Dope Sheet, a Perspective view, a top view and a Hypergraph view all set up in a particular manner.

1   Add a new layout of your own

- Go to the view panel's **Panels** menu and select **Saved Layouts → Edit Layouts...**

  In the Edit window, you can add a new saved layout and edit the various aspects of the layout.

2   Add a new layout to the list

- Select the **Layouts** tab and click on **New Layout**.
- Select and edit the layout's name.
- Press the **Enter** key.

3 Edit the configuration of a saved layout

- Press the **Edit Layouts** tab.

- Choose a configuration, then **click+drag** on the separator bars to edit the layout's composition.

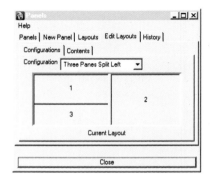

Layout Editor

- Press the **Contents** tab.

- Choose a panel type for each of the panels set up in the configuration section.

Tip: *There is quick access to preset layouts, panel types and layout configuration through the toolbox on the left side of the Maya UI.*

Display options

Using the **Shading** menu on each view panel, you can choose which kind of display you want for your geometry.

1 Change your panel display

- Go to the panel's **Shading** menu and select one of the options.

  OR

- Click in a panel to set it as the active panel and use one of the following hotkeys to switch display types:

  4 for wireframe;

  5 for smooth shaded.

Layout toolbox

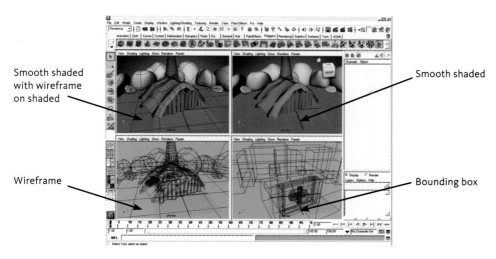

Smooth shaded
with wireframe
on shaded

Smooth shaded

Wireframe

Bounding box

Various display styles

Texturing and lighting

Another important option found on this menu is hardware texturing. This option allows you to visualize textures and lighting interactively in the view panels.

1   Hardware texturing

- Build a shader that uses textures.

- Go to the panel's **Shading** menu and select **Hardware Texturing**.

  OR

- Press the **6** hotkey.

2   Display different textures

It is possible to display different texture maps on your surface during hardware texturing. For example, you could display the color map or the bump map if those channels are mapped with a texture.

- Select the material that is assigned to your objects.

- In the Attribute Editor, scroll down to the **Hardware Texturing** section and set the **Textured channel** to the desired channel.

- You can also set the **Texture Resolution** in the Attribute Editor for each material node so that you can see the texture more clearly in your viewport.

3   Hardware lighting to your scene

- Add a light to your scene by going to the panel's **Lighting** menu and select one of the options.

  OR

- Press the **7** hotkey for all lighting.

Hardware lighting and texturing

High quality rendering

When high quality interactive shading is turned on, the scene views are drawn in high quality by the hardware renderer. This lets you see a very good representation of the final render without having to software render the scene.

1   Turn on high quality rendering

- Go to the panel's **Renderer** menu and enable **High Quality Rendering**.

Display smoothness

By default, NURBS surfaces are displayed using a fine smoothness setting. If you want to enhance playback and interactivity, you can have the surfaces drawn in a lower quality.

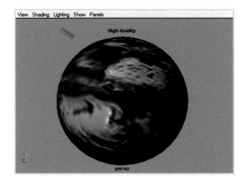

High Quality Rendering

1 Change NURBS smoothness:

- Go to the **Display** menu and under **NURBS** choose one of the smoothness options.

  OR

- Use one of the following hotkeys to switch display types:

  1 – for rough;

  2 – for medium;

  3 – for fine.

Fine

Medium

Rough

NURBS smoothness

Tip: *To speed up camera movement in a scene with heavy NURBS geometry, go to* **Window** → **Settings/Preferences** → **Preferences...** *in the* **Display** *section to enable the* **Fast Interaction** *option. This option shows the rough NURBS smoothness any time a camera is moving.*

Smooth Mesh Preview

Use one of the following hotkey to switch display types of polygonal objects:

1 - for the polygon display;

2 - for the polygon cage and smooth preview;

3 - for the smooth preview only.

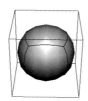

Smooth Mesh Preview

Note: *When in smooth display, you can still go in component mode and tweak the geometry's vertices*

Show menu

The **Show** menu is an important tool found on each view panel's menu. This menu lets you restrict or filter what each panel can show on a panel-by-panel basis.

Restricting what each panel shows lets you display curves in one window and surfaces in another to help edit construction history. Or, you can hide curves when playing back a motion path animation while editing the same curve in another panel.

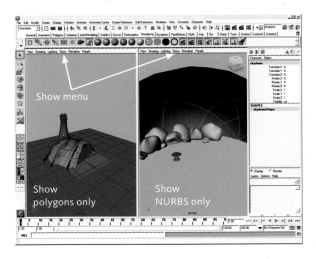

The Show menu

UI preferences

The Maya workspace is made up of various UI elements that assist you in your day-to-day work. The default workspace shows all of them on screen for easy access.

1 Reduce the UI to only view panels and menus
- Go to the **Display** menu and select **UI Elements** → **Hide All UI Elements**.

With less UI clutter, you can rely more on hotkeys and other UI methods for accessing tools while conserving screen real estate.

2 Return to a full UI
- Go to the **Display** menu and select **UI Elements** → **Show All UI Elements**.

Tip: *You can use the **Ctrl+space bar** to toggle between these UI settings.*

Menus

Most of the tools and actions you will use in Maya are found in the main menus. The first six menus are always visible, while the next few menus change depending on which UI mode you are in.

Menus and menu pop-ups that display a double line at the top can be *torn off* for easier access.

1 Tear off a menu

- Open the desired menu, then select the double line at the top of the menu.

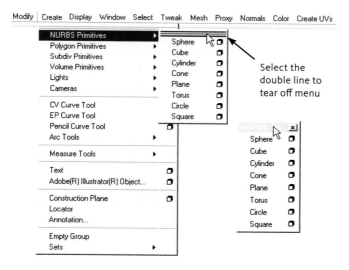

A tear-off menu

Menu sets

There are five menu sets in Maya Complete: *Animation, Polygons, Surfaces, Dynamics* and *Rendering*. Each menu set allows you to focus on tools appropriate to a particular workflow.

1 Choose a menu set:

- Select the menu set from the pop-up menu found at the left of the Status Line bar.

Choose a menu set using hotkeys:
- While pressing the h key LMB+drag over any viewport and choose the desired UI mode from the radial marking menuChoose a menu set using function keys:
- Press **F1** – to invoke **Help**
- Press **F2** – for **Animation**
- Press **F3** – for **Polygons**
- Press **F4** – for **Surfaces**
- Press **F5** – for **Dynamics**
- Press **F6** – for **Rendering**

Shelves

Another way of accessing tools and actions is by using the shelves. You can move items from a menu to a shelf to begin combining tools into groups based on your personal workflow needs.

1 **Add a menu item to a shelf:**
- Press **Ctrl+Shift** and select the menu item. It will appear on the active shelf.

2 **Edit the shelf contents and tabs:**
- Go to the **Window** menu and select **Settings/Preferences** → **Shelf Editor**

   OR
- Select the **Shelf Editor** from the arrow menu located to the left of the shelves.

3 **Remove a menu item from a shelf:**
- **MMB+drag** the shelf icon to the trash icon located at the far right of the shelves.

Status Line

The Status Line, located just under the Maya main menu, provides feedback on settings that affect the way the tools behave. The display information consists of:

- The current menu set
- Icons that allow you to create a new scene, open a saved one, or save the current one
- The selection mode and selectable items
- The snap modes
- The history of the selected lead object (visible by pressing the input and output buttons)
- The construction history flag

- The render into a new window and IPR buttons
- The Quick Selection field and Numeric Input field

1   Collapse part of the shelf buttons

- Press the small handle bar next to a button set.

Selection mode

Collapsing handle

Select modes before collapsing

Select modes button collapsed

Hotbox

As you learned, tapping the spacebar quickly pops a pane between full screen and its regular size, but if you press and hold the spacebar, you gain access to the hotbox.

The hotbox is a UI tool that gives you access to as much or as little of the Maya UI as you want. It appears where your cursor is located and offers the fastest access to tools and actions.

1   Access the hotbox

- Press and hold the spacebar.

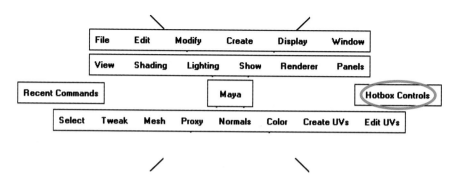

The hotbox with four quadrants marked

The hotbox offers a fully customizable UI element that provides you with access to all of the main menus as well as your own set of marking menus. Use the **Hotbox Controls** to display or show as many or as few menus as you need.

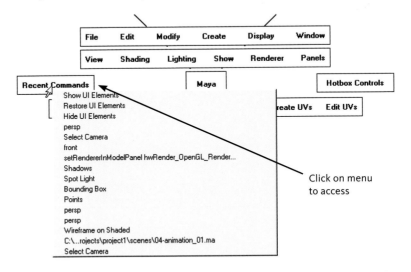

Accessing the recent commands menu

Hotbox marking menus

You can access marking menus in five areas of the hotbox. Since each of these areas can have a marking menu for each mouse button, it is possible to have fifteen menus in total. You can edit the content of the marking menus by going to the **Window** menu and selecting **Settings/Preferences** → **Marking Menu Editor**

1   Access the center marking menu

- Press the **spacebar**.
- **Click+drag** in the center area to access the desired menu.

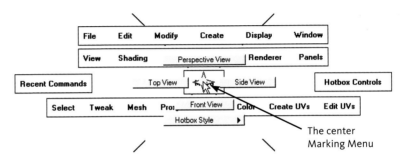

The center marking menu

2   Access the edge marking menus

- Press the **spacebar**.

- **Click+drag** in either one of the north, south, east or west quadrants to access the desired marking menu.

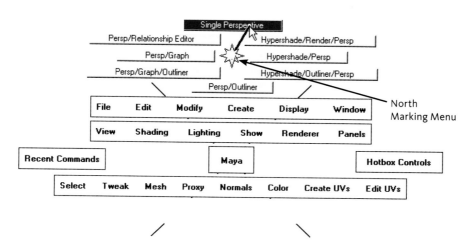

A quadrant-based marking menu

Customizing the hotbox

You can customize the hotbox to make it as simple or complex as you need. You can choose which menus are available and which are not.

If you want, you can reduce the hotbox to its essentials and focus on its marking menu capabilities.

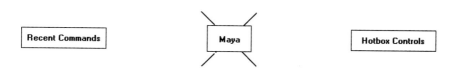

A reduced hotbox layout

Alternatively, you could hide the other UI elements, such as panel menus, and use the hotbox to access everything. You get to choose which method works best for you.

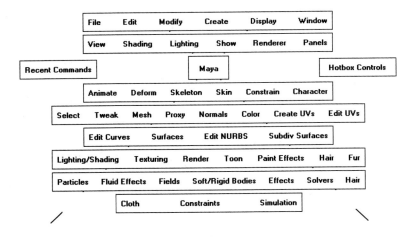

A complete hotbox layout

1 **Customize the hotbox**

- Use the **Hotbox Controls**.

 OR

- Use the center marking menu.
- Choose an option from the **Hotbox Styles** menu.

Tool manipulators

To the left of the workspace you have access to important tools. These include the **Select**, **Move**, **Rotate**, **Scale** and **Show Manipulator** tools. Each of these is designed to correspond to a related hotkey that can be easily remembered using the QWERTY keys on your keyboard.

These tools will be used for your most common tool-based actions, like selecting and transforming.

QWERTY tool layout

Note: *The Y key drives the last spot on the QWERTY palette which is for the last tool used. The advantages of this will be discussed later in this lesson under the heading Tools and Actions.*

Universal Manipulator

The **Universal Manipulator** lets you transform geometry in translation, rotation or scaling, both manually and numerically. A single click on any of the manipulators will display a numeric field allowing you to type in a specific value.

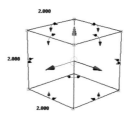

Universal manipulator

Soft Modification Tool

The **Soft Modification Tool** lets you push and pull geometry as a sculptor would on a sculpture. The amount of deformation is greatest at the center of the push/pull, and gradually falls off further away from the center. The corresponding action is **Deform →
Soft Modification**.

Transform manipulators

One of the most basic Maya node types is the *transform node*. This node contains attributes focused on the position, orientation and scale of an object. To help you interactively manipulate these nodes, there are three transform manipulators that make it easy to constrain along the main axes.

Each of the manipulators uses a color to indicate their axis. RGB is used to correspond to X, Y, Z. Therefore, red is for X, green for Y and blue for Z. Selected handles are displayed in yellow.

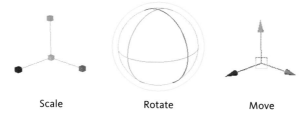

| Scale | Rotate | Move |

Transform manipulators

To explore some of the options available with manipulators, you will use the transform manipulator.

1 **Use a transform manipulator in view plane**

   • **Click+drag** on the center of the manipulator to move freely along all axes.

2 **Constrain a manipulator along one axis**

   • **Click+drag** on one of the manipulator handles.

3 **Constrain a manipulator along two axes**

   • Hold the **Ctrl** key and **click+drag** on the axis that is aligned with the desired plane of motion.

   This now fixes the center on the desired plane, thereby letting you click+dragon the center so that you can move along the two axes. The icon at the center of the manipulator changes to reflect the new state.

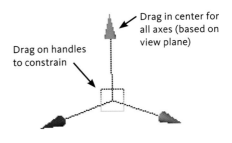

Drag in center for all axes (based on view plane)

Drag on handles to constrain

The move manipulator

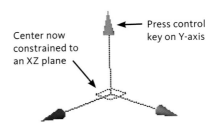

Press control key on Y-axis

Center now constrained to an XZ plane

4 **Go back to the default view plane center:**

   • Press the **Ctrl** key and click on the center of the transform manipulator.

Working along two axes

Note: *The ability to constrain in two axes at one time is available for the move and scale manipulators.*

Using the mouse buttons

You can interact directly with manipulators by using the left mouse button (LMB) to select objects.

The **MMB** is for the active manipulator and lets you **click+drag** without direct manipulation.

1 **Select objects**

   • Set up selection masks.

   • Click with the **LMB**.

2   Select multiple objects

- Use the **LMB** and **click+drag** a bounding box around objects.

3   Add objects to the selection

- Press **Ctrl+Shift** while you select one or multiple objects.

4   Manipulate objects directly

- **Click+drag** on a manipulator handle.

5   Manipulate objects indirectly

- Activate a manipulator handle.

- **Click+drag** with the **MMB**.

Shift gesture

The manipulators allow you to work effectively in a Perspective view panel when transforming objects.

If you want to work more quickly when changing axes for your manipulators, there are several solutions available.

1   Change axis focus using hotkeys

- Press and hold on the transform keys:

    w - for move

    e - for rotate

    r - for scale

- Choose an axis handle for constraining from the marking menu.

2   Change axis focus using Shift key

- Press the **Shift** key.

- **Click+drag** with the **MMB** in the direction of the desired axis.

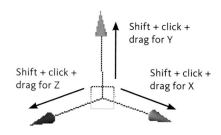

Shift + click + drag for Y

Shift + click + drag for Z

Shift + click + drag for X

Transform manipulators

Set pivot

The ability to change the pivot location on a transform node is very important for certain types of animation.

1 **To change your pivot point:**

- Select one of the manipulator tools;

- Press the **Insert** key (**Home** on Macintosh);

- **Click+drag** on the manipulator to move its pivot;

- Press **Insert** to return to the manipulator tool (**Home** on Macintosh).

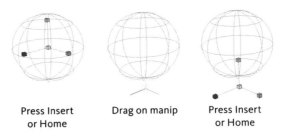

Press Insert   Drag on manip   Press Insert
or Home   or Home

Setting pivot using Insert / Home key

Channel Box

Another way of entering accurate values is through the Channel Box. This powerful panel gives you access to an object's transform node and any associated input nodes.

If you have multiple objects selected, then your changes to a channel will affect every node sharing that attribute.

To put one of the selected objects at the top of the Channel Box so that it is visible, choose the desired node from the Channel Box's **Object** menu.

If you want to work with a particular channel, you can use the **Channels** menu to set keys, add expressions and complete other useful tasks. You can also change the display of Channel Box names to short MEL-based names.

> **Note:** *To control what channels are shown in the Channel Box, go to the* **Window** *menu, and choose* **General Editors → Channel Control***.*

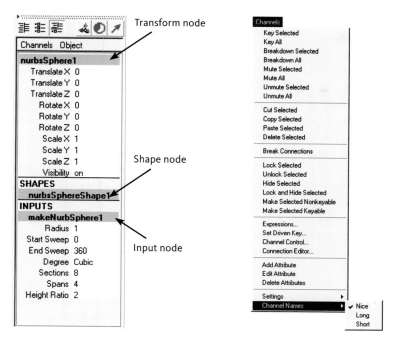

Transform node

Shape node

Input node

The Channel Box   *Channel's menu*

Channel Box and manipulators

One of the features of the Channel Box is the way in which you can use it to access manipulators at the transform level.

By default, the Channel Box is set to show manipulators every time you tab into a new Channel Box field. You will notice that as you select the channel names such as *Translate Z* or *Rotate X*, the manipulator switches from translate to rotate.

One fast way to edit an attribute is to invoke the virtual slider by selecting the name of the desired channel in the Channel Box, then using the **MMB+drag** in a view panel to change its value.

There are three options for the Channel Box manipulator setting:

Default manipulator setting

This setting lets you activate the appropriate field in the Channel Box, and then modify the values with either the left or middle mouse button.

To use the default method, complete the following steps:

- Click on the desired channel name or input field, then **click+drag** directly on the active manipulator with the **LMB**.

  OR

- Click on the desired channel name or input field, then **click+drag** in open space with the **MMB**.

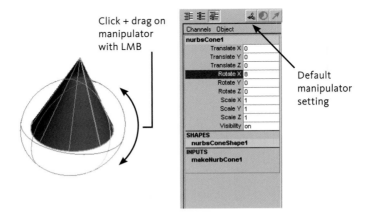

Click + drag on
manipulator
with LMB

Default
manipulator
setting

Channel Box default manipulator setting

No-manipulator setting

You can click on the manipulator icon over the Channel Box to turn manipulation off, which leaves the Channel Box focused on coordinate input. With this setting, you cannot use the middle or left mouse buttons for manipulation. To manipulate objects in this mode, you must do one of the following:

- Click in the channel's entry field and type the exact value.

  OR

- Use one of the normal transform tools such as **Move**, **Rotate** or **Scale**.

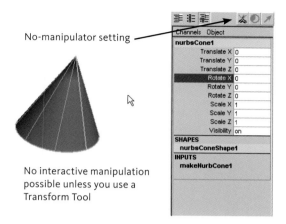

No-manipulator setting

No interactive manipulation possible unless you use a Transform Tool

Channel Box no-manipulator setting

No-visual manipulator setting

A third option found on this manipulator button returns manipulator capability to the Channel Box—but now you will not see the manipulator on the screen.

- Click on the desired channel name or within the channel's input field.

- **Click+drag** in open space with the **MMB**.

    You can now use the two new buttons that let you edit the speed and drop-off of the manipulations.

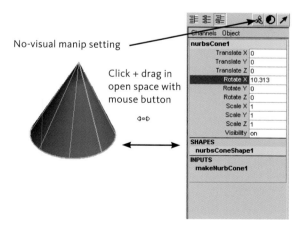

No-visual manip setting

Click + drag in open space with mouse button

Channel Box no-visual manipulator setting

The first button that becomes available with the *No-visual* setting is the speed button which lets you **click+drag** with your **MMB** either slow, medium or fast.

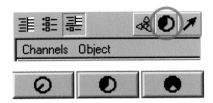

Channel speed controls

> **Tip:** *You can also combine* **MMB+dragging** *with the* **Ctrl** *key for slow or* **Shift** *key for fast value changes.*

The second button is the drop-off button which lets you choose between a linear motion as you **click+drag** with the **MMB**, or a **click+drag** that is slow at first and faster as you drag further.

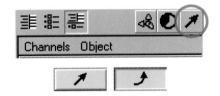

Channel drop-off options

Attribute Editor

The Channel Box lets you focus on attributes that are keyable using **Set Key**, but the Attribute Editor gives you access to all the other attributes/channels.

The Attribute Editor is used for all nodes in Maya. This means that shaders, textures, surfaces, lattices, Render Settings, etc. can all be displayed in this one type of window.

1 Open the Attribute Editor window

- Select a node.
- Go to the **Window** menu and select **Attribute Editor**.

2 Open the Attribute Editor panel

- Select a node.

  Go to the **Display** *menu and select* **UI Elements** → **Attribute Editor**.

  The Channel Box is now replaced by an Attribute Editor panel.

When you open up the Attribute Editor, you not only get the active node, but also related nodes based on dependency relationships. In the example below, a sphere's transform, shape and *makeNurbSphere* nodes are all present. These are the same input and shape nodes shown in the Channel Box.

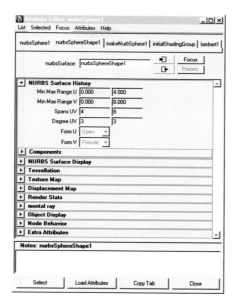

A typical Attribute Editor

Tip: You can also press the **Ctrl + a** hotkey to open the Attribute Editor. You can set your preference for having the Attribute Editor in a panel or in its own window through **Window → Settings/Preferences → Preferences** and click on the **Interface** section to modify the **Open Attribute Editor** option.

Numeric input

To add specific values to your transformations, you can use the numeric input boxes. This allows you to apply exact absolute or relative values to the attributes associated with the current manipulator.

1   Enter absolute values

- Select the **Absolute Transform** option from the input field menu.

- Enter values and press **Enter** on your keyboard.

  The selected objects will be moved based on the input and the current manipulator.

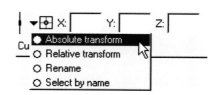

The input field menu

2   **Enter relative values**

- Select the **Relative Transform** option from the input field menu.

- Enter values and press **Enter** on your keyboard.

Note: *You are not required to enter zero values.*

Selecting

One of the most important tasks when using Maya is your ability to select different types of nodes and their key components.

For instance, you may need to be able to select a sphere and move it, or to select the sphere's control vertices and move them. You may also need to distinguish between different types of objects so that you can select only surfaces or only deformers.

Selection masks

To make selecting work, you have a series of selection masks available to you. This allows you to have one Select Tool that is then *masked* so that it can only select certain kinds of objects and components.

The *selection mask* concept is very powerful because it allows you to create whatever combination of selection types that you desire. Sometimes, you only want to select joints and selection handles, or maybe you want to select anything but joints. With selection masks, you get to set up and choose the selected options.

The selection UI

The UI for selecting offers several types of access to the selection masks. You can learn all of them now and then choose which best suits your way of working down the line.

Grouping and parenting

When working with transform nodes, you can create more complex structures by building hierarchies of these node types.

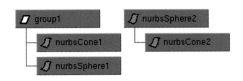

To build these structures, you can choose to *group* the nodes under a new transform node or you can *parent* one of the nodes under the other so that the lower node inherits the motion of the top node.

Grouped and parented nodes

Selection modes

At the top of the workspace, you have several selection mask tools available. These are all organized under three main types of select modes. Each type gives you access to either the hierarchy, object type or components.

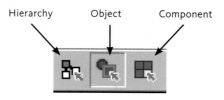

The select modes

Scene hierarchy mode

Hierarchy mode gives you access to different parts of the scene hierarchy structure. In the example shown below, the leaf node and the root node are highlighted. This mode lets you access each of these parts of the hierarchy. You can select root nodes, leaf nodes and template nodes using the selection masks.

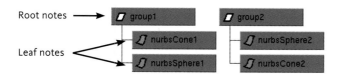

Hierarchy types

Object mode

Object mode lets you perform selections based on the object type. Selection masks are available as icons which encompass related types of objects.

With your **RMB**, you can access more detailed options that are listed under each mask group. If you create a partial list, the mask icon is highlighted in orange.

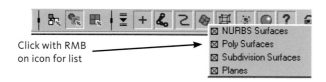

Object mode with selection masks

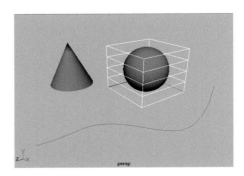

A lattice object and a curve object selected

Pop-up menu selection

When objects overlap in a view, the pop-up menu selection lets you display a pop-up list of the objects to select. **LMB** click the overlap area to display the menu. Your selection is highlighted in the scene viewports as you select an item in the list.

- This option is disabled by default. To turn it on, select **Window** → **Settings/ Preferences** → **Preferences** and click on the **Selection** section to enable **Pick chooser**.

Selection pop-up menu

Component mode

The shape nodes of an object contain various components such as control vertices or isoparms. To access these, you need to be in Component mode.

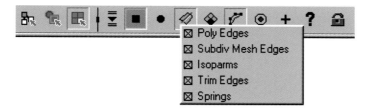

Component selection masks

When you select an object in this mode, it first highlights the object and shows you the chosen component type—you can then select the actual component.

Once you go back to Object mode, the object is selected and you can work with it. Toggling between Object and Component modes allows you to reshape and position objects quickly and easily.

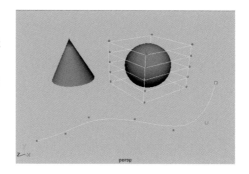

CV components and lattice point components

Tip: *To toggle between Object and Component modes, press the **F8** key.*

RMB select

Another way of accessing the components of an object is to select an object, then press the **RMB**. This brings up a marking menu that lets you choose from the various components available for that object.

If you select another object, you return to your previous select mask selection. This is a very fast way of selecting components when in hierarchy mode, or for components that are not in the current selection mask.

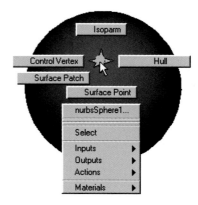

The RMB select menu

Combined select modes

In front of the selection mask mode icons is a pop-up menu that gives you different preset mask options. These presets let you combine different object and component level select options.

An example would be the NURBS option. This allows you to select various NURBS-based mask types such as surfaces, curves, CVs, curve control points and isoparms.

> **Note:** *In this mode, if you want to select CVs that are not visible by default, you must make them visible by going to the* **Display** *menu and selecting* **NURBS → CVs.**

When using a combined select mode, objects and components are selected differently. Objects are selected by **click+dragging** a select box around a part of the object, while components can be selected with direct clicking.

> **Note:** *If you have CVs shown on an object and the select box touches any of them, you will select these components instead of the object. To select the object, you must drag the select box over part of the surface where there are no CVs.*

TOOLS AND ACTIONS

In Maya, a large group of menu items can be broken down into two types of commands: *tools* and *actions*, each working in their own particular manner. Almost every function can be set as a tool or action.

Tools

Tools are designed to remain active until you have finished using them. You select a tool, use it to complete a series of steps, then select another tool. In most cases, the Help line at the bottom of the workspace can be used to prompt your actions when using the tool.

Earlier you were introduced to the **Y** key on the QWERTY toolbox. By default, this button is blank because it represents the last tool used. When you pick a tool from the menus, its icon inserts itself into the QWERTY menu.

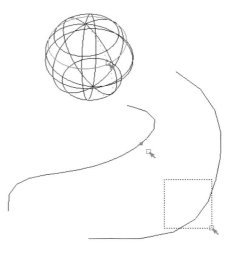

NURBS select options

1   As tool option

- Pick a menu item and go to the options.

- Under the **Edit** menu, select **As Tool**.

  By default you will remain in this tool until you pick another tool. There is also an option that will deselect the tool after completion.

2   Return to the last tool used

- Press the **Y** key.

Actions

Actions follow a selection-action paradigm. This means that you first have to pick something and then act on it. This allows you to choose an action, return to editing your work and refine the results immediately.

Actions require that you have something selected before acting on it. This means that you must first find out what is required to complete the action.

1   Find out selection requirements of an action

- Move your cursor over a menu item.

- Look at the Help line at the bottom-left of the interface.

  *If you have the Help line UI element visible, the selection requirements are displayed. For instance, a **Loft** requires curves, isoparms or curves on surfaces while **Insert Isoparm** requires isoparms to be picked.*

2   Complete the action

- If the tool is not already set as an action, select **Edit** → **As Action** from the menu item's options.

- Use either pick modes or the **RMB** pick menu to make the required selections.

- Choose the action using the hotbox, shelf or menus.

  The action is complete and the focus returns to your last transform tool.

Tip: *If a menu item contains the word "Tool" such as "Align Curves Tool," it uses tool interaction. If the word "Tool" is not mentioned, the menu item is set as an action. This dynamically updates according to your preferences.*

2D fillet as an action

A good example of a typical action is a 2D fillet. As with all actions, you must start with an understanding of what the tool needs before beginning to execute the action.

Two curves for filleting

1   **Draw two curves**

- Select **Create → CV Curve Tool**.

- Place several points for one curve.

- Press **Enter** to complete.

- Press the **y** key to refocus on Curve Tool.

- Draw the second curve so that it crosses the first.

- Press the **Enter** key to complete.

2   **Find out 2D fillet requirements**

- In the **Surfaces** menu set, move your cursor over the **Edit Curves → Curve Fillet** menu item without executing it.

- Look in the Help Line to determine what kind of pick is required.

    The Help Line says: "Select curve parameter points."

3   **Pick the first curve point**

- Click on the first curve with the **RMB**.

- Pick **Curve Point** from the selection marking menu.

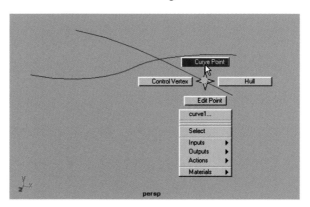

RMB pick of curve parameter point

- Click on the curve to place the point on the side you want to keep.

4   Pick the second curve point

- Click on the second curve with the **RMB**.

- Pick **Curve Point** from the selection marking menu.

- Press the **Shift** key and click on the curve to place the point on the side of the curve you want to keep.

  The **Shift** *key lets you add a second point to the selection list without losing the first curve point.*

Note: *You must first use the marking menu and then the* **Shift** *key to add a second point to the selection list, otherwise the selection menu will not appear.*

Two curve points in place

5   Fillet the curves

- Select **Edit Curves** → **Curve Fillet** → ❑, to open the tool options.

- Turn the **Trim** option **On**.

- Click on the **Fillet** button.

Fillet Tool options window

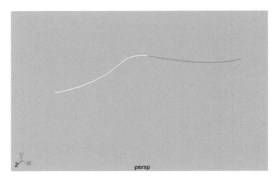

Final filleted curves

2D fillet as a tool

With this example you will use the menu item as a tool rather than an action.

1   Draw two curves

- In a new scene, draw two curves as in the last example.

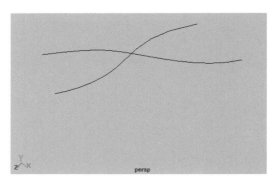

Two curves for filleting

2   Change curve fillet to tool

- Select **Edit Curves** → **Curve Fillet** → ❑.

- Select **Edit** → **As Tool** from the options window.

- Set **Trim** to **On**.

- Press the **Fillet Tool** button.

> **Note:** *Notice the menu item now says "Curve Fillet Tool."*

3   Pick the first curve

- Click with the **LMB** on the first curve.

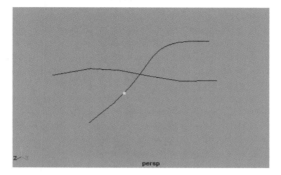

First curve selected

4   Pick the second curve

- Click with the **LMB** on the second curve.

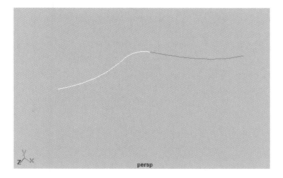

Final filleted curves

Conclusion

You now know how to navigate the Maya UI and how tools and actions work. The skills you learned here will be applied throughout the rest of this book. You have the knowledge now to determine how you want to use the interface. Experiment with the different techniques taught here as you work through the Learning Maya projects.

The instructions for the following projects will not specify whether or not you should use the hotbox or menus to complete an action—the choice will be yours.

In the next lesson, you will explore the Dependency Graph. You will learn about the different nodes and how to build them into hierarchies and procedural animations.

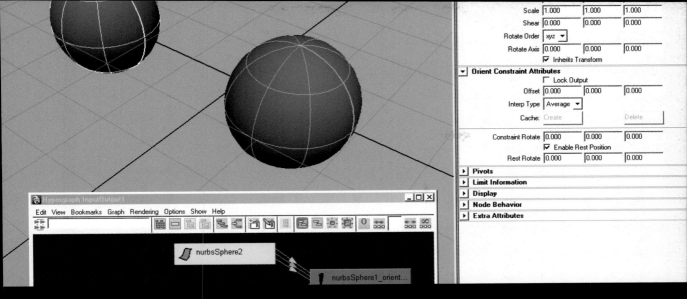

Lesson 06
The Dependency Graph

In the first five lessons of this book, you encountered many nodes that helped you animate and render your scene. You were introduced to input nodes, hierarchy nodes, shading networks and texture nodes. These nodes, among others, represent key elements within Maya—each node contains important attributes that help you define and animate your scenes.

In this lesson, you are going to explore nodes, attributes and connections by animating objects at various levels. You will explore how attributes are connected by Maya and how you can connect them yourself. You will also learn how to distinguish scene hierarchies from object dependencies.

This lesson might seem a bit abstract at first, but in the end you will see how the various nodes contribute to an animated scene that will help you in later lessons.

In this lesson you will learn the following:

- About hierarchies and dependencies
- About connections
- About construction history

Maya architecture

The Maya architecture functionality is defined by a node-based system, known as the *Dependency Graph*. Each node contains attributes that can be connected to other nodes. If you wanted to reduce Maya to its bare essentials, you could describe it as *nodes with attributes that are connected*. This node-based approach gives Maya its open and flexible procedural characteristics.

Hierarchies and dependencies

If you understand the idea of *nodes with attributes that are connected*, you will understand the Dependency Graph. Building a primitive sphere is a simple example involving the Dependency Graph.

1   Set up your view panels

To view nodes and connections in a diagrammatic format, the Hypergraph panel is required along with a Perspective view.

- Select **Panels → Layouts → 2 Panes Side by Side**.
- Set up a Perspective view in the first panel.
- Set up a Hypergraph in the second panel by selecting **Panels → Panel → Hypergraph Panel → Hypergraph: Hierarchy.**
- Dolly into the Perspective view to get closer to the grid.

2   Create a primitive sphere

- Select **Create → NURBS Primitives → Sphere**.
- Press **5** to turn on smooth shading.

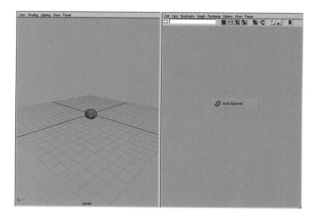

New sphere

3   View the shape node

In the Hypergraph panel, you are currently looking at the scene view. The scene view is focused on *transform nodes*. This type of node lets you set the position and orientation of your objects.

Right now, only a lone *nurbsSphere* node is visible. In fact, there are two nodes in this hierarchy, but the second is hidden by default. This hidden node is a *shape node* which contains information about the object itself.

- In the Hypergraph, select **Options** → **Display** → **Shape nodes**.

  You can now see the transform node, which is the positioning node, and the shape node which contains information about the actual surface of the sphere. The transform node defines the position of the shape below:

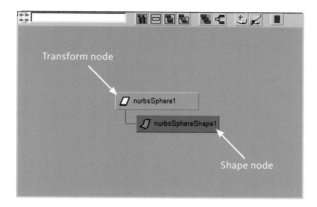

Transform and shape nodes

- In the Hypergraph panel, select **Options** → **Display** → **Shape nodes** to turn these **Off**.

  Notice that when these nodes are expanded, the shape node and the transform node have different icons.

  When collapsed, the transform node takes on the shape node's icon to help you understand what is going on underneath.

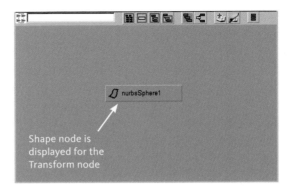

Transform node on its own

4   **View the dependencies**

To view the dependencies that exist with a primitive sphere, you need to take a look at the up and downstream connections.

- In the Hypergraph panel, click on the **Input and Output Connections** button.

The original transform node is now separated from the shape node. While the transform node has a hierarchical relationship to the shape node, their attributes are not dependent on each other.

The input node called makeNurbSphere is a result of the original creation of the sphere. The options set in the sphere's tool option window have been placed into a node that feeds into the shape node. The shape node is dependent on the input node. Changing values for the input node will affect the shape of the sphere.

You will also see the initial shading group connected to the sphere. This is the default grey Lambert that is applied to all new objects.

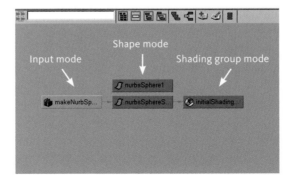

Sphere dependencies

5   Edit attributes in the Channel Box

In the Channel Box, you can edit attributes belonging to the various nodes. Every node type can be found in the Channel Box. This lets you affect both hierarchical relationships and dependencies.

If you edit an attribute belonging to the *makeNurbSphere* node, then the shape of the sphere will be affected. If you change an attribute belonging to the *nurbsSphere* transform node, then the positioning will be altered. Use the Channel Box to help you work with the nodes.

- For the transform node, change the **Rotate Y** value to **45**.

- For the *makeNurbSphere* input node, change the **Radius** to **3**.

> **Note:** *You can set attribute values to affect either the scene hierarchy or the Dependency Graph.*

Shading group nodes

In earlier lessons, the word *node* was used a great deal when working with shading groups. In fact, shading group nodes create dependency networks that work the same way as shape nodes.

1   Create a shading network

When you create a material, it automatically has a shading group connected to it.

- Select **Window → Rendering Editors → Hypershade**

- In the Hypershade window, select **Create → Materials → Phong**.

- **Assign** this material to the sphere.

- Select the sphere in the Perspective panel and click on the **Input and Output Connections** button.

    In the Hypergraph view, you will notice how the input node is connected to the shape node, which relates to the Phong shading group.

    A line is now drawn between the sphere's shape node and shading group node. This is because the shading group is dependent on the surface in order to render.

    Every time you assign a shading network to an object, you make a Dependency Graph connection.

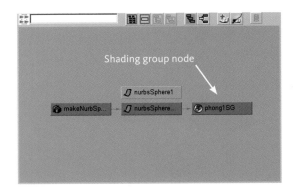

Shading group dependencies

- Select the *nurbsSphere1* node and the *phong1SG* node in the Hypergraph.
- Again, click on the **Input and Output Connections** button.

  You can now see how the phong material node and the sphere's shape node both feed the shading group. You can move your cursor over any of the connecting lines to see the attributes that are being connected.

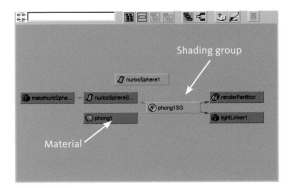

Assigned shading group

2   Open the Attribute Editor

You have seen how the nodes in the Hypergraph and Channel Box have been used to view and edit attributes on connected nodes. Now you will see how the Attribute Editor displays nodes, attributes and connections.

- Click on the **Scene Hierarchy** button in the Hypergraph panel to go back to a scene view.
- Select the *sphere*'s transform node.

- Press **Ctrl+a** to open the Attribute Editor.

  In this integral window, you will see several tabs, each containing groups of attributes. Each tab represents a different node. All the tabs displayed represent parts of the selected node's Dependency Graph that are related to the chosen node. By bringing up several connected nodes, you have easier access to particular parts of the graph.

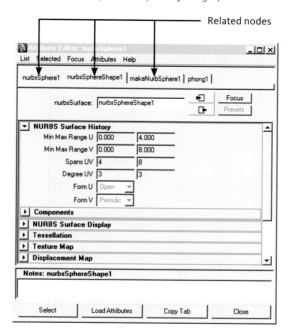

Nodes and attributes in the Attribute Editor

Note: *The Attribute Editor lets you focus on one part of the Dependency Graph at a time.*

Making connections

To help you understand exactly what a Dependency Graph connection is, you are going to make your own connection and see how it affects the graph.

1   Open the Connection Editor

- Select the *sphere*.

- Select **Window → General Editors → Connection Editor...**

- Click on the **Reload Left** button.

  The selected transform node is loaded into the left column. All of the attributes belonging to this node are listed.

Note: *There are more attributes here than you see in the Channel Box. The Channel Box only shows attributes that have been set as keyable. Other attributes can be found in the Attribute Editor.*

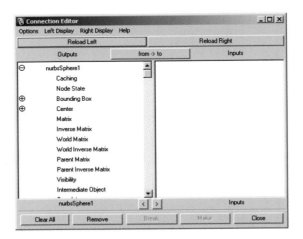

Transform node in Connection Editor

2   **Add phong as the input node**

- In the Hypergraph, select **Rendering** → **Show Materials**.
- Select the *phong1* material node.
- In the Connection Editor, click on the **Reload Right** button.

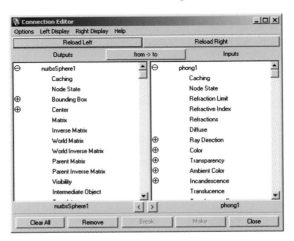

Material node in Connection Editor

3   Make connections

You will now connect some attributes from the transform node to the material node.

- In the left column, scroll down until you find the *Translate* attributes.
- Click on the plus (+) sign to expand this multiple attribute and see the *Translate X, Y* and *Z* attributes.
- In the right column, scroll down until you find the *Color* attribute.
- Click on the plus (+) sign to expand this multiple attribute and see the *Color R, G* and *B* attributes.
- Click on the **Translate X** attribute in the left column.
- Click on the **Color R** in the right column.

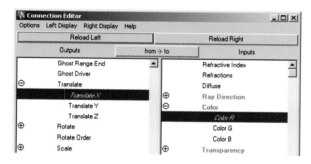

Connected attributes

- Use the same method to connect the following attributes:

   Translate Y to **Color G**;

   Translate Z to **Color B**.

4   View the connections

- In the Hypergraph panel, select the *phong1* node and click on the **Input and Output Connections** button.

- Move your cursor over one of the arrow connections between the transform node and material node.

   The connection arrow is highlighted and the connected attributes are displayed. You now see the diagrammatic results of your action.

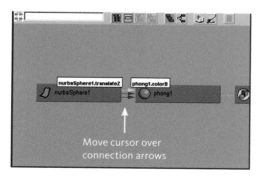

Viewing attribute connections

5 Move the sphere

You should see the effect of your connections when moving the sphere in the Perspective view.

- In the Perspective view, select the *sphere*.
- **Move** the sphere along the **X-axis**.

  The color of the sphere changes to red. By increasing the value of the translation along X, you add red to the color.

- Try moving the sphere along each of the three main axes to see the colors change.

Adding a texture node

While it is a fun and educational exercise to see the material node's color dependent on the position of the ball, it may not be very realistic. You will now break the existing connections and map a texture node in their place.

1 Delete connections

You can delete the connections in the Hypergraph view.

- In the Hypergraph view panel, select one of the three connection arrows between the transform node and the material node.
- Press the **Backspace** or **Delete** key to delete the connection.
- **Repeat** for the other two connections between these nodes.

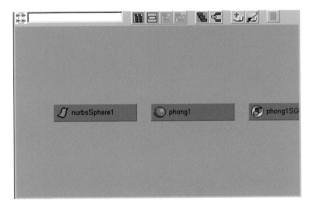

Broken connections

2 Add a checkered texture map

You will now use the Attribute Editor to help add a texture to the existing shading group.

- Click on the *phong1* material node.

- Press **Ctrl+a** to open the Attribute Editor.
- Click on the **Map** button next to **Color**.
- Choose a **Checker** texture from the **Create Render Node** window.
- **MMB** in the Perspective view to make it active and press **6**.

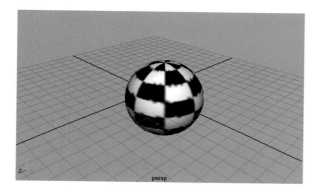

Textured sphere

In the Hypergraph, you can see the dependencies building up for the shading group. The texture is built using two nodes: the checker node, which contains the procedural texture attributes, and the placement node, which contains attributes that define the placement of the texture on the assigned surfaces.

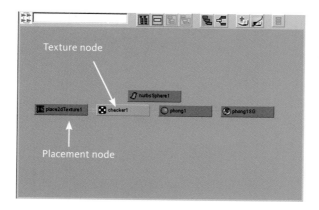

Shading group network

Animating the sphere

When you animate, you are changing the value of an attribute over time. You use keys to set these values at important points in time, then tangent properties to determine how the attribute value changes in-between the keys.

The key and tangent information is placed in a separate animation curve node that is then connected to the animated attribute.

1   Select the sphere

- In the Hypergraph panel, click on the **Scene Hierarchy** button.
- Select the *nurbsSphere* transform node.

2   Return the sphere to the origin

Since you moved the sphere along the three axes earlier, it's a good time to set it back to the origin.

- Select the sphere's **Translate** attributes through the Channel Box by clicking on the **Translate X** value and dragging to the **Translate Z** value.

  Doing so will highlight all three translate values, allowing you to enter a single value to change all of them at once.

- In the Channel Box, type **0** and hit **Enter**.

  Make sure all three translation values changed simultaneously.

- Make sure to also set all **Rotate** values to **0** and all **Scale** values to **1**.

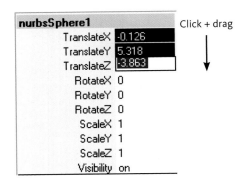

Click + drag

Click+drag on the scale values

3   Animate the sphere's rotation

- In the Time Slider, set the playback range to **120** frames.
- Go to frame **1**.
- Click on the **Rotate Y** attribute name in the Channel Box.
- Click with your **RMB** and select **Key Selected** from the pop-up menu.

  This sets a key at the chosen time.

- Go to frame **120**.
- In the Channel Box, change the **Rotate Y** attribute to **720**.
- Click with your **RMB** and select **Key selected** from the pop-up menu.

- **Playback** the results.

  The sphere is now spinning.

4   View the dependencies

- In the Hypergraph panel, click on the **Input and Output Connections** button.

  You will see that an animation curve node has been created and then connected to the transform node. The transform node is shown as a trapezoid to indicate that it is now connected to the animation curve node. If you move the mouse cursor over the connection arrow, you will see that the connection is to Rotate Y.

  If you select the animation curve node and open the Attribute Editor, you will see that each key has been recorded along with value, time and tangent information. You can actually edit this information here, or use the Graph Editor where you get more visual feedback.

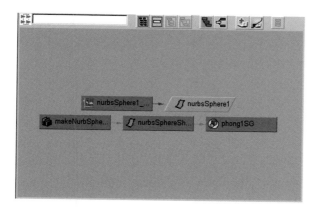

Connected animation curve node

Procedural animation

If the Maya procedural nature is defined as *nodes with attributes that are connected*, then a procedural animation would be set up by animating attributes at various levels of a Dependency Graph network.

You will now build a series of animated events that build on each other to create the final result.

1   Create an edit point curve

- Hide everything in your scene by selecting **Display → Hide → All**.
- Select **Create → EP Curve Tool**.
- Press and hold the **x** hotkey to turn on grid snap.

- Draw a curve as shown below:

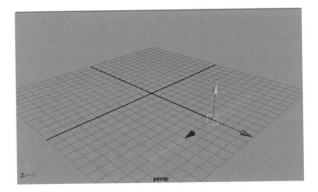

New curve

- When you are finished, press **Enter** to finalize the curve.
- Select **Modify → Center Pivot**.

Note: *The pivot of a new curve is centered to the origin by default.*

2   **Duplicate the curve**

- Select **Edit → Duplicate**.
- **Move** the new curve to the opposite side of the grid.

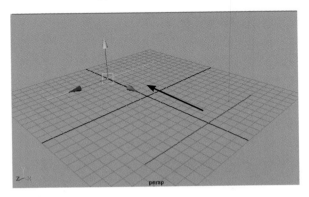

Moved curve

3 Create a lofted surface

A lofted surface can be created using two or more profile curves.

- **Click+drag** a selection box around both of the curves.
- Select **Surfaces → Loft**.

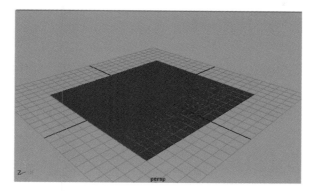

Lofted surface

4 Change your panel display

- In the Hypergraph panel, select **Panels → Perspective → persp**.
- In the new Perspective panel, select **Show → None** and then **Show → NURBS Curves**.

Now you have two Perspective views. One shows the surface in shaded mode and the second shows only the curves. This makes it easier to pick and edit the curves in isolation from the surface itself.

5 Edit CVs on the original curves

- Select the first curve.
- Click with your **RMB** to bring up the selection marking menu and select **Control Vertex**.
- **Click+drag** a selection box over one of the CVs and **Move** it down.

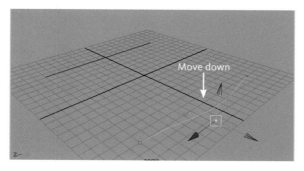

Edited profile curve

In the original Perspective view, you can see the effect on the lofted surface. Since the surface was dependent on the shape of the curve, you again took advantage of the Dependency Graph.

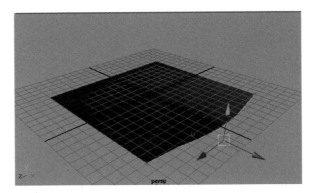

Resulting surface update

Note: *The dependencies associated with models are sometimes referred to asconstruction history. By updating the input shape, you have updated the history of the lofted surface.*

Curve on surface

You will now build a curve directly onto the surface. This curve will become dependent on the shape of the surface for its own shape.

The surface was built as a grid of surface lines called *isoparms*. These lines help define a separate coordinate system specific to each surface. Whereas world space coordinates are defined by X, Y and Z, surface coordinates are defined by U and V.

1   Make the surface live

So far, you have drawn curves into the world space coordinate system. You can also make any surface into a *live* surface and draw into the UV space of the surface.

- Select the lofted surface.

   The CVs on the curve disappear and you are able to focus on the surface.

- Select **Modify** → **Make Live**.

   Live surface display changes to a green wireframe.

- Select **Display** → **Grid** to turn off the ground grid.

2   Draw a curve on the surface

- Select **Create → EP Curve Tool**.

- **Draw** a curve on the live surface.

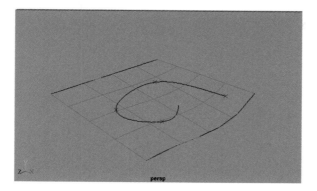

New curve on surface

3   Move the curve on surface

- Press the **Enter** key to complete the curve.

- Select the **Move Tool**.

  The move manipulator looks a little different this time. Rather than three manipulator handles, there are only two. One is for the U direction of the surface and the other is for the V direction.

- **Click+drag** on the manipulator handles to move the curve around the surface space.

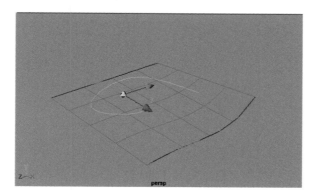

Moving the curve on surface

Tip: *This UV space is the same one used by texture maps when using 2D placement nodes.*

4 **Revert live surface**

   • Click in empty space to clear the selection.

   • Select **Modify** → **Make Not Live**.

   With nothing selected, any live surfaces are reverted back to normal surfaces.

Tip: *You can also use the Make Live button on the right of the snap icons in the Status bar.*

Group hierarchy

You are now going to build a hierarchy by grouping two primitives, then animating the group along the curve-on-surface using path animation.

1 **Create a primitive cone**

   • Select **Create** → **NURBS Primitives** → **Cone**.

2 **Create a primitive sphere**

   • Select **Create** → **NURBS Primitives** → **Sphere**.

   • **Move** the sphere above the cone.

3 **Group the two objects**

   • Select the cone and the sphere.

   • Select **Edit** → **Group** or use the **Ctrl+g** hotkey.

   • Select **Display** → **Transform Display** → **Selection Handles**.

   The selection handle is a special marker that will make it easier to pick the group in Object selection mode.

New primitive cone

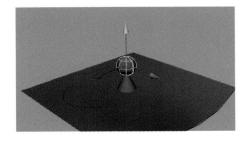

Second primitive object

Grouped objects with selection handle

> **Note:** *Selection handles have higher selection priority than curves and surfaces.*

Path animation

To animate the new group, you will attach it to the curve on surface. You can use the curve on surface to define the group's position over time.

1   Attach to the curve on surface

- With the group still selected, press the **Shift** key and select the curve on surface.
- Go to the **Animation** menu set.
- Select **Animate** → **Motion Paths** → **Attach to Motion Path** → ❑.
- In the Option window, make sure that the **Follow** option is turned **Off**.
- Click **Attach**.
- **Playback** the results.

As the group moves along the path curve, you will notice that it is always standing straight up.

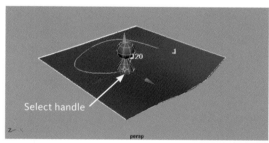

Path animation

2   Constrain to the surface normal

You will now constrain the orientation of the group to the normal direction of the lofted surface. The normal is like the third dimension of the surface's UV space.

- Click on the loft surface to select it on its own.
- Press the **Shift** key and select the grouped primitives using the selection handle.
- Select **Constrain** → **Normal** → ❑.
- In the **Option** window, set the following:

    Aim Vector to **0**, **1**, **0**;

    Up Vector to **1**, **0**, **0**.

- Click **Add** to create the constraint.
- **Playback** the results.

Note: *If your group is upside down, it could be because the surface normals are reversed. To fix this, select your plane and select* **Edit NURBS → Reverse Surface Direction**.

Now the group is orienting itself based on the normal direction of the surface. The group is dependent on the surface in two ways. Firstly, its position is dependent on the path curve, which is dependent on the surface for its shape. Secondly, its orientation is directly dependent on the surface's shape.

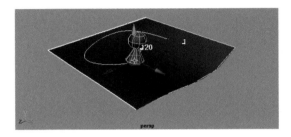

Constrained orientation

Layer the animation

The various parts of the Dependency Graph can all be animated to create exciting results. To see the Dependency Graph in motion, you will animate different nodes within the network to see how the dependencies react.

1   Edit the loft curve shape

Since the shape of the surface is dependent on the original loft curves, you will start by animating the shape of the second curve.

- Select the second loft curve.

Tip: *You may want to use the second Perspective panel, which is only displaying curves.*

- Click with your **RMB** to bring up the selection marking menu and select **Control Vertex**.

Control vertices define the shape of the curve. By editing these, you are editing the curve's shape node.

- **Click+drag** a selection box over one of the CVs and **Move** it up to a new position.

  As you move the CV, the surface updates its shape, which in turn redefines the curve-on-surface and the orientation of the group. All the dependencies are being updated.

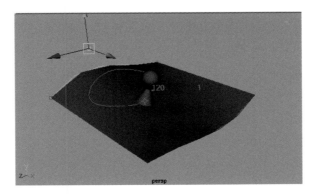

Updating the dependencies

2 Set keys on the CV position

- Go to frame **1**.
- Press **s** to set a key.
- Go to frame **120**.
- Press **s** to set a key.
- Go to frame **60**.
- **Move** the CV to a new position.
- Press **s** to set a key.
- **Playback** the results.

  You can see how the dependency updates are maintained as the CV is animated. You are animating the construction history of the lofted surface and the connected path animation.

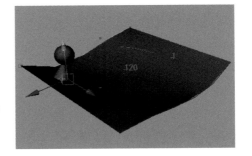

Animated history

3 Animate the curve-on-surface

To add another layer of animation, you will key the position of the curve-on-surface.

- Select the curve-on-surface.
- Go to frame **1**.
- Press **s** to set key.

- Go to frame **120**.
- **Move** the curve-on-surface to another position on the lofted surface.

  Press **s** *to set key.*

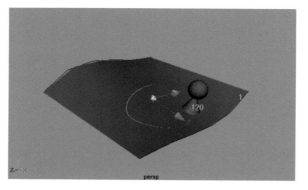

Animated curve on surface

4 Assign the phong shading group

To make it easier to see the animating objects, apply the checker shading group created earlier to the primitive group.

- Select the primitive group using its selection handle.
- Go to the **Rendering** menu set.
- Select **Lighting/Shading → Assign Existing Material → phong1**.
- **Playback** the scene.

5 View the dependencies

Of course, you can view the dependency network that results from all these connections in the Hypergraph view, which will probably be a bit more complex than anything you have seen so far.

- Select the primitive group that is attached to the motion path.
- Open the Hypergraph panel and click on the **Input and Output Connections** button.

  The resulting network contains the various dependencies that you built during this example.

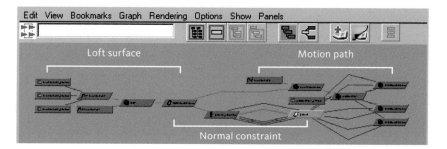

The dependency network

Conclusion

The procedural qualities of Maya are tied to how the Dependency Graph uses nodes, attributes and connections. You can see how deep these connections can go and how they are maintained throughout the animation process. Similar techniques can be used on other node types throughout Maya.

Obviously, you don't have to use the Hypergraph and the Connection Editor to build, animate and texture map your objects. In most cases, you will be thinking more about the motion of your character's walk or the color of their cheeks. It is still a good idea to know that the Dependency Graph supports everything you do and can always be used to your advantage.

In the next project, you will model, texture, set up and animate a penguin character.

Project 02

In this project, you will create a character named BigZ, one of the penguins from the Sony Pictures Animation Inc. movie *Surf's Up*. You will begin by modeling and texturing his skin using several polygonal tools. Once that is done, you will set up his skeleton and rig it so that you can fully animate him. You will then test the rig by keyframing a simple walk cycle.

Lesson 07
Polygonal Modeling

In this lesson, you will create BigZ, one of the penguins from the movie *Surf's Up*. The character will be created starting from primitives. You will use many polygonal tools and deformers until the desired shape is achieved. As you learned in the first project, it will be possible to edit the construction history of modeling actions to update the model as you go. As well, you can edit the results throughout the lesson until you delete the history.

In this lesson you will learn the following:

- How to model starting from a cube primitive
- How to model using polygon proxy
- How to mirror geometry
- How to work with polygonal components
- How to edit the topology of a polygonal model
- How to work with procedural modeling attributes
- How to change edge normals
- How to use a lattice deformer

Set up your project

Since this is a new project, you must set a new directory as your current project directory. This will let you separate the files generated in this project from other projects. If you want to look at the final scene for this lesson, refer to the scene *07-bigz_05.ma*.

1 Set the project

As you have already learned, it is easier to manage your files if you set a project directory that contains sub-directories for different types of files that relate to your project.

- If you copied the support files onto your drive, go to the **File** menu and select **Project → Set...**

  A window opens, pointing you to the Autodesk® Maya® projects directory.

- Click on the folder named *project2* to select it.

- Click on the **OK** button.

  This sets the project2 directory as your current project.

  OR

- If you did not copy the support files on your drive, create a new project called *project2* with all the default directories.

2 Make a new scene

- Select **File → New Scene**.

Starting the penguin

You will build the penguin starting from a polygonal cube primitive. Facets will be extruded to create the more complex biped shape required and will then be refined to create the penguin shape.

It is important to understand what you will be doing throughout this lesson, so you must plan ahead and breakdown the task into simple stages. The following explains how you will approach the character modeling.

Torso

The cube primitive will be the pelvis area of the penguin. You will then extrude faces up to create the torso, neck and head.

Legs

Starting from the pelvis geometry, you will extrude the polygon faces to create the legs.

Arms

Starting from the torso geometry, you will extrude polygon faces to create and refine the arms.

Later in the lesson, you will ensure that your model is symmetrical by mirroring it.

> **Tip:** It is a good idea to look at reference images from this project and from the gallery in this book to give you an idea of the finished product.

1   Primitive cube

- Select **Create → Polygon Primitives → Cube**.

- Press **5** to **Smooth Shade All**.

- **Rename** the cube to *body*.

- From the **Inputs** section of the Channel Box, set the **Subdivisions Width** of the *polyCube1* node to **2**.

  Doing so will define polygonal edges going down the central line of the character.

> **Tip:** As a general convention, you should always model your characters facing the scene's positive Z-axis.

- **Move** the cube up and **scale** it to roughly match the image to the right, which represents the waist of the character:

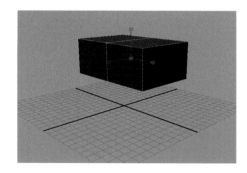

Start primitive cube

> **Tip:** When modeling, don't be afraid to model big. You do not want to be stuck working on a tiny model. Use the grid as a reference to represent the floor. You can always edit the proportions of your character later on.

2 Extrude faces

Before extruding the faces, you need to make sure that the **Keep Faces Together** option is enabled. When this option is **On**, it extrudes chunks of facets instead of each facet individually. The following is an example of **Keep Faces Together** both **On** and **Off**:

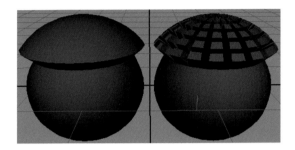

The Keep Faces Together effect

Note: *During the process of modeling the character, make sure that you do not accidentally select, deselect or modify faces that are behind the current view of the object. If you do, use Ctrl to deselect unwanted components.*

- Select the **Polygons** menu set by pressing **F3**.
- Make sure the option **Edit Mesh → Keep Faces Together** is set to **On**.
- Go into **Component** mode with faces displayed by pressing **F11,** or by setting the selection mask in the Status Bar as follows:

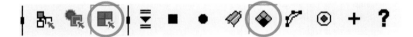

Component mode with faces enabled

- Select the two top faces on the cube, then select **Edit Mesh → Extrude**.
- **Move** the faces up in the **Y-axis**.
- **Scale** them up uniformly a little bit.
- **Repeat** the last three steps to get geometry similar to the image to the right.

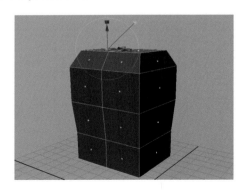

Waist and torso of the penguin

- **Extrude** three more times to make the neck, the middle of the head and the top of the head of the penguin.

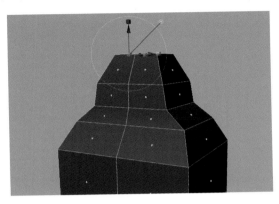

Neck and head of the penguin

Note: *You can preview smooth geometry by pressing the* **1**, **2** *or* **3** *hotkeys with polygonal geometry selected.*

3 Subdiv Proxy

So far, you need a bit of imagination in order to see the penguin's shape. Subdiv Proxy is a simple tool that allows you to see a smoothed version of your model while still modeling on the cube from the previous steps.

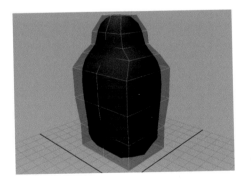

- Go into **Object** mode.
- With the *body* selected, select **Proxy** → **Subdiv Proxy**.

Doing so displays the original geometry, known as the proxy, with transparency, and displays the smoothed resulting

The proxy and smoothed geometry

geometry within it. Whenever you update the proxy geometry, the smoothed version will automatically update. Once you have refined the proxy cage to your needs, you can either get rid of the smoothed version and keep working on the proxy geometry or vice-versa.

Tip: *You should never tweak the smoothed version of the geometry directly.*

- Press the **[`] hotkey** (the key on the upper left corner of your keyboard), to toggle between the proxy and smoothed geometry.
- Press **Ctrl+`** to toggle between the original geometry and the Subdiv Proxy.

4 Extruding the legs

Now that you can see the rough shape of the penguin's body, you need to extrude the legs. Here, you will extrude both legs at the same time.

- Select the proxy geometry and display its faces.
- Select the two faces from underneath the pelvis to start extruding the legs.
- Turn **Off** the **Edit Mesh → Keep Faces Together**.

  You will now be able to extrude both faces at the same time, still creating independent legs.
- Select **Edit Mesh→ Extrude**.
- **Move** and **scale** the extruded faces down to the penguin's knees.

> **Note:** *When you manipulate the handle associated with one face, the other face reacts equally. Extrusions work according to the normals of the original faces. Normals are lines that run perpendicular to the surface. To view polygon surface normals, select* **Display → Polygons → Face Normals**.

- **Extrude** again to create the pant borders.
- **Extrude** and **scale** the faces to create the ankle inside the pants.
- **Extrude** and **move** the faces down to create the heels
- **Rotate** the faces from the last extrusion by about **45 degrees** in order to flow the next extrusion into the feet.
- **Extrude** to create the base of the feet.

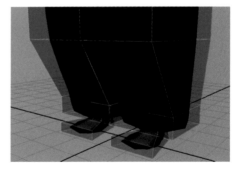

Leg extrusions

5 Extruding the arms

Since you should be concentrating only on the basic shape of the character, you will stop refining the legs here and go right into extruding the arms.

- Select the faces on either side of the top torso.

> **Tip:** *While selecting, remember to use* **Shift** *to toggle the new selection,* **Ctrl** *to deselect and* **Ctrl+Shift** *to add to the new selection.*

- **Extrude** once and **scale** the faces down so the arms start with small shoulders.
- **Extrude** the arms up to the elbows and roughly **tweak** the placement of the new faces.

Note: *You may have to tweak one arm at a time in order to get to the following result. Don't worry if the changes are not perfectly symmetrical, you will be mirroring the geometry later in this lesson.*

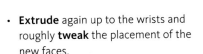

- **Extrude** again up to the wrists and roughly **tweak** the placement of the new faces.
- **Extrude** one last time to create the tip of the hand, and roughly **tweak** the placement of the new faces.

6   Save your work

- Save your scene as *07-bigz_01.ma*.

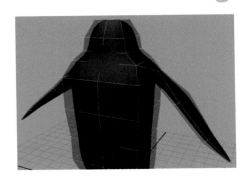

The extruded arms

Shaping the penguin

Now that the basic shape of the penguin is established, you can concentrate on moving polygonal vertices around to refine the general silhouette of the penguin.

Tip: *For a quick look at the silhouette of the character, you can press **7** on your keyboard. Without lights in your scene, this makes an instant black silhouette.*

1   Tweak the proxy

In order to define the shape of the penguin a little better, you do not need to add geometry yet. Instead, you can edit the proxy geometry's vertices.

- Select the proxy geometry.
- Go into **Component** mode with **vertices** displayed.

Component mode with vertices enabled

- **Double-click** on the **Move Tool** in the Toolbox to bring up its options.

- In the Move Tool options, set the following:

  Reflection to **On**;

  Center to **Origin**;

  Reflection axis to **X**;

  Tolerance to **0.1**.

- Click on the **Close** button.

- Select a vertex on the proxy geometry and **move** its position.

  Because of the reflection option in the Move Tool, the corresponding symmetrical vertex is also moved.

- **Tweak** the global shape of the character using the proxy geometry.

  It is important to tweak the proxy geometry in order to have the smoothed geometry look good.

Tip: *You should try to do symmetrical edits for this section of the lesson. It is not critical to always do them, but it will help you experience different tools and workflows. If you don't do symmetrical edits, try to always modify the same side of the model.*

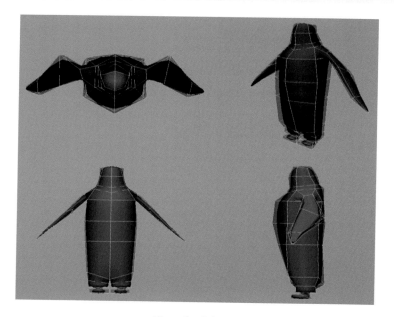

The refined shape

2   Modeling tips

- With vertices selected, you can press the arrows on your keyboard to traverse the geometry components.

- Make sure to always look through different views when modeling. You can stay in the Perspective view, but be sure to use the **View Cube** located in the upper right corner.

The View Cube

You can turn on the wireframe on shaded option by selecting **Shading → Wireframe on Shaded**. This will allow you to see the underlying geometry on the smoothed geometry.

- Try to not move the central line of vertices on their X-axis. This will make your work easier when you mirror the geometry.

Refine the penguin

You should now need more geometry to play with in order to get the penguin to the next level. Here, you will add to the existing geometry in order to better define key areas such as the tail, feet and hands.

1   Chamfer a vertex

Before you can extrude the tail of the penguin, you will need an actual polygon face to extrude the tail from. The Chamfer command allows you to select a vertex and do the proper face division in order to convert that vertex into a face.

- Select the one vertex located at the lower back of the penguin.

  This is the vertex from which you will extrude the tail.

- Select **Edit Mesh → Chamfer Vertex**.

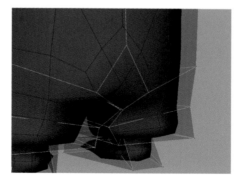

The Chamfered vertex

Tip: *In the construction history of the polyChamfer node, you can change the width of the chamfered vertex.*

- **Tweak** the positioning of the newly created vertices to make the new face more of a hexagonal shape as follows:

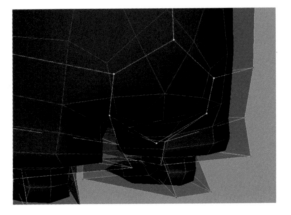

Proper tail face shape

Tip: *Select all the tail face vertices and use the Scale Tool to make the face perfectly flat on its Z-axis.*

2 **Extrude the tail**
- **Extrude** the tail face **twice** as follows:

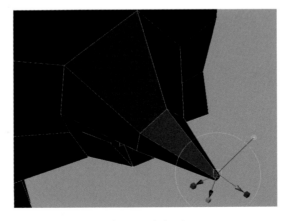

The extruded tail

> **Tip:** *If you cannot find the vertex that will be at the bottom of the hexagonal shape, press* **4** *turn off* **Smooth Shade All**. *You will find the vertex between the penguin's legs.*

3 Splitting a polygon

The last face on the tip of the tail should be split vertically in order to comply with the central line dividing your character along the chest, neck and head.

- Select **Edit Mesh → Split Polygon Tool**.
- **Click+drag** to the top edge of the hexagonal face.
- **Click+drag** to the bottom edge of the hexagonal face.

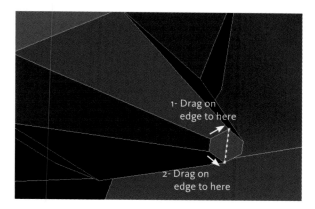

The face split

- Hit **Enter** to complete the action.

  Doing so inserts a vertical edge that starts from the top vertex and splits the face down to the bottom vertex.

4 Flatten the feet

As you can see, the smoothed penguin model does not have flat feet. This can be fixed by extruding an additional face underneath the feet.

- Select the faces under both feet.
- Select **Edit Mesh → Extrude**.

  Doing so forces the smoothed version of the geometry to be flatter in that area.

- Using the extrude manipulator, **scale** the faces so they are smaller.

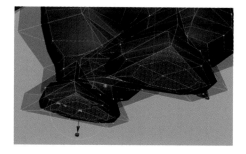

The flat foot soles

5   Toes

The feet of the character are very simplistic at this time. You will now extrude three claws coming out of the webbed feet.

- With the proxy selected, press **Ctrl+`**.

  This reverts the Subdiv Proxy functionality to the body geometry only.

- **Zoom in** on the foot of the right side of your character.

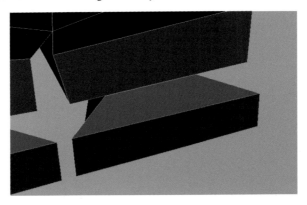

The low-resolution foot

- Select the face on the front of the foot where the claws should be extruded.
- Select **Edit Mesh → Extrude**, then **scale** and adjust vertices as follows:

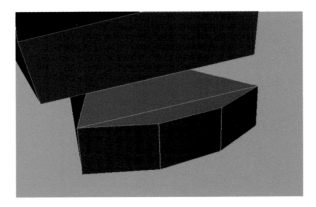

Faces for claw extrusions

- Select the three faces on the front of the foot.
- Select **Edit Mesh → Extrude** twice and **tweak** the resulting shape as follows:

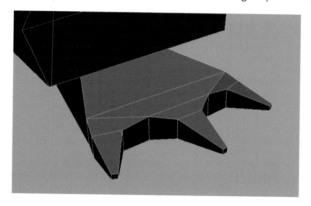

The final shape of the foot

Mirror geometry

Mirroring geometry is a very important step when modeling since it saves you a lot of time when creating a symmetrical model.

The last few steps done to extrude the webbed foot were not reflected on the other foot. Rather than redoing all the work for the other side, it is simpler to create a mirrored version of your geometry. This will also simplify your work once you begin modeling the character's face.

1   Delete one half

You will now delete one half of the model and duplicate the remaining half using instance geometry.

- Make sure to display the original *body* geometry. If you still see the smooth proxy, press **Ctrl+`** with the proxy selected to go back to the original low-resolution model.

- From the *front* view, press **4** to display the model in wireframe.

- Select all the faces on the left side of the character.

All the left faces selected

Tip: *Be careful to select the tiny face at the tip of the tail.*

- Hit the **Delete** key on your keyboard.

2   Duplicate instance

- Go back into Object mode and select the *body* geometry.
- Select **Edit** → **Duplicate Special** → □.
- In the duplicate options, select **Edit** → **Reset Settings**, and then set the following:

   Geometry Type to **Instance**;

   Scale X to **-1**.

- Click the **Duplicate Special** button.

   The model is duplicated as a mirrored instance. An instanced object uses the same geometry as the original object, except that it can have a different position, rotation and scaling in space. Any adjustments done on one side will simultaneously be done on the other side.

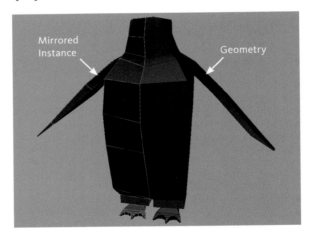

The model with instance

3   Save your work

- Save your scene as *07-bigz_02.ma*.

Refine the head

Perhaps the most important part of the character is the face. This exercise will go through some steps in order to refine the head, but most of the work will have to be done by yourself, since this is an artistic task which cannot easily be explained step–by-step.

Several new tools will be explained here with some key examples that will require experimentation. If you would like to use the final scene of this exercise as a reference, look for the scene *07-bigz_03.ma* from the support files.

1   Delete the construction history

After all the operations done thus far on the model, the construction history list is starting to look impressive in the Channel Box, but it is useless. Now is a good time to delete the history on your model and from the entire scene.

- Select **Edit → Delete All by Type → History**.

2   Insert Edge Loop Tool

The head is now very simplistic and the first step is to add more geometry to play with. You will add several edge loops for the head.

Note: *An edge loop is defined by a continous line of connected edges. The edges perpendicular to an edge loop are called an edge ring.*

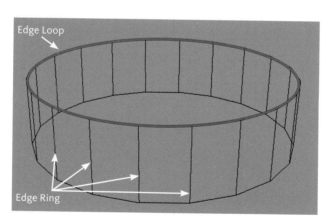

The difference between an edge loop and an edge ring

- With the *body* geometry selected, select **Edit Mesh → Insert Edge Loop Tool**.
- **Click+drag** on any vertical edge in the top facial area.
- **Release** the mouse button to execute the tool.

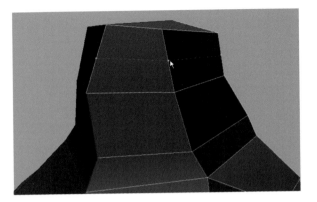

Insert an edge loop

3 Offset Edge Loop Tool

- With the *body* geometry selected, select **Edit Mesh → Offset Edge Loop Tool**.

  This tool allows you to simply add two edge loops on either side of an existing edge loop.

- **Click+drag** on any horizontal edge at the top of the neck.

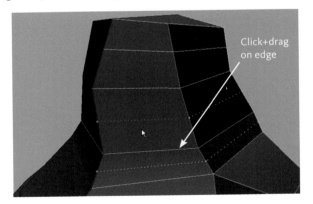

Offset edge loop

- **Release** the mouse button to execute the tool.

4   Delete edges

If you need to delete edges, it is possible to simply select them and press the delete key on your keyboard. However, working this way leaves vertices on the perpendicular edges that are not wanted. In order to compensate for this, there is a specialized command that can be used to correctly delete edges and vertices.

- Select **Select → Select Edge Loop Tool**.

  This tool requires you to double-click on an edge in order to select its related edge loop.

- **Deselect** any edges by clicking in an empty space in the viewport.

- **Double-click** on one of the bottom edges from which you used the offset command in the last step.

  The entire edge loop is selected.

- Select **Edit Mesh → Delete Edge/Vertex**.

  The entire edge loop is properly deleted.

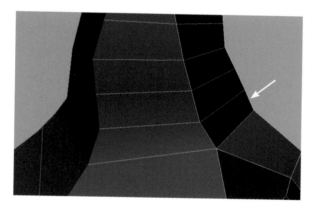

The deleted edge loop

5   Insert an edge loop

There are several ways to access the different modeling commands other than with the menus. If you like working with the menus, keep doing so, but the following is an alternative that involves a hotkey and a marking menu.

- Deselect any edges from the *body* geometry.

- **Pick** one of the horizontal edges on the side of the head.

- Hold down the **Ctrl** key and then **RMB** on the geometry.

  This brings up a polygonal modeling marking menu.

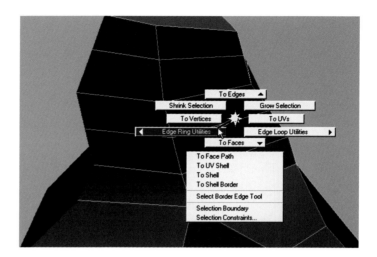

The modeling marking menu

- From the marking menu, select **Edge Ring Utilities**.

  Doing so automatically pops up a second marking menu related to edge rings.

- Select **To Edge Ring and Split**.

  The command automatically selects the related edge ring about the chosen edge, and then does a split on those edges.

  Notice that when inserting and splitting edge loops or rings, the tool keeps splitting across polygonal faces with four sides. If it encounters polygonal faces with more than or fewer than four sides, the tool stops splitting more edges. This can be very useful, but it can also go through your entire character before it stops splitting edges. In this example, notice how the edges split the toes, thus adding unwanted extra geometry.

The edge ring split goes across the entire model

6   Split polygons

In order for you to control how many edges are split and the path the tool is taking, there is an option that allows you to pick the edge to split. The following is an example of such an application.

- **Undo** the last command.

- Select **Edit Mesh** → **Insert Edge Loop Tool** → ❑.

- In the shown window, turn **Off** the **Auto Complete** option.

- Click the **Close** button.

- **Pick** the central horizontal edge on the top of the head.

  The tool now requires you to pick subsequent edges in order to define an edge loop.

- **Pick** an edge on the hips of the model.

  The tool displays the solved edge loop.

The solved edge loop

Note: *You can keep selecting other edges to define a longer edge loop. The edges do not need to be part of the same edge ring.*

Lesson 07: Polygonal Modeling

- **Pick** an edge on the ankle of the model.
- Instead of going into the toes like in the previous step, **split** straight down into the foot sole edge.
- Continue splitting across the foot sole and up into the crotch.

The specific path to split the foot

- Hit the **Enter** key when you are ready to insert the proposed edge loop.

7   Tweak the inserted vertices

There is now much more geometry to refine in the head area. This is where the artistic work comes in, and where you must use your own judgment to define the head to your liking. In the following, you will use different options in the Subdiv Proxy command.

- **Delete** the instanced geometry.
- Select the *body* geometry.
- Select **Proxy → Subdiv Proxy → ❑.**
- Set the following in the option window:

  Mirror Behavior to **Full**;

  Mirror Direction to **−X**;

  Merge Vertex Tolerance to **0.1**.

  Since your geometry has been split in half, setting this option will automatically make a mirrored and merged geometry.

- Click the **Smooth** button.
- Select the proxy geometry.

- Go into Component mode with vertices enabled.
- **Tweak** the head vertices as follows:

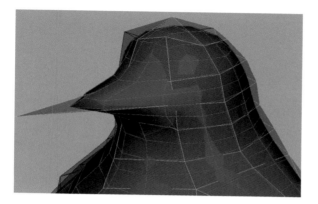

The refined head

8   Tweak the rest of the body

- Refine the model using the vertices that were added to the model thus far.

9   Save your work

- Save your scene as *07-bigz_03.ma*.

Keep on modeling

You now have a good understanding of polygonal modeling basics. By continuing to refine the penguin character, you will see that the time spent experimenting will provide invaluable experience. Throughout the modeling process, you can explore trial and error processes that will eventually achieve great solutions. At some point, you will be able to visualize the different steps to take without ever touching the model.

The following are some general directions to finish modeling the head of the character. To see the final scene of this exercise, look for the scene *07-bigz_04.ma* from the support files.

1   Removing the proxy

The proxy geometry is a great way to create a general shape for your character, but at some point, you will need to refine the smoothed version. Proxy geometry will need to be deleted when refining the higher resolution model.

- Select **Edit → Delete All by Type → History**.

Doing so removes any history between the proxy and smooth geometry.

- Select the *body* proxy geometry and its mirrored instance, and then hit the **Delete** key.
- **Rename** the high-resolution geometry to *body*.

High-resolution refinements

The high-resolution model

2 Tweak the vertices

Now that you have more vertices defining your character, you can play with the shape of the penguin.

Tip: *Don't be afraid of moving vertices one by one. You will most likely end up moving each vertex by hand for the entire model anyway.*

While you are tweaking the vertices around the eyes and beak, try to delimiter the different facial areas with edges. Doing so will help you see the different parts of the face, and it will also make it easier to split polygons to get even more resolution.

3 Add divisions

You must now concentrate on splitting and refining only one half of the model.

- **Delete** half the model and create a mirrored **instance** as shown previously.
- Use the **Split Polygon Tool** to insert new edges where required in order to better define certain areas.
- Use the **Delete Edge/Vertex** to remove unwanted edges where you will split new faces.

Tip: *As a rule, try to always create four-sided polygons when splitting geometry. Doing so will spare you problems later on.*

- **Extrude** the eye socket faces and **scale** them slightly toward the inside to add circular edges in the eye area.

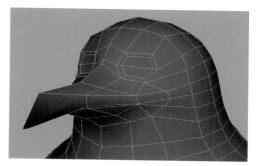

Edges inserted

4   Soft normals

The extrusion and polygon splits create hard edges by default.

The following shows how to soften polygonal normals.

- With the *body* geometry selected, select **Normals → Soften Edge**.

Soft and hard edges comparison

5   Mouth

To simplify your work, you will not see how to model the inner mouth in this lesson. Instead, concentrate on modeling the beak borders in order to clearly define the lips.

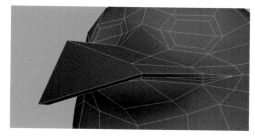

The beak

6 Merging the model

At this point, you can continue refining the model, or call it final and go on with the rest of the project. The following shows how to mirror and merge the actual geometry in order to create a final complete body.

- **Delete** the instanced geometry.
- Select the *body* geometry.
- Select **Mesh** → **Mirror Geometry** → ❏.
- In the options, specify the **Mirror Direction** to be **–X**.
- Click the **Mirror** button.

  The geometry is mirrored and then merged together to create a full body.

7 Merging edges

It is possible that, through the process of modeling, you moved central vertices off the mirror plane, causing the geometry to have open edges along the central axis. The following shows how to merge those edges.

- Select the *body* geometry.
- Select **Display** → **Polygons** → **Border Edges**.

  Doing so causes border edges to be displayed with a thicker wireframe line.

- Press **4** to see your model in wireframe.

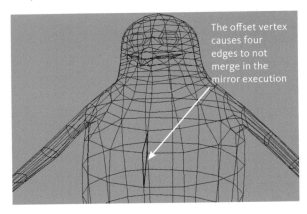

The offset vertex causes four edges to not merge in the mirror execution

An open edge

- Select **Edit Mesh** → **Merge Edge Tool**.

  This tool allows you to pick two edges and force them to merge together.

- **Choose** any of the opened thicker edges.

  Possible edges to be merged with are highlighted in pink.

- **Choose** the pink edge located on the other half of the model.
- Hit **Enter** to merge the edges.

  The edges should now be closed.

- **Repeat** the previous steps for any other open edges.

8   Final steps

- With the *body* geometry selected, select **Normals → Soften Edge**.
- Select **Edit → Delete All by Type → History**.

9   Save your work

- Save your scene as *07-bigz_04.ma*.

Proportions

Sometimes when modeling, you sit back and look at your work thinking you could improve the proportions of the model. An easy way to change a model's proportions is to create and modify a lattice deformer. A lattice surrounds a deformable object with a structure of points that can be manipulated to change the object's shape. Once you are happy with the new proportions, you can simply delete the history, thus freezing the deformations on the model.

1   Create a lattice deformer

- Select the *body* geometry.
- From the **Animation** menu set, select **Create Deformers → Lattice**.

  A large lattice box is created around your model.

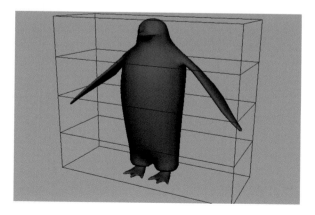

The lattice deformer

- In the Channel Box with the lattice selected, set the *ffd1LatticeShape* node as follows:

    S Divisions to **5**;

    T Divisions to **5**;

    U Divisions to **3**.

    Doing so will change the amount of subdivisions in the lattice deformer, which in turn adds more lattice points to deform the surface with. This will allow more control over the deformations.

Tip: *You may adjust these settings to better fit your geometry and divide the model into body part sections.*

2   **Deform the lattice box**

- **RMB** on the lattice object in the viewport to bring up the lattice context menu and select **Lattice Point**.

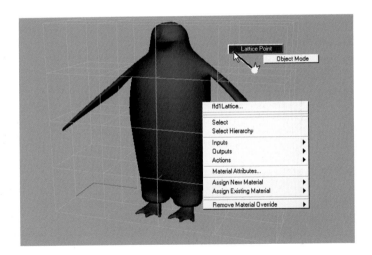

The lattice context menu

- Select lattice points and **transform** them just as you would do with vertices.

    Notice how the lattice points deform the geometry.

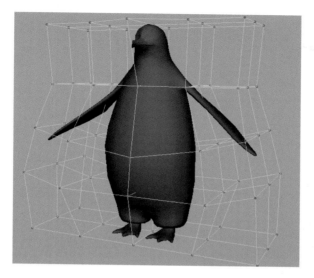

Lattice effect

- Find the best proportions possible.

> **Tip:** *This is a good time to place the character's feet on the world grid, if they are not already there. Also, make sure to place the model's center of gravity on the Z and X-axes.*

3 Delete the deformer

If you simply deleted the lattice deformer, the geometry would snap right back to its original shape. In order to keep the deformation and freeze the geometry with that shape, you need to delete its history, which will automatically delete the deformer.

- Select the *body* geometry.
- Select **Edit → Delete by Type → History**.

Final touches

The body of the penguin looks great, but BigZ is still missing key components such as eyes and hair. Those objects will be created in a simplistic manner, starting from NURBS primitives.

Just like the rest of this lesson, you will model only half the geometry and then mirror it over to the other side.

1   **The Eyeball**

- Select **Create** → **NURBS Primitives** → **Sphere**.

- **Rename** the sphere to *eyeball*.

- **Translate** and **scale** the eyeball to the proper eye location.

- **Rotate** the eyeball by **90** degrees on its **X-axis**.

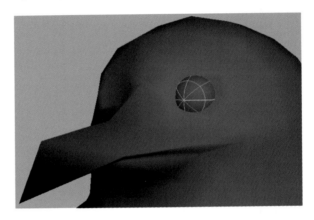

The eyeball in place

2   **The Eyelid**

- With the *eyeball* selected, select **Edit** → **Duplicate Special** → ❑.

- In the shown window, select **Edit** → **Reset Settings**, then turn **On** the **Duplicate input graph** option.

  This option duplicates the geometry along with all its inputs, such as construction history, which will be used here.

- Click the **Duplicate Special** button.

- **Rename** the duplicate to *eyelid*.

- From the Channel Box, **rotate** the eyelid by **-90** degrees on its **Y-axis**.

- **Scale** the eyelid so that it is a little bigger than the eyeball.

- In the Channel Box, highlight the *makeNurbsSphere2* input node.

- Set the **Start Sweep** to **10** and the **End Sweep** to **330**.

  The eyelid will use its construction history in order to simplify the eye blinks.

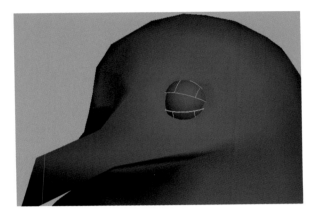

The eyelid

Note: *Advanced modelers should be creating realistic looking eyes by modeling the eyelids starting from the original polygonal geometry. This will not be covered in this book.*

3   Mirror the eyeball

- Select the *eyeball* and *eyelid*.
- Press **Ctrl+g** to **group** them all together.
- With the new group selected, select **Edit → Duplicate Special → ❑**.
- In the shown window, turn **On** the **Duplicate input** graph option.

  Doing so will duplicate the required construction history on the eyelid, which will be needed later for eye blinking.

- Click the **Duplicate Special** button.
- In the Channel Box with the duplicated group still selected, set **ScaleX** to **-1**.

  You now have eyes for both sides of the character.

4   **Hair**

- **Create** a **NURBS plane** primitive.
- Set the **Patches V** attribute in the makeNurbsPlane input node from the Channel Box to **5**.
- **Rename** the cone to *hair1*.
- **Place** and **tweak** the hair's shape as follows:

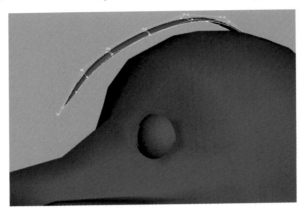

The first hair

- **Duplicate** the hair in order to create a good-looking hair style.

Hair style

> **Note:** *From now on, do not delete the construction history for the entire scene since the eyelids require it for blinking. If you want to delete the history, do it only for the selected models.*

5   Save your work

- Save your scene as *07-bigz_05.ma*.

The final model

Conclusion

In this lesson, you learned how to model a complete character out of basic polygonal primitives. In the process, you used several polygonal modeling tools to create the shape and details. As you noticed, each tool created an input node for which you were able to modify the construction history. You also used the lattice deformer, which is a great tool to know about.

In the next lesson, you will texture the penguin. This will allow you to experiment with polygonal texture tools and techniques.

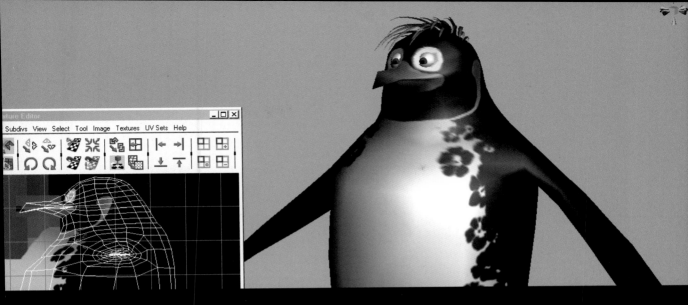

Lesson 08
Polygonal Texturing

You now have a polygonal mesh that requires texturing. Even though polygons have a default setting for UV parameters onto which textures can be applied, in this lesson, you will adjust these to get the best possible result. You can use special polygon tools to assign and modify these kinds of values on the model.

You will first apply texture projections in order to create UV coordinates on the mesh. Then, you will texture the penguin using the 3D Paint Tool to paint directly on the model.

In this lesson you will learn the following:

- How to use the UV Texture Editor
- How to project UVs on polygons
- How to manipulate projections
- How to unfold UVs
- How to grow and reduce the current selection
- How to assign and paint textures using the 3D Paint Tool
- How to remove unused shading groups

Texturing polygonal surfaces

The penguin will be textured using multiple shading groups and texture maps. You will start by positioning a texture on the main body geometry, which will be accomplished using useful polygon texturing tools. Once that is done, you will texture the eyes and hair of the character. Feel free to continue using your own file, or start with *07-bigz_05.ma* from the last lesson.

1 UV Texture Editor

The UV Texture Editor is where you can see the UVs of your model. UVs are similar to vertices except that they live in a flat 2D space. The UVs determine the coordinates of a point on a texture map. In order to properly assign a texture to a polygonal model, the UVs need to be unfolded somewhat like a tablecloth.

- Select the *body* geometry.

- Select **Window** → **UV Texture Editor**.

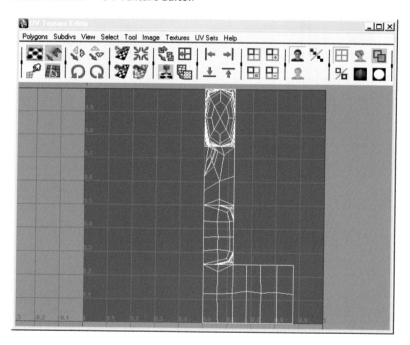

The UV Texture Editor

Displayed in the UV Texture Editor are the UVs for the selected geometry. Those UVs are now irregular and will result in a very poor texture mapping.

2   Create and assign a body shader

- **Open** the Hypershade window.

- **Create** a *blinn* material node.

  Blinn is the simplest material that, once properly set up, can look like fur.

- **Rename** the material node to *bodyM*.

- **Assign** the *bodyM* material to the *body* geometry.

- Turn **on** the **Hardware Texturing** in the Perspective view to see your work in the upcoming steps.

3   Map a checker to the color

- Open the Attribute Editor for the *bodyM* material.

- **Map** the **Color** attribute with a **Checker** texture node.

Irregular texture placement due to poor UVs

Note: *The checker texture is just a temporary texture in order to better see the UV placement on the model.*

4   Planar mapping

In order to start correcting the texture mapping of the character, you will use a planar projection.

- With the *body* geometry selected, select **Create UVs → Planar Mapping → ❑** from the Polygons menu set.

- In the option window, select **Project from X-axis.**

- Click the **Project** button.

A large projection plane icon surrounds the object, which projects the texture map along the X-axis. You can see the texture mapped onto the surface with hardware texturing.

Planar projection

5   Projection manipulators

The projection manipulator allows you to transform the projection to better suit your geometry.

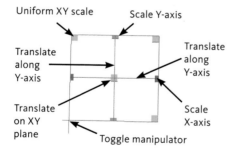

Planar projection manipulator

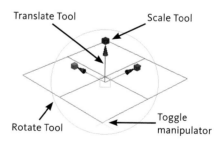

Other planar projection manipulator

You can toggle the manipulator type for a conventional all-in-one manipulator by clicking on the *red T.*

Note: *If the projection manipulator disappears, reselect the geometry, click on the polyPlanProj input node in the Channel Box and select the Show Manipulator Tool, or press the **t** hotkey.*

6   UV Texture Editor

If you change the positioning of the manipulator from the previous step, you will see that the UVs of the model in the UV Texture Editor have been updated to be projected according to the manipulator in the viewport.

- In the UV Texture Editor menu bar, select **Image** → **Display Image** to toggle the display of the checker texture to **Off**.

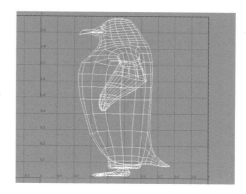

The projected UVs

> **Note:** *The view of the object and the loaded texture are both initially displayed in the Texture Editor with a square proportion—regardless of the proportion of the planar projection positioned in the 3D space of the model and the proportion of the texture image file.*

Modifying UVs

It is important to prevent overlapping of the UVs where it is not wanted. For instance, if you make a planar projection from the front of the model, the UVs would overlap on the front and back of the model. If you make the belly of the character another color, the back would also change.

In this example, you made the projection from the side because the character should be symmetrical on its X-axis. The problem with the current UVs is that the arms are overlapping with the belly and could cause unwanted texture results later in this lesson.

Since UVs can be tweaked as needed through the UV Texture Editor, you will now alter the UVs manually.

1   Select the arm UVs

- In the UV Texture Editor with the penguin's UVs displayed, **RMB** and select **UV** from the context menu.

  Doing so sets the current selection mask to UVs only.

- **Click+drag** a selection rectangle over the penguin's paw.

  The UVs of both paws are now selected because their UVs are overlapping.

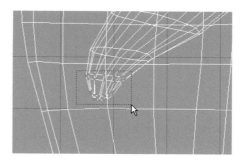

Selecting the paw UVs

- From the main Maya interface, select **Select** → **Grow Selection Region** >.

  The neighbor UVs on the model are selected, which increases the current selection.

Tip: You can press **Shift+>** *to increase the selection and* **Shift+<** *to shrink the current selection.*

- Select **Select** → **Grow Selection Region** >, or press **Shift+>** a few more times until you have the arm selected up to the shoulder.

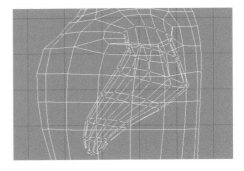

The entire arm UVs selected

Note: *By doing this, you actually selected both arms. You cannot see this in the UV Texture Editor, but you can in the viewports.*

2 Unfolding the arm UVs

The goal of this step is to minimize the arm overlapping from the rest of the body. You could do this entire step manually by moving the UVs one by one, but in order to speed up the process, you will automatically unfold the selected UVs.

- From the UV Texture Editor, select **Polygons** → **Unfold** → ❑.
- In the Unfold options, make sure that **Pin UVs** is enabled and that **Pin Unselected UVs** is chosen.

  By setting those options, you specify to the tool that you want only the selected UVs to be unfolded.

- Click the **Apply and Close** button.

3   Moving UVs

- Press **r** to use the **Scale Tool** and tweak the UVs in the UV Texture Editor.

- You can press **Ctrl+<** to shrink the current selection in order to scale up the other row of UVs.

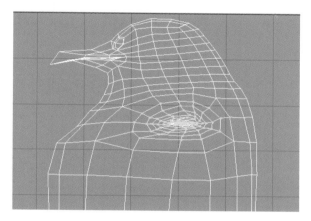

Unfolding and scaling the UVs

Note: *The placement of the UVs doesn't need to be perfect since the arms will be the same color overall.*

- Close the UV Texture Editor.

Note: *Another technique is to cut the UVs and move the arm aside the rest of the body, but this will not be covered in this book.*

4   Save your work

- Save your scene as *08-bigzTxt_01.ma.*

3D Paint Tool

A great way to create custom texture is to paint a texture directly on a model in the viewport. The 3D Paint Tool allows you to paint using default paintbrushes or Paint Effects brushes. You can use the tool to outline details to be painted in separate software, or to create a final texture directly in Maya.

> **Tip:** As you are working with the 3D Paint Tool, you might want to change the way the UVs are laid out to minimize texture stretching and overlapping.

1   Open the 3D Paint Tool

- Select the *body* geometry.
- Select the **Rendering** menu set by pressing **F6.**
- Select **Texturing → 3D Paint Tool → ❑.**

  This will open the tool's option window.
- Scroll down to the **File Textures** section.
- Make sure **Attribute to Paint** is set to **Color.**
- Click the **Assign/Edit Textures** button.

  This will open the new texture creation options.
- Set **Image Format** to **Tiff (tif).**
- Set both the **Size X** and **Size Y** to **512.**

> **Tip:** For more definition in your textures and (and if your computer can handle it), you might want to boost up the texture resolution to 1024x1024 or even 2048x2048.

- Click the **Assign/Edit Textures** button.

  Doing so will duplicate the currently assigned texture and save it in your project in the 3dpainttextures folder. As you paint on the geometry, only this new texture will be automatically updated.

2   Set the initial color

You will now paint a color over the old checkered pattern.

- In the 3D Paint Tool settings, change the **Color** attribute in the **Flood** section to be **black.**
- Click on the **Flood Paint** button.

  The penguin is now totally black.

3   Set erase image

To make sure that you can erase your drawing and come back to the original texture, you need to set the erase image as the current texture.

- Scroll to the **Paint Operations** section and click on the **Set Erase Image** button.

4   Paint on geometry

- Under the **File Textures** section, turn **On** the **Extend Seam Color** option.

  This option will make sure that there are no seams visible when painting.

- Scroll at the top of the 3D Paint Tool and make sure the second **Artisan** brush is enabled in the **Brush** section.

- When you put your mouse cursor over the geometry in the viewport, if the brush size is too big or too small for painting, set its **Radius (U)** in the option window, or hold the **b** hotkey and **drag** the radius of the brush in the viewport.

- Change the **Color** attribute from the **Color** section to **white**.

- **Paint** directly on the geometry to change the color of the penguin's belly.

The painted belly

5   Paint options

Under the **Paint Operations** section, you can set various paint operations like Paint, Erase, Clone, Smear and Blur. You can also set the Blend Mode, which affects the way new strokes are painted on your texture. Those options can be very useful for tweaking your texture.

- Continue painting the penguin with different colors on the different parts of his body such as the neck, beak, eye sockets, feet, ears and arms.

Fully painted penguin

6   Paint Effects

- Scroll to the **Brush** section of the tool and enable the first **Paint Effects** brush.

- To choose a template brush, click on the **Get Brush** button to pull up the Visor.

Paint Effects:

Get Brush button

> **Note:** *Sometimes, painting directly on the geometry creates artifacts—due to things such as seams, color, texture resolution, UV placement, UV overlapping, etc. One way of correcting this is by editing the texture later on in a paint program.*

- In the Visor, scroll to the **Pens** directory and choose the brush called **inkSplash.mel.**
- Experiment by painting on the geometry.

Paint Effects strokes

7 Screen projection

When painting with a Paint Effects brush, you will notice that the brush icon in the viewport looks stretched. This is because the brush bases itself on the object's UVs, which are stretched. To correct the problem, you need to enable the screen projection option.

- Expand the **Stroke** section in the **3D Paint Tool** window.
- Turn **On** the **Screen Projection** attribute.
- **Paint** on geometry.

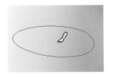

Stretched brush

> **Note:** *When painting with Screen Projection, you are painting using the current camera view. This can be very useful in some cases, but can also create stretched textures when painting on geometry parallel to the view.*

8   Reference strokes

You might find it easier to draw only reference strokes in Maya and then use a paint program to refine the look of the texture. To do so, you will draw where you want to add texture details on the object, and then open the texture in a paint program. Once you are finished with the texture, you can reload it in Maya.

9   Save textures

You have not yet saved the texture just drawn to disk, making it inaccessible to another program.

- To save the texture manually, click the **Save Textures** button in the **File Textures** section.

    OR

- To save the texture automatically on each stroke, turn **On** the **Save Texture on Stroke** checkbox in the **File Textures** section.

10   Edit the texture

You can now edit your texture from the *3dpainttextures* directory in a paint program. When you have finished modifying the texture, save the new image out.

The final texture

- Back in Maya, in the texture's Attribute Editor, click the **Reload File Textures** button to update the fur texture for the new version.

The final texture on the model

> **Tip:** *If you saved the file under a different name or in a different location, browse to get the modified texture.*

Final touches

Since the character's geometry consists of several other objects as well, you should also be texturing those. Note that the eyes and hair were made out of NURBS surfaces, so they will not require extra UV steps. The texturing of NURBS surfaces will be shown in more detail in the third project.

1   Create and assign an eye shader

- **Open** the Hypershade window.
- **Create** a *phong* material node.

  Phong is the material that suits the shiny eyes best.

- **Rename** the material node to *eyeM*.
- **Assign** the *eyeM* material to both *eyeballs*.

2   Map a ramp to the color

- Open the Attribute Editor for the *eyeM* material.
- **Map** the **Color** attribute with a **Ramp** texture node.

- **Rename** the ramp node to *eyeColor*.

3 Tweak the ramp

- In the Attribute Editor for the *eyeColor*, set the following:

    Type to **U Ramp**.

    Interpolation to **None**.

- **Tweak** the ramp's colors like the image to the right.

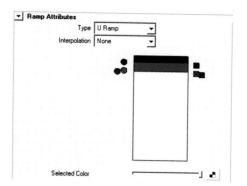

4 Create and assign an eyelid shader

- **Create** a *blinn* material and **rename** it to *eyelidM*.

- Set the **Color** of the material to be a color similar to the surrounding eye color of the penguin.

- **Assign** the *eyelidM* to the *eyelid* objects.

The textured eyes

5   Create a hair shader

- **Create** a *Blinn* material and **rename** it to *hairM*.

- **Assign** the *hairM* to all the *hair* objects.

- **Map** the **Color** of the material with a **ramp** going from **black** to **brown**.

- Set the material to be **semi-transparent** by opening the Attribute Editor for the hairM shader and move the slider beside the **Transparency** attribute a little to the right.

The hair material

Optimizing the scene

To maintain a good workflow, you should clean up your scene once texturing is complete. For instance, you might want to delete all unused shading networks in the scene.

1   Delete unused nodes

- From the Hypershade window, select **Edit → Delete Unused Nodes**.

  Maya will go through the list of render nodes and delete anything that is not assigned to a piece of geometry in the scene.

2   Optimize scene size

- Select **File → Optimize Scene Size**.

  Maya will go through the entire scene and remove any unused nodes.

3   Delete the history

- Select all the objects except the *eyelids*.

- Select **Edit → Delete by Type → History**.

4   Save your work

- The final scene *08-bigzTxt_02.ma* can be found in the support files. BigZ's texture is called *body.tif* and is located in the *3dpainttextures* directory.

Conclusion

You now have a good understanding of texturing polygons. You have experimented with a projection and some polygonal tools and actions. There is much more to learn concerning polygon texturing, so feel free to experiment on your own.

In the next lesson, you will learn about creating joint chains, which is the first step for animating a character.

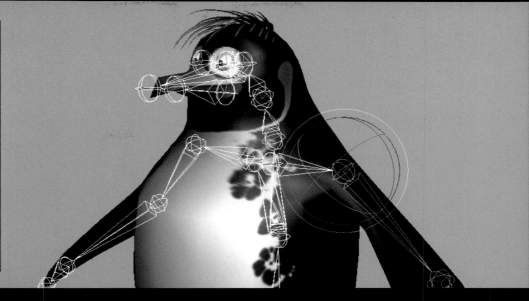

Skeleton	
Joint Tool	▢
IK Handle Tool	▢
IK Spline Handle Tool	▢
Insert Joint Tool	
Reroot Skeleton	
Remove Joint	
Disconnect Joint	
Connect Joint	▢
Mirror Joint	▢
Orient Joint	▢
Retargeting	▶
Joint Labelling	▶
Full Body IK	▶
Set Preferred Angle	▢
Assume Preferred Angle	▢
✔ Enable IK Handle Snap	
Enable IK/FK Control	
Enable Selected IK Handles	
Disable Selected IK Handles	

Lesson 09
Skeleton

In this lesson you will create the skeleton hierarchy to be used to bind the geometry and to animate the penguin character. In order to create a skeleton, you need to draw joints to match the shape of your character. The geometry is then bound to the skeleton and deformations are applied.

In this lesson you will learn the following:

- How to create skeleton joints

- How to navigate around a joint hierarchy

- How to edit joint pivots

Drawing a skeleton chain

In this exercise, you will draw skeleton chains. Even if this operation appears to be simple, there are several things to be aware of as you create a joint chain.

1   Joint Tool

- Open a new scene and change the view to the *side* Orthographic view.
- From the **Animation** menu set, select **Skeleton** → **Joint Tool** → ❑.

  The tool's option window is displayed.

- Change the **Orientation** attribute to **None**.

Note: *This attribute will be explained later in this exercise.*

- Click the **Close** button to close the tool window.
- In the side view, **LMB+click** two times to create a joint chain.
- Press **Enter** to exit the tool.

2   Joint Hierarchy

- Open the Hypergraph.

  Notice the joint hierarchy, which is composed of two nodes.

3   Adding joints

- Click on the **Joint Tool** icon in the toolbox or press the **y** hotkey to access the last tool used.
- **LMB** on the end joint of your previous chain.

  The tool will highlight the end joint.

- **LMB+click** two times to create a Z-like joint chain.

  The new joints are children of the joint selected in the previous step.

- You can **MMB+drag** to change the last joint placement.
- Press **Enter** to exit the tool.

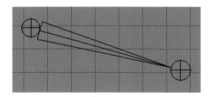

A simple joint chain

Joint hierarchy

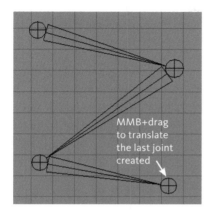

New joint chain

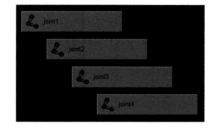

Joint hierarchy

4 Automatic joint orientation

When using the automatic orientation, all three joint axes are aligned according to the right-hand rule. For example, if you select an orientation of XYZ, the positive X-axis points into the joint's bone and toward the joint's first child joint, the Y-axis points at right angles to the X-axis and Z-axis, and the Z-axis points sideways from the joint and its bone.

Note: *If you look closely at the joints in the Perspective view, you can see these axes and where they are pointing.*

- **Double-click** on the **Joint Tool** icon in the toolbox.

  The tool's option window is displayed.

- Change the **Orientation** attribute to **XYZ**.

- **Close** the tool window.

- Create a second joint chain similar to the first one.

  Notice that as you draw the joints, they are automatically oriented toward their child.

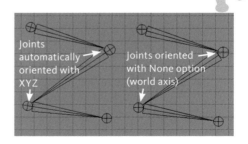

Joint orientation

Lesson 09: Skeleton

5 Joint rotation axis

To better understand the effect of the joint orientation, you need to rotate in local mode and compare the two chains you have created.

- **Double-click** on the **Rotate Tool** icon in the toolbox.

  The tool's option window is displayed.

- Select **Local** as the **Rotation Mode**.

  This specifies that you want to rotate nodes based on their local orientation rather than using the global world axis.

- **Close** the tool window.

- Select the second joint of both chains and see the difference between their rotation axes as you rotate them.

  Notice that when the joint is properly oriented, it moves in a more natural way.

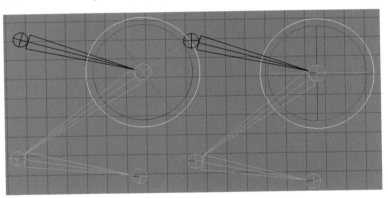

Joint rotation axis

Complex joint chain

When you create a complex joint chain, you can use some features intended to simplify your work. For instance, you can navigate in a hierarchy of joints as you create them. You can also use a command to reorient all the joints automatically.

1 Navigate in joint hierarchy

- **Delete** all the joint chains in your scene.

- Make the *top* view active.

- Press the **y** hotkey to access the **Joint Tool**.

Note: *Make sure the tool* **Orientation** *is set to* **XYZ**.

- **Draw** three joints as follows:

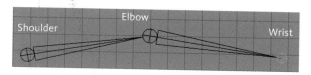

Arm chain

- **Draw** a thumb made of two joints.

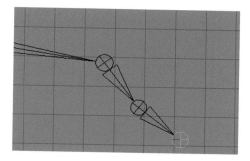

Thumb joints

- Press the **up arrow** twice on your keyboard to put the selection on the wrist joint.

  The arrows let you navigate in the hierarchy without exiting the Joint Tool.

- **Draw** the index joints and press the **up arrow** again.
- **Draw** the remaining fingers as follows:

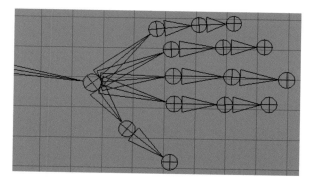

Completed hand

2 Snap to grid

- Press the **up arrow** until the selection is on the shoulder joint.
- Hold down the **x** hotkey to snap to grid and add a spine bone.
- Press **Enter** to exit the Joint Tool.

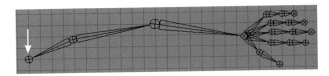

Spine bone

3 Reroot a skeleton

In the last step, you created a spine bone that is the child of the shoulder bone. This is not a proper hierarchy since the spine should be the parent of the shoulder. There is a command that allows you to quickly reroot a joint chain.

- Select the *spine* bone, which was the last joint created.
- Select **Skeleton → Reroot Skeleton**.

The spine is now the root of the hierarchy.

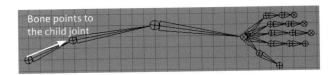

Spine joint as root

4 Mirror joints

Another very useful feature is the ability to mirror a joint chain automatically.

- Select the *shoulder* bone.
- Select **Skeleton → Mirror Joint → ❑**.
- In the option window, specify **Mirror Across** the **YZ** plane.
- Click the **Mirror** button.

Both arms

Penguin skeleton

You are now ready to create a skeleton for the penguin from the last lesson. To do so, you need to determine the proper placement of each joint. Once that is done, you will need to set a proper joint orientation so that when you rotate a joint, it rotates in an intuitive manner. If you do not take great care for placement and orientation, you will have difficulty animating the character later on.

1   Open scene

- Open the file *08-bigzTxt_02.ma*.

- While in Smooth Shaded mode, select **Shading → X-Ray** from the panel menu.

2   Character spine

In this step, you need to determine a good placement for the pelvis bone, which will be the root of the hierarchy. Once that is done, it will be easy to create the rest of the spine bones.

- Select **Skeleton → Joint Tool**.

- Make the *side* view active.

- **LMB** to create the *pelvis* joint.

  It is recommended that the pelvis joint be aligned with the hips.

- **LMB** to draw three equally spaced joints, which will represent the *spine*, *spine1* and *neck* joints.

- **LMB** to draw two equally spaced joints, which will represent the *neck1* and *head* joints.

- Lastly, **LMB** to draw the *nose* joint.

- Hit **Enter** to complete the joint chain.

- **Rename** each joint properly.

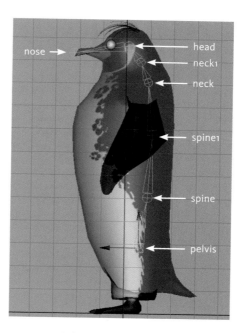

Pelvis, spine and head joints

> **Note:** *A spine could be made of more bones, but this is not required in this example. The nose joint would normally be used only to get a visual representation of the head when the geometry is hidden, but you might as well use it to deform the beak to create a cartoony animation.*

3   Create a leg

You now need to create the legs of the character. The new joint chain will be in a separate hierarchy, but you will connect it to the pelvis later on.

- Select **Skeleton → Joint Tool**.

- **Click+drag** the *hip* joint to its proper location.

   The hip joint should be centered on the hip geometry, very close to the pelvis joint.

- **Draw** the remaining *knee*, *ankle* and *toe* joints, and create an extra joint on the tip of the foot, which should be called *toesEnd*.

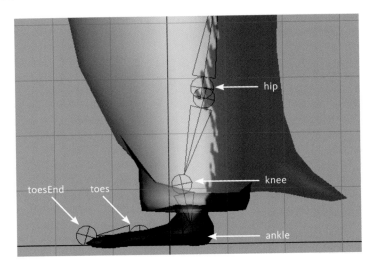

Leg joints

- Press **Enter** to exit the tool.

- Change to the *front* view.

   Notice that all the bones you created were drawn centered on the X-axis. That was correct for the spine, but not for the leg.

- **Translate** the *hip* joint on the X-axis to fit the geometry as follows:

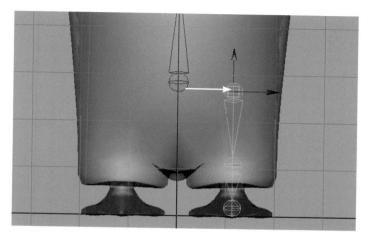

Front view

4   Connect and mirror the leg

- Select the *hip* joint, then **Shift-select** the *pelvis* joint.
- Select **Skeleton → Connect Joint → ❑**.
- Change the **Mode** option to **Parent Joint**.
- Hit the **Connect** button.

  The leg is now parented to the pelvis.

Note: *You could also parent using the* **p** *hotkey, but joints have a special connection that are not created when using the* **Parent** *command. The* **Connect Joint** *command does make this special connection.*

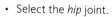

- Select the *hip* joint.
- Select **Skeleton → Mirror Joint → ❑**.
- Set the following:

    Mirror across to **YZ**;

    Mirror function to **Orientation**.

  This option will cause the legs to have the same behavior.

- Click on the **Mirror** button.

  If your character was modeled symmetrically, it should now have two legs properly placed.

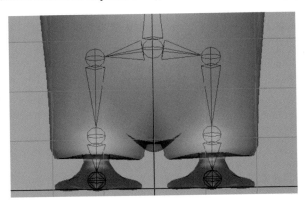

Completed lower body

- **Rename** all the joints appropriately.

> **Note:** *Make sure to prefix the joints on the left side with l, and the ones on the right side with r. For example, if you name the ankle, you may want to call it lAnkle.*

5   **Arm and hand joints**

- Select **Display → Animation → Joint Size...**
- Set the **Joint Size** to **0.25**.

  Doing so will reduce the display size of the joints in the viewport, making it easier to place joints close together, such as the finger joints.

- From the *front* view, **draw** a joint to represent the *clavicle* between the *spine1* and *neck* joints, then **draw** the *shoulder* joint.

The clavicle and shoulder joints

- Change to the *top* view.
- **Move** the *clavicle* on the **Z-axis** to better fit the geometry.
- **Draw** the character's *elbow*, *wrist* and *wristEnd* joints.

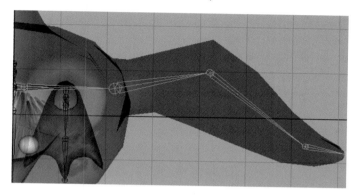

The arm and hand joints

- Change to the *front* view.
- **Move** down the joints on the **Y-axis** to better fit the geometry.
- Make sure the joints are properly positioned in the *Perspective* view.

Tip: *It is a better workflow for joint placement to rotate the joints rather than translating them.*

- **Rename** all the joints correctly.

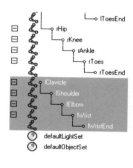

Joints correctly placed

> **Tip:** *It might be easier to set the display in the viewport as X-Ray with Wireframe on Shaded.*

6   Joint pivot

In some cases, you might want to adjust the position of a joint without moving all of its children. You can use the **Insert** key (**Home** key on Macintosh) to move a joint on its own.

For instance, if the angle defined by the shoulder, elbow and wrist joints is not appropriate, you can correct the problem by moving a joint on its own.

- Select the *elbow* joint.
- Select the **Move Tool**.
- Press the **Insert** key (**Home** on Macintosh).
- **Move** the pivot of the *elbow* joint.
- Press the key again and exit the Move Pivot manipulator.

7   Connect and mirror the arm

- Select the *clavicle* joint, then **Shift-select** the *spine1* joint.
- Select **Skeleton → Connect Joint**.

  The arm is now parented to the spine1 joint.

- Select the *clavicle* joint.
- Select **Skeleton → Mirror Joint → □.**
- In the option window, make sure to set **Mirror function** to **Behavior.**

  This option will cause the arms to have mirrored behavior.

- Click on the **Mirror** button.

Proper arms

8   Details

- Select the **Joint Tool**.
- From the *side* view, click on the *head* joint to highlight it.

  Doing so tells the tool that you want to start drawing joints from the head joint.

- **Draw** one joint for the *eye* and two for the *jaw* as follows:

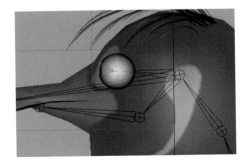

The new head joints

- **Draw** two joints for the *tail* starting from the *pelvis*.
- **Rename**, **translate** and **mirror** the new joints when needed.

Joint orientation

Now that the penguin has a skeleton, you need to double-check all the joint orientations using the Rotate Tool. In this case, most of the joint orientations will be correct by default, but there will be times when you will need to change some orientations to perfect your skeleton.

1   Hide the geometry

- From the *Perspective* view, select **Show → Polygons** and **Show → NURBS Surfaces** to hide them.

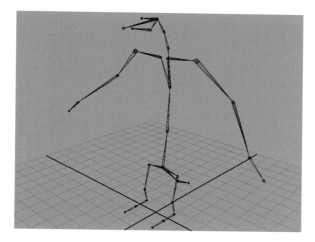

Complete skeleton

2   Default rotation values

It is recommended that all rotations of a joint hierarchy be zeroed out. This means that when the skeleton is in the current default position, all the joint rotations are zero.

- Select the *pelvis* joint.

- Select **Modify → Freeze Transformations**.

  If you rotated bones in previous steps, their rotations are now zeroed out.

Note: *Unlike geometry, joint translations cannot be zeroed or else they would all be at the origin.*

3 **Reorient all joints**

You can reorient all the joints in a hierarchy automatically to your preferred orientation, such as XYZ.

- Select the *pelvis* joint.

- Select **Skeleton** → **Orient Joint** → ❑.

- Make sure the **Orientation** is set to **XYZ**, then click the **Orient** button.

  All the joints are now reoriented to have the X-axis pointing toward their children.

4 **Local rotation axes**

The automatic orientation of the joints is not always perfect. Depending on how your skeleton was built, it can flip certain local rotation axes and you need to manually fix those pivots.

- Select the *pelvis* joint.

- Press **F8** to go into Component mode and enable the **?** mask button.

Local rotation axes mask

All the local rotation axes are displayed in the viewport for the selected hierarchy.

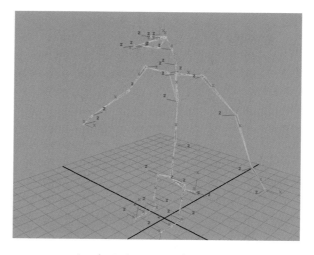

Local rotation axes in the viewport

5   Manually set the local rotation axes

It might seem confusing at the moment, but changing the local rotation axes is quite easy. There is one axis per joint, and if you dolly closer to a joint, you will see that the axis respects the left-hand rule, where the X-axis points toward the first child joint.

The left-hand rule

In certain cases you will not want the automatic orientation setting. Problems usually arise when you select multiple bones and rotate them at the same time. For instance, if you selected the entire spine and neck joints you would notice an odd rotation, since their rotation axes are not aligned.

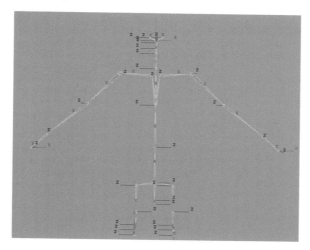

Bad rotation axes

X rotation on the upper body is not in the same orientation as the X rotation of the lower body since Z points in different directions.

To fix the problem, manually select an incorrect local rotation axis and rotate it into a good position.

- Still in Component mode with the local rotation axis displayed, select the *hips* and *spine* local rotation axes by clicking on them and holding down the **Shift** key.

- **Double-click** the **Rotate Tool**.

- In the tool's options, set **Snap rotate** to **On** and **Step size** to **90**.
- **Rotate** on the **X-axis** by **180 degrees**.

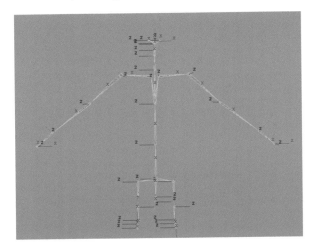

The corrected rotation axis

- In the **Rotate Tool**'s options, set **Snap rotate** to **Off**.
- Go back in Object mode and try rotating the hips, spine, neck and head together.

  The problem seen earlier is now solved.

Note: *It is normal that mirrored joints have an inverted local rotation axis. This is a welcome behavior set in the Mirror Joint command, which allows animation to be mirrored from one limb to another.*

6 Test the skeleton

You should now test your skeleton to see if everything is rotating as expected. If you notice incorrect local rotation axes, attempt to correct them manually by following the steps outlined above. Typical problematic areas are the knees and ankles, since the joint chains are made in a Z shape.

Note: *The end joint's local rotation axis usually isn't important since it might not be intended for animation.*

7   Save your work

- Save your work as *09-bigzSkeleton_01.ma.*

Conclusion

You now have greater experience creating skeleton chains and navigating skeleton hierarchies. You have learned how to move and rotate joints, and how to use joint commands such as reroot, connect, mirror and orient. Finally, you have manually changed local rotation axes, which is the key to creating a good skeleton.

In the next lesson, you will bind the penguin geometry to the skeleton and explore different techniques and tools used for character rigging.

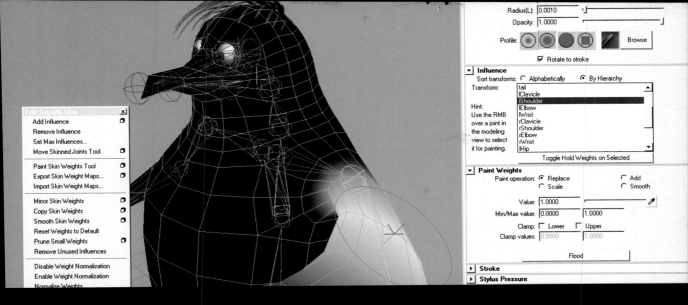

Lesson 10
Skinning

To get your character's geometry to deform as you move joints, you must bind it to the skeleton. There are many skinning techniques to bind a surface. In this lesson, you will first experiment with basic examples, which will help you to understand the various types of skinning. You will then use this understanding to bind the penguin character.

In this lesson you will learn the following:

- How to bind using parenting
- How to use rigid binding
- How to use the Edit Membership Tool
- How to edit rigid bind membership
- How to use flexors
- How to use lattice binding
- How to use smooth binding

Parent binding

Perhaps the simplest type of binding is to parent geometry to joints. This type of binding is very fast and needs no tweaking, but requires the pieces of a model to be separate. For instance, an arm would need to be split into two parts: an upper arm and a lower arm. There are other scenarios where parenting is appropriate, for example, a ring on a finger, or the eyes of a character.

1   Create a simple scene

- Open a new scene and change the view to the *top* Orthographic view.
- **Draw** three joints defining an arm.
- Change the view to the *Perspective* view.
- Create two polygonal cylinders and place them over the bones, as follows:

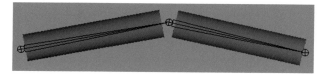

Basic parenting setup

2   Parent the geometry

- Select the *left cylinder*, then **Shift-select** the *left bone*.
- Press the **p** hotkey to **Parent** the cylinder to the bone.
- Repeat the last two steps to **Parent** the *right cylinder* to the *right bone*.

Note: *Notice that the geometry is now a child of the joints in the Outliner.*

3   Test joint rotations

- Select the bones and rotate them to see the result of the parenting.

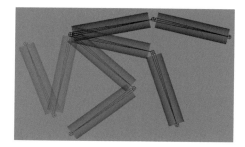

Joints rotation

Note: *Notice that when selecting, bones have a higher selection priority than geometry. To select a bone, simply make a bounding box selection over the bone and geometry.*

Rigid binding

Rigid binding works like the parenting method, except that it affects the geometry's components. By rigid binding geometry on bones, the vertices closer to a certain bone will be instructed to follow that bone. This type of binding usually looks good on low resolution polygonal geometry or NURBS surfaces, but can cause cracking on dense geometry. The following are two examples using rigid binding:

1   Create a simple scene

- Open a new scene and change the view to the *top* Orthographic view.
- **Draw** three joints defining an arm.
- Select the first joint and press **Ctrl+d** to duplicate the joint chain.
- **Move** the joint chains side by side.
- From the *Perspective* view, create a *polygonal cylinder* and a *NURBS cylinder*.
- Place each cylinder so it entirely covers a joint chain.
- Set the polygonal cylinder's **Subdivisions Height** to **10**.
- Set the NURBS cylinder's **Spans** to **10**.

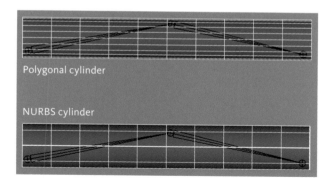

Example scene setup

2   **Rigid bind**
   - Select the *first joint chain*, then **Shift-select** the *polygonal cylinder*.
   - Select **Skin → Bind Skin → Rigid Bind**.
   - Select the *second joint chain*, then **Shift-select** the *NURBS cylinder*.
   - Select **Skin → Bind Skin → Rigid Bind**.

3   **Test joint rotations**
   - Select the bones and rotate them to see the result of the rigid binding on both geometry types.

     The polygonal object appears to fold in on itself, since a vertex can only be assigned to one bone. The NURBS object seems much smoother because the curves of the surface are defined by the CVs, which are bound to the bones just like the polygonal object.

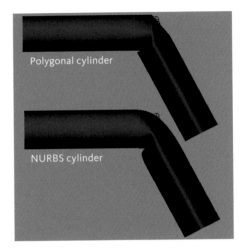

Polygonal cylinder

NURBS cylinder

Rigid binding

> **Note:** *Notice in the Outliner that the geometry is not parented. The binding connects the geometry's vertices to the joints.*

4   **Edit Membership Tool**
   When using rigid bind, you might want to change the default binding so that certain points follow a different bone. The Edit Membership Tool allows you to specify the cluster of points affected by a certain bone.

   - Select **Edit Deformers → Edit Membership Tool**.
   - Click on the *middle bone* of the first joint chain.

     You should see all the vertices affected by that joint highlighted in yellow. Vertices affected by other bones are highlighted using different colors to distinguish them.

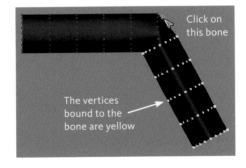

Click on this bone

The vertices bound to the bone are yellow

The Edit Membership Tool

- Using the same hotkeys as when you select objects, toggle points from the cluster using **Shift**, remove points from the cluster using **Ctrl** and add points to the cluster using **Shift+Ctrl**.

- **Repeat** the same steps for the NUBRS geometry to achieve a better deformation.

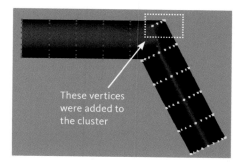

Added polygon vertices

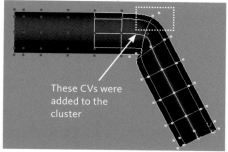

Added NURBS vertices

Flexors

Flexors are a type of deformer designed to be used with rigid bound surfaces. By creating a flexor for a joint, you can smooth out the binding region between two bones, thus preventing geometry from cracking. Flexor points can also be driven by Set Driven Keys to modify their positions as the bone rotates. For instance, you can refine an elbow shape when the elbow is folded.

1 Creating flexors

- From the previous scene, reset the rotations of the bones to their default positions.
- Select the *middle joint* for the first joint chain.
- Select **Skin → Edit Rigid Skin → Create Flexor...**

An option window is displayed.

- Make sure the **Flexor Type** is set to **Lattice**.
- Turn **On** the **Position the Flexor** checkbox.
- Click the **Create** button.

A flexor is created at the joint's position and is selected so that you can position it correctly.

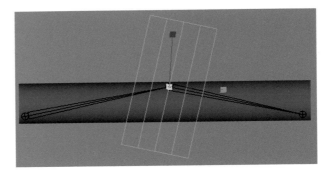

The flexor deformer

- **Translate** and **scale** the flexor to cover the bending region.

2   Test joint rotations
- Select the *middle bone* and rotate it to see the result of the flexor on the geometry.

  Notice that the bending area of the polygonal geometry is now much smoother.

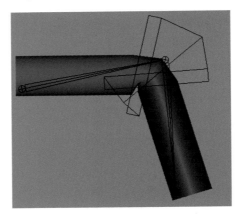

The bent geometry using a flexor

> **Tip:**   *If necessary, hide the flexor object by toggling* **Show → Deformers***, so you can see the deformations more clearly.*

3   Set Driven Keys
- **Zero** the rotation of the bones.
- Select **Animate → Set Driven Key → Set...**

- In the **Driver** section, load the *middle joint* and select the **Rotate Y** attribute.
- Select the *flexor* and press **F8** to display its points.
- Select all the flexor's lattice points and click the **Load Driven** button in the Set Driven Key window.
- Highlight all the driven objects in the **Driven** section and highlight the **XYZ values** on the right side.
- Click the **Key** button to set the normal position.
- Go back into Object mode and **rotate** the *middle joint* on the **Y-axis** by about **80** degrees.
- Select the *flexor* and press **F8** to display its points.
- **Move** the flexor points to confer a nice elbow shape on the cylinder.
- Click the **Key** button to set the bent position.

Note: *The points on the flexor might not move exactly as expected since they are using the local space of the middle bone.*

4   **Test joint rotations**

- Select the *middle bone* and rotate it to see the result of the driven flexor on the geometry.

  Notice that you can achieve a much better crease by using a driven flexor.

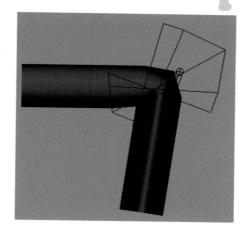

Driven flexor

Lattice binding

Another way to achieve nice skinning using rigid bind is to create a lattice deformer on the geometry and rigid binding the lattice to the bones. This technique can achieve a very smooth binding, using the simplicity of the rigid binding to your advantage.

1 **Detach a skin**

- Select the *polygonal cylinder* from the previous exercise.

- Select **Skin → Detach Skin**.

  The geometry returns to the original shape and position it was in before being bound.

- Select the *middle joint* and zero its rotation.

- Select the *flexor* and press **Delete** on your keyboard, as it is no longer required.

2 **Create a lattice**

- Select the *polygonal cylinder*, then select **Deform → Create Lattice**.

  A lattice is created and fits the geometry perfectly.

- Increase the number of lattice subdivisions by going to the **Shapes** section in the Channel Box and setting its **T Divisions** attribute to **9**.

3 **Rigid bind the lattice**

- With the lattice still selected, **Shift-select** the *first bone* of the joint chain.

- Select **Skin → Bind Skin → Rigid Bind**.

4 **Test joint rotations**

- Select the *middle bone* and rotate it to see the result of the lattice on the geometry.

  At this time, the binding is not much different than a normal rigid binding.

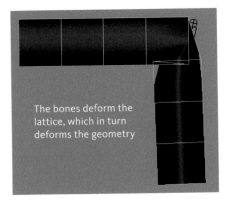

The bones deform the lattice, which in turn deforms the geometry

The bound lattice

5 Adjust the lattice

- Select the *lattice* object.

- In the **Outputs** section of the Channel Box, highlight the *ffd1* node.

- Set the following:

  Local Influence S to **4**;

  Local Influence T to **4**;

  Local Influence U to **4**.

  The deformation of the geometry is now much smoother.

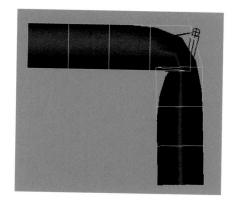

The smoothed influences of the lattice

6 Edit membership

It is now much easier to edit the membership of the lattice points rather than the dense geometry vertices.

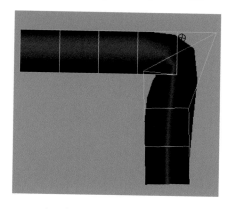

The edited rigid bind membership

7 Driven lattice

If the Edit Membership Tool does not provide enough control over the deformation of the geometry, you can use driven keys to achieve a much better deformation for the elbow and the elbow crease, just like in the previous flexor exercise. You can also use driven keys to bulge the bicep.

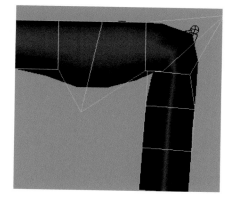

Driven lattice

Smooth binding

The most advanced type of skinning is called smooth binding. Smooth binding allows an object vertex or CV to be influenced by multiple bones, according to a certain percentage. For instance, a vertex's influence can follow a particular bone at 100%, or that influence can be spread across multiple bones in varying percentages, such as 50%-50% or 25%-75%. Doing so will move the vertex accordingly between all the influence bones.

1 **Set-up the scene**

- Using the scene from the previous exercise, set the *middle joint* rotation to zero.

- Select **Edit → Delete All by Type → History** to remove the lattice object.

2 **Smooth bind**

- Select the *first joint*, then **Shift-select** the *polygonal cylinder*.

- Select **Skin → Bind Skin → Smooth Bind**.

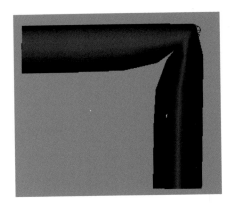

Default smooth binding

3 **Test joint rotations**

- Select the *middle bone* and rotate it to see the result of the smooth binding on the geometry.

4 **Edit smooth bind influence**

Modifying the influences of each bone on each vertex can be a tedious task, but you can use the *Paint Skin Weights Tool* to paint the weights of the vertices directly on the geometry in the viewport. The *Paint Skin Weight Tool* will display an influence of 100% as white, an influence of 0% as black and anything in-between as grayscale. This makes it easier to visually edit the influence of bones on the geometry.

- Select *polyCylinder* and go to **Shading → Smooth Shade All**.

- Select **Skin → Edit Smooth Skin → Paint Skin Weights Tool → ❑**.

The painting option window opens and the geometry gets displayed in grayscale.

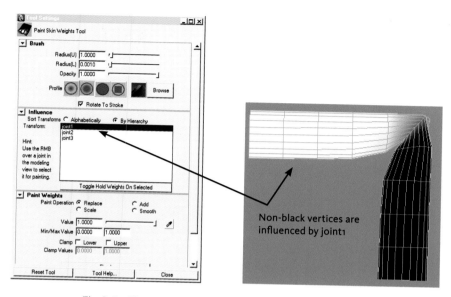

The Paint Skin Weights Tool and the weights on the geometry

Painting skin weights requires a solid understanding of bone influences. Since the tool is based on the Artisan Tool, you can edit the skin weighting on your own. Smooth binding, along with its various related tools, will be covered in greater detail in the intermediate *Learning Maya 2008 | The Modeling & Animation Handbook.*

Binding the penguin

Since the penguin is mostly composed of deformable skin objects, you will bind its geometry using smooth binding. You will also use binding for the eyes and claws. You could parent those objects directly to the skeleton, but it is an easier workflow to keep geometry in one hierarchy and the character skeleton in another.

1   Open the last lesson scene

- Open the file *09-bigzSkeleton_01.ma.*
- **Save** the file as *10-bigzSkinning_01.ma.*

2   Set Preferred Angle

When binding geometry on a skeleton, you need to test the binding by rotating the bones. By doing so, you should be able to return the skeleton to its default position quickly. Maya has two easily accessible commands called *Set Preferred Angle* and *Assume Preferred Angle.* These commands allow you to first define the default skeleton pose, then return to that pose whenever you want.

Note: *The preferred angle also defines the bending angle for IK handles.*

- Select the *pelvis* joint.
- In the viewport, **RMB** over the *pelvis* joint to pop up the contextual marking menu.
- Select **Set Preferred Angle**.

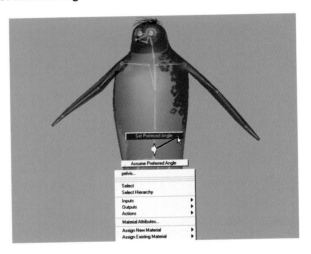

Joint marking menu

Note: *These commands are also available in the **Skeleton** menu.*

3 Assume Preferred Angle

- **Rotate** several joints to achieve a pose.
- Select the *pelvis* joint.
- In the viewport, **RMB** over the *pelvis* joint and select **Assume Preferred Angle**.

   The skeleton should return to its preferred angle (set in the previous step).

4 Bind the body

- Select **Skin** → **Bind Skin** → **Smooth Bind** → ❑.
- In the smooth bind options, change **Bind To** to **Selected Joints**.

> **Tip:** It is recommended that you select the joints to which you want to bind the geometry, in order to avoid having unwanted influence from other bones.

- Select the following joints, which should play an important role in the binding of the penguin:

pelvis	lClavicle	lHip
spine	lShoulder	lKnee
spine1	lElbow	lAnkle
neck	lWrist	lToes
neck1	rClavicle	
head	rShoulder	rHip
jaw	rElbow	rKnee
tail	rWrist	rAnkle
		rToes

- **Shift-select** the *body* geometry.
- Click the **Bind Skin** button in the smooth bind option window.

  You will notice that the wireframe of the bound geometry is now purple, which is a visual cue to show the connection to the selected joint.

- **Rotate** the *pelvis* joint to see if the geometry follows correctly.

5 Smooth bind the eyeballs

- Select the *lEyeball* geometry, then **Shift-select** the *lEye* joint.
- Select **Skin → Bind Skin → Smooth Bind**.
- **Repeat** the previous steps to bind the right eye.
- **Rotate** the *eye* joints to see if the geometry follows correctly.

6 Rigid bind the eyelids

- Select the *lEyelid* and *rEyelid* geometry, then **Shift-select** the *head* joint.
- Select **Skin → Bind Skin → Rigid Bind → ❑**.
- In the rigid bind options, change **Bind To** to **Selected Joints**.
- Click the **Bind Skin** button.
- **Rotate** the *head* joints to see if the geometry follows correctly.
- **Repeat** to rigid bind the hair geometry.

7 Ensure everything is bound

- To ensure all the geometry is bound, select the *pelvis* joint and translate it.

  You will easily notice if a piece is left behind.

- Pose the character to see the effect of the binding and note problematic areas.

> **Note:** *Do not translate any bones except the root joint (pelvis). The preferred angle command only keeps rotation values.*

8 Reset the skeleton position

- **Undo** the last movement to bring the skeleton back to its original position.

  OR

- Select the *pelvis* joint, then select **Skeleton → Assume Preferred Angle**.

  Doing so will ensure all the skeleton rotations are set to their preferred values.

9 Save your work

- **Save** your scene as *10-bigzSkinning_01.ma*.

10 Paint Skin Weights Tool

Once the geometry is bound to the skeleton, you must refine the weighting so that every joint bends the geometry as expected. Perhaps the easiest way to edit a smooth skin is to use the Paint Skin Weights Tool. This tool works just like the 3D Paint Tool, except that you paint bone influences in greyscale instead of colors, where white is fully influenced by a joint and black is not influenced at all by a joint.

Since painting skin weights is considered as an advance topic, this lesson will not cover the painting weights workflow. Consider experimenting on your own with this tool.

- To see the final skinned character scene file, open the scene *10-bigzSkinning_02.ma*.

The entirely bound character

Joint degrees of freedom and limits

A character is usually unable to achieve every possible pose. In this case, the penguin's articulation works in a similar way to the human body. Some joints cannot be rotated a certain way or exceed a certain rotation limit. Bending joints too much or in the wrong way might cause the geometry to interpenetrate or appear broken. Joints have many options to let you control how they are bent by the animator.

1   Degrees of freedom

By default, all three rotation axes on a joint are free to rotate. If you need to, you can limit the degrees of freedom on a joint. In the case of the penguin, the elbows and knees cannot bend in all three directions due to the nature of a biped skeleton. Therefore, you need to limit these joints' rotations to a single axis.

- Select the *lElbow* joint.

- Notice on which axis the joint should be allowed to bend.

The elbow should rotate only on the Y-axis

The elbow rotation axes

Tip:	*The **Rotate Tool** must be in **Local** mode.*

- Open the Attribute Editor and scroll to the **Joint** section.
- Turn **Off** the **X** and **Z** checkboxes for the **Degrees of Freedom** attribute.

    *Notice that the **Rotate X** and **Rotate Z** attributes in the Channel Box are now locked.*

2 Joint limits

A joint limit allows you to specify the minimum and maximum values allowed for a joint to rotate. In this case, the elbow joint needs to stop rotating when it gets fully bent or fully extended.

- Select the *lElbow* joint.
- **Rotate** the joint to bend it on the **Y-axis** and stop just before it interpenetrates with the upper arm.
- In the Attribute Editor, open the **Limit Information** section.
- In the **Rotate** section, turn **On** the **Rot Limit Y Min** attribute.
- Click on the **<** button to put the **Current** value in the **Min** field.
- **Rotate** the *lElbow* joint on the **Y-axis** the other way and stop when the arm is perfectly straight.
- Back in the Attribute Editor, turn **On** the **Rot Limit Y Max** attribute.
- Click on the **>** button to put the **Current** value in the **Max** field.

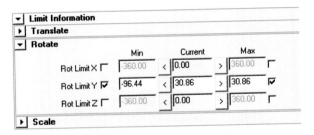

The lElbow rotation limits

3 Remainder of skeleton limits

You can now set the freedom and limitations on the penguin skeleton as you would like them to be.

4 Save your work

The completed version of the bound penguin can be found in the support files as *10-bigzSkinning_03.ma*.

Conclusion

You have now explored the various skinning types required to bind a character to its skeleton. You have also learned how to change a joint's degrees of freedom and set limit information.

In the next lesson, you will learn about the blendshape deformer which will be used for facial animation.

Lesson 11
Blend Shapes

In this lesson you will create a blend shape deformer, which is a type of deformer that blends between different geometry shapes. This will allow you to model facial expressions for the penguin to be used for animation.

In this lesson you will learn the following:

- How to sculpt surfaces by painting with Artisan
- How to use different brush operations
- How to create blend shapes
- How to mix blend shapes

Sculpting a surface

You will now test the Artisan Sculpt Tool. You will use the tool on a sphere to get a feel for it. Once you are more familiar with the tool, you will apply brush strokes to the penguin geometry.

1 Make a test sphere

- **Create** a polygonal primitive sphere.

- Set its construction history for both **Subdivisions Axis** and **Subdivisions Height** to **60**.

- To better see the effect of your painting in the viewport, assign a new phong material to the sphere by selecting **Lighting/Shading** → **Assign New Material** → **Phong** from the **Rendering** menu set.

- Press the 5 key to turn on **Smooth Shade All**.

2 Open the Sculpt Polygons Tool

- With the *pSphere* selected, select
Mesh → **Sculpt Geometry Tool** → ❑
from the **Polygons** menu set.

  This opens the **Tool Settings** *window, which includes every Artisan sculpting option.*

- Click on the **Reset Tool** button to make sure that you are starting with Artisan's default settings.

- Set the following attributes:

  Under **Brush***:*

  Radius (U) to **0.2**.

  Under **Sculpt Parameters:**

  Max Displacement to **0.1**.

- Place the Tool Settings window to the right of the *sphere* and keep it open.

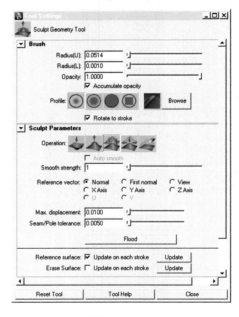

Tool Settings window

3 Paint on the surface

- Move your cursor over the *pSphere* geometry.

  The cursor icon changes to show an arrow surrounded by a red circular outline. The arrow indicates how much the surface will be pushed or pulled, while the outline indicates the brush radius. Artisan's brush icon is context sensitive. It changes as you choose different tool settings.

• **Click+drag** on the *sphere*.

You are now painting on the surface, pushing it toward the inside.

Tip: *Artisan works more intuitively with a tablet and stylus, since the input device mimics the use of an actual paintbrush.*

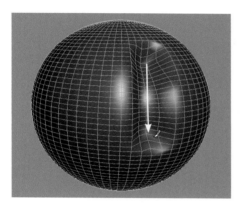 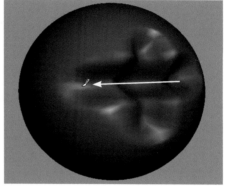

First brush stroke   *Second brush stroke*

4   **Change the Artisan display**

• Open the **Display** section in the Tool Settings window.

• Click on **Show Wireframe** to turn this option **Off**.

Now you can focus on the surface without displaying the wireframe lines.

5   **Paint another stroke**

• **Paint** a second stroke across the mask surface.

Now it is easier to see the results of your sculpting.

The sculpting tools

You will now explore some of the Artisan sculpting operations to see how they work. So far, you have been pushing on the surface. Now you will learn how to pull, smooth and erase.

1   **Pull on the surface**

• In the Tool Settings window, scroll to the **Sculpt Parameters** section.

• Under **Operation**, click on **Pull**.

• **Tumble** around to the other side of the sphere.

• **Paint** on the surface to create a few strokes that pull out.

2 **Smooth out the results**

- Under **Operation**, click on **Smooth**.

- Under **Brush**, change the **Radius (U)** to **0.6**.

  This increases the size of your brush. You can see that the red outline has increased in size. This is the brush feedback icon.

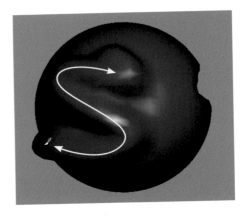

Pulling the surface with several brush strokes

 Tip: *You can hold the **b** hotkey and **click+drag** in the viewport to interactively change the brush size.*

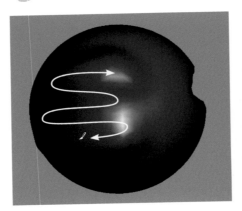

Smoothing the brush strokes　　　　　　*Erasing the brush strokes*

- **Paint** all of the strokes to smooth the details.

  If you stroke over an area more than once, the smoothing becomes more evident.

3 **Erase some of the brush strokes**

- Under **Operation**, click on the **Erase** option.

- **Paint** along the surface to begin erasing the last sculpt edits.

4   Flood

- Under **Operation**, click on the **Pull** option.

- In the **Sculpt Parameters** section, click on the **Flood** button.

  This uses the current operation and applies it to the entire surface using the current opacity setting.

- Under **Operation**, click on the **Erase** option.

- In the **Sculpt Parameters** section, click on the **Flood** button.

  The sphere comes back to its original shape.

Fully erased surface

Updating the reference surface

When you paint in Artisan, you paint in relation to a *reference surface*. By default, the reference surface updates after every stroke so that you can build your strokes on top of one another. You can also keep the reference surface untouched until you decide to update it manually.

1   Change the brush attributes

- Under **Operation**, click on **Pull**.

- Set the following attributes:

  Under **Brush***:*

  Radius (U) to **0.2**.

  Under **Sculpt Parameters:**

  Max Displacement to **0.2**.

2   Pull the surface with two strokes

- **Paint** on the surface to create two crossing strokes that pull out.

  The second stroke is built on top of the first stroke. Therefore, the height of the pull is higher where the two strokes intersect.

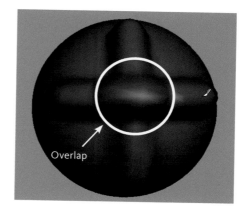

Painting with reference update

3   Change the reference update

- In the Tool Settings window, scroll down in the **Sculpt Parameters** section, and turn **Off** the **Reference Surface: Update On Each Stroke**.

4 **Paint more overlapping strokes**

- **Paint** on the surface to create a few strokes that pull out.

  *This time, the strokes do not overlap. The reference surface does not update, therefore the strokes can only displace to the **Maximum Displacement** value. You cannot displace beyond that value until you update the reference surface.*

5 **Update the reference layer**

- Still in the **Sculpt Parameters** section, click on the **Update** button next to **Reference Surface**.

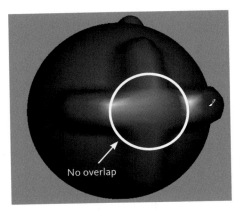

Painting with no reference update

6 **Paint on the surface**

- **Paint** another stroke over the last set of strokes.

  The overlapping strokes are again building on top of each other.

7 **Flood erase the surface**

- Under **Operation**, click on the **Erase** option.

- Click on the **Flood** button.

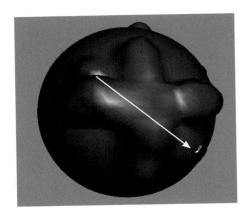

Painting on updated reference layer

Sculpting the penguin

You will now use the Artisan Sculpt Tool to create a few facial shapes for the penguin. You will first duplicate the body of the penguin in order to have multiple copies to use for the blend shape deformer.

1 **Scene file**

- Continue with your own scene file from the previous lesson.

  OR

- Continue with *10-bigzSkinning_03.ma*.

2 Skin envelope

Before you start making blend shapes, you must ensure that the geometry is in its original position. One way to get the skin back to its exact original position is to turn off the skin's influence.

- Select the penguin's *body.*
- In the Channel Box, highlight the *skinCluster* node.
- Set **Envelope** to **0**.

Doing so temporarily turns off the skinCluster, thus removing any influence of the skeleton and placing the geometry back to its exact original position.

3 Duplicate the penguin

The blend shape deformer requires the original untouched penguin and penguin duplicates to be deformed.

- **Hide** the joints in the viewport.
- Select all of the penguin's geometry.
- Press **Ctrl+d** to **Duplicate** it all.
- Highlight every locked attribute in the Channel Box, then **RMB** and select **Unlock Selected**.
- Press **Ctrl+g** to **Group** all the geometry together.
- **Move** the new group next to the original character.
- **Rename** the new *body* geometry to *smile.*
- **Duplicate** the group you have just created and **rename** the *body* geometry forthe following:

> sad;
> browUp;
> browDown.

Highlight and unlock the attributes

Tip: *It is good to duplicate the other objects like the eyes, since you will be able to use them as a reference for when you model the blend shapes. Never modify objects other than the one intended for deformation.*

The duplicates

- Select the penguin's original body.
- In the Channel Box, highlight the *skinCluster* node.
- Set **Envelope** to **1**.

4   Sculpt the smile shape

You will use Artisan to paint and deform the smile geometry.

- With the *smile* geometry selected, select **Mesh** → **Sculpt Geometry Tool** → ❑ from the Polygons menu set.
- Click on the **Reset Tool** button to make sure that you are starting with Artisan's default settings.
- Set the following attributes:

Under **Brush***:*

>   **Radius (U)** to **0.4**.

Under **Sculpt Parameters***:*

>   **Operation** to **Pull**;

>   **Reference Vector** to **Y-axis**;

>   **Max Displacement** to **0.1**.

Under **Stroke:**

>   **Reflection** to **On**.

This option allows you to sculpt only one side of the geometry to create the complete shape.

Under **Display***:*

>   **Show Wireframe** to **Off**.

This last option will turn off the wireframe display on the geometry. It is up to you whether to turn this on or off.

> **Note:** *In the previous test sphere example, you were painting using the normals of the surface as the direction to be pushed and pulled. In this case, you will pull along the Y-axis, which will move the vertices up.*

- **Paint** directly on the model to get a shape similar to the following:

Smile shape

5   **Sculpt the other shapes**

- **Repeat** the previous steps to sculpt the three other shapes and any other shape you would want.

Sad shape

Brow up shape

Brow down shape

Blend shape deformer

In order to make character animation more realistic, you will need facial animation. This will be done using a deformer that will blend between the original penguin geometry and the geometry displaying emotion that you just created. That kind of deformer is called a *blend shape deformer*. Blend shapes are very useful in 3D, especially to animate facial expressions on characters, but they can also be used for plenty of other things.

1 Creating the deformer

- Select, in order, the *smile, sad, browUp* and *browDown* shapes and then **Shift-select** the original *body* shape.

Note: *It is important to select the original object last.*

- From the **Animation** menu set, select **Create Deformers → Blend Shape → ❏.**
- In the blend shape option window, make sure to set **Origin** to **Local**.
- Select the **Advance** tab and make sure **Deformation Order** is set to **Front of chain**.
- Click the **Create** button.

Note: *The Front of chain option tells Maya that you need the blend shape deformer to be inserted before any other deformers, such as the skinCluster.*

2 Testing the deformer

- Select the original body geometry.

  In the Channel Box, you should see a blendShape1 node and its construction history.

- Highlight the *blendShape1* node.

  Notice that the attributes have the same names as the geometry you duplicated earlier. These attributes control the blending between the original shape and the sculpted ones.

- Highlight the *smile* attribute's name.
- **MMB+drag** from left to right to access the virtual slider and see the effect of the deformer on the geometry.
- Experiment blending more than one shape at a time to see its effect.

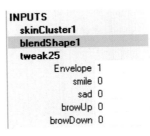

The blendshape node

3 **Tweaking the blend shape**

Since construction history still links the blend shape with the deformed surface, you can still tweak the sculpted geometry as needed.

- Make modifications on any of the sculpted geometry with the Artisan Sculpting Tool.

Sad and browDown shapes mixed together

Tip: *Your changes must be made on the sculpted blend shape geometry and not on the original geometry.*

4 **Delete targets**

- Select all the duplicated groups used to create the blend shapes.

- Press **Backspace** or **Delete** to dispose of them.

Note: *When you delete blend shape targets, Maya keeps the blend values in the blend shape node instead of using the geometry in the scene. Because of this, it is important to not delete the history on the model unless you want to get rid of the blend shapes.*

5 **Save your work**

- **Save** your scene as *11-bigzBlendshapes_01.ma*.

Conclusion

You are now more familiar with the very useful blend shape deformer, as well as the Artisan Sculpting Tool. You now have the skills to create extremely powerful deforming animations, such as lip-synching, facial expressions and reactive animations.

In the next lesson, you will refine your character set-up by using IK handles, constraints and custom attributes. You will also create a reverse foot setup that will help maintain the character's feet on the ground.

Lesson 12
Inverse Kinematics

In this lesson, you will add IK (inverse kinematics) handles and constraints to the existing penguin skeleton in order to make the character easier to animate. You will also create a reverse foot setup, which simplifies floor contact when animating, and hand manipulators, which will help lock hands upon contact with the environment. Lastly, you will learn about pole vector constraints.

In this lesson you will learn the following:

- How to add single chain IK handles
- How to add rotate plane IK handles
- How to create a reverse foot setup
- How to use point, orient and parent constraints
- How to use pole vector constraints

IK handles

There are several types of IK handles and you will experiment with two types in this lesson: the Single Chain IK and the Rotate Plane IK. The difference between these two is that the single chain IK handle's end effector tries to reach the position and orientation of its IK handle, whereas the rotate plane IK handle's end effector only tries to reach the position of its IK handle.

Single Chain IK

A single chain IK handle uses the single chain solver to calculate the rotations of all joints in the IK chain. Also, the overall orientation of the joint chain is calculated directly by the single chain solver.

1   Open the last penguin scene

- **Open** the file *11-bigzBlendshapes_01.ma*.

2   Joint rotation limits

For better results using IKs, it is not recommended to have rotation limits on joints that are part of an IK handle. Limiting joint rotations will prevent the IK solver from finding good joint rotations and may cause it to behave unexpectedly.

- **Remove** rotation limits and enable all degrees of freedom for the arm and leg joints, if any.

> **Note:** *Rotation limits and degrees of freedom are especially useful on joints intended to be animated manually.*

3   Single Chain IK

- Select **Skeleton → IK Handle Tool → ❏**.

  The tool's option window will be displayed.

- Change the **Current Solver** to **ikSCsolver**.

- Click on the **Close** button.

- In the viewport, click on the *lShoulder* bone.

  The joint will be highlighted. This is the start joint.

- Click on the *lWrist* bone.

  The IK handle is created, starting at the shoulder and going down to the wrist of the character.

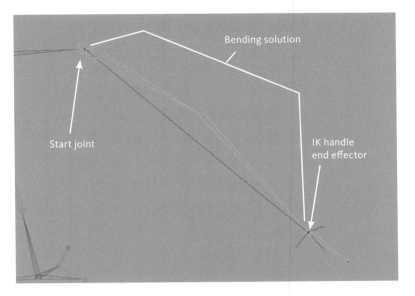

In the Hypergraph, you can see the end effector connected to the hierarchy and the IK handle to the side. The end effector and the IK handle are connected, along with the appropriate joints at the dependency node level. When you control the handle, you control the whole IK chain.

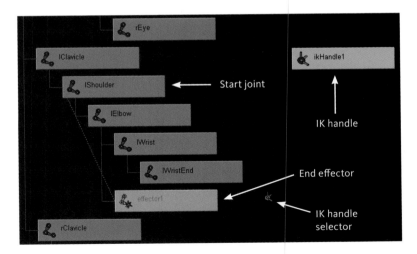

Hypergraph

4 Experiment with the IK handle

- Press **w** to enter the **Translate Tool**.
- **Translate** the IK handle and notice the resulting bending of the arm.

> **Tip:** *If the IK handle does not bend the arm or if it bends it the wrong way, it is because the angle in the arm joint chain was not appropriate. To remedy the situation, delete the IK handle, bend the arm appropriately, and then recreate the IK.*

- Press **e** to enter the **Rotate Tool**.
- **Rotate** the IK handle and notice the resulting bending of the arm.

  Rotating the IK handle will change the bending solution, but will not affect the wrist's rotation. You will create a hand setup in a later exercise.

- **Rename** the IK handle *lArmIk*.

5 Preferred angle

- With the IK selected, **RMB** in the viewport and select **Assume Preferred Angle**.

  The arm joints and the IK handle will move back to the preferred angle set in the previous lesson.

6 Right arm IK

- **Create** another single chain IK for the right arm and rename it *rArmIk*.

> **Tip:** *IK handles have a higher selection priority than joints and geometry. To pick an IK handle, simply make a selection bounding box over it.*

Rotate Plane IK

A rotate plane IK handle uses the rotate plane solver to calculate the rotations of all joints in its IK chain, but not the joint chain's overall orientation. Instead, the IK rotate plane handle gives you direct control over the joint chain's orientation via the pole vector and twist disk, rather than having the orientation calculated by the IK solver.

> **Note:** *The twist disc is a visual representation showing the vector defining the chain's overall orientation. You will experiment with the twist disk in the following steps.*

1   Rotate Plane IK

- Select **Skeleton** → **IK Handle Tool** → ❑.

- Change the **Current Solver** for **ikRPsolver**.

- Turn **On** the **Sticky** option.

   This option snaps the IK to its effector at all time.

- Click on the **Close** button.

- In the viewport, click on the *lHip* bone.

- Click on the *lAnkle* bone.

   The IK handle gets created, starting at the hip and going down to the ankle of the character.

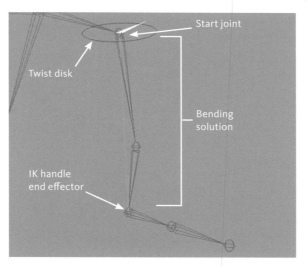

Rotate plane IK

2   Experiment with the IK handle

One differentiating feature of this type of IK handle is the ability to control the twist of the solution using the *Twist* and *Pole Vector* attributes.

- **Move** the IK handle up.

- Press **t** to show the IK handle manipulators.

- **Move** the pole vector manipulator located next to the twist disk.

   This manipulator affects the pointing direction of the IK chain.

- Highlight the **Twist** attribute in the Channel Box and **MMB+drag** in the viewport.

This attribute also affects the pointing direction of the IK chain, but overrides the pole vector attributes.

- **Rename** the IK handle *lLegIk*.

3   Reset the IK handle's position

- With the IK selected, **RMB** in the viewport and select **Assume Preferred Angle**.

4   Right leg IK

- **Create** another rotate plane IK for the right leg.
- **Rename** the IK handle *rLegIk*.

5   Save your work

- **Save** the file as *12-bigzIK_01.ma*.

Reverse foot

When you animate a walking character, you need one of the character's feet to plant itself while the other foot is lifted into position. In the time it is planted, the foot needs to roll from heel to toe. A reverse foot skeleton is the ideal technique for creating these conditions.

1   Draw the reverse foot skeleton

- Change the viewport to a *four view* layout.
- Dolly on the feet of the penguin in all views.
- Select **Skeleton → Joint Tool**.

  *The **Orientation** of the tool should be set to **XYZ**.*

- In the side view, create the first joint on the heel of the penguin's foot geometry.

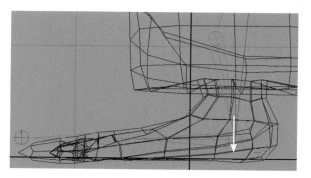

The heel joint

- In the *front* view, **MMB+drag** the new joint to align it with the rest of the foot joints.

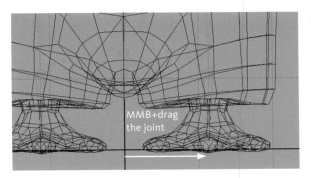

Move the heel joint

- In the Perspective view, turn **Off** the geometry display by selecting **Show → Polygons**.
- Hold down the **v** hotkey to enable **Snap to Point**.
- **Draw** three other bones, snapping them to the *toesEnd*, *toes* and *ankle* joints

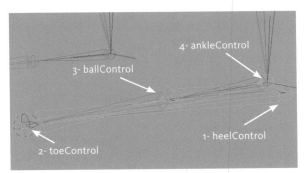

The complete reverse foot

- Press **Enter** to exit the tool.
- **Rename** the joints as shown in the previous image.

Set up the reverse foot

To control the foot and have a proper heel-to-toe rotation, you will now constrain the IK handle, ankle and toe joints to the reverse foot chain. This will allow you to use the reverse foot chain to control the foot and leg.

Lesson 12: Inverse Kinematics

2 Point constrain the IK handle

- Select the *ankleControl* joint on the reverse foot chain.
- **Shift-select** the IK handle.

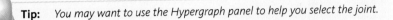

Tip: *You may want to use the Hypergraph panel to help you select the joint.*

- Select **Constrain → Point**.

  The point constraint forces an object to follow the position of a source object. The IK handle is now positioned over the reverse foot's ankleControl joint.

3 Test the reverse foot chain

- Select the *heelControl* joint.
- **Move** the joint to test the foot setup so far.

  The ankle moves with the reverse foot chain, but the joints do not stay properly aligned.

- **Undo** your moves.

4 Orient constrain the toes

To align the rest of the foot, you will orient constrain the *toes'* joint to the reverse foot.

- Select the *toeControl* joint on the reverse foot chain.
- **Shift-select** the *toes'* joint from the leg chain.
- Select **Constrain → Orient → ❏.**
- In the orient constraint options, turn **On** the **Maintain Offset** option.

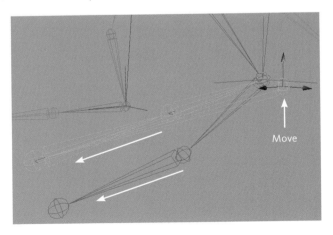

Orient constrained toes' joint

- Click the **Add** button.

  The orient constraint forces an object to follow the rotation of a source object. The Maintain Offset option forces the constrained object to keep its position.

- **Move** the *heelControl* joint to test the foot setup so far.

- **Undo** your moves.

5   Orient Constrain the ankle joint

You will now repeat these last few steps for the *ankle* joint.

- Select the *ballControl* joint on the reverse foot chain.

- **Shift-select** the *ankle* joint from the leg chain.

- Select **Constrain → Orient**.

  Now the foot joints and reverse foot joints are aligned.

6   Test the movement of the reverse foot

- **Rotate** the different joints of the foot setup to test them.

  Notice how you can easily achieve the motion of peeling the foot off the floor. You can also easily roll the toes or the heel on the floor, which would otherwise be very difficult to achieve.

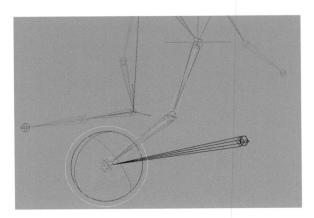

Orient constrained foot setup

- **Undo** your moves to bring the foot setup back to its original position.

Creating the heel-to-toe motion

You can now control the rotation of the foot by rotating the various control joints on the reverse foot. Instead of requiring the rotation of several joints to achieve a heel-to-toe motion, you will use Set Driven Key to control the roll using a single attribute on the *heelControl* joint.

1   **Add a Roll attribute**

- Select the *heelControl* joint.

- Select **Modify** → **Add Attribute...**

- Set the following values in the Add Attribute window:

    Long Name to **roll**;

    Data Type to **Float**;

    Minimum to **-5**;

    Maximum to **10**;

    Default to **0**.

- Click **OK** to add the attribute.

    You can now see this attribute in the Channel Box. The minimum and maximum values give reasonable boundary values for the roll.

2   **Prepare the Set Driven Key window**

- Select **Animate** → **Set Driven Key** → **Set...**

- Select the *heelControl* joint and click **Load Driver**.

- In the **Driver** section, highlight the **roll** attribute.

- Select the *heelControl, ballControl* and *toeControl* joints and click **Load Driven**.

3   **Key the heel rotation**

- In the **Driven** section, highlight **heelControl** and the **rotate Z** attribute.

- Click on the **Key** button to set the starting rotation.

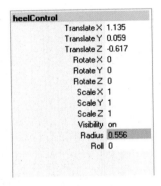

The roll attribute in the Channel Box

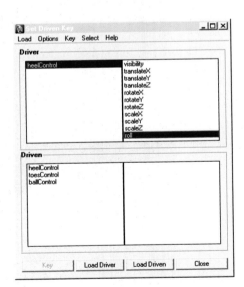

Set Driven Key window

- In the Channel Box, set the **roll** value to **-5**.
- Set the **Rotate Z** to **20**.

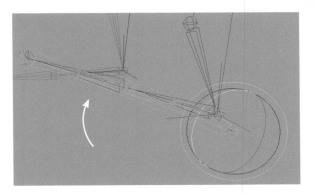

Foot rotated back on heel

- Again, click on the **Key** button.
- You can now test the **roll** attribute by clicking on its name in the Channel Box and **MMB+dragging** in the viewport. You can see that the foot rolls from the heel to a flat position.
- Set the **Roll** attribute to **0**.

4   Key the ball rotation

- In the **Driven** section, click on **ballControl** and then on **rotate Z**.
- Click on the **Key** button to set the starting rotation.
- Click on **heelControl** in the **Driver** section and set the **roll** value to **10**.
- Click on **ballControl** and set the **Rotate Z** to **30**.

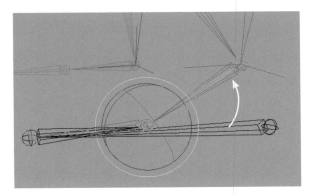

Foot rotated forward on ball

- Again, click on the **Key** button in the Set Driven Key window.
- Click on **heelControl** and set the **Roll** value back to **0**.

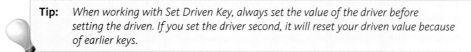

Tip: *When working with Set Driven Key, always set the value of the driver before setting the driven. If you set the driver second, it will reset your driven value because of earlier keys.*

5 **Key the toe rotation**

- In the **Driven** section, click on **toeControl** and then on **rotate Z**.
- Click on the **Key** button to set the starting rotation.
- Click on **heelControl** and set the **roll** value to **10**.
- Click on **toeControl** and set the **Rotate Z** to **30**.

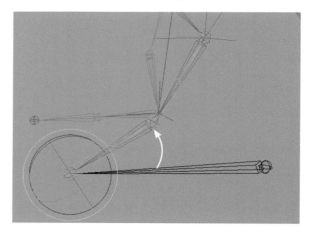

Foot rotated forward on toe

- Again, click on the **Key** button.

6 **Test the foot roll**

- Select the *heelControl* joint.
- Click on the **roll** attribute name in the Channel Box and **MMB+drag** in the viewport to test the roll.
- Set the **roll** back to **0**.
- Click the **Close** button in the Set Driven Key window.

7   **Right foot setup**

Create another reverse foot setup for the right leg.

- Select the *heelControl* joint.

- Select **Edit** → **Duplicate Special** → ❑.

- In the options, turn **On** the **Duplicate** input graph option.

- Click the **Duplicate Special** button.

    By duplicating the input graph, you will keep the driven keys you have just made.

- In the Channel Box, change the value of the **TranslateX** attribute to be the same value, but **negative**.

- **Recreate** the different constraints for the right foot.

- **Rename** all the joints appropriately with their left and right prefixes.

8   **Test the setup**

- Select the *pelvis* joint.

- **Move** and **rotate** the *pelvis* to see the effect of the constrained IK handles.

- **Undo** the last step to bring the pelvis back to its original position.

Moving the pelvis joint

9   **Save your work**

- **Save** the scene as *12-bigzIK_02.ma*.

Hand setup

It is good to be able to plant the feet of your character, but it would also be good to control the hand rotations. In this exercise, you will create a basic hand setup that will allow you to control the hand rotations.

1   Change the arm IK type

Single plane IKs are best used when you don't need to bother with the hands' rotation or with the bending solution. This means that they are not ideal for the type of control you are looking for in this case. You will need to delete the ones you have on the arms and create new rotate plane IKs.

- Select the two arm IK handles.

- Press **Delete** on your keyboard.

- Select **Skeleton → IK Handle Tool**.

    The IK type should already be set to ikRPsolver.

- **Create** IK handles for both arms.

- **Rename** the IK handles properly.

The hand manipulator

2   **Create a hand manipulator**

- Select **Show** → **NURBS Surfaces** to show all the NURBS surfaces in the viewport.
- Select **Create** → **NURBS Primitives** → **Circle**.
- **Rename** the circle *lHandManip*.
- Press **w** to access the **Translate Tool**.
- Hold down the **v** hotkey and snap the *circle* to the *lWrist* of the skeleton.
- **Rotate** and **scale** the circle to fit the wrist.
- Select **Modify** → **Freeze Transformations**.

3   **Constrain the IK handle**

- With the *circle* still selected, **Shift-select** the *lArmIk* handle.
- Select **Constrain** → **Parent**.

  The parent constraint forces the constrained object to follow a source object, just as if it were parented to it.

4   **Constrain the wrist**

- Select the *circle*, then **Shift-select** the *lWrist* joint.
- Select **Constrain** → **Orient**.

5   **Test the wrist manipulator**

- **Move** and **rotate** the *lHandManip* to see how it affects the arm and hand.
- **Move** and **rotate** the *pelvis* joint to see how it affects the arm and hand.

  Notice how the hand stays planted wherever it is. This is exactly the behavior you are looking for.

- **Undo** the last steps to return the *pelvis* and *lHandManip* to their original locations.

6   **Create a pole vector constraint**

- Select **Create** → **Locator**.
- Hold down **v** to enable **Snap to Point**, then snap the locator on the *lElbow* joint.
- **Move** the *locator* back on the **Z-axis** by about **5 units**.
- With the *locator* selected, **Shift-select** the *lArmIk* handle.
- Select **Constrain** → **Pole Vector**.

  *The pole vector constraint will connect the locator's position to the IK handle's **Pole Vector** attribute. By doing this, you can now control the rotation of the arm using a visual indicator.*

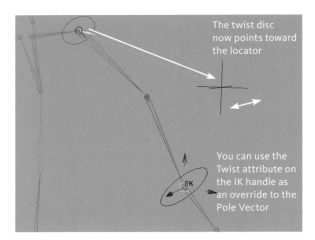

The twist disc now points toward the locator

You can use the Twist attribute on the IK handle as an override to the Pole Vector

A pole vector locator

- **Rename** the locator to *lArmPv*.

7 Right hand manipulator

- **Create** the same type of manipulator on the right hand.

The completed IK setup

8   Save your work

- **Save** the scene as *12-bigzIK_03.ma.*

Conclusion

In this lesson, you learned the basics of how to use IK handles in a custom setup. You experimented with some of the most popular tricks, such as the reverse foot setup and manipulators. You also used the twist attribute and pole vector constraints, which are required for any good IK handle animation.

In the next lesson, you will refine the current character set-up even more. Steps will include creating an eye set-up, locking and hiding non-required attributes, adding and connecting custom attributes, and creating a character set. Doing so will make your character rig easier to use, limiting manipulation errors that could potentially break it. You will also generate a higher resolution version of the geometry.

Lesson 13
Rigging

Rig hierarchy

When you look in the Outliner, your character's hierarchy should be clean, well named and simple to understand. For instance, all the set-up nodes should be parented together under a master node. You can then use that master node for the global placement of the character in a scene.

1   Open the last scene

- **Open** the file *12-bigzIK_03.ma*.

2   Geometry group

- Select all the bound geometry in your scene.

Tip: *It might be simpler to select the geometry and geometry groups from the Outliner.*

- Press **Ctrl+g** to group it all together.
- **Rename** the group *geo*.

3   Create a master node

- Change the current view to the top view.
- Select **Create** → **EP Curve** → ❑.
- Change the **Curve Degree** for **1 Linear**.
- Click the **Close** button.
- Hold down **x** and draw a four-arrows shape as indicated:

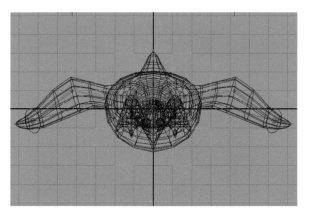

The master node curve

- Hit **Enter** to complete the curve.
- **Rename** the curve *master*.

4   **Hierarchy**
   - Select **Panels** → **Saved Layouts** → **Persp/Outliner**.

   - In the Outliner, select all character set-up nodes and **Parent** them to the *master* node.

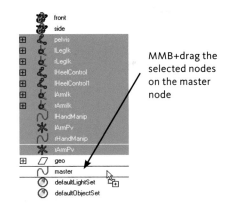

MMB+drag the selected nodes on the master node

Parent set-up nodes to master

Note: *Do not parent bound geometry or the geometry group to the master node.*

There should now be only two main groups in the Outliner, which are geo and master.

5   **Node names**
   - Make sure all nodes are named correctly.

Note: *It is recommended to have unique names for all your objects.*

6   **Visibility layers**
   - In the Layer Editor, click on the **Create a new layer** button.
   - **Rename** the new layer *setupLayer*.
   - Select the *master* node in the *Perspective* view, then **RMB** on the *setupLayer* and select **Add Selected Objects**.

     All the character rig nodes can now be hidden by hiding the setupLayer.

   - Click the **Create a new layer** button and **rename** the new layer to *geoLayer*.
   - Select the *geo* node in the *Perspective* view, then **RMB** on the *geoLayer* and select **Add Selected Objects**.

Selection sets

Selection sets are meant to simplify the selection process of multiple objects. In the penguin set-up, it would be nice to select all the spine and neck joints at once in order to be able to bend the character's back easily.

Lesson 13: Rigging

1   **Select the spine and neck**

• Select the *spine*, *spine1*, *neck*, *neck1* and *head* joint.

2   **Create a set**

• Select **Create → Sets → Quick Select Set…**

• In the Create Quick Select Set window, enter the name *spineSet*.

• Click the **OK** button.

If you scroll down in the Outliner, there
will be a set called spineSet.

  spineSet

The new set

3   **Use the selection set**

• Select *spineSet* in the Outliner.

• **RMB** to pop up a contextual menu and choose **Select Set Members**.

All the objects in the set are selected.

• Press **e** to access the **Rotate Tool**.

• **Rotate** all the joints simultaneously.

Rotate all joints simultaneously

Tip: *If you notice that some joint local rotation axes are not aligned correctly, you can go*
into Component mode and adjust them, even after a skin is bound.

4 **Edit a selection set**

It would probably be best if the head was not selected at the same time as the other joints when you need to rotate the character's back. The following will remove the head from the selection set.

- **Undo** the last rotation.

- Select **Window → Relationship Editors → Sets**.

- On the left side of the Relationship Editor, click on the **+** sign next to the *spineSet* to expand it.

  All the objects in that set are displayed.

- Still in the left side of the Relationship Editor, highlight the *head* joint from the set *spineSet*.

- Select **Edit → Remove Highlighted from Set**.

> **Note:** *When you highlight a set in the Relationship Editor, its members are highlighted on the right side of the panel. Toggle objects on the right side to add them to or remove them from the current set.*

- **Close** the Relationship Editor.

5 **Save your work**

- **Save** your scene as *13-bigzRig_01.ma*.

Custom attributes

As you will notice by working in the current rig, some attributes are not easy to access. You should place useful attributes on strategic nodes for easy access.

Since you control the arm and leg IK handles using custom set-ups, it is a good idea to place useful IK attributes on the hand manipulator and the reverse foot bones.

1 **Add new attributes**

- Select the *lHandManip*, the *rHandManip*, the *lHeelControl* and the *rHeelControl*.

- Select **Modify → Add Attribute...**

- Set the following:

  Long Name to **twist**;

  Data Type to **Float**;

  Default to **0**.

- Click the **Add** button.

This will add the Twist attribute to all selected nodes. The Add Attribute window will remain open for further attribute additions.

- Set the following:

    Name to **ikBlend**;

    Data Type to **Integer**;

    Minimum to **0**;

    Maximum to **1**;

    Default to **1**.

- Click the **OK** button.

2   Connect the new attributes

- Select **Window → General Editors → Connection Editor**.
- Select the *lHandManip*.
- In the Connection Editor, click on the **Reload Left** button.
- Scroll down and highlight the **Twist** attribute.
- Select the *lArmIk*.
- In the Connection Editor, click on the **Reload Right** button.
- Scroll down and highlight the **Twist** attribute.

    You have just connected the Twist attribute of the hand manipulator to the left arm IK handle Twist attribute.

- Highlight the ikBlend attribute on the left side of the editor.
- Highlight the ikBlend attribute on the right side of the editor.

    The ikBlend attribute of the hand manipulator is now connected to the left arm IK handle ikBlend attribute.

3   Repeat

- **Repeat** the previous steps in order to connect the remaining *rHandManip*, *lHeelControl* and *rHeelControl* attributes to their respective IK handles.
- Click the **Close** button to close the Connection Editor.

> **Note:** *If you intend to use the joint in both IK and FK, make sure to turn on the IK FK Control attribute found in the IK Solver Attributes section of the Attribute Editor for the IK handles.*

4 Hide the IK handles

Since you have connected the *Twist* and *IK Blend* attributes of the IK handles to their manipulators, the IK handles can now be hidden since they are no longer required to be visible or selected.

- Select the *lArmIk*, the *rArmIk*, the *lLegIk* and the *rLegIk*.

- Set the **Visibility** attribute in the Channel Box to **Off** by typing in **o** in the Channel Box.

  All the IK handles are now hidden.

- Highlight the **Visibility** attribute's name.

- **RMB** in the Channel Box and select **Lock Selected**.

  Doing so will prevent the IK handles from being displayed, even when using the **Display** → **Show** → **All** *command.*

Selection handles

There are several nodes that you will need to select when animating the character. Unfortunately, these nodes can be hidden under geometry or difficult to pick in the viewport. This is where a selection handle becomes helpful.

1 Show selection handles

- Select the *lHeelControl*, the *rHeelControl* and the *pelvis* joints.

- Select **Display** → **Transform Display** → **Selection Handles**.

- Clear the current selection.

- **Click+drag** a selection box over the entire character in the viewport.

  Since selection handles have a very high selection priority, only the three selection handles get selected.

2 Move selection handles

- Go into **Component** mode.

- Make sure only the selection handle mask is enabled.

The selection handle mask

- Select the selection handles for the *lHeelControl*, the *rHeelControl* and the *pelvis* joints.

- Press **w** to enable the **Translate Tool**.

- **Translate** the selection handles toward the back of the **Z-axis** until they are outside the geometry.
- Go back into **Object** mode.

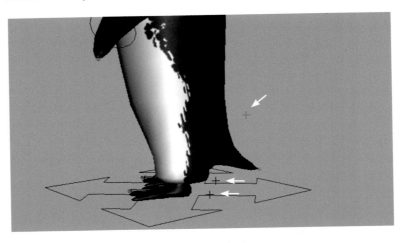

The selection handle outside the geometry

3 Save your work

- **Save** your scene as *13-bigzRig_02.ma*.

Eye set-up

The eyes of the penguin need to be able to look around freely. To do so, you will create an aim constraint, which forces an object to aim at another object. You will also need to define a new attribute for blinking.

1 LookAt locator

A locator will be used to specify a point in space where the eyes will be looking.

- Select **Create → Locator** and **rename** it *lookAt*.
- **Snap** the locator to the *head* joint.
- **Move** the locator in front of the penguin about **10 units** on the **Z-axis**.
- **Parent** the *lookAt* locator to the *master* node.

The lookAt locator

2   Freeze transformations

In order to be able to easily place the *lookAt* locator at its default position, you should freeze its transformations.

- Select the *lookAt* locator.
- Select **Modify → Freeze Transformations**.

3   Aim constraint

- Select *lookAt*, then from the Outliner, **Ctrl-select** the *lEye* joint from the Outliner.

> **Note:** *You might have to expand the hierarchy in the Outliner using the + sign to reach the desired node.*

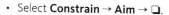

- Select **Constrain → Aim → ❑**.
- Turn **On** the **Maintain Offset** checkbox, then click the **Add** button.
- **Repeat** for the *rEye* joint.

4   Experiment with lookAt

- Select the *lookAt* locator and move it around to see how the *eyeball* reacts.

The eyes looking at the locator

5   Eye blink attribute

It would be good to have a *blink* attribute on the locator, to make it easy to blink the penguin's eyes.

- Select the *lookAt* locator and select **Modify → Add Attribute**...

- Set the following in the new attribute window:

> **Long Name** to *blink*;
>
> **Data Type** to **Float**;
>
> **Minimum** to **0**;
>
> **Maximum** to **2**;
>
> **Default** to **1**.

- Click the **OK** button to add the new attribute.

6   Eye blink driven keys

- Select the **Animate → Set Driven Key → Set**...

- Load the *lookAt* node and the *blink* attribute as the driver.

- Select both *eyelid* geometries, then highlight the *makeNurbsSphere* in the Channel Box.

- Click on the **Load Driven** button.

- Highlight the two *makeNurbsSphere* nodes and highlight their *startSweep* and *endSweep*.

- Click the **Key** button.

- Set the **blink** attribute to **0**, then set the **sweep** attributes to set the eye closed.

- Click the **Key** button.
- Set the **blink** attribute to **2**, then set the **sweep** attributes to set the eye wide open.
- Click the **Key** button.

7   Test the eye blink
- Test the **Blink** attribute using the virtual slider.

Jiggle deformer

The Jiggle deformer will make vertices jiggle as the geometry is moving. You will use a jiggle deformer on the belly of the penguin so that it wobbles as he is walking.

1   Paint Selection Tool
- Select the *body* geometry.
- In the Toolbox, **double-click** on the **Paint Selection Tool**.
- **Paint** on the *body* geometry to easily select the belly vertices.

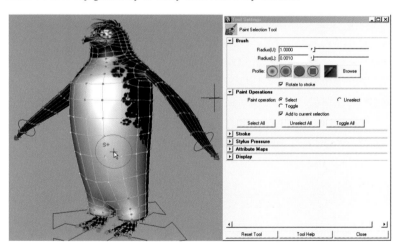

The vertices to be used with the jiggle deformer

Tip: *Use the Unselect paint operation to select unwanted vertices.*

Lesson 13: Rigging

Project 02

2   **Create a jiggle deformer**
- Select **Create Deformers** → **Jiggle Deformer** → ❏.
- In the option window, set the following:

    Stiffness to **0.2**;

    Damping to **0.2**;

    Ignore Transform to **On**.

- Click the **Create** button.

    The jiggle1 deformer will be added to the penguin's input history in the Channel Box.

3   **Smooth the jiggle influence**

With the default value, all the vertices selected are fully affected by the jiggle deformer. It is better to create a nice gradient effect by smoothing the jiggle's weight.

- Go into Object mode and select the *body* geometry.
- Select **Edit Deformers** → **Paint Jiggle Weights Tool** → ❏.
- Change the **Paint Operation** to **Smooth.**
- Click on the **Flood** button repeatedly **5** or **6** times to get the following:

The jiggle influence

- **Close** the tool window.

4 Test the jiggle deformer

In order to test the jiggle deformer, take some time to keyframe a very simple animation and then playback the scene. The attributes of the jiggle deformer to tweak can be found in the Channel Box, when the *body* geometry is selected.

Once testing is over, remove the animation and make sure all the joints are at their preferred angle.

> **Tip:** *Make sure to always set your Playback Speed to Play Every Frame when playing a scene with dynamics. Doing so will ensure an acurate representation of the final effect.*

5 Save your work

- **Save** your scene as *13-bigzRig_03.ma.*

Lock and hide nodes and attributes

Many nodes and attributes in the character rig are not supposed to be animated or changed. It is recommended that you double-check each node and attribute to see if the animator requires them. If they are not required, you can lock and hide them.

The Channel Control window allows you to quickly set which attributes are displayed in the Channel Box and which ones are locked.

1 Lock geometry groups

Since all the geometry is bound to the skeleton, it must not be moved. All the geometry attributes should therefore be locked.

- Select **Window → Hypergraph: Hierarchy**.
- Make sure all nodes are visible in the Hypergraph by enabling **Options → Display → Hidden Nodes** to **On**.
- Select the *geo* group.
- Select **Edit → Select Hierarchy** from the main menu.
- In the Channel Box, highlight the **Translate**, **Rotate** and **Scale** attribute names.
- **RMB** in the Channel Box and select **Lock and Hide Selected**.

2 Channel Control Editor

- Select **Window → General Editors → Channel Control**.

  Under the **Keyable** *tab, all the keyable attributes shown in the Channel Box are displayed. If you highlight attributes and then click on the* **Move >>** *button, the selected attributes will be*

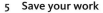

moved in the **Nonkeyable Hidden** column. Notice that only the **Visibility** attribute is still visible in the Channel Box.

In the same manner, under the **Locked** tab, you can move the wanted attributes from the **Locked** column to the **Non-Locked** column and vice versa.

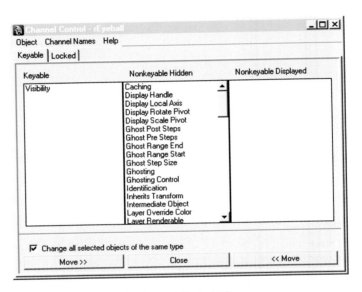

The Channel Control Editor

3 Hide end joints

End joints are usually not animated.

- Select all the end joints on your skeleton, except the eye joints.

- Set their **Visibility** attributes to **Off**.

- **Lock and hide** all the end joints on your skeleton.

  An end joint is the last joint in a joint chain. They are usually created only for visual reference and often never used.

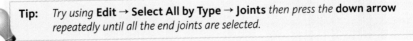

Tip: Try using **Edit → Select All by Type → Joints** then press the **down arrow** repeatedly until all the end joints are selected.

4   **Lock joints**

Joints can usually rotate, but should not be translated or scaled. There are exceptions, such as *joint* roots, that usually need to be able to translate.

- **Lock and hide** the **Translate, Scale** and **Visibility** attributes for all the joints in the scene, except for *pelvis, lHeelControl* and *rHeelControl,* which require translation.

> **Tip:**   *Try using* **Edit → Select All by Type → Joints**.

- **Lock and hide** the **Scale** and **Visibility** attributes for the *pelvis, lHeelControl* and *rHeelControl.*

5   **Rest of set-up**

You should spend some time checking each node in your character rig hierarchy to lock and hide unwanted attributes or nodes. When you don't know what an attribute does, you should at least set it to non-keyable, so that it doesn't appear in the Channel Box. This will prevent it from being keyframed accidentally.

6   **Master scale**

You should make sure to set the *master*'s scaling attributes to non-keyable, but you should not lock these attributes. By doing so, you can be sure no keyframes will be made on the global scaling of the character, but you will still be able to change the penguin's scaling to fit its environment.

7   **Save your work**

- **Save** your scene as *13-bigzRig_04.ma.*

High-resolution model

When animating a character, it is good to have the choice of displaying either the high-resolution or low-resolution model. In this case, the penguin geometry is already quite low-resolution and it would be good to have a high-resolution version of the model to visualize the final result of your animation.

Here you will use a polygonal smooth node and connect it to a new attribute on the character's master. Once that is done, you will be able to crank up the penguin's resolution easily.

1   **Smooth polygons**

- Select the *body* geometry.
- Select **Mesh → Smooth**.

Project 02

High resolution geometry

2   **Smooth attribute**

- Select the *master* node.

- Select **Modify** → **Add Attribute...**

- Set the following in the new attribute window:

    Long Name to *smooth*;

    Data Type to **Integer**;

    Minimum to **0**;

    Maximum to **2**;

    Default to **0**.

- Click the **OK** button to add the new attribute.

- Using the Connection Editor, connect the new **Smooth** attribute to the *polySmoothFace1*'s **Divisions** attribute.

- **Test** the new attribute.

    You can now easily increase or decrease the resolution of the model.

Creating character sets

In the next lesson, you will use keyframing techniques to make the penguin walk. To organize all animation channels needed for keyframing, you can create character sets. These sets let you collect attributes into a single node that can then be efficiently keyed and edited as a group.

1 Create a main character node

- Select the *master* node.
- Select **Character** → **Create Character Set** → ❑ from the Animation menu set.
- Set the following:

    Name to *penguin*;

    Hierarchy below selected node to **On**;

    All keyable to **On**.

- Click **Create Character Set**.

This character is now active and visible next to the Range Slider. It was created with all the keyframable attributes for the entire master hierarchy.

2 Remove unnecessary attributes from the character set

- Select the *penguin* character set from the Outliner.

All the character's attributes are listed in the Channel Box.

If you scroll in the Channel Box, you will notice that some attributes are already connected (colored). They are being driven by constraints, therefore, they are not needed in the character.

Character menu

The character node

- Use the **Ctrl** key (**Apple** key on Macintosh) to highlight all of the colored attributes in the Channel Box for the *penguin* character set.
- Select **Character** → **Remove from Character Set**.

Those attributes are now removed from the character set.

3 Save your work

- **Save** your scene as *13-bigzRig_05.ma*.

Conclusion

You now have a biped character all hooked up and ready for a stroll. You made your character rig simpler for an animator to use and virtually unbreakable. You also created an attribute to set the resolution of the model, which will be very useful for visualizing animation.

In the next lesson, you will animate the penguin using the character rig and character set. It will put both your rigging and animation skills to the test.

Lesson 14
Animation

Reference

Instead of working directly with the file from the last lesson, you will reference the penguin. A reference refers to another scene file that is set to read-only and loaded into the current scene. It allows you to animate the character, leaving the rig file untouched. That way, if you update the rig file, the file referencing it will also get updated.

1   **Create a reference**

- Select **File → New Scene**.

- Select **File → Create Reference → ❏.**

   Doing so will open the Create Reference options.

- Under **Name Clash Options**, set **Resolve all nodes with this string:** *penguin.*

   This will prefix all the reference nodes with the string penguin.

Note: *For simplicity, the penguin prefix will not be cited.*

- Click on the **Reference** button.

- In the browse dialog that appears, select the file *13-bigzRig_05.ma,* then click **Reference**.

   The file will load into the current one.

   Notice the small diamond icon in the Outliner and the red names in the Hypergraph. This means that the penguin nodes are loaded from a reference file as read-only.

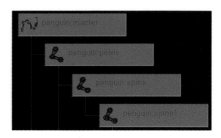

Referenced nodes in the Outliner and Hypergraph

Note: *If you need to bring changes to the character set-up from the last lesson, you will need to open the rig file, make your changes, then save the file. Once that is done, you will need to open the animation file again so the new referenced rig gets reloaded. Be careful—if you remove nodes or attributes in the rig file that are animated in the animation file, their animation will be lost.*

2 **Layers**

- Turn the visibility **On** for the *geoLayer* and the *setupLayer*.
- Make sure the **smooth** attribute on the *master* node is set to **0**.

  You should now see only the low-resolution model along with its rig.

3 **Change the view panels**

- Select **Panels → Layouts → Two Panes Stacked**.
- Change the top panel to a *side* view and the bottom panel to a *Perspective* view.
- For the *side* view, select **View → Predefined Bookmarks → Left Side**.
- In the *side* view, turn **Off** both **Show → NURBS Surfaces** and **Show → Polygons**.

  This panel will be used to watch the movements of the rig.

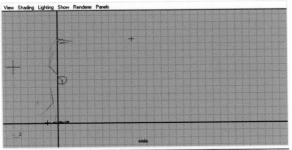
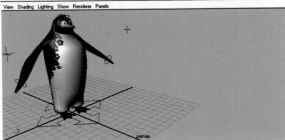

View panel layout

Animating a walk cycle

To create a walk, you will start with a single cycle. To create a cycle, you will need the start position and end position to be the same. There are several controls that need to be keyed, including the position of the feet, the roll of the feet, and the rotation of the pelvis.

Animate the feet sliding

You will now key the horizontal positions of the feet to establish their forward movement. This will result in a sliding motion of the feet.

> **Note:** *The animation values specified here depend on the scale of your character. To follow this lesson properly, either open the required support file or adjust the values to compensate.*

1 Set your time range

- Set the **Start Time** and **Playback Start Time** to **0**.

- Set the **End Time** and **Playback End Time** to **20**.

  This will give you a smaller time range to work with as you build the cycle. The cycle will be a full stride, using two steps of 10 frames each.

2 Active character

- In the **Current Character** menu next to the Range Slider, select *penguin*.

  Now any keys you set will be set on all the attributes of this character node.

Active Character menu

3 Position and key the lower body start pose

You will key the starting position of the character in the position of a full stride.

- Go to frame **0**.

- Select the *lHeelControl* selection handle and set the following:

  Translate Z to **4** units;

  Roll to **-5**.

- Select the *rHeelControl selection handle* and set the following:

  Translate Z to **0** units;

  Roll to **10**.

Tip: *Make sure the Translate Tool is set to be in World coordinates.*

- Set the *pelvis* **translate Z** to **3** units.
- **Move** the *pelvis* down until the knees bend.

Note: *Leave the arms behind for now. Later, you will add secondary animation.*

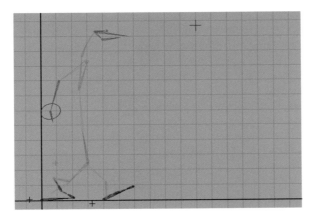

Lower body position

- Press **s** to set a key on all the channels of the *penguin* character.

  The entire character gets keyframed since the penguin character is selected in the Current Character menu at the bottom right of the interface.

4   Position and key the right foot

- Go to frame **10**.
- Set the *rHeelControl* **translate Z** to **8** units and **roll** to **-5**.

  This translation value is exactly double the value of the initial left foot key. This is important to ensure that the two feet cycle together later.

- Set the *lHeelControl* **roll** to **10**.
- Set the *pelvis* **translate Z** to **7** units.

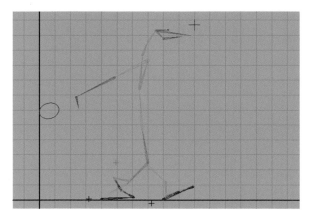

Right leg position

- Press **s** to set a key on all the channels of the *penguin* character.

5   Position and key the left foot

You will move the left foot into a position that is similar to the starting position.

- Go to frame **20**.
- Set the *lHeelControl* **translate Z** to **12** units and **roll** to **-5**.

  Again, the value is set using units of 4. This will ensure a connection between cycles later.

- Set the *rHeelControl* **roll** to **10**.
- Set the *pelvis* **translate Z** to **11** units.

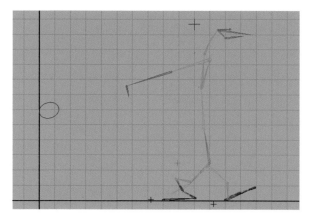

Left leg position

• Press **s** to set a key on all the channels of the *penguin* character.

Edit the animation curves

To refine the in-between motion of the feet, you can use the animation curves to view and change the tangent options for the feet.

1   View the curves in the Graph Editor

You will edit the animation curves produced by the keys in the Graph Editor.

• Clear the selection.

• Select **Window** → **Animation Editors** → **Graph Editor**.

• In the Graph Editor, highlight the *penguin* character.

• Select **View** → **Frame All**.

• Press the **Ctrl** key (**Apple** key on Macintosh) to select *lHeelControl.TranslateZ* and *rHeelControl.TranslateZ* in the Outliner section of this window.

• Select **View** → **Frame Selection**.

The pattern of the animation curves you have created should look as follows:

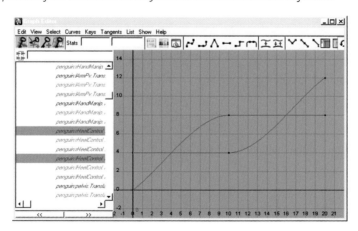

Animation curves in Graph Editor

• **Playback** the animation to see the motion.

> **Note:** *If you open the Graph Editor when the feet are selected, you will see an animation channel with keys set in the negative direction. This is the animation curve connecting the Rotate Z of the foot to the Roll attribute.*

2   **Edit the curve tangents on the feet**

The curve tangent type should be changed so that the steps cycle smoothly. The default tangent type is *Clamped*.

• Select the two animation curves for *lHeelControl.TranslateZ* and *rHeelControl.TranslateZ*.

• Select **Tangents → Flat**.

The visual difference between clamped and flat tangents in the Graph Editor is subtle. Look at the start and end keyframes on the curves. The flat tangents will create a smooth hook-up for the cycle between the start frame and end frame.

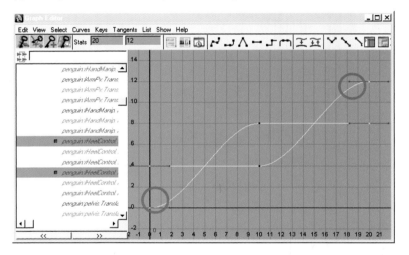

Flat tangents

Animate the feet up and down

You will now key the vertical raising and lowering of the feet to establish the stepping action.

1   **Turn on Auto Key**

You will now use **Auto Key** to help with the raising of the feet. The Auto Key feature will automatically keyframe any attributes on the selected nodes that already have at least one keyframe, and for which the value is changing.

• Click on the **Auto Keyframe** button in the right side of the Time Slider to turn it **On**.

• Open the **Animation Preferences** window, using the button just to the right of the **Auto Keyframe** button.

• In the **Timeline** category, make sure the **Playback speed** is set to **Play every frame**.

- Click on the **Animation** category under the **Settings** category and set the following under the **Tangents** section:

  Default in tangent to **Flat**;

  Default out tangent to **Flat**.

  This will set all future tangents to flat.

- Click on the **Save** button.

2   Raise the right foot at mid-step

Key the high point of the raised foot in the middle of a step.

- Go to frame **5**.

- Select the *rHeelControl*.

- **Translate** the foot about **0.2** units up along the **Y-axis**.

  This sets a new key for the Y-axis channel of the foot using Auto Key.

3   Raise the left foot at mid-step

- Go to frame **15**.

- Select the *lHeelControl*.

- **Move** the foot about **0.2** units up along the **Y-axis**.

  Again, a key is automatically set.

- **Playback** the results.

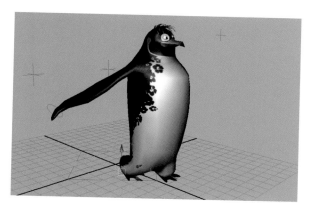

The character is walking

4   Save your work

- **Save** your scene as *14-bigzWalk_01.ma*.

Animate the pelvic rotations

To create a more realistic action, the pelvis' position and rotation will be set to work with each step. You will again set keys for the translation and rotation of the pelvis using Auto Key.

1 Set the pelvis Y rotation

You will now animate the pelvis rotation to give the walk a little more motion.

- Go to frame **0**.

- Select the *pelvis* node using its selection handle.

- In the *top* view, **rotate** the *pelvis* using the rotation handle in a clockwise direction by about **-10 degrees**.

  This points the left hip towards the left foot and the right hip towards the right foot.

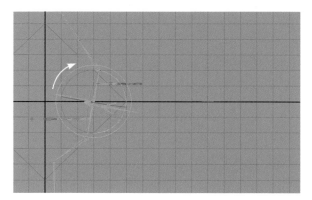

Rotate pelvis toward left foot

2 Rotate in the opposite direction

- Go to frame **10**.

- **Rotate** the pelvis in the opposite direction by about **10 degrees**.

3 Copy the first Y rotation

- Go to frame **0**.

- In the Time Slider, **MMB+drag** the current time to frame **20**.

  The display has not changed, but the time has changed.

- With the *pelvis* still selected, highlight the **Rotate X** attribute in the Channel Box, then **RMB** and select **Key Selected**.

  By doing so, you have manually set a keyframe on the rotateX value of the pelvis from frame 0 to frame 20.

- **Refresh** the Time Slider by dragging anywhere in the time indicator.

Notice that the pelvis' **Rotate X** *attribute has the exact same value at frame* **20** *that it does at frame* **0**.

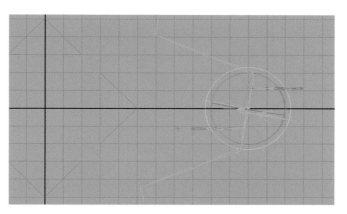

Copied rotation value at frame 20

4   **Pelvis in front view**

- Go to frame **5**.

- In the *front* view, **Rotate** the *pelvis* on its **Y-axis** by about **3** degrees so that the right hip is rising with the right leg.

- **Translate** the *pelvis* on the **X-axis** by about **0.4** units so that the weight of the penguin is on the left leg.

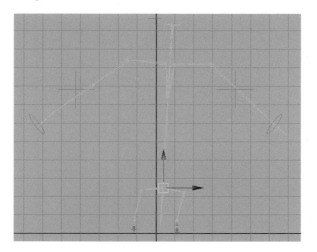

Offset pelvis with right foot raised

- Go to frame **15**.
- **Rotate** the *pelvis* on the **Y-axis** in the opposite direction as the left foot raises.
- **Translate** the *pelvis* on the **X-axis** so that the weight of the penguin is on the **right leg.**

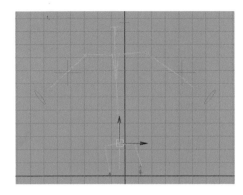

Offset pelvis with left foot raised

5   Edit the keys

To prepare the file for creating cycles later, you will need to ensure that the rotations match at the start and end of the cycle.

- Make sure the *pelvis* is selected.
- In the Graph Editor, press the **Ctrl** key and highlight the **Translate X**, **Rotate X** and **Rotate Y** attributes.
- Select **View** → **Frame All**.

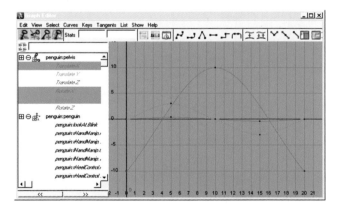

Pelvis curves

Since you copied frame 0 of the pelvis' X rotation onto frame 20 in Step 3, the start and end values of the animation curve are a perfect match. If they were different, you could have fixed the curve in the Graph Editor so that the cycled motion is smooth.

Add a bounce to the walk

To create a bouncing motion for the walk, you will add keyframes to the Y translation of the *pelvis* node.

1 Edit the pelvis height

- In the Graph Editor, highlight the *pelvis.TranslateY* channel.

2 Insert keys

- Select the **Insert Keys Tool** found in the Graph Editor.

- Select the **translateY** curve, then with your **MMB** insert a key at frame **5** and frame **15**.

3 Edit the Y translation value of the keys

- Press **w** to select the **Move Key Tool**.

- Select the new keys at frame **5** and frame **15** by holding down **Shift** and select the two keyframes.

- **Click+drag** with the **MMB** to move these keys to a value of about **2.7** to add some bounce to the walk.

> **Tip:** *If the current time in the Time Slider is either on frame 5 or 15, you will see the effect of the change directly on the character. Make sure the value you are using doesn't hyperextend the legs.*

- Press **a** to frame the curve.

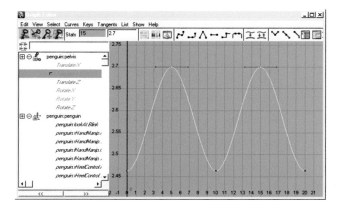

Pelvis Y Translate channel

Refine the heel rotation

When you created the reverse foot set-up, you spent a great deal of time preparing the foot for the *heel-to-toe* motion that occurs when walking. So far, you have only rolled the feet so the legs would not snap. You are now going to refine the animation of the foot rotations.

1   Set a key on the left foot's roll

As you playback, you will notice that the feet don't pound on the ground after the heel contact.

- Select the *lHeelControl* using its selection handle.
- Go to frame **2**.
- Set the *lHeelControl*'s **Roll** attribute to **0**.
- Go to frame **5**.
- Set the *lHeelControl*'s **Roll** attribute to **0**.

2   Set a key on the right foot's roll

- Select the *rHeelControl* using its selection handle.
- Go to frame **12**.
- Set the *rHeelControl*'s **Roll** attribute to **0**.
- Go to frame **15**
- Set the *rHeelControl*'s **Roll** attribute to **0**.

3   Playback the results

The leg animation is now finished, but you might notice that the knees overextend between keyframes. In order to fix these snaps, do not try to add more keyframes right away. Instead, try to change the existing animation. If you clearly see that no keyframe changes can fix the problem, then you can alter the animation by adding keyframes.

> **Tip:**   *You should always try to keep the required amount of keyframes to a minimum and group them on the same frame if possible. Later in the animation process, the animation curves can become quite complex and having fewer keyframes makes it easier to modify.*

4   Save your work

- **Save** your scene as *14-bigzWalk_02.ma*.

Animate the arm swing

The character needs some motion in his arms. To do this, you will animate the translation of the arm manipulators to create an animation that can be cycled.

To add some secondary motion, you will also set keyframes on the rotation of the head.

1   Set keys for the start position

- Go to frame **0**.
- Show the *geoLayer* to see the character's geometry.
- **Move** and **rotate** the *lHandManip* behind the body and low down.
- **Move** the *lArmPv* to bend the elbow to a good angle.
- **Move** and **rotate** the *rHandManip* in front of the body and up.
- **Move** the *rArmPv* to bend the elbow to a good angle.

  Now the arms are opposite to how the feet are set up. This makes the swinging motion work with the feet.

Arm positions

- Select the *head* joint and **rotate** it around the **Y-axis** by about **10-degrees**.

  This has the head and hips moving in opposite directions, where the head always aims straight forward.

Lesson 14: Animation

Project 02

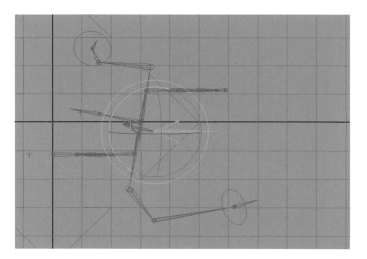

Top view of head rotation

2   Copy keys for the end position

In order to create a smooth transition for the arm cycle, you must have matching values at the start and end of the cycle.

- Select the *lArmPv*, *rArmPv*, *lHandManip* and *rHandManip* nodes.

- In the timeline, **MMB+drag** and move the Time Slider to frame **20**.

  The character will not move when you scrub along the timeline when the **MMB** *is pressed.*

- Highlight the **translation** and **rotation** attributes in the Channel Box.

- **RMB** and select **Key Selected** from the pop-up menu.

  This sets keyframes only on the attributes you have selected in the Channel Box.

Note: *Because you have multiple nodes selected, you can see three dots after the node's name in the Channel Box. This indicates that other nodes are active, and that they will also receive the keyframes.*

- **Refresh** the Time Slider at frame **20**.

  You will see that you have set keyframes at the current position on the manipulators, but they are not following the penguin.

Note: *You can also use the Dope sheet to copy and paste selected keyframes, or you can cut and paste keyframe values from the Graph Editor.*

3 Add to attributes

You must now set the right offset to the values already in the Translate Z attributes of the arm manipulators and pole vectors. The Channel Box can allow you to enter a simple mathematical expression in the attribute value field.

- Go to frame **20**.

- With the *lArmPv*, *rArmPv*, *lHandManip* and *rHandManip* nodes selected, type *+=8* in the **Translate Z** attribute in the Channel Box, then hit **Enter**.

  Doing so adds 8 units to whatever value is in the attribute for each node.

4 Set keys for the head

Use the method outlined in Step 2 to set the last keyframe for the head rotation.

- Select the *head* joint.

- **MMB+drag** the Time Slider from frame **0** to frame **20**.

- **LMB** over the *head* **Rotate Y** attribute in the Channel Box to highlight it.

- **RMB** and select **Key Selected** from the pop-up menu.

5 Set keys for the middle position

- Go to frame **10**.

- **Move** the arm manipulators opposite to the *legs*.

- **Rotate** the *head* joint opposite to the *hips*.

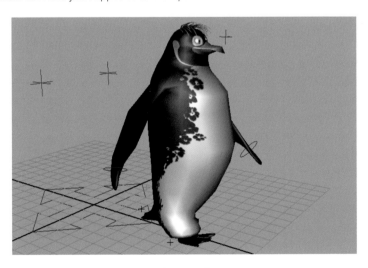

Arm positions at frame 10

6   Keyframe the in-between

- Make sure to set a good position for the arms at frames **5** and **15**.

7   Fix the arm manipulator curves

- In the Graph Editor, select the arm manipulator's **Translate** and **Rotate** attributes.
- Select all keyframes between frame **5** and **15**.
- Select **Tangents → Spline**.

8   Delete the static channels

If a curve is flat its whole length, the value of the attribute it represents doesn't change. This attribute is a static channel. Static channels slow Maya processing, so it's beneficial to remove them.

- Select **Edit → Delete All By Type → Static Channels**.

9   Turn off Auto Key

10   Save your work

- **Save** your scene as *14-bigzWalk_03.ma*.

Cycle the animation

So far, you have animated one full step for the walk cycle. Next, you will use the Graph Editor to complete the cycle.

1   Set your time range

- Set the **Start Time** and **Playback Start Time** to **0**.
- Set the **End Time** and **Playback End Time** to **300**.

2   View all curves in the Graph Editor

- Select **Window → Animation Editors → Graph Editor.**
- Select *penguin* from the Outliner portion of the window to see all the animation curves for the character.

3   View the cycle

In order to check if the cycle works smoothly, you can display the curves' infinity and set it to cycle.

- In the Graph Editor, select **View → Infinity**.
- Select all the animation curves.

- Select **Curves** → **Pre Infinity** → **Cycle with Offset**.
- Select **Curves** → **Post Infinity** → **Cycle with Offset**.

  Cycle with Offset appends the value of the last key in the cycled curve to the value of the first key's original curve. You can now see what the curves are like when cycled.

- **Play** the animation for the entire **300** frames.

4 Adjust the curves

- Zoom on the curves and adjust the tangents so that the connection between the curves and cycle is smooth.
- If needed, adjust the tangency of the keyframes on frames **0** and **20**.

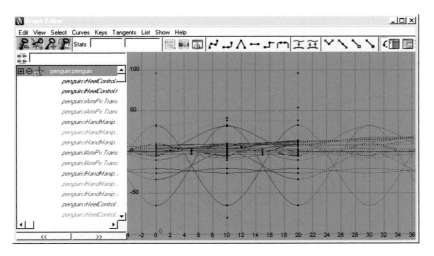

Animation cycle

- Go to frame **300.**

  At this frame, you should clearly see if there are any problems with the offset of your cycle where an object keeps moving farther and farther away.

- Fix any problems in your cycle by changing either frame **0** or **20**.

  You should not set a keyframe outside the cycle's boundary otherwise you will break up the cycle.

Bake the keyframes

Ultimately, you will use this animation inside the Trax Editor, so you will bake the keyframes of the post infinity onto the curves. The Trax Editor cannot use post infinity curves from the Graph Editor, so you will generate the actual keyframes by baking them.

1   **Select the penguin character**

• In the Graph Editor, select *penguin*.

2   **Bake the keyframes**

• In the Graph Editor, select **Curves** → **Bake Channel** → ❑.

• Set the following options:

> **Time Range** to **Start/End**;
>
> **Start Time** to **0**;
>
> **End Time** to **120**;
>
> **Sample** by **5**;
>
> **Keep Unbaked Keys** to **On**;
>
> **Sparse Curve Bake** to **On**.

• Click the **Bake** button.

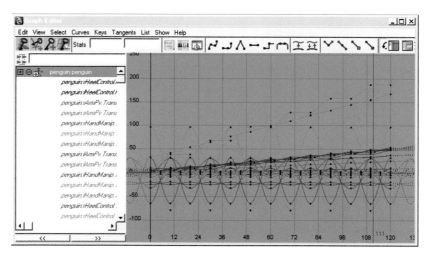

Baked curves

3 **Save your work**

- **Save** your scene as *14-bigzWalk_04.ma*.

Create a Trax clip file

The animation is finished, but since you will be working with the Trax Editor later in this book, you will now create a Trax clip file and export it for later use.

4 **Open the Trax Editor window**

- Select **Window** → **Animation Editors** → **Trax Editor**.

- Make sure the *penguin* character is set as current.

- In the Trax Editor, enable **List** → **Auto Load Selected Characters**.

  You should not see anything in the Trax Editor at this time.

5 **Create a clip**

- From the Trax Editor, select **Create** → **Animation Clip** → ❏.

- Set the following options:

  Name to *walk;*

  Leave Keys in Timeline to **Off**;

  Clip to **Put Clip in Trax Editor and Visor**;

  Time Range to **Animation Curve**;

  Include Subcharacters in Clip to **Off**;

  Create Time Warp Curve to **Off**;

  Include Hierarchy to **On**.

- Click the **Create Clip** button.

- Press **a** in the Trax Editor to frame all.

  A clip is created and placed in the Trax timeline. A corresponding clip source file called walkSource is also placed in the Visor.

  Until you export the clip, it can only be accessed through this scene file.

Lesson 14: Animation

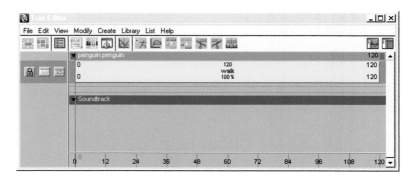

Walk clip in the Trax Editor

6   Export the clip

- Select **File → Visor...**
- Select the **Character Clips** tab to see the clip source.

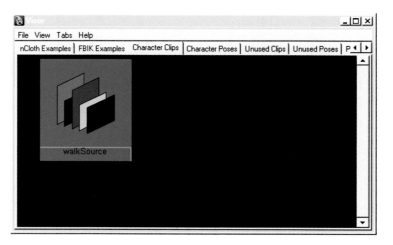

Walk source clip in Visor

- Select the *walkSource* clip.
- **RMB** on the clip and select **Export.**

  A pop-up menu will browse to the clips directory of your current project.

- **Export** the clip as *bigzWalkExport*.

  Now you can import this clip into another scene. You will do so later in this book.

- **Close** the Visor**.**

7 **Save your work**

- **Save** your scene as *14-bigzWalk_05.ma.*

Conclusion

Congratulations, you have completed a walk cycle! You learned how to reference a file, and then you animated the penguin using a character set. You produced a perfect cycle and exported a Trax clip.

In the next project you will build a crab from NURBS, texture it and rig it up so that BigZ can interact with it.

IMAGEGALLERY

SONY PICTURES
animation

Project 03

In this project, you will model Mikey, the bird from *Surf's Up* movie, which will interact with BigZ. You will begin by modeling, texturing and rigging the NURBS bird. Once that is done, you will test various deformers, animate a wave and use Paint Effects to add vegetation to the beach. Finally, you will add lights to your scene and experiment with the different renderers available in Autodesk® Maya®.

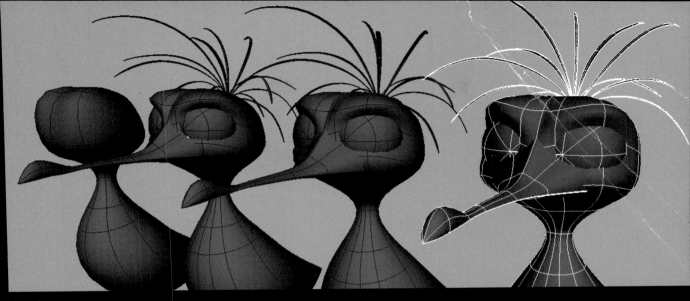

Lesson 15
NURBS Modeling

This lesson will introduce you to modeling with NURBS (Non-Uniform Rational B-Spline) surfaces.
You will create curves and build surfaces to construct Mikey, a bird character from the Sony
Pictures Animation Inc. movie *Surf's Up*.

In this lesson you will learn the following:

- How to detach and attach surfaces

Set up your project

Since this is a new project, it is recommended to set a new current project directory.

1 Set the project

- If you copied the support files onto your drive, go to the **File** menu and select **Project → Set...**

  A window opens, pointing you to the Maya projects directory.

- Click on the folder named *project3* to select it.

- Click on the **OK** button.

  This sets the project3 directory as your current project.

  OR

- If you did not copy the support files on your drive, create a new project called *project3* with all the default directories.

2 Make a new scene

- Select **File → New Scene**.

Body and head

The first step for modeling Mikey is to shape up his body. This will be a simple exercise that will introduce several useful NURBS tools.

1 Body sphere

You will now create the body starting from a primitive sphere.

- Select **Create → NURBS Primitives → Sphere.**

- **Translate** the *sphere* up by **17** units**.**

- **Rotate** the *sphere* on its **Y-axis** by **90** degrees.

  Doing so places the NURBS sphere's seam on the back of the character. The seam is shown as a thicker line on the sphere's wireframe while in shaded mode.

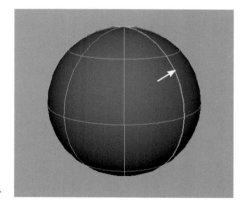

A NURBS seam

When modeling with NURBS, it is important to carefully place the seam for two reasons. First, when attaching and detaching surfaces, it is better to have seams aligned on every surface. Second, when texturing, it is better to hide the seams as much as possible since this is where the opposite texture edges meet. For this character, the body seam will be in the middle of the back.

2   Shape the body

- From the *side* view, tweak the sphere so it resembles a bird's body.

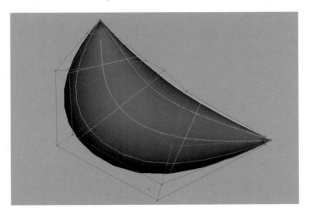

The bird's body

> **Tip:**   *Make sure to place the poles of the sphere at the tail and neck locations. As you will see in the next lesson, poles create texture stretching, so you need to hide them as much as possible.*

3   Head sphere

- Select **Create** → **NURBS Primitives** → **Sphere again.**

- **Translate** the *sphere* up by **24** units.

- **Rotate** the *sphere* on its **Y-axis** by **90** degrees.

- From the side view, tweak the sphere so it resembles the image to the right.

  Just as with the body, carefully place the poles in the neck and on the back of the head, where the hair will come out.

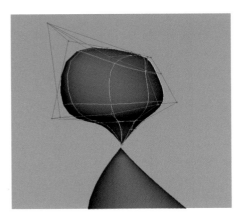

The bird's head

Lesson 15: NURBS Modeling

4 Global shape

- Take some time to adjust the shape of the bird in the other views.

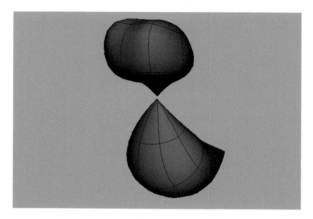

The shape of the bird so far

5 Detach surfaces

Since the head and body should meet at the neck, you will now detach two surfaces in order to remove the poles located at the neck. Once that is done, you will be able to connect the body to the head.

- **RMB** on the *body* and select **Isoparm**.

- **Click+drag** on the horizontal isoparm to define a new isoparm where the neck opening is needed.

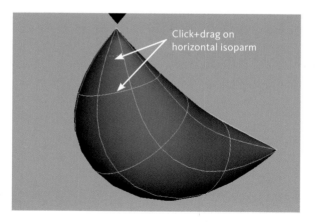

The defined isoparm

- Select **Edit NURBS** → **Detach Surfaces.**
- **Delete** the separated surface located in the neck**.**

The neck opening

- **Repeat** this step to create the neck opening for the head.

6 Duplicate surface curve

At this point, you have a body and head, but the neck is missing. You will now duplicate the isoparm of the neck in order to better define the shape of the neck surface.

- **RMB** on the *body* surface and select **Isoparm.**
- Click on the **isoparm** at the neck opening to select it.

Note: *When you click directly on an isoparm to select it, the isoparm gets highlighted with a continuous yellow line. If you* **click+drag** *on an isoparm, a dotted yellow line shows you the isoparm at the cursor's position.*

- Select **Edit Curves** → **Duplicate Surface Curves.**

A curve is created, representing exactly the surface isoparm. Doing so will spare you the trouble of using a NURBS circle to create the neck surface.

- Select **Modify** → **Center Pivot.**

Note: *New curves and surfaces always have their pivot at the origin.*

- **Translate** the curve up and **scale** it down to represent the middle part of the neck.

7   Loft

The Loft tool creates a surface by linking several profile curves. This is the perfect tool to generate the neck surface.

- **RMB** on the *body* surface and select **Isoparm.**

- Click on the **isoparm** at the neck opening to select it.

- **Shift-select** the middle neck curve.

- **RMB** on the *head* surface and select **Isoparm.**

- **Shift-select** the **isoparm** at the neck opening to select it.

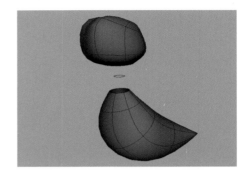

The middle neck curve

> **Note:** *You must select the appropriate curves or isoparms so that the loft is created correctly.*

- Select **Surfaces → Loft**.

The new surface is created by linking the selected curves.

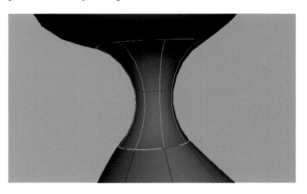

The neck loft

> **Tip:** *Because of construction history, you can still manipulate the curve, body or head geometry and the neck surface will update properly.*

8   Attach surfaces

You will now attach the three surfaces together so the entire body is a single piece of geometry.

- Select the *body* and the *neck* surfaces.

- Select **Edit NURBS → Attach Surfaces.**

  The two pieces should now have become a single surface.

- Select the *body* and the *head* surfaces.

- Select **Edit NURBS → Attach Surfaces.**

  The entire body is now a single surface.

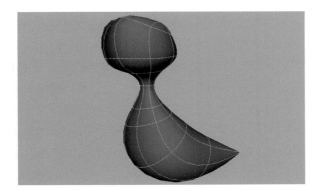

The entire body surface

9   Clean up

- **Delete** any obsolete nodes from the Outliner.

- **Rename** the surface to *body*.

- With the *body* selected, select **Modify → Freeze Transformations**.

- Select **Edit → Delete All by Type → History**.

  Doing so will clean up all the construction history left by the various tools used so far.

10   Save your work

- **Save** the scene as *15-mikey_01.ma*.

Refine the head

You will now learn how to insert new isoparms on a surface in order to increase its level of detail. Doing so will allow you to create the eye sockets. You will also create the eyeballs, beak and hair.

1   Add isoparms

- **RMB** on the *body* surface and select **Isoparm.**

- **Click** on the vertical central isoparm and drag to define a new isoparm in the middle of the eye patch.

- Hold down **Shift** and **repeat** the previous step to define the same isoparm but on the opposite side of the head.

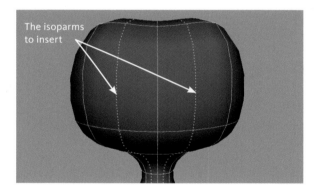

The NURBS context menu

Note: *Don't worry if the isoparms are not perfectly symmetrical to each other, you will eventually delete one half of the body and mirror it to keep the model symmetrical.*

- Select **Edit NURBS → Insert Isoparms.**

Note: *Since the body is a single surface, the new isoparms go across the entire geometry. Be careful to not insert too many isoparms for a localized area. Doing so will increase the topology of the entire surface.*

- **Repeat** the previous step to define a new isoparm going horizontally across the eye patches.

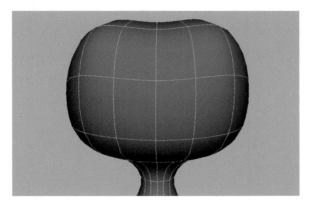

The new facial topology

2 Create the eyes

- Using the newly inserted CVs, tweak the shape of the *head* to narrow the nose area and carve the eye sockets.

- **Create** a primitive sphere and place it at the eye location.

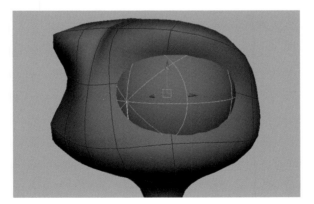

The eye in place

- **Rotate** the eyeball on it's **X-axis** by **90** degrees and on it's **Z-axis** by **-90** degrees.

- With the eyeball selected, press **Ctrl+d** to **duplicate** it

- Press **Ctrl+g** to create a **group** with the new eyeball, then set its **Scale X** to **-1**.

  Since the group's pivot is centered on the scene's origin, doing so will mirror the eyeball over to the other side of the head.

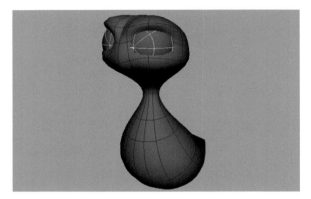

The character with both eyes

3   Beak side profile

You will now create the beak of the bird. You will do so by drawing profile curves and lofting them.

- Select **Create → EP Curve Tool.**

- From the side view, **draw** the following beak profile curve:

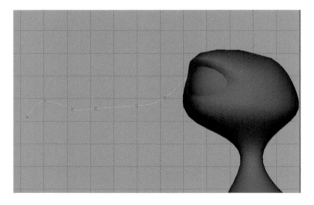

The beak profile curve

4   Beak top profile

The upcoming loft operation works best if the curves used have the same number of CVs, spread across the curve at similar distance. Here, instead of drawing a new curve, you will duplicate the existing one and rotate it to create the top profile curve.

- Select the new curve and press **Ctrl+d** to duplicate it.
- Select **Modify → Center Pivot**.
- **Rotate** it by **-90** degrees on it's **Z-axis**.
- From the *top* view, **tweak** the shape of the beak profile curve to look as follows:

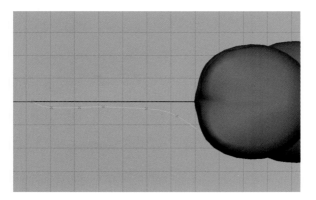

The top profile curve

- **Translate** the last curve on its **Y-axis** to fit the base of the first profile curve.
- Select the CV at the tip of the upper profile curve, then prss the **c** hotkey to **snap to curve** and **click+drag** the CV to the tip of the first profile curve.
- **Tweak** the rest of the beak curve to your liking.

5   Beak loft

- **Group** and **mirror** the last curve to the other side of the beak.

  You should now have three profile curves to loft the beak surface.

> **Note:** *If you don't snap the tip of the beak's curves together, there will be a small hole at the tip of the beak.*

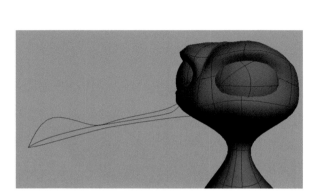

The beak curves

- Select the three curves and then select **Surfaces → Loft.**

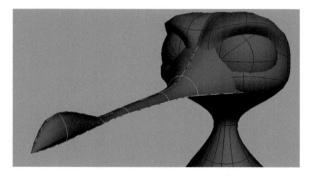

The beak loft

6 Refine the beak

- With the new loft selected, highlight the *loft1* node from the **Inputs** section of the Channel Box.

- Set the **Section Spans** attribute to **2**.

  Doing so will increase the number of isoparms on the loft.

- **Tweak** the shape of the surface to your liking.

7 Creating the lower beak

You will now create the bottom piece of the beak.

- Select the two profile curves at the base of the beak.

> **Tip:** *It might be easier to hide the NURBS surfaces temporarily or to select them from the Outliner.*

- Select **Surfaces** → **Loft** to loft them together.

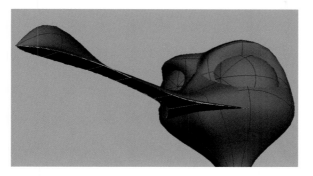

The bottom piece of the beak

- With the new loft selected, highlight the *loft2* node from the **Inputs** section of the Channel Box**, and s**et the **Section Spans** attribute to **2**.
- **Tweak** the shape of the surface to your liking.

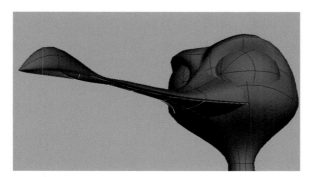

The refined beak shape

- **Move** the pivot of the lower beak surface to the jaw area.

  Doing so will allow you to test the rotation of the lower jaw to see how it looks when opening.

> **Note:** *You can insert isoparms at the borders of the beak and curve them toward the inside to get a smoother beak edge result.*

8 Create the hair profile curves

This step will add hair to Mikey that will be similar to that made for BigZ in the last project. The only difference is that you will use different tools to make it.

- Select **Create → EP Curve Tool.**

- From the *side* view, **draw** the following hair profile curve:

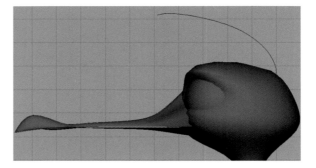

The hair profile curve

- From the *top* view, **draw** a smaller hair profile curve to look like the following:

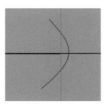

The top hair profile curve

9 Extrude the hair

- Select the tiny curve from the last step, then **Shift-select** the first hair profile curve.

- Select **Surfaces → Extrude → ❑.**

- In the option window, set the following:

   Style to **Flat;**

   Result position to **At path**.

- Click the **Extrude** button.

A hair surface is created, which follows the hair profile curve. Notice that the hair starts out rounded up and finishes flat.

- **Tweak** the shape of the hair so the tip is pointed.

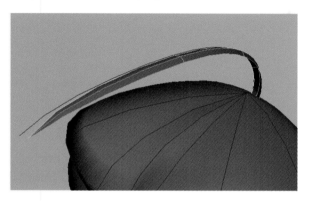

The final hair shape

10 Duplicate the hair

- **Duplicate** the hair from the last step to create the following hair style:

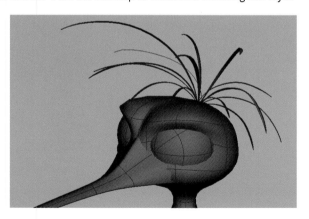

Mikey's hair style

11 Clean up

- **Delete** any obsolete nodes from the Outliner.

- **Rename** each node correctly.

- Use **Modify → Freeze Transformations** on all nodes.

- Select **Edit → Delete All by Type → History**.

> **Tip:** *Since you don't require any construction history, it is good to frequently clean up your scene.*

12 Save your work

- **Save** the scene as *15-mikey_02.ma*.

Legs

Since Mikey's legs are quite simple, you will now model one using simple primitives, and then mirror the other one.

1 Thigh primitive

- **Create** a NURBS cylinder primitive for the thigh.
- Make sure the cylinder has **2 spans** in the Channel Box.
- **Tweak** the shape of the cylinder as follows:

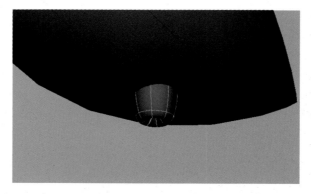

The thigh

> **Tip:** *Make sure to place the seam on the inside of the leg.*

2 Leg primitives

- **Create** another NURBS cylinder primitive for the upper leg.
- **Create** a NURBS sphere for the knee.
- **Duplicate** the upper leg cylinder to create the lower leg and stretch it so it goes down to the floor grid.

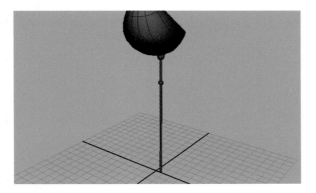

The leg pieces

3 **Foot primitives**

- **Duplicate** the knee sphere and **translate** it down to the ankle.
- **Tweak** the shape of the sphere so it is flat where it touches the floor.
- **Create** a NURBS cone primitive to model a toe.
- Make sure the cone has **2 spans** in the Channel Box.
- **Rotate** the cone by **90** degrees on its **X-axis**.
- **Shape** the cone as follows:

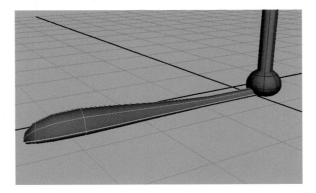

The first toe

- **Duplicate** the first toe and **rotate** it to have two toes at the front and one toe at the back of the foot.

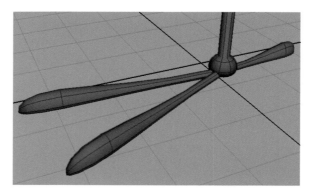

The final foot

Tip: *Hold down the d hotkey to translate the pivot at the ankle before rotating.*

4 Move a seam

If you modeled the toe with the seam at another location than underneath it, it might be hard for you to change the seam's location now that the toes are modeled. The following is a simple tool that will change a seam of location.

- **RMB** on the toe and select **Isoparm**.
- Click to select the longitudinal isoparm underneath the toe.
- Select **Edit NURBS → Move Seam.**

  The tool recalculates the shape of the model in order to place the seam at the desired location.

- **Repeat** this step to relocate any other seams that are not at the proper location.

5 Mirror the leg

- Select every leg surface.
- Press **Ctrl+g** to **group** them together.
- Press **Ctrl+d** to **duplicate** the leg group.
- Set its **Scale X** to **-1**.

  Doing so will mirror the second leg.

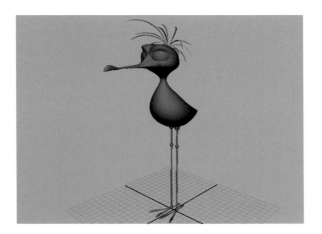

The completed model

6 Clean up

- **Rename** each node correctly.
- Use **Modify → Freeze Transformations** on the leg groups.
- Select **Edit → Delete All by Type → History**.

7 Save your work

- **Save** the scene as *15-mikey_03.ma*.

Mirror the body

In case you did asymmetrical changes to the body shape, you will now detach, mirror and attach the NURBS surface. This same workflow can be used for any other symmetrical NURBS surface.

1 Detach the body

- **RMB** on the body and select **Isoparm**.
- Select the central isoparm on the back of the surface.
- Select **Edit NURBS → Detach Surfaces.**
- Select the central isoparm on the front of the surface.
- Select **Edit NURBS → Detach Surfaces.**

You should now have two distinct halves.

> **Note:** *You cannot do this operation in one step since on the first detach, the tool rebuilds the model as if the geometry were open. If you have more than one isoparm selected, the first isoparm will open the surface, and the second isoparm will be lost.*

- **Delete** one half of the model.
- **Duplicate** the remaining half and set its **Scale X** to **-1**.

2 Attach the body

- With the two halves selected, select **Edit NURBS → Attach Surfaces.**

> **Tip:** *If the attach tool uses opposite border isoparms, you can pick the two isoparms to attach before executing the tool.*

3 Close the surface

Since the body is now a single surface, you cannot attach the remaining gap together. Instead, you need to close the surface.

- With *body* selected, select **Edit NURBS → Open/Close Surfaces → ❑.**
- In the option window, set Shape to Blend.

This option tells the tool that you want to blend the two opened isoparms together rather than simply connecting them.

- Click the **Open/Close** button.

The surface is now completely closed.

4 Rebuild the surface

The seam on your model might not be where you want it at this time. If you tried to use the move seam tool, you might get unexpected results because of the way the surface is currently built. You will therefore need to rebuild the surface.

- With *body* selected, select **Edit NURBS → Rebuild Surfaces → ❑.**
- In the option window, set the following:

    Rebuild type to **Uniform**;

    Direction to **U and V**;

    Keep to **CVs**.

- Click the **Rebuild** button.

The surface will be rebuilt so the isoparms are uniformly spaced. You can now move the seam on the surface.

> **Note:** *Rebuilding a surface corrects its topology and its parameterization, but it will also affect its shape. You might have to refine the resulting surface.*

- **RMB** on the body and select **Isoparm**.
- Click to select the longitudinal isoparm in the back.
- Select **Edit NURBS** → **Move Seam.**

  The seam will move to the desired location.

5   Finalize the model

> **Tip:**   *To speed up the display in the viewport, you can select some NURBS geometry and press 1 to set the NURBS display to coarse.*

6   Clean up the scene

7   Save your work

- **Save** the scene as *15-mikey_04.ma.*

Conclusion

In this lesson, you experimented with several NURBS curves and surface tools. NURBS modeling for simple objects can be straightforward, but modeling organic and complex shapes requires much more experience and planning.

In the next lesson, you will assign materials and textures to Mikey.

Lesson 16
NURBS Texturing

In this lesson, you will learn about NURBS texturing. NURBS surfaces use a different UV system than polygons because they are square and can automatically compute square UV mapping. Be aware that NURBS poles are really entire borders at the same location.

In this lesson you will learn the following:

Texturing NURBS

Unlike polygonal geometry, UV mapping is not required on NURBS geometry since texture coordinates are determined by the U and V directions of the NURBS surface itself.

1   Checker texture

In order to view the default UV maps, you will create both a Lambert and checker texture, and then assign them to the body geometry.

- In the Hypershade, create a Lambert material.
- **Map** the **Color** of the new material with a **Checker** texture.

> **Tip:**   *Make sure the create option at the top of the Create Render Node window is set to* **Normal**.

- Press **6** on your keyboard to enable the **Hardware Texturing**.
- **Assign** the new material to the *body*.
- See how the texture is mapped.

On equally proportionate surfaces (as close to square as possible), the checker texture won't appear to be too stretched, but on long and thin surfaces, such as the neck, the texture will look stretched. Also, where a NURBS surface has a pole, the texture will look pinched.

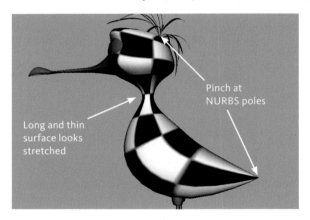

NURBS texture mapping

2   Assign a ramp texture

- Open the Attribute Editor for the Lambert material created in the last step.
- At the top of the attribute list, set **Type** to **Blinn**.

Doing so changes the type of the material without creating a new shader.

- Still in the Attribute Editor, **RMB** on the **Color** attribute's name and select **Break Connection**.

This breaks the link between the shader and the checker.

- **Map** the **Color** of the material with a **Ramp** texture.

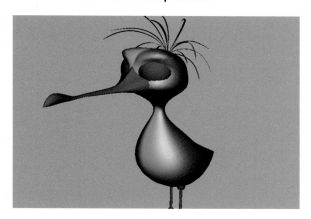

The assigned ramp texture

Notice how the texture is automatically mapped on the NURBS surfaces.

- **Rename** the material *bodyM*.
- **Tweak** the *bodyM*'s **Specular Shading** to your liking.

3   Body color

Mikey should be dark brown at the head and in the back, with a lighter belly. You will be able to texture Mikey's body quite well using only procedural textures.

With the Attribute Editor, change the colors so the back of the body is a dark brown and the front a light brown.

- Select the color marker at the top of the ramp widget.
- Click in the color swatch of the **Selected Color** attribute.
- Set a **dark brown** color.
- Before accepting the color, click the **arrow** button at the top of the Color Chooser window.

Doing so will save the color in one of the color presets for future usage.

- Select the color marker at the bottom of the ramp widget.

- Click the color preset you have just saved.

  You are now certain that the top and bottom of the ramp have the exact same color. As a result, the seam in the back of the body will be invisible.

- Select the color marker in the middle of the ramp widget.

- Set a **light brown** color.

- Click the **arrow** button at the top of the Color Chooser window to save another color preset.

- Click anywhere in the ramp widget to create a new color marker.

- Set its color to be the same light brown as the previous color marker.

- Click the **Accept** button.

- **Tweak** the *ramp* so it looks as follows:

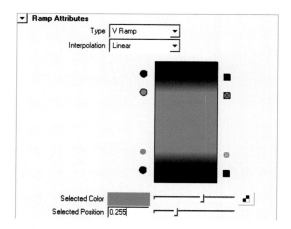

The ramp set-up

4   Head color

The head of the character should be a dark brown. Right now, the ramp from the previous step colors the face with a light brown. In order to fix this, you will map a new ramp in the Color Gain attribute of the first ramp.

- In the Attribute Editor for the ramp texture, scroll down to the **Color Balance** section.

- **Map** the **Color Gain** attribute with a **Ramp** texture.

- Set the new ramp texture's **Type** to **U Ramp**.

  This creates a ramp aligned perpendicularly to the first ramp.

• **Tweak** the *ramp* so it looks as follows:

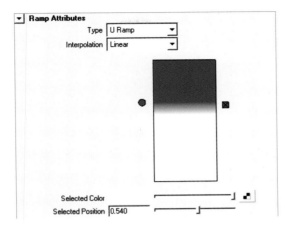

The new ramp set-up

Note: *The colors mapped into the Color Gain of a texture act as multipliers to the existing colors.*

The body color

5 Fractals

At this time, the overall look of the body is a little dull. In order to break up the even colors, you will map a fractal in the Color Gain of the new ramp.

• In the Attribute Editor for the new ramp, scroll down to the **Color Balance** section.

Lesson 16: NURBS Texturing

- **Map** the **Color Gain** attribute with a **Fractal** texture.
- Set the following:

  Amplitude to **0.2**;

  Threshold to **0.5**;

  Ratio to **0.8**;

  Frequency Ratio to **2.5**;

  Inflection to **On**.

The fractal effect

Note: *You will need to render the scene in order to see the exact effect of the fractal on the body*

6 Eyeball material

- **Create** a **Phong** material.
- **Assign** the new shader to both *eyeballs*.
- **Map** the **Color** attribute with a **File** texture.
- Click the **Browse** button for the **Image Name** attribute.
- Select the *mikey_eyeball.tif* texture file from the *sourceimages* folder.

The eye texture

7 Texture placement

In order for the eye texture to properly fit your model, you must align the iris with the pole at the front of the eyeball. If the iris of the eye is not located at the right place, you will need to rotate it using the texture placement node.

- Select the *place2dTexture* node for the file texture you have just created.

- Set the **RotateUV** attribute to **180** degrees.

The colored eyeballs

Note: *If this setting doesn't fix the iris placement, try rotating by 90 degree increments until you get the right look.*

Interactive Placement Tool

The Interactive Placement Tool is designed to ease the placement of textures onto NURBS surfaces. This tool allows you to interactively set the different placement values of a 2D texture using an all-in-one manipulator.

The following explains how to use this tool:

- Select a *place2dTexture* node of a texture used by a NURBS surface.

- In the Attribute Editor, with the file texture's *place2dTexture* tab selected, click on the **Interactive Placement** button.

  *Doing so will access the **NURBS Texture Placement Tool**. This tool displays a red manipulator on the NURBS geometry, which allows you to interactively place the texture in the viewport.*

> **Note:** *You can also access the* **NURBS Texture Placement Tool** *via the* **Texturing** *menu when a NURBS surface is selected.*

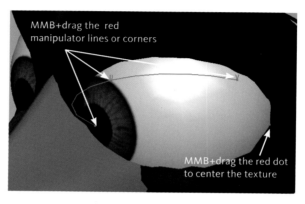

MMB+drag the red
manipulator lines or corners

MMB+drag the red dot
to center the texture

The interactive placement manipulator

> **Note:** *Notice the value of the place2dTexture node updates as you drag the manipulator. You can also set the place2dTexture values manually. If you have assigned the same shader to other surfaces, they will also be modified.*

Finish texturing the character

You can now spend some time shading and creating textures for the remaining pieces of the Mikey's geometry. Once you are satisfied with the results, you must make sure your scene is cleared of obsolete shading nodes.

1   Texture the rest of the character

> **Note:** *If you would like to paint details on a procedural texture, you will have to convert the shading network to a file texture. This will be explained later when texturing subdivision surfaces.*

2   Optimize scene size

- Select **File → Optimize Scene Size**.

    Doing so will remove any unused texture nodes.

The final Mikey

3 Save your work

- **Save** your file as *16-mikeyTxt_01.ma*.

Conclusion

You now have experience texturing NURBS surfaces and have learned how to use cascading procedural textures. You should now be comfortable creating textures from scratch using only Maya nodes. In the next project, you will learn about projections and conversion to file textures, which can also apply to NURBS texturing and can greatly broaden the possibilities not covered in this lesson.

In the next lesson, you will set up Mikey for animation.

Lesson 17
Rigging

In this lesson, you will rig Mikey for animation. This character rig will be slightly different from the penguin character's since the geometry is simpler. You will first organize the character's hierarchy. Once that is done, you will create a simple skeleton and skin the geometry using rigid binding.

In this lesson you will learn the following:

- How to rename multiple objects all at once
- How to change prefixes on mirrored joint chains
- How to snap objects together using constraints
- How to use rigid binding
- How to edit the membership of a skin deformer

Hierarchy

The first thing to do before rigging a model is to make sure that all of its nodes are in a good hierarchy where everything is easy to find and well named.

1 Scene file

- **Open** your scene from the last lesson.

  OR

- **Open** the scene file named *16-mikeyTxt_01.ma* from the support files.

2 Rename multiple objects

When you create content, you should be renaming nodes fairly frequently. Since you usually need to rename all the nodes one-by-one, you will learn a way to rename several nodes simultaneously.

- Select all the objects that should have similar names, such as the character's hair.

- In the top right corner of the interface, set the **Rename** option in the input field as follows:

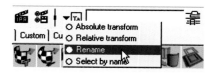

Rename option

- Enter *hair* in the input field andpress **Enter**.

  Each and every selected object will be assigned a unique name starting with the defined string, followed by a unique number.

Note: *The order of selection defines the order of the numbers appended to each name.*

- Take some time to appropriately **rename** every node in the scene.

3 Hierarchy

- **Group** every object together and rename the group to *geo*.

4 Skeleton

- Select **Skeleton** → **Joint Tool**.

- From the *side* view, **draw** a skeleton for the character as follows:

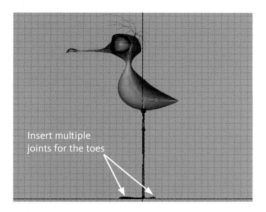

Insert multiple
joints for the toes

The basic skeleton

As you are drawing the different joints, try to visualize how the joint pivot will affect the deforming geometry.

Tip: *Don't forget to use the arrows on your keyboard to navigate in the skeleton while creating the different limbs.*

- From the other viewports, **move** the leg joint chain into its proper location in the model.
- **Rename** every joint accordingly, with the *l* or *r* prefix for *left* or *right* side of the body.

Tip: *Use the input field to rename the toes quickly.*

- **Duplicate** the toe joint chain to accommodate the third toe.

5 Mirror the leg

- With the leg joint chain selected, select **Skeleton → Mirror Joint → ❑.**
- In the option window, set the following:

   Mirror across to **YZ**;

   Mirror function to **Behavior**;

   Search for to *l*;

   Replace with to *r*.

   These options will ensure that the left prefix changes to a right prefix.

- Click the **Mirror** button.

Lesson 17: Rigging

> **Note:** *Double-check the names of the new joint chain since some names might have been altered by the search and replace function.*

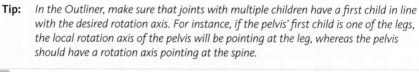

6 Place and mirror the eye joint

The eye joint should be placed at the exact center of the eyeball since it is perfectly round. You will now use a trick to align the eye joint to the eyeball.

- Select the left eyeball surface, then **Shift-select** the left eye joint.
- Select **Constrain → Point.**

  The eye joint will move at the pivot location of the eyeball. You can now delete the constraint since it is no longer required.

- Select the point constraint from the **Outliner** or select the eye joint and press the **down arrow** on your keyboard.
- Press the **Delete** key on your keyboard to delete the constraint node.
- **Mirror** the eye joint to the other side of the head.

7 Reorient all joints

At this point, you might have translated or rotated joints. Since this affects a joint's local rotation axis, you will now need to reorient them.

- Select the *pelvis* joint.
- Select **Modify → Freeze Transformations.**

  Doing so will remove any transformation values from the Channel Box.

- Select **Skeleton → Orient Joint.**

  Doing so will reorient the joints so each local rotation axis points at the joint's first child.

> **Tip:** *In the Outliner, make sure that joints with multiple children have a first child in line with the desired rotation axis. For instance, if the pelvis' first child is one of the legs, the local rotation axis of the pelvis will be pointing at the leg, whereas the pelvis should have a rotation axis pointing at the spine.*

8 Set preferred angle

- **RMB** on the *pelvis* joint and select **Set Preferred Angle.**

  Doing so saves the current pose of the skeleton.

9 Save your work

- **Save** your scene as *17-mikeyRig_01.ma.*

Skinning

You are now ready to skin Mikey's geometry to the skeleton using rigid binding. Rigid binding assigns each surface point to a single influence joint. This type of skinning could potentially break dense geometry when bending, but since NURBS geometry tends to bend smoothly when there are few CVs, rigid binding will do the trick.

1   Skin the body

- Select the *body*, then **Shift-select** the *pelvis*.

- Select **Skin → Bind Skin → Rigid Bind → ❑.**

- Make sure **Bind to** is set to **Complete skeleton,** then click the **Bind Skin** button.

- **Test** the effect of the joint rotation on the body geometry.

Test the binding

2   Edit Membership Tool

When testing the body's binding, you might notice that some points are not assigned to the proper joint. You will use the Edit Membership Tool to correct this.

- Select the *body* geometry.

- Select **Edit Deformers → Edit Membership Tool.**

- **Click on the** *pelvis* **joint to highlight it.**

  Doing so tells the tool that you want to edit the membership for the pelvis joint on the body skin.

- **Click+drag** to add CVs to the joint influence.

> **Tip:** Use the **Ctrl** key to deselect, **Shift** to toggle and **Ctrl+Shift** to add CVs to the joint influence. Be careful not to remove all influence from a given point since this point will not get deformed with the rest of the geometry.

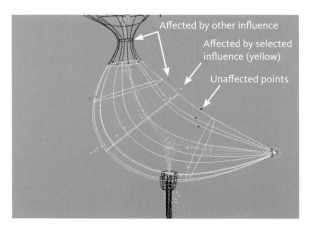

Affected by other influence

Affected by selected influence (yellow)

Unaffected points

Editing the membership of CVs

3 More rigid binding

Geometry that is not intended to deform can be rigid bound to a unique joint. The following will help you bind geometry to the selected joint.

- Select **Skin → Bind Skin → Rigid Bind → ❑.**
- Make sure **Bind to** is set to **Selected joints.**
- Still in the option window, select **Edit → Save Settings.**
- Click the **Close** button**.**
- **Rigid bind** the *beakTop* to the *head* joint.
- **Rigid bind** the *hair* to the *head* joint.
- **Rigid bind** the *beakBottom* to the *jaw* joint.
- **Rigid bind** the left *upperLeg* to the *lLeg* joint.
- **Rigid bind** the left *knee* and *shin* to the *lKnee* joint.
- **Rigid bind** the left *ankle* to the *lAnkle* joint.
- **Repeat** to bind the right leg.

Note: *You could also parent the geometry directly in the skeleton, but it is preferable to keep the set-up and geometry in separate hierarchies. You could also parent constrain the geometry to its joints, but that wouldn't allow you to scale the entire set-up later on.*

4 Other skinning

The toes and thigh will need to be bound to more than one joint.

* Select the geometry for one of the *toes*, then **Shift-select** each related toe joint, except the tip.

* **Edit** the membership of each toe so it bends properly.

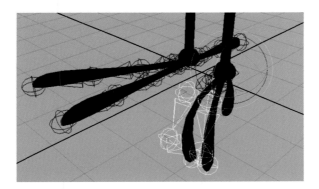

The skinned toes

* **Rigid bind** the *thigh* geometry to both the *pelvis* and *leg* joints.

* **Edit** the membership of the *thigh* surfaces if required.

5 Eye skinning

Since the eyeballs need to be skinned to a tip joint, you cannot use rigid binding. You will have to smooth bind the eyes to their respective joints.

* Select the left *eyeball* and the *lEye* joint.

* Select **Skin → Bind Skin → Smooth Bind → ❑.**

* Make sure **Bind to** is set to **Selected joint.**

* Click the **Bind Skin** button.

* **Repeat** for the right eyeball.

6   Test the binding

- **Translate** the *pelvis* joint to see if everything follows.
- **Pose** the character to see if you need to change something in your skinning.

A character pose

7   Save your work

- **Save** your scene as *17-mikeyRig_02.ma*.

Animation rig

You should now create a character rig similar to the one made for BigZ in the second project. Use what you have learned so far to create Mikey's animation rig. The following are some general guidelines.

1   Rigging the legs

Set up the legs using Rotate Plane IKs and pole vectors.

> **Note:** *If you have created the leg joints in a perfectly straight line, it is possible that the IK won't bend the leg since it doesn't know in which direction to bend the knee. One solution would be to slightly translate the joint in the direction you would like it to bend using the Insert key.*

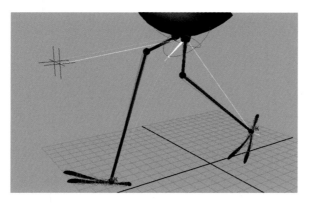

The leg IKs

2 Reverse foot

Create reverse foot set-ups. Their creation will be exactly like BigZ's, except that you will need to orient constrain the joints for two toes. Also create set driven keys for the **Roll** attribute.

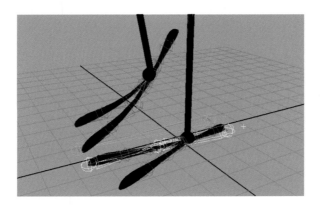

The reverse foot set-ups

3 Eyes

Create a *lookAt* locator and set the eye joints to aim at it. Create NURBS spheres with construction history for the eyelids and incorporate them into the character.

The lookAt set-up

4   Master node

Create a master node and parent every other set-up node to it.

The master node

5   Visibility layers

- **Create** a **new layer** and **rename** it to *setupLayer*.
- Select the *master* node and **add** it to the *setupLayer*.
- **Create** a **new layer** and **rename** it to *geoLayer*.
- Select the *geo* group and **add** it to the *geoLayer*.

6   Lock and hide attributes

- Make sure to **lock and hide** attributes that are not required to be changed by the animator.

7   Create a character set

- Create a Character Set named *mikey.*

8   Save your work

- **Save** your scene as *17-mikeyRig_03.ma.*

Conclusion

Mikey is now ready to be animated. You have gained some more experience with character rigging, which will greatly help you understand and plan ahead for animation tasks.

In the next lesson, you will learn how to fill your environment with one of the most powerful Maya tools—Paint Effects.

Lesson 18
Paint Effects

For this next stage, you will generate lots of content for BigZ's environment. The Paint Effects Tool gives you access to preset brushes, ranging from grasses to trees and buildings to lightning bolts, which can be customized for your own scenarios.

In this lesson, you will use several Paint Effects brushes and test render your scene.

In this lesson, you will learn the following:

· How to paint on canvas

· How to paint on geometry

· How to optimize the way Paint Effects are displayed in the viewport

· How to share, blend and customize brushes

· How to save brush presets

· How to auto-paint a surface

Paint on canvas

In order to experiment with various Paint Effects brushes, you will create a nature scene with palm trees, flowers and grass. First, you will test the tool on a canvas.

1   Open a new scene

2   Paint in the Paint Effects window

- Press **8** on your keyboard to display the Maya Paint Effects canvas window.

- Select **Paint → Paint Canvas**.

  This will set the canvas to a 2D paint mode.

- In the Paint Effects window, select **Brush → Get Brush**.

  The Visor will open, letting you browse through the various template Paint Effects brushes.

- Open any brush folder, select a brush and paint on the canvas.

  You can now experiment with different brushes.

- Select **Canvas → Clear**.

3   Change the background color

- Select **Canvas → Clear → ❑**.

- Set the **Clear Color** to **light blue**, then press the **Clear** button.

> **Note:** *You can also import an image as a starting point by selecting* **Canvas →**
> **Open Image**.

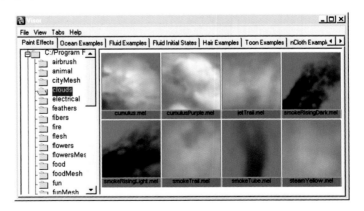

The Visor

4   Paint your image

- In the Visor window, open the *clouds* folder.

- Select the *jetTrail.mel* brush and paint some clouds onto your image.

> **Note:** *Hold down* **b** *and* **LMB+drag** *to change the size of the current brush.*

- Continue painting elements onto your image using the different preset brushes.

- If you make a mistake, you can **undo** the last brush stroke by selecting **Canvas** → **Canvas Undo**.

Test image

5   Save the image

- When you are finished with your image, you can save it by selecting **Canvas** → **Save As** → ❑.

- In the Option window, you can decide whether or not you want use the **Save Alpha** option.

- Click on **Save Image** and name your image.

  If you want, you can then use this image as an image plane or as a texture.

> **Note:** *To set a saved image as an image plane, simply select the camera for which you would like to add a background image, then from the camera panel select* **View** → **Image Plane** → **Import Image**.

- Return to a single perspective layout by clicking its icon in the Toolbox.

Lesson 18: Paint Effects

Paint Effects strokes

You will now learn how to paint strokes on geometry and how strokes can share the same brush. As well, you will learn how to scale Paint Effects.

1 Scene file

- **Open** the scene *04-animationBasics_01.ma* from the first project's *scenes* directory.

2 Delete the animation

- Go to frame **1**, then select **Edit → Delete All by Type → Channels.**

  Doing so will delete the animation in the entire scene.

3 Visibility layer

- **Create** a new **layer**.

- **Rename** it to *envLayer*.

- **Add** the *environmentGroup* to the new layer.

4 Paint trees

- Press **F6** to select the **Rendering** menu set.

- With the *ground* selected, select **Paint Effects → Make Paintable.**

  Doing so will allow you to paint directly on the surface.

- Select **Paint Effects → Get Brush**...

- In the Visor, select the **treesMesh** directory, then click on the **palmLight. mel** brush preset.

  Clicking on a brush preset in the Visor automatically accesses the Paint Effects Tool.

- Hold down **b** and **click+drag** to resize the brush.

- **Paint** a single stroke on the *ground* to create a palm tree.

A Paint Effects palm tree

5 Test render the scene

- Select **Render → Render Current Frame.**

The rendered palm tree

6 **Optimized display**

When working with Paint Effects, you can clutter your scene and computer with a lot of objects in no time. The following will change the display of a stroke in the viewport.

- Select the palm tree stroke.

- In the **Shapes** section of the Channel Box, set **Draw As Mesh** to **Off**.

    Rather than displaying meshes when painting the Paint Effects, only reference lines will be used. This drastically reduces the display refresh of the viewport, but does not affect the scene rendering.

- Select **Paint Effects** → **Paint Effects Tool** → ❑.

- In the option window, turn **Off** the **Draw as Mesh** option.

- **Paint** some more palm trees around the house.

More trees

> **Tip:** To reduce the viewport refresh rate even more, you can also set the stroke's **Display Percent** to a lower value. This attribute specifies how many of the Paint Effects you want to see interactively in the viewport.

7 Share one brush

At the moment, every stroke that you have drawn uses a different brush, letting you customize each one individually. To scale down the trees simultaneously, you can set up the strokes so they share the same brush.

- Open the Outliner.

  You should see all the different strokes you have drawn on the ground.

- Select all the *strokePalmLight* strokes.

- Select **Paint Effects** → **Share One Brush**.

  Now all the strokes use the same brush. Modifying this brush will change all the trees at the same time.

8 Scale the trees

- Press **Ctrl+a** to open the Attribute Editor for any of the selected strokes.

- Select the *palmLight* tab.

  This is the brush shared among all the strokes.

- Set the **Global Scale** attribute to your liking.

9 Test render the scene

10 Save your work

- **Save** your scene as *18-paintEffects_01.ma*.

Customize brushes

In this exercise, you will blend brushes together and customize your own brushes. You will also save your custom brush presets on your shelf for later use.

1 Blending brushes

- Select **Paint Effects** → **Get Brush**...

- In the Visor, select the **grasses** directory, then click on the *astroturf.mel* brush preset.

- Still in the Visor, **RMB** on the *grassBermuda.mel* brush preset.

  This will display a menu letting you blend the current brush with the new one.

- Select **Blend Brush 50%**.

  This will blend the second brush with the first brush, giving the stroke a little bit of profile from both brushes.

- **RMB** again on the *grassBermuda.mel* brush preset and select **Blend Shading 5%**.

  This will blend the shading of the two brushes together.

2   Paint the new brush

- **Paint** one stroke of the new brush on the ground on either side of the house.

- In the Channel Box Set the **Display Percent** attribute of the Paint Effect stroke to **50**.

- Set the **Global Scale** of the Paint Effect brush as desired.

- Select all the *strokeGrassBermuda* strokes.

- Select **Paint Effects →
  Share One Brush**.

3   Customizing brushes

- In the Attribute Editor, select the *grassBermuda* tab.

  Doing so will display all the Paint Effects attributes for the current brush and the current stroke.

The painted grass

- Try changing some of the values to see their affect on the current stroke. The following are some examples:

  Tubes → Creation → Tubes Per Step;

  Tubes → Creation → Length Min;

  Tubes → Creation → Length Max;

  Tubes → Creation → Tubes Width1;

  Tubes → Creation → Tubes Width2;

  Tubes → Creation → Width Rand;

  Tubes → Creation → Width Bias;

  Behavior → Forces→ Gravity.

Tip: *You may have to render the stroke in order to see changes.*

Lesson 18: Paint Effects

- **Reduce** the quality of the brush to speed up rendering time:

    Brush Profile → **Brush Width** to **3**;

    Brush Profile → **Flatness1** to **1**;

    Brush Profile → **Flatness2** to **1**;

    Tubes → **Creation** → **Tubes per Step** to **25**;

    Tubes → **Creation** → **Segments** to **1**;

    Tubes → **Growth** to **Branches** only.

4   Get brush settings from stroke

In order to draw more customized grass, you need to update the current template brush with the settings of the stroke you just modified.

- With the stroke selected, select **Paint Effects** → **Get Settings from Selected Stroke**.

    This will set the customized grass brush as the current template brush.

5   Save custom brushes

You can save the current template brush for later use. The brush can be saved either to your shelf or the Visor.

- Select **Paint Effects** → **Save Brush Preset...**

- Set the following in the Save Brush Preset window to save to current shelf:

    Label to **Custom Grass;**

    Overlay Label to **grass;**

    Save Preset to **To Shelf.**

> **Note:** *The preset will be saved to the currently selected shelf, so make sure you select the appropriate shelf before executing these steps.*

OR

- Set the following in the Save Brush Preset window to save to a Visor directory:

    Label to **Custom Grass;**

    Overlay Label to **grass;**

    Save Preset to **To Visor;**

    Visor Directory to **brushes** from your *prefs* directory.

- Click the **Save Brush Preset** button.

> **Note:** *You can obtain an image for your new brush only through the Paint Effects Canvas panel.*

6 Automatically paint a surface

If you do not need to paint strokes by hand, you can use the **Paint Effects → Auto Paint** command. This will automatically paint onto a surface according to the options set. For instance, you could cover a rock with lichen or flowers in a single click.

7 Paint some more plants

Add some ferns and flowers to your scene.

8 Scene set-up

- Open the Outliner.

- **Group** the strokes together and **rename** the group to *pfxGroup*.

- **Create** a new layer called *pfxLayer* and add *pfxGroup* to it.

The final render

> **Tip:** *To speed up the rest of the project, you can hide the pfxLayer.*

9 Save your work

- **Save** your scene as *18-paintEffects_02.ma*.

Conclusion

You have now experienced one of the software's greatest tools, but you have only scratched the surface of the power available in Paint Effects. Learning how to use the Paint Effects Canvas, how to paint on objects and how to customize your brushes will serve you well as you become more and more familiar with the tool. There are so many ways to use Paint Effects to generate scene content that there should be no reason for your future scenes to look dull and empty.

In the next lesson, you will learn how to convert Paint Effects and how to use deformers.

Lesson 18: Paint Effects

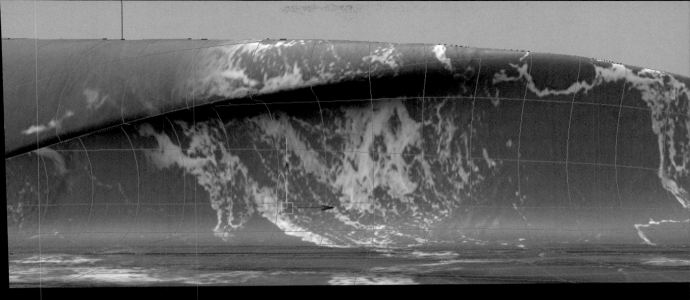

Lesson 19
Deformers

Deformers can be used for numerous reasons—for character set-up and animation, for facial
expressions, for modeling and for creating dynamic surfaces. In this lesson, you will be introduced
to various deformers to experiment with using a Paint Effects tree converted to polygons. These
deformers will change the tree's shape while still keeping an organic feel to the geometry.

In this lesson, you will learn the following:

- How to convert Paint Effects to polygons

- How to use wire deformers

Convert Paint Effects

To begin, you will need geometry to deform. In this lesson, you will be using a polygonal tree originally from Paint Effects. Most Paint Effects strokes can be converted to geometry and even animated dynamically.

For the sake of this lesson, you will only be using the output geometry of the conversion as a surface to deform.

1   Open a new scene

2   Paint a tree

- From the **Rendering** menu set, select **Paint Effects → Get Brush**.

- Under the **TreesMesh** directory, click on the palmLight.mel brush preset.

- **Paint** a single palm tree at the origin.

Paint Effects tree

3   Convert to polygons

- With the stroke selected, select **Modify → Convert → Paint Effects to Polygons → ❏**.

- In the options, turn **On** the **Quad output** option.

- Click on the **Convert** button.

4   Combine the model

If your model is composed of multiple meshes, for instance the leaves, branches and trunk, it will be simpler to combine them all together.

- Select the entire tree meshes.

- Select **Mesh → Combine.**

5 **Delete history**

Some Paint Effects brushes are animated by default, and when you convert the Paint Effects to polygons, the construction history keeps the ability to animate the mesh automatically. In this lesson, you will not require construction history.

> **Note:** *Try to play your scene to see the Paint Effects animation. If the playback is too slow, try to display the stroke as wireframe or playblast the scene.*

- Select **Edit → Delete All by Type → History**.

  The mesh has now lost its connection to the Paint Effects stroke and is now a static model.

- **Delete** the stroke from the Outliner.

6 **Center the tree**

- Select the tree mesh and **move** it so it grows straight up from the origin.

- **Freeze** its transformations.

- **Rename** it to *tree.*

7 **Save your work**

- **Save** the scene as *19-deformer_01.ma.*

Wire deformer

You will now modify the tree using a wire deformer. A wire deformer is used to deform a surface based on a NURBS curve. You will use that type of deformer for one of the tree branches.

1 **Draw a curve**

- Select **Create → EP Curve Tool**.

- From a *side* view, **draw** a curve along the trunk, then press **Enter**.

- **Tweak** the curve to follow the trunk in other views.

2 **Create the wire deformer**

- From the Animation menu set, select **Create Deformers → Wire Tool**.

  The Wire Tool requires two steps. First you must select the deformable surfaces, then you must select the NURBS curve to be the deformer.

The curve to be used as a deformer

Lesson 19: Deformers

- Select the *tree* geometry and press **Enter**.
- Select the NURBS curve and press **Enter**.

The wire deformer is created.

3 Edit the shape of the curve

- With the *curve* selected, press **F8** to go into Component mode.
- Select some CVs and **move** them to see their effect on the geometry.

The default wire deformer effect

4 Edit the deformer attribute

As with any other deformers, the attributes of the wire deformer can be changed through the Channel Box.

- In the Channel Box, select the *wire1* history node.
- Highlight the **Dropoff Distance** attribute in the Channel Box.
- Hold down **Ctrl**, then **MMB+drag** in the viewport to see its effect.

The effect of the wire deformer changes across the geometry.

Note: *Holding down the* **Ctrl** *key makes the virtual slider change with smaller increments.*

5 Edit the deformer membership

The **dropoff** has a nice effect, but the deformer might be affecting some undesired components. You can correct that by defining the membership of the geometry to the deformer.

- Select **Edit Deformers → Edit Membership Tool**.

- Select the *curve* to highlight the vertices affected by it.

  All the vertices of the tree geometry will be highlighted yellow.

- Hold the **Ctrl** key and **deselect** the branch vertices.

  Vertices that are no longer deformed will move back to their original positions.

The deformer's membership

Tip: *You can also use* **Edit Deformers → Paint Set Membership Tool** *to easily define the membership of the vertices.*

---

6 Experiment

Now that the deformer no longer affects the branches, you can set its **dropoff** to a higher value.

- Go back to **Object** mode.
- Press **q** to exit the **Edit Membership Tool** and enable the **Pick Tool**.
- Select the *curve* and try to change other deformer attributes from the Channel Box.
- Experiment with moving the *curve*'s CVs to see the effect of the deformer.

Point on curve and cluster deformer

The wire deformer is working well to deform the tree, but it is not practical to deform the curve for animation. Several other types of deformers can be used to deform the curve itself. Here you will experiment with the *point on curve* deformer and the *cluster* deformer.

1   **Point on curve deformer**

The point on curve deformer will create a locator linked to a curve edit point.

- **RMB** on the *NURBS curve* and select **Edit Point**.

   Unlike CVs, edit points are located directly on the curve.

- Select the edit point located at the base of the trunk.

- Select **Create Deformers** → **Point on Curve**.

   A locator is created at the edit point's position.

- Select **Modify** → **Center Pivot** to center the pivot of the *locator*.

- **Move** the locator to see its effect on the curve.

The point on curve deformer

Note: *Rotating a point on curve deformer has no effect on the curve.*

2   **Cluster deformer**

The point on curve works well, but has its limitations. For instance, it can only control one edit point at a time, and it cannot be used for rotation. The cluster deformer will create a handle that controls one or more vertices. When a cluster has multiple vertices in it, it can also be rotated.

- **RMB** on the *NURBS curve* and select **Control Vertex**.

- Select the two CVs in the middle of the trunk.

Tip: *It might be easier to locate the CVs by also displaying hulls.*

- Select **Create Deformers** → **Cluster**.

*A cluster handle is displayed with a **C** in the viewport.*

The cluster handle

- **Move** and **rotate** the *cluster handle* to see its effect on the curve and the tree.

Note: *Both the point on curve locator and cluster handle can be animated like any other node.*

Soft Modification Tool

The *Soft Modification Tool* lets you push and pull geometry as a sculptor would push and pull a piece of clay. By default, the amount of deformation is greatest at the center of the deformer, and gradually falls off moving outward. However, you can control the fall-off of the deformation to create various types of effects.

1 **Scene file**
   - **Open** the scene *19-deformer_01.ma* without saving your previous changes.

2 **Create the deformer**
   - **RMB** on the *tree* surface and select **Vertex**.
   - Select some vertices at the base of the tree.
   - Click on the **Soft Modification Tool** in the toolbox, or select **Create Deformers** → **Soft Modification**.

   *An **S** handle similar to the cluster handle will be created. The tool's manipulator will also be displayed and the influence of the deformer is shown. Yellow indicates areas that are fully deformed, while black areas are not deformed at all.*

The influence of the deformer

3   **Edit the deformer**

   • **Move**, **rotate** and **scale** the deformer to see its effect on the geometry.

   • Press **Ctrl+a** to open the Attribute Editor for the deformer.

   The various deformer options can be edited here.

   • Set the **Falloff Radius** to **2.0**.

   • Click on the button next to the **Falloff Curve** graph.

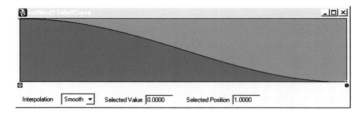

Falloff curve

   • See the effect of the deformer on the geometry.

4   **Modeling with Soft Modification Tool**

   When modeling a high resolution model, such as a character's face, you can create multiple Soft Modification deformers to achieve a final shape. The deformers can even overlap.

5   **Delete Soft Modification deformers**

   If you want to delete the deformer, simply select its **S** handle and **delete** it. If you want to keep the shape of the geometry but remove the deformers, you must delete the model's history.

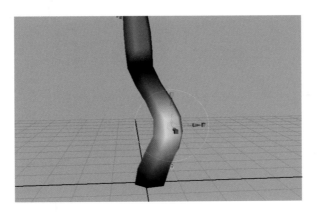

The modified influence

> **Note:** *The Soft Modification effect works best on high resolution models.*

Non-linear deformers

Maya has several *non-linear deformers*. Non-linear deformers can affect one surface, multiple surfaces or parts of a surface, and are very simple to use. In this exercise, you will experiment with all the non-linear deformers.

1 **Scene file**

  • **Open** the scene *19-deformer_01.ma* without saving your previous changes.

2 **Bend deformer**

  • Select the *tree* geometry, then select **Create Deformers → Nonlinear → Bend**.

   The Bend handle is created and selected.

  • In the Attribute Editor, highlight the *bend1* input.

   All the attributes for this deformer type are listed.

  • Experiment and combine the different attributes to see their effect on the geometry.

> **Tip:** *Most of the attributes have visual feedback on the deformer's handle in the viewport. You can also use the* **Show Manipulator Tool** *to interact with the deformer in the viewport.*

  • **Moving**, **rotating** and **scaling** the handle will also affect the location of the deformation.

Lesson 19: Deformers

uses, including simplifying modeling tasks,
which would be otherwise difficult to achieve. In this case, it could be used to simulate wind animation.

- When you finish experimenting, select the deformer and **delete** it.

3 Flare deformer

- Select the *tree* geometry, then select **Create Deformers → Nonlinear → Flare**.

  The Flare handle is created and selected.

- In the Attribute Editor, highlight the *flare1* input.

- Experiment by moving, rotating, scaling and combining the different attributes to see their effect on the geometry.

  This deformer is also versatile and can be used to simplify modeling tasks.

- When you finish experimenting, select the deformer and **delete** it.

4 Sine deformer

- Select the *tree* geometry, then select **Create Deformers → Nonlinear → Sine**.

  The Sine handle is created and selected.

- In the Attribute Editor, highlight the *sine1* input.

- Experiment by moving, rotating, scaling and combining the different attributes to see their effect on the geometry.

This deformer can have several

Flare deformer

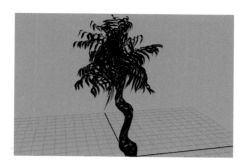

Sine deformer

 Tip: *The **Offset** attribute is great for animating a waving effect.*

This deformer can help achieve refined randomization and could be used to simulate a flag animation or waves on a shore.

- When you finish experimenting, select the deformer and **delete** it.

5 Squash deformer

- Select the *tree* geometry, then select **Create Deformers → Nonlinear → Squash**.

The Squash handle is created and selected.

- In the Attribute Editor, highlight the *squash1* input.

- Experiment by moving, rotating, scaling and combining the different attributes to see their effect on the geometry.

This deformer is useful for adding stretch and squash to an animated object.

- When you finish experimenting, select the deformer and **delete** it.

6 Twist deformer

- Select the *tree* geometry, then select **Create Deformers → Nonlinear → Twist**.

The Twist handle is created and selected.

- In the Attribute Editor, highlight the *twist1* input.

- Experiment by moving, rotating, scaling and combining the different attributes to see their effect on the geometry.

This deformer can add twisting animation to an object, among other uses.

- When you finish experimenting, select the deformer and **delete** it.

Squash deformer

Twist deformer

7 Wave deformer

- Select the *tree* geometry, then select **Create Deformers → Nonlinear → Wave**.

The Wave handle is created and selected.

- In the Attribute Editor, highlight the *wave1* input.

- Experiment by moving, rotating, scaling and combining the different attributes to see their effect on the geometry.

Lesson 19: Deformers

*As you can see, this deformer can have
several uses, such as creating a rippling
effect for water.*

- When you finish experimenting, select
the deformer and **delete** it.

8 Experiment

Spend some time deforming the tree as
you wish. Keep in mind that you can add
multiple deformers to the same object.

If you want to animate the tree later on,
consider keeping the deformers in the scene and making an animation set-up.

Wave deformer

Deformation order

The deformation order of a surface is very important to take into consideration. For instance, if
you apply a *sine* deformer and then a *bend* deformer, the results are different than if you apply
a *bend* deformer and then a *sine* deformer.

The deformation order does not only apply to non-linear deformers. For instance, a rigid
binding and a polygonal smooth will have a different effect than a polygonal smooth and a
rigid bind.

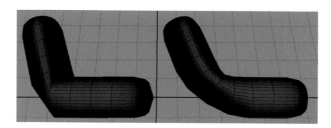

Smooth/Rigid bind vs Rigid bind/Smooth

Note: *In the previous statement, a rigid bind followed by a smooth would evaluate much
faster and give better results than a smooth followed by a rigid bind, since the rigid
binding would have to skin a higher resolution model.*

1 **New Scene**

- Select **File** → **New**.

2 **Create a cylinder**

- Select **Create** → **Polygon Primitives** → **Cylinder**.

- Edit the *cylinder* as follows:

3 **Apply deformers**

- Select the *cylinder*, then select **Create Deformers** → **Nonlinear** → **Bend**.

- Select the *cylinder*, then select **Create Deformers** → **Nonlinear** → **Sine**.

4 **Edit the bend deformer**

- Select the *cylinder*.

- In the Channel Box, highlight the *bend1* deformer.

- Set the **Curvature** attribute to **2**.

5 **Edit the sine deformer**

- Select the *cylinder*.

- In the Channel Box, highlight the *sine1* deformer.

- Set the **Amplitude** attribute to **0.1**.

- Set the **Wavelength** attribute to **0.35**.

6 **List input for the cylinder**

- **RMB** on the *cylinder*.

- Select **Inputs** → **All Inputs...**

  Doing so will display a window with all the history nodes affecting the cylinder.

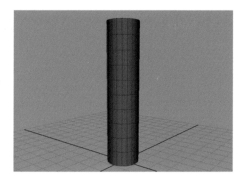

Example cylinder

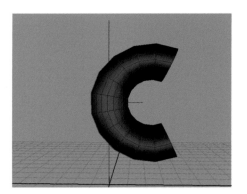

Bend deformer effect

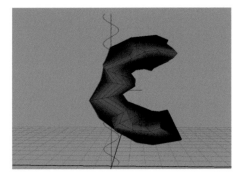

Sine and bend deformer effect

Lesson 19: Deformers

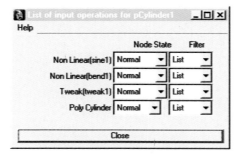 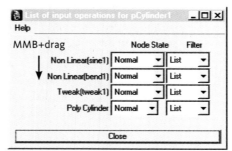

List of input for cylinder   *List of input for cylinder*

7   Change the order of deformation

- In the Input window, **MMB+drag** the *Non Linear(sine1)* item over the *Non Linear(bend1)* item to change their order.

8   Result of the new order of deformation

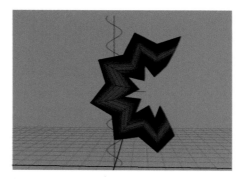

New deformation order effect

Layering deformers

As you have learned so far in this lesson, deformers can be used individually for modeling or animation. In addition, you can layer multiple deformers to create an animation specific to your needs.

1   Scene file

- **Open** the scene *19-wave_01.ma* from the *support_files*.

  This scene file contains only a NURBS plane and deformers to create a tidal wave.

2   Understand

- **RMB** on the *wave* plane.

- Select **Inputs → All Inputs...**

  As you can see, there are four different deformers affecting the surface, which are in a very particular order to give the proper results.

- In the list of inputs window, set the **Node State** of the deformers to **Has No Effect**.

  Doing so temporarily disables the deformers.

Wave created from deformers

- **Enable** the deformers one by one to see their layered effect.

  First, the sine deformer raises a blade out of the water. Second, the flare deformer gradually increases the wave's height. Third, the bend deformer creates the barrel. And finally a wave deformer ripples the overall surface.

3 Experiment

- Try to translate the NURBS plane to see how it is dynamically following the wave shape to give the impression that the wave is moving forward.

- Try to change the settings on the different deformers to see their effects.

- **Animate** the entire scene so the NURBS plane moves on its **Z-axis** and so the wave gradually gains height and creates a nice barrel for BigZ to surf in.

4 Save your work

- The animated scene file is *19-waveAnim_01.ma*.

Conclusion

You should now be comfortable using basic deformers. Being aware of the results created by the deformation order will allow you to reorder them if needed.

In the next lesson, you will learn about lighting and effects, which can greatly improve the quality of your rendered scene.

Lesson 20
Lights and Effects

In the real world, it is light that allows us to see the surfaces and objects around us. In computer graphics, digital lights play the same role. They help define the space within a scene and, in many cases, help to set the mood or atmosphere. As well, several other effects besides lighting can be added to the final image in order to have it look more realistic. This lesson explores and explains some of the basic Maya effects.

In this lesson you will learn the following:

- How to add lighting to your scene
- How to enable shadows
- How to add light fog and lens flare
- How to set up motion blur
- How to batch render an animation
- How to use fcheck

References

When you first animated BigZ, you saw how to create a reference. You will now open that same animation file, but this time you will also reference the environment.

1 Scene file

- **Open** the scene file *14-bigzWalk_05.ma* from the second project's *scenes* directory.

2 **Create references**

- Select **File → Reference Editor** from the main interface menu.

- Select **File → Create Reference → ❏** from the main interface menu or from the Reference Editor.

   This will prefix all the reference nodes with the string set.

- Click on the **Apply** button.

- In the browse window, select the file *18-paintEffects_02.ma*, and then click **Reference**.

   The file will load into the current one.

- Set **Resolve all nodes with this string:** *mikey.*

- Click on the **Reference** button.

- In the browse dialog that appears, select the file *17-mikeyRig_03.ma*, and then click **Reference**.

Note: *You may have to re-link textures that are not automatically found. To do so, simply open the Hypershade, select the Texture tab and change the path of the texture through the Attribute Editor.*

3 **Scaling**

Looking at the three elements in your scene, you can clearly see that there is a scaling issue between the files.

- Select the *environmentGroup.*

Tip: *Make sure the group's pivot is located at the origin before scaling.*

- Set its **scale X**, **Y** and **Z-axes** to **1.5** or any other appropriate value.

   The set should now be proportionate to BigZ.

- Select the Mikey *master.*

- Set its **scale X**, **Y** and **Z-axes** to **0.4** or any other appropriate value.

The entire scene

Note: *If the top node's scale attributes are non-keyable and unlocked, they will not show in the Channel Box, but the Scale Tool will still work. Alternatively, you can access the scale attributes in the Attribute Editor. If the scale attributes of the node are locked, you need to unlock them in the referenced file and re-open this file again.*

4   Save your work

- **Save** this scene to *20-lightsEffects_01.ma*.

Placing a point light

To create the primary light source in the scene, such as the sun, you will use a point light. This light type works exactly like a lightbulb, with attributes such as color and intensity.

1   Create a point light

- Select **Create → Lights → Point Light**.

    This places a point light at the origin.

- With the light still selected, **translate** the point light high up in the sky, in front of the house.

The light placement

 Tip: *Make sure that you don't place the light outside the sky dome.*

2 Turn on hardware lighting (if possible)

One step beyond hardware texturing is *hardware lighting*. This lets you see how the light is affecting the surface that it is shining on.

- Press the **6** hotkey to display textures in the viewport.
- Select **Lighting** → **Use All Lights** or press the **7** hotkey.

You will see the scene being lit by the point light.

The hardware lighting enabled

3 **Test render the scene**

- From the **Rendering** menu set, select **Render → Render Current Frame**.

Notice the rendered image is dark without much contrast.

The rendered scene

Placing a directional light

So far, you used a point light to create a sun, but this kind of light is not adequate for sunlight and shadows because in reality, the sun is so far away that the rays coming from it are parallel to each other.

As a second light source in the scene, you will use a directional light. This light type mimics a light source so far away that rays are parallel, which is exactly what you need.

1 **Create a directional light**

- Select **Create → Lights → Directional Light**.

This places a directional light at the origin.

2 **Edit the directional light's position**

The Show Manipulator Tool provides a manipulator for the light's *look at point* and *eye point*. You can edit these using the same method as you would with a typical transform manipulator.

- Press the **t** key to access the **Show Manipulator Tool**.

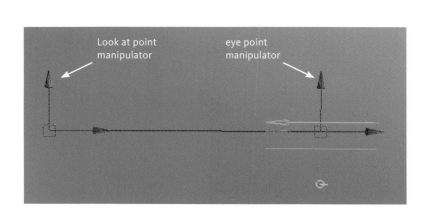

Show Manipulator Tool

- **Click+drag** on the manipulator handles to reposition the light in the direction in which the sunlight should hit the set.

New light position

3 Shadows

- In the Attribute Editor, expand the **Shadows** section for the directional light.

- **Enable** shadow casting by checking the **Use Depth Map Shadows** attribute.

- **Render** the scene.

  Notice that you don't see the effect of the directional light anymore. This is because the directional light is from an infinite distance, so the sky dome places the entire set in shadow. To correct this, you can disable shadow casting on the sky dome surface.

- Select the *skydome* surface and open its Attribute Editor.

Project 03

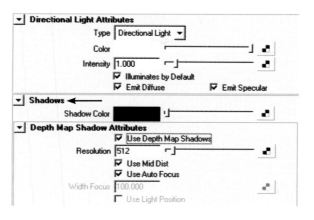

Shadows section in the Attribute Editor

- Under the **Render Stats** section, set the following:

  Casts Shadows to **Off**;

  Receive Shadows to **Off**.

- **Render** the scene again.

  You should now see shadows.

Shadows in the rendered image

4   Refine the shadows

Right now, the shadow resolution is a little coarse. The following shows how to increase the depth map shadow resolution:

- Open the Attribute Editor for the *directionalLight1*.

Lesson 20: Lights and Effects

- In the **Depth Map Shadow Attributes** section, set the following:

  Resolution to **1024** or even **2048,** rather than **512**;

  Filter Size to **2**.

  Doing so will first increase the resolution of the shadow maps, and will then apply a blur filter to smooth out the shadow even more.

- **Render** the scene again to see how this makes the shadow smoother.

5 Adding ambient lighting

In the real world, light rays bounce off surfaces, particles and atmosphere, making the global lighting level of a set brighter. In order to mimic this, you could add several directional lights pointing from the back and from below, but instead you will use an ambient light, which can accomplish this effect.

- Select **Create → Lights → Ambient Light**.

- In the Channel Box, set the **Intensity** attribute to **0.5**.

- **Place** the light at the opposite side of the scene.

- **Render** the scene.

  Notice how the geometry that previously had a side in complete shadow is now much more visible. Also notice how the global light level raised to what you would think of as daylight.

The ambient light effect

Light effects

The point light used for the sun doesn't help much at this time. When the rendered camera is looking directly at bright light, a light glow and lens flare would add realism to your renders. You will now add light effects to your point light.

1 Light FX

- Open the Attribute Editor for the *pointLightShape1*.
- Scroll down to the **Light Effects** section.
- Click on the **map** button next to the **Light Glow** attribute.

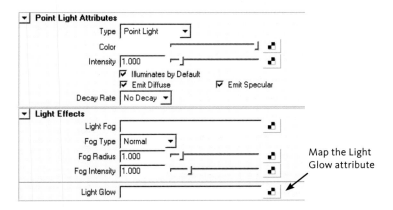

Light Glow attribute

Maya will automatically create, select and display an opticalFX node in the Attribute Editor.

- Set the *opticalFX1* attributes as follow:

    Lens flare to **Enabled**;

    Glow Type to **Linear**;

    Halo Type to **Lens Flare**.

    Under **Lens Flare Attributes,** set **Flare Intensity** to **2**.

- **Place** the camera to look directly at the sun from inside the house.
- **Render** your scene to see the lens flare.

Lesson 20: Lights and Effects

Never look directly at the sun!

2   **Save your work**

- **Save** your scene as *20-lightsEffects_02.ma*.

Rendering animation

Now that you have defined the lighting in your scene and you are happy with your test rendering, it is time to render an animation. This is accomplished using the Maya *batch renderer*. In preparation, you will add motion blur to your scene, in order to simulate the blur generated in live action film and video work.

1   **Render Settings**

Render Settings are a group of attributes that you can set to define how your scene will render. To define the quality of the rendering, you need to set the Render Settings.

- In the Render View window, click with your **RMB** and choose **Options** → **Render Settings...**

   OR

- Click the **Render Settings** button located at the top right of the main interface.

- Select the **Maya Software** tab.

- Open the **Anti-aliasing Quality** section if it is not already opened.

- Set the **Quality** preset to **Intermediate Quality**.

   Anti-aliasing is a visual smoothing of edge lines in the final rendered image. Because bitmaps are made up of square pixels, a diagonal line would appear jagged unless it was anti-aliased.

2 Set the image output

To render an animation, you must set up the scene's file extensions to indicate a rendered sequence. You must also set up the start and end frames.

- Select the **Common** tab in the Render Settings window.

- From the **Image File Output** section, set the following:

  File Name Prefix to *beach*.

  This sets the name of the animated sequence.

  Frame/Animation Ext *to:*

  name.#.ext.

  This sets up Maya to render a numbered sequence of images.

  Start Frame to **1**;

  End Frame to **50**;

  By Frame to **1**.

  This tells Maya to render every frame from 1 to 50.

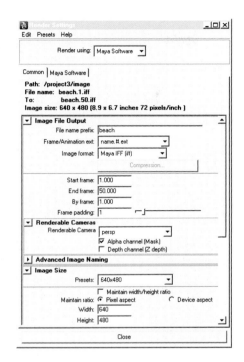

Render Settings

3 Turn on motion blur

- Select the **Maya Software** tab.

- Under the **Motion Blur** section, click on the **Motion Blur** button to turn it **On**.

- Set the **Motion Blur Type** to be **2D**.

  This type of motion blur renders the fastest.

> **Tip:**   *If you want to see more motion blur in your renders, you can set the* **Blur length** *to* **2** *in the* **Motion Blur** *section of the Render Settings.*

4 Place your camera

- In the Perspective view panel, select **View** → **Camera Settings** → **Resolution Gate**.

- **Place** the camera so you can see your animation from frame **1** to **50**.

5 Save your work

- **Save** your scene as *20-lightsEffects_03.ma*.

Lesson 20: Lights and Effects

Motion blur on BigZ

6   Batch render the scene

- Press **F6** to change to the **Rendering** menu set.

- Select **Render** → **Batch Render**.

- If, for any reason you want to cancel the current batch render, select **Render** → **Cancel Batch Render**.

7   Watch the render progress

- The sequence will be rendered as a series of frames. You can look in the Command Feedback line or through the **Window** → **General Editor** → **Script Editor** to see the status of the current rendering process.

Tip: *Once a batch render is launched, you can safely close Maya without interrupting the batch render.*

8   View the resulting animation

After the rendering is complete, you can preview the results using the *fcheck* utility.

- To open the *fcheck* utility, go in your programs, and then go to **Autodesk Maya 2008** → **FCheck.**

- In FCheck, select **File** → **Open Sequence**.

- Navigate to the *project3\images* folder.

- Select the file *beach.1.iff* and click **Open**.

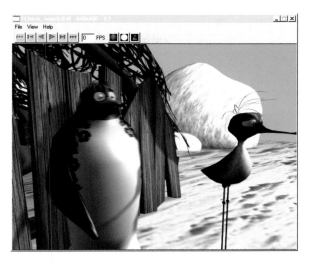

Animation previewed with fcheck utility

The animation will load one frame at a time, and once in memory, it will play it back in realtime.

Tip: To learn more about the capabilities of fcheck for previewing your animations, enter `fcheck -h` in a command shell or select the Help menu.

Conclusion

You are now familiar with the basic concepts of lighting and rendering a scene. You began by enabling various light options such as shadows, light glow and lens flare. Then, you added 2D motion blur just before launching your first animation batch render. Once your render was complete, you viewed it in the fcheck utility.

In the next lesson, you will learn about rendering tasks and experiment with different renderers.

Lesson 21
Rendering

This lesson will make extensive use of the Maya Interactive Photorealistic Renderer (IPR). This tool allows you to create a rendering of the scene that can then be used to interactively update changes to the scene's lighting and texturing. You will see how fast and intuitive it is to texture your scene with the IPR.

So far in this book, you have been using only the Maya software renderer to render your scenes. In this lesson, you will also learn about three additional rendering types: Maya Hardware, Maya Vector and mental ray® for Maya. Each has its own strengths and you should determine which rendering engine to use on a per project basis, depending on the final application.

In this lesson you will learn the following:

- How to render a region and display snapshots

- How to open and save images

- How to display an image's alpha channel

- How to start the IPR

- How to make connections in the Hypershade

- How to enable high quality rendering in a viewport

- How to render with mental ray®

- How to render with Maya Vector

- How to render with Maya Hardware

Rendering Features

You are now ready to refine the rendering of your scene. In this section, you will experiment with the Render view features, such as snapshots, image storage and region rendering.

1 **Scene file**

- Continue with the scene file you were using in the last lesson.

OR

- **Open** the scene *20-lightsEffects_03.ma*.

2 **Panel set-up**

- In the *Perspective* view, select **Panels → Saved Layouts → Hypershade/Render/Persp**.
- Frame BigZ's *eyes* in the *Perspective* view.
- **RMB** click in the *Render* view and select **Render → Render → Persp**.

Note: *You can change the size of the panels by* **click+dragging** *on their separators.*

Tip: *You may want to turn off* **Motion Blur** *in the* **Render Settings** *window to see the image more clearly.*

3 **Keep and remove image**

When test rendering a scene, it is good to be able to keep previously rendered images for comparison with the changes you implement.

- To keep the current render for reference, select **File → Keep Image in Render View** or click the **Keep Image** button.

  Notice a slider bar appears at the bottom of the Render view.

- In the *Perspective* view, select the eyeball geometry.
- In the Hypershade, click on the **Graph material on selected objects** button.

Note: *Here, you will be modifying the eyeball textures when the character is referenced. This way, your changes will only be in that scene file and not in the original scene file.*

- In the **Create Maya Node** section, scroll down and set the **2D Textures** option to **Normal** and click on the **File** node.
- **Double-click** on the *file1* node to open the Attribute Editor.

- Click the **Browse** button and select the *eyeball.tif* texture from the *sourceimage* folder.
- In the Hypershade Work Area, **MMB+drag** the *file1* node onto the *eyeM* material.

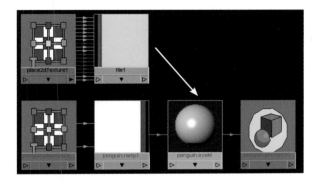

Dragging to create a connection

- Choose **Color** from the context menu to map the file in the color of the material.
- Make sure the *place2dTexture* node places the iris correctly on the eyeball.
- In the *Render* view, **render** the model again.
- Click the **Keep Image** button.
- Open the Attribute Editor for the *file1* node.
- Under the **Color Balance** section, change the **Color Offset** to change the eye color.
- **Render** the model again.
- Once the rendering is done, scroll the image bar at the bottom of the *Render* view to compare the previous render results.
- Scroll the image bar to the right (the older image), and select **File → Remove Image from Render View** or click the **Remove Image** button.

This will remove the currently displayed image stored earlier.

The eye render

> **Note:** *You can keep as many images as you want in the Render view. The images will be kept even if you close and reopen the Render view window.*

4   Region rendering

You might think it is a waste of time to render the entire image again just for the small portion of the image that changed. With the Render view, you can render only a region of the current image.

- Select a region of the current image by **click+dragging** a square directly on the previously rendered image.

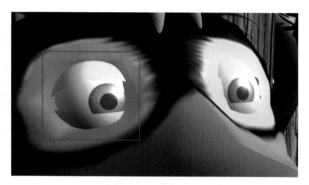

Select a region of the rendered image

- Click on the **Render Region** button to render the selected region.
- To automatically render a selected region, **RMB** and enable the **Options** → **Auto Render Region**.

With this option, every time you select a region on the rendered image, it will automatically be rendered.

> **Note:** *You can still keep an image that has a region render in it.*

5   Snapshots

If your scene is long, you might not want to wait for a complete render before selecting a region to render. The Render view allows you to take a wireframe snapshot of the image to render so that you can easily select the region you want.

- **RMB** in the Render view and select **Render** → **Snapshot** → **Persp**.

  A wireframe image is placed in the Render view for reference.

- Select the region you would like to render.

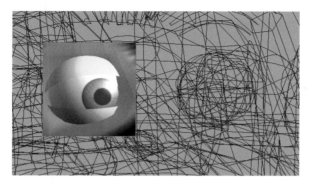

A snapshot in the Render view

6   Open and save images

You can open renders or reference images directly in the Render View.

- To open a reference image, select **File** → **Open Image**.

- **Browse** to the reference image *eyeReference.tif* located in the *images* folder of the current project.

The eye reference

Tip: *Keep reference images in the Render view to easily compare them with the render.*

You can also save your renders to disk from the Render view.

- To save your current Render view image, select **File** → **Save Image**.

Lesson 21: Rendering

7   Display the alpha channel

When rendering, you often want to display the image's alpha channel to see if it will composite well onto another image.

- Select the penguin geometry group.
- Select **Display** → **Hide** → **Hide Unselected Objects**.
- Select **Display** → **Show** → **Lights**.
- Frame the character and render your scene.
- Once the render is finished, click on the **Display Alpha Channel** button located at the top of the Render view.

The character's alpha channel

Note: *In an alpha channel, black is totally transparent, white is completely opaque and grey tones are semi-transparent. The above image is slightly blurred because of motion blur.*

- To go back to the colored images, click on the **Display RGB Channels** in the Render view.

IPR

To give you access to interactive updating capabilities, you will set up an IPR rendering. An IPR rendering creates a special image file that stores not only the pixel information about an image, but also data about the surface normals, materials and objects associated with each of these pixels. This information is then updated as you make changes to your scene's shading.

1   IPR set -up

- From the *Render* view panel, click on the **Render Settings** button.

- Click on the **Maya Software** tab.

- From the **Anti-aliasing Quality** section, set **Quality** to **Production Quality**.

  For IPR, you can use the best settings if desired. Your initial IPR rendering will be slower, but the interactive updates will still be fast.

- Close the Render Settings window.

2   IPR render

- From your *Render* view panel, select **IPR → IPR Render → persp**.

  Now what seems to be a regular rendering of the scene appears. Notice the message at the bottom of the Render view saying: Select a region to begin tuning.

- **Click+drag** to select an area of the IPR rendering that will cover the entire character.

  This is the area that will be updated as you make changes.

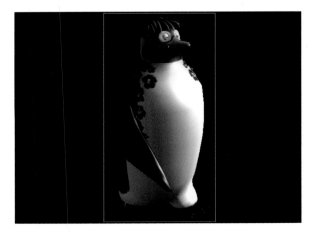

Initial IPR rendering

Note: *You can still change the region by* **click+dragging** *again in the Render view.*

3   Tweak your materials

- In the Render panel, **double-click** on the character's *body*.

  Doing so will automatically bring up the Attribute Editor for the bodyM material.

Note: *Doing so doesn't actually select the material node.*

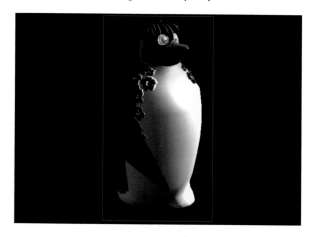

- Click the **Select** button at the bottom of the Attribute Editor to select the *bodyM* material node.

- Graph the *bodyM* shading network in the Hypershade by clicking the **Input and output connections** button.

- **Drag** the *peguin file1* onto the *bodyM* material and **drop** it in the **specularColor** attribute.

- **Drag** the *peguin file1* onto the *bodyM* material and **drop** it in the **bump map** attribute.

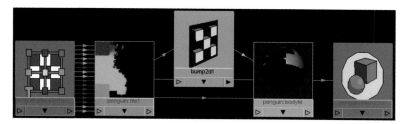

The updated shading network

Notice how the IPR updates every time you bring a change to the shading group.

- Select the *bump2D* node and change the **Bump Depth** to **0.2**.

IPR update

4 Stop the IPR

- **Stop** the IPR by clicking on the button located at the top right of the Render view.

5 Drag and drop feature

- Select the *eyeball* geometry and **graph** its shading network.

- In the Hypershade, select the *eyeM* material.

Pause   File size   Stop

↓   ↓   ↓

II IPR: 37MB **(IPR)**

IPR functions

- Select **Edit → Duplicate → Shading Network** in the Hypershade

Doing so duplicates the entire selected shading network(s).

- Click the **Rearrange graph** button to order the work area.

- Frame the eyes in the *Perspective* view and **launch** another IPR.

- Select the render region surrounding the eyes.

- With your **MMB**, drag the new eyeM in the Render view and drop it on one of the *eyeballs*.

Each eye now has a separate material assigned.

Note: *Dropping a material directly in the IPR has the same effect as dropping it on a model in a viewport.*

6 IPR and the Attribute Editor

- Open the Attribute Editor.

- Single click on any object in the IPR image and see the Attribute Editor update to show the related material node.

The IPR updates the Attribute Editor

7 Refresh the IPR image

When you have models outside the IPR region, you can refresh the entire image without losing your selected region.

- To refresh the entire image, click on the **Refresh the IPR Image** button.

The entire image gets redrawn and your original region is maintained.

8 IPR lighting

You can also use the IPR window to explore different lighting scenarios. Changing the light direction or properties will cause the IPR to redraw accordingly.

> **Note:** *When you don't have any lights in your scene, the IPR creates a directional light for you by default. The defaultLight node gets deleted when you stop an IPR rendering.*

- Select any light from the Outliner.
- Change the light intensity or color to see the IPR update with the new lighting.

New light color and intensity in IPR

9 IPR shadows

The IPR might not update certain shadow tweaks. To correct this, do the following:

- Select **IPR → Update Shadow Maps**.

The IPR updates and the shadows are re-rendered.

- **Stop** the IPR.

High Quality Rendering

When high quality rendering is turned on, the scene views are drawn in high quality by the hardware renderer. This lets you see a very good representation of the final render's look without having to software render the scene.

1 Enabling high quality rendering

- In the Perspective view, press **5**, **6** or **7**.

Note: *High quality rendering is not available while in wireframe.*

- Enable **Renderer → High Quality Rendering**.
- Enable **Lighting → Shadows**.

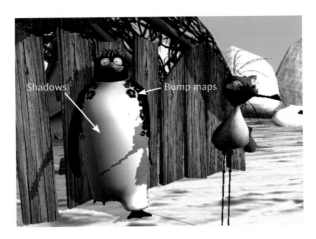

High quality rendering

Tip: *If you require faster playback or camera tumbling while using high quality rendering, turn on **Shading → Interactive Shading.***

Note: *If the surfaces appear black even when you have lights in your scene you might need to reverse the surface so the normals point outwards.*

mental ray

Perhaps the most complex and powerful rendering type available in Maya is mental ray ®. It offers many solutions for the creation of photorealistic renders, such as Global Illumination, caustic reflections and refractions, support for High Dynamic Range Imaging (HDRI), custom shaders and motion blurred reflections and shadows.

In this exercise, you will open an existing scene that includes the penguin with animation, reflection and lighting. Using mental ray, the shadows will have motion blur and the motion blur on the penguin will be reflected into a mirror.

1 Scene file

- Select **File** → **Open** and choose *21-rendering_01.ma* without saving changes to the previous scene.

2 Open the Render Settings

- Select **Window** → **Rendering Editors** → **Render Settings...**
- In the **Render Settings** window, select **Render Using** → **mental ray**.

   Doing so changes the renderer to mental ray instead of Maya software.

 Tip: *If mental ray is not available, you must load the Mayatomr.mll plug-in in the* **Window** → **Settings/Preferences** → **Plug-ins Manager**.

3 Set the rendering options

To render the animation, you must set up the scene's file extensions to indicate a rendered sequence. You must also set up the start and end frames.

- Click on the **Common** tab.
- From the **Image File Output** section, set the following:

   File Name Prefix to *mentalRay*

   This sets the name of the animated sequence.

   Frame/Animation Ext *to:*

   name.#.ext

   This sets up Maya to render a numbered sequence of images.

   Start Frame to **1;**

   End Frame to **10;**

   By Frame to **1.**

4 Set up the mental ray Render Settings for motion blur

- Under the **mental ray** tab, select **Quality → ProductionMotionblur**.

  This image quality preset automatically turns on high quality motion blur. It also sets up raytracing, as well as high quality anti-alias and texture sampling values for mental ray.

5 Perform a test render

- Go to frame **10**.

- Make the *Perspective* view active.

- Select **Render → Render Current Frame...**

mental ray ® rendering

Note: *Notice that the reflection and shadows in the scene have a motion blur.*

6 Batch render

- Select **Render → Batch Render**.

Tip: *If you have a computer with multiple processors, it is recommended that you set* **Use all Available Processors** *to* **On** *in the batch render options, since the render can be time-consuming.*

- When the render is complete, select **Render → Show Batch Render...** This will activate the fcheck utility to play back the animated sequence.

  OR

- From the browser, select one of the frames of the animation, then click **Open**.

Lesson 21: Rendering

Maya Vector

The Maya Vector renderer can output files in 2D vector format. It can also be used to create stylized flat renderings seen in illustrations and 2D animation.

Using the previous scene, you will set up a Maya Vector render.

1 **Set up the depth map shadows**

- Select *pointLight1* and open the Attribute Editor.
- Under the *spotLightShape1* tab, expand the **Shadows** section.
- Set **Use Depth Map Shadows** to **On**.
- Change the **Shadow Color** to a **dark grey**.

2 **Open the Maya Vector Render Settings**

- Select **Window** → **Rendering Editors** → **Render Settings** ...
- In the **Render Settings** window, select **Render Using** → **Maya Vector**.

3 **Set up the Maya Vector options**

- Select the **Maya Vector** tab.
- In the **Fill Options** section, set the following:

   Fill objects to **On**;

   Fill style to **Single color**;

   Show back faces to **On**;

   Shadows to **On**;

   Highlights to **On**;

   Reflections to **On**.

- In the **Edge Options** section, select the following:

   Include edges to **On**;

   Edge weight preset to **3.0 pt**;

   Edge style to **Outlines**.

4 **Perform a test render**

- Make the Perspective view active.
- Select **Render** → **Render Current Frame**...

Maya Vector rendering

Note: *You may experience compatibility issues with the Maya Vector renderer on Intel-based Macs.*

5   Batch render

- **Repeat** step **7** from the previous exercise to render the sequence.

Maya Hardware

Not to be confused with the Hardware Render Buffer, which will be introduced in the next project, the Maya hardware renderer allows you to create broadcast resolution images faster than with the software renderer.

In many cases, the quality of the output will be high enough to go directly to broadcast, but some advanced shadows, reflections and post-process effects cannot be produced with the hardware renderer. The final image quality of the Maya hardware renderer is significantly higher than that of the viewport and Hardware Render Buffer.

1   Set up the depth map shadows

- Make sure the **Use Depth Map Shadows** attribute for the *pointLight1* is still **On** from the previous exercise.

2   Open the Maya Hardware Render Settings

- Select **Window** → **Rendering Editors** → **Render Settings...**

- In the **Render Settings** window, select **Render Using** → **Maya Hardware**.

• Select the **Maya Hardware** tab.

• Under the **Quality** section, set **Presets** to **Production Quality.**

• Under the **Render Options** section, set **Motion Blur** to **On**.

3 Perform a test render

• Make the *Perspective* view active.

• Select **Render** → **Render Current Frame...**

You cannot see a reflection in the mirror since the raytracing feature is unavailable with the hardware renderer. However, the renderer is otherwise capable of fast, high quality rendering, including texture mapped reflections, depth map shadows and motion blur.

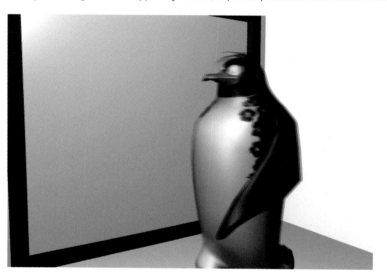

Maya hardware render

Note: *You might need to reverse some surfaces in order to render them correctly.*

4 Batch render

• **Repeat** step **7** from the mental ray exercise to render the sequence.

Conclusion

You have now completed this short introduction to the rendering engines available in Maya. The Maya IPR helps speed up the creative process and allows you to explore fast shading, lighting and texturing possibilities. For more mental ray ®, Maya Vector, Maya hardware and Maya software rendering tutorials, see the Maya online documentation.

In the next project, you will model using the third surface type available in Maya—subdivision surfaces. You will also experiment with more animation, rigid bodies and particles.

Project 04

In this project, you will model and texture BigZ's surfboard and medallion using subdivision (SubD) surfaces tools. You will then try more animation techniques using Trax, motion paths, particles and dynamics. Finally, you will learn about MEL scripting so you can automate some tasks and simplify your everyday work.

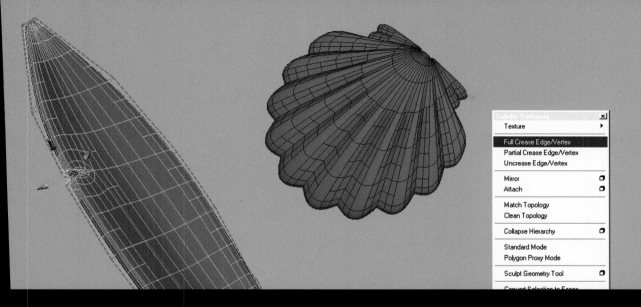

Lesson 22
SubD Modeling

Initial set-up

Start a new file within the project4 directory copied onto your system.

1 Set the current project

- Select **File** → **Project** → **Set...**
- Select the *project4* directory.

2 Create a new scene

- Select **File** → **New Scene**.

Modeling a surfboard

In order to learn about subdivision surfaces, you will model a simple surfboard to be used by BigZ later in this project. You will start with a polygonal cube primitive. You will then convert the cube to a subdivision surface. The basic form will be constructed using the *Subdivision Surfaces' Poly Proxy Mode*.

Poly Proxy mode creates an unshaded polygonal cage around the subdivision surface, similar to the one used by the Smooth Proxy polygonal tool. This cage can be edited using the same set of tools as a regular polygon. The subdivision surface will remain smooth and maintain the history of edits made on the proxy object.

1 Primitive cube

- Select **Create** → **Polygon Primitives** → **Cube**.
- Set the modeling view to **Shading** → **Smooth Shade All**.
- Change the construction history of the cube as follows:

  Width to **5**;

  Height to **1**;

  Depth to **20**;

  Subdivisions Width to **2**;

  Subdivisions Height to **1**;

  Subdivisions Depth to **6**.

- **Translate** the cube above the grid.

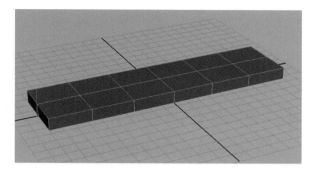

The start cube

2 **Convert to subdivision surface**

- With the cube selected, select **Modify** → **Convert** → **Polygons to Subdiv**.

- Press the **3** hotkey for a smooth display of the surface.

- **Rename** the surface *board*.

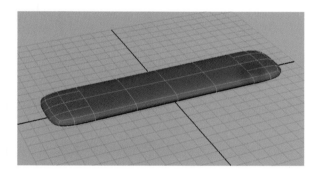

Smooth shaded subdivision surface

> **Note:** *You could create a SubD primitive from the* **Create** → **Subdiv Primitives** *menu, but you would not have primitive construction history. This is the reason why you have started from a polygonal cube.*

3 **Poly Proxy mode**

- Press **F4** to enable the **Surfaces** menu set.

- Select **Subdiv Surfaces** → **Polygon Proxy Mode**.

- In the **Outliner**, set **Display** → **Shapes** to **On.**

- Click the **+** sign next to *board* to display the shape nodes beneath.

*A new node called boardShapeHistPoly
has been created and grouped
underneath the board node. This is the
proxy node that you will edit using the
polygon toolset.*

4   Tweak the vertices

The marking menu of subdivision surfaces
allows quick selection of subdivision tools
and will be used extensively throughout
this lesson.

Outliner with the proxy object selected

- **RMB** over the *board*

- Select **Vertex** from the marking menu.

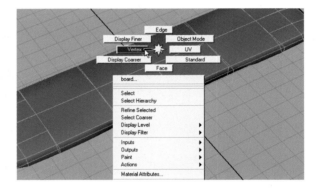

Marking menu display

- From the *top* and *side* views, shape the outline of the board.

- Select the central vertices and **translate** them down so the board takes a scoop shape.

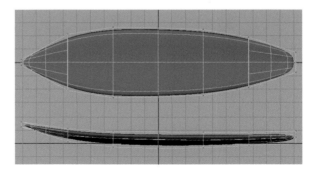

The basic shape of the board

5 **Edge loops**

- Go into **Object** mode.

- Press **F3** to select the **Polygons** menu set.

- With the *board* selected, select **Edit Mesh** → **Offset Edge Loop Tool**.

- **Click+drag** on the central edge of the *board* to insert symmetrical edge loops across its length.

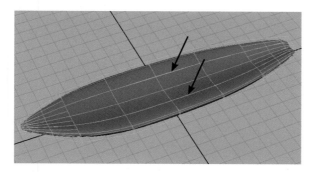

The inserted edge loops

6 **Extrude three fins**

Underneath the board, you will extrude three small fins. The central fin, located on the central axis, will require two polygonal faces.

- Select **Edit Mesh** → **Insert Edge Loop Tool**.

- **Click+drag** to insert **two** edge loops across the width of the back of the board.

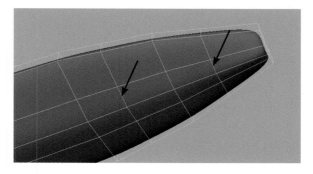

The inserted edge loops for the fins

- Make sure to enable **Edit Mesh** → **Keep Faces Together**.

- **RMB** on the *board* and select **Face**.

- Select the bottom **four** faces where the three fins should be.

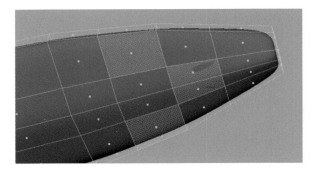

The faces to extrude

- Press **F3** to enable the **Polygons** menu set.
- Select **Edit Mesh** → **Extrude**.
- **Scale** the faces on their **X-axis** so they are narrower.
- **Extrude** the faces **twice** as follows:

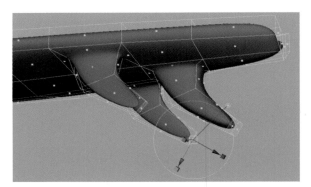

The fin extrusions

Note: *At this time, the geometry doesn't look exactly like it should, but this will be fixed later in the lesson.*

7 Tweak the central fin

You may notice the central fin is wider than the other ones since it was extruded from two faces. You will now correct this.

- **RMB** on the *board* and select **Vertex**.
- Select the central vertices on the fin.

Tip: *You may go into wireframe mode to ease the selection process.*

- **Scale** the vertices on their **X-axis** to narrow the central fin.

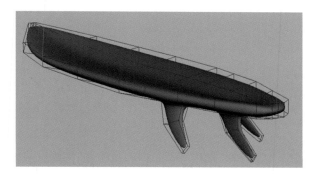

The board so far

8   Save your work

- **Save** your scene as *22-board_01.ma*.

Standard mode

So far, you have been using Poly Proxy mode to create a smooth subdivision surface by editing a few faces and edges on a simple polygon mesh. The polygonal cage surrounding the subdivision surface has provided enough detail to this point.

Now, you will leave Poly Proxy mode and edit the model using Standard mode. You will see in the rest of the lesson that in Standard mode you can edit vertices, faces and edges. As well, you can adjust edge or vertex creases and achieve a greater level of detail using the hierarchical levels of refinement available with subdivision surfaces.

Creases

When defining an edge or a vertex to be creased, the underlying subdivision surface is changed in order to get the geometry closer to the defined edge or vertex.

Lesson 22: SubD Modeling

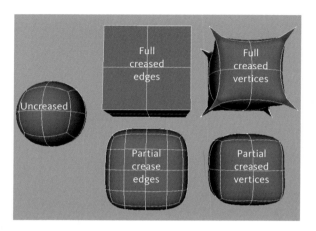

Different crease examples

1   **Leave Poly Proxy mode**

   • Select the *board*.

   • Select **Subdiv Surfaces** → **Standard Mode** from the **Surfaces** menu set.

   This eliminates the Poly Proxy mode geometry. The proxy can be regenerated and edited by accessing **Subdiv Surfaces** → **Poly Proxy Mode** *again if necessary, but the construction history will not be rebuilt.*

2   **Display subdivision surface edges**

   • **RMB** over the subdivision surface and select **Edges** from the marking menu.

   This displays edges at the same coordinates as the proxy vertices and refers to the roughest level of subdivision surface refinement. Edges of subdivision surfaces look similar to NURBS hulls and can help realize the shape defining the surface. They can also be selected individually, just like polygonal edges.

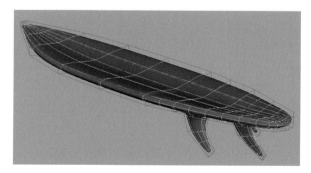

Subdivision surface edges

3   **Partial creases**

- Select the two edge loops defining the outside of the board.

- Select **Subdiv Surfaces → Partial Crease Edge/Vertex**.

   A partial crease will define and sharpen the surface outlined by the selected edges or vertices. Notice the creased edges are displayed with hashed lines.

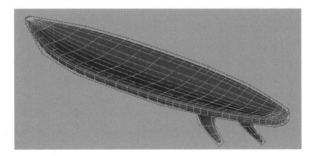

The partial creases

Note: *Notice how the subdivision surface's topology was increased in order to reflect the changes.*

4   **Full creases**

- Select the edge loops where the fins meet with the board.

- Select **Subdiv Surfaces → Full Crease Edge/Vertex**.

   Notice how the fins now connect to the board with right angles.

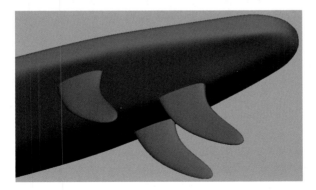

Fully creased edges

5   **Save your work**

- **Save** your scene as *22-board_02.ma*.

Lesson 22: SubD Modeling

Tweak the board shape

The geometry you have built is completed, but you could refine it further. You will now go back into Polygon Proxy mode and split some more faces.

1   Polygon Proxy mode

- **RMB** on the *board* and select **Polygon**.

    This is a faster way to switch between Standard and Polygon mode.

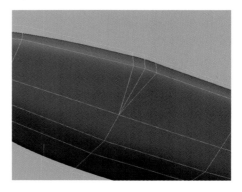

The new edges on the side of the board

2   Split polygonal faces

- Select **Edit Mesh → Split Polygon Tool** from the Polygons menu set.

- Add some new edges to be used to create a dent on the side of the board.

3   Crease

- **RMB** on the *board* and select **Standard**.

- **RMB** on the *board* and select **Edge**.

- **Move** the vertical edge towards the inside of the board.

- Select all the edges defining the dent.

- Select **Subdiv Surfaces → Partial Crease Edge/Vertex**.

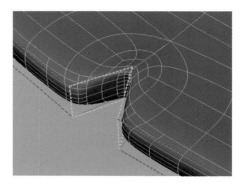

The board's dent

4   Refine the model

- Spend some time refining the board using both the Polygonal Proxy and Standard modes.

5   Overrides

Since the board is basically ready to be animated, you will now add animation overrides. It is important to have animation overrides when animating any object as a whole. For instance, the board will later be constrained when BigZ picks it up, and then later animated following a motion path. Since the attributes will be locked by those connections, you will not be able to add any refinement to the motion of the object. With overrides, you can use lower nodes to add some custom animation such as rotation or translation.

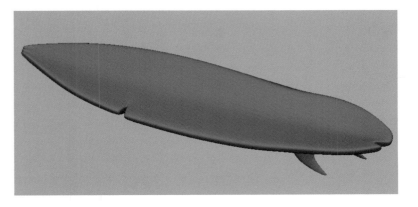

The final board shape

- Select the *board*.

- Press **Ctrl+g** to group it **three times**.

- **Rename** the top group to *master*.

- **Rename** the first child group to *transOverride*.

- **Rename** the second child group to *rotOverride*.

6   Save your work

- **Save** your scene as *22-board_03.ma*.

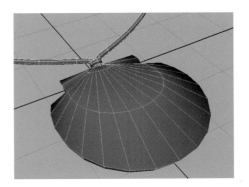

The board overrides

Refine a medallion

In order to experiment more with the subdivision surfaces tools, you will now refine an existing model to be used for BigZ's shell medallion. This will allow you to model with a finer level of detail on the SubD model.

1   Scene file

- **Open** the scene file *22-medallion_01. ma* from the support files.

  This scene contains a pre-modeled medallion and strap.

BigZ's necklace

2   Convert to subD

- With the *medallion* selected, select
  **Modify → Convert →
  Polygons to Subdiv**.

- Press the **3** hotkey for a smooth display
  of the surface.

- **Rename** the surface to *medallion*.

3   Display finer levels of detail

- **RMB** on the *medallion* and
  select **Vertex**.

  *You should now see the vertices of the
  surface at the base level. The base level
  components are basically the same as
  those in Polygon mode.*

- **Tweak** the shape using vertices and
  notice how the surface reacts.

  *You will soon realize that there are not
  enough components to refine the
  seashell's shape.*

- **RMB** on the *medallion* and select
  Display Level → 1.

  *Doing so changes the displayed level of
  components. You were previously on
  the base display level (0), and now the
  second level of refined components is
  displayed (1). Notice how only the back of the medallion requires second level components
  in order to achieve the required shape.*

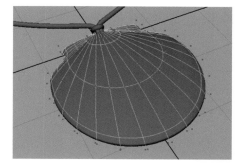

Base level vertices

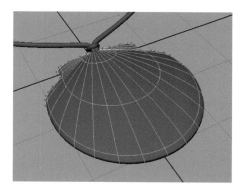

Level 1 vertices

> **Note:** *Notice that every time you refine the components, only the components available in
> that display level are shown.*

4   Refine components

At this point, you want to tweak the shape of the seashell so it is embossed, but there
are not enough level 1 components to use. You will now increase the number of level 1
components.

- **RMB** on the *medallion* and select **Display Coarser**.

  You are now back on level 0.

- Select all the vertices.

- **RMB** on the *medallion* and select **Refine selected**.

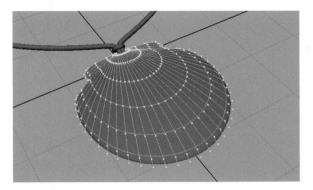

Finer vertices

5   Create more detail

- While in wireframe, **select** a row of vertices every three rows.

  These vertices will be used to create an embossed shape.

- **Deselect** the vertices underneath and at the back of the shell.

- **Scale** the vertices to get the following shape:

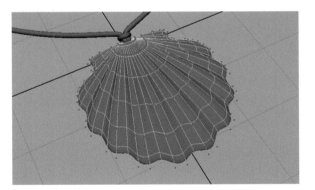

The embossed seashell

Note: *It is possible that gaps appears when editing the subdivision surfaces. To resolve this, simply press the 3 hotkey to increase the surface's smoothness.*

6 Lower display level

- **RMB** on the *medallion* and select **Display Level** → **o.**

  Doing so brings you back to the base level of refinement. You now have access to all the original vertices on the surface.

- Try to move vertices from the base level.

  Notice how the vertices in finer levels are updating accordingly, and are totally dependent on the lower level components.

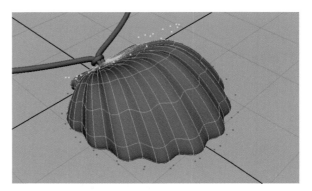

Moving lower level components

Tip: *It is not recommended to add topology in Polygon mode when finer components have been changed in Standard mode. Doing so produces unpredictable results.*

7 Creases

- **Undo** any changes you made in the last step.

- **RMB** on the medallion and select **Display Level** → **1.**

- Select the edges located in the grooves of the seashell, then select **Subdiv Surfaces** → **Full Crease Edge/Vertex.**

  Note how the surface updates to add more topology on finer component levels to reflect the changes.

Note: *Even when undoing refinement actions, the subdivision surface will keep its refined resolution. You will see how to clean up the model later in this lesson.*

- You can review the added components by selecting **Display Level** → **2** and higher.

Creased geometry

8   Clean up the model

When modeling with subdivision surfaces, geometry will be automatically added to your model and sometimes this geometry will not be necessary. In order to remove the extra information, you can clean the surface's topology.

- Select the model, and then select **Subdiv Surfaces → Clean Topology**.

Unused components are automatically removed from the surface.

9   Save your work

- **Save** your scene as *22-medallion_02.ma*.

Conclusion

You have now gone through the process of modeling complex forms with subdivision surfaces. You learned how to refine components and how to crease edges and vertices.

In the next lesson, you will texture BigZ's surfboard and medallion.

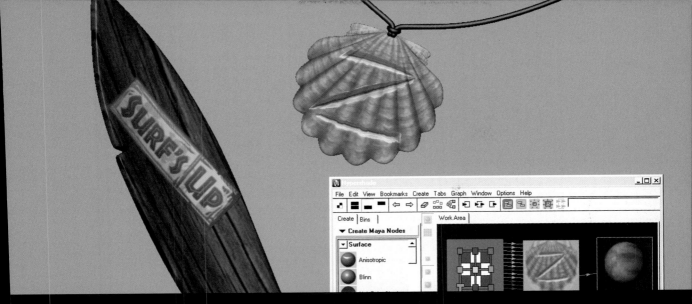

Lesson 23
SubD Texturing

In this lesson, you will texture the SubD models from the last lesson. You will see that SubD texturing is quite similar to polygonal UV mapping learned in Lesson 8. In order to try new techniques, you will learn how to project textures onto a surface and how to convert a shading network to a single file texture. You will also learn how to import and export shading networks. Finally, you will import the medallion into BigZ's scene file.

In this lesson, you will learn the following:

- How to manipulate SubD UVs
- How to create and tweak texture projections

Projections

You will now create a shading network to project a logo on BigZ's surfboard.

1 Scene file

- **Open** the scene *22-board_03.ma*.

  This scene contains the SubD surfboard from Lesson 22.

2 Correct the UV placement

The UV placement of the SubD surface is not appropriate for proper texturing. You will now use automatic mapping to lay out the UVs in a better way.

- With the board selected, select **Subdiv Surfaces** → **Texture** → **Automatic Mapping.**

  This will help to better visualize assigned textures.

3 Projected texture

- **Open** the Hypershade.

- **Create** a **Phong** material and assign it to the surfboard.

- **Rename** the material to *boardM*.

- Open the Attribute Editor for the *boardM*.

- Click on the **Map** button for the **Color** attribute.

- In the Create Render Node window, make sure to select the **As projection** option.

- Click the **File** button to create a projected file texture.

  Notice the place3dTexture1 icon located at the origin in your scene and in the Hypershade.

- Select the *file1* texture node, then in the Attribute Editor, click on the **Browse** icon next to the **Image Name** attribute.

- Select the file named *logo.tif* from the *sourceimages* directory in the *support_files* of the current project or any other logo you might want.

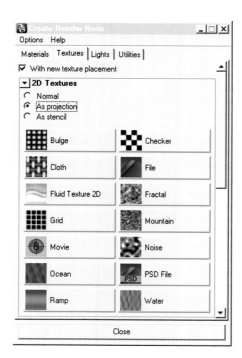

The Create Render Node window

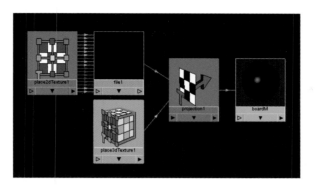

The projection network in the Hypershade

4 Place the projection

The projection of the texture is determined by the 3D texture placement node located at the origin. At this time, the texture is not projected correctly on the surfboard. You will now correct this.

- Select the *place3dTexture* node from the viewport.

- **Rotate** it by **-90** degrees on its **X-axis**.

- **Rotate** it by **90** degrees on its **Y-axis**.

- In the Attribute Editor, click the **Fit to Group BBox**.

  The projection node will move to fit the bounding box of the surfaces using this texture.

5 Increase the texture display quality

The viewport display of a projected texture is quite low since a projection is very heavy to refresh. Until you finish placing the projected logo, you will increase the display resolution.

- Select the *boardM* shader.

- In the Attribute Editor, set the **Texture Resolution** from the **Hardware Texturing** section to **Highest**.

The projected logo

Lesson 23: SubD Texturing

>
>
> **Tip:** *In the Attribute Editor for the projection node under the **Extra Attributes** section, you can set the **Resolution** of the texture to be higher or to match your texture size. Doing so will increase the quality of the display in the viewport but does not affect the render quality.*

6 Place the projection

- Select the *place3dTexture* node.

- Click the **Interactive Placement** button in the Attribute Editor, or press **t** on your keyboard to access the placement tool.

- **Scale** and **rotate** the projected logo as you would like.

The logo placement

7 Projection options

At this time, the texture repeats itself outside the projection box and is projected inverted on the other side of the board. There are options you can use to disable this functionality.

- Select the *place3dTexture* node.

- In the Channel Box, highlight the *projection1* node from the **Outputs** section.

- Set **Wrap** to **Off**.

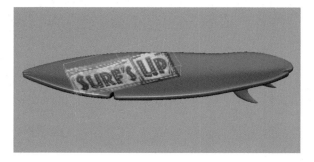

No texture wrapping

Note: *The projection manipulator changes when you set* **Wrap** *to* **Off**. *This is because you can now define the depth of the projection and prevent the texture from being inverted on the other side of the surface.*

- **Move** the manipulator up on its **Y-axi**s and **rotate** it slightly so the texture doesn't get projected underneath the board.

Note: *Depending on the shape of your geometry, it might be impossible to get the texture to be projected only at the location you want. In that case, you will need to convert the projection to a file texture and correct it in a paint program. You will see how to convert to a file texture in the next exercise.*

8   Change the default color

As you can see, grey is the default color used by a projection when wrapping is off. The default color fills all space outside the texture's range. You will now change this color to blue so it mixes well with the logo.

- Select the *projection1* node from the Hypershade and open its Attribute Editor.

- Under the **Color Balance** section, click the **Default Color** swatch.

- In the Color Chooser window, change **HSV** to **RGB**.

- Change the range next to **RGB** to **0 to 255**.

  Doing so allows you to manually enter an **RGB** *color value ranging from* **0** *to* **255***.*

- Set the **RGB** values to **16**, **78** and **151** respectively.

  This is the exact color used on the boundary of the logo texture.

- Click the **Accept** button.

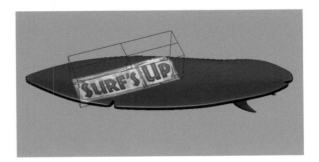

The changed default color

9 **Map the default color**

You could also map the **Default Color** with another file texture of wood to give a wooden look to the surfboard.

- **Map** the **Default Color** of the *projection1* node with another projected **file** texture.

- In the new file texture node, browse for the *wood.tif* texture from the *sourceimages* directory.

- **Place** the second projection manipulator to fit the surfboard as follows:

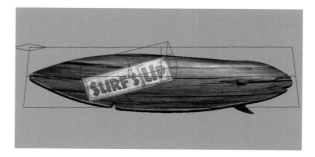

The wood projection

10 **Save you work**

- **Save** your scene as *23-boardTxt_01.ma*.

Convert to texture

Since the logo shading network is becoming fairy complex and heavy to compute in the viewport, you will convert the network to a single file texture.

The shading network will then be much simpler to render since the texture will perfectly fit the UVs of the surfboard geometry.

1 **Convert to shading network**

Autodesk® Maya® software can convert a complex shading network into a single texture file.

- Select the *boardM* material and **Shift-select** the *board* geometry.

- From the Hypershade, select **Edit** → **Convert to File Texture (Maya Software)** → ❏.

- In the option window, set the following:

    UV Range to **Entire Range**;

    X Resolution to **512**;

    Y Resolution to **512**;

    Image Format to **Tiff (tif)**.

- Click the **Convert and Close** button.

  Maya software will convert the network to a texture and will create and assign a new network using only a single texture. The new texture is automatically saved in the current project's sourceimages folder.

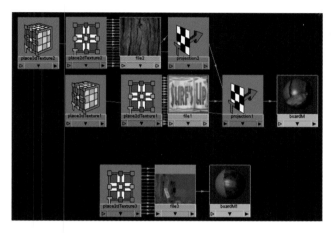

Before and after the conversion

Tip: *You must make sure that the UVs of the surface can accommodate a single texture to cover all of its geometry. If some UVs overlap, the texture might not reflect exactly what you have just created.*

2 **Delete unused render nodes**

- In the Hypershade, select **Edit →
  Delete Unused Nodes.**

  Doing so will delete the earlier shading network since it is no longer required.

3 **Edit the converted texture**

If required, you can edit the converted texture found in the *sourceimages* folder of the current project to fix any problems with the projections and then reload your file texture to see your changes.

The converted file texture

4 **Save you work**

- **Save** your scene as *23-boardTxt_02.ma.*

Texture reference objects

Projected textures work well on static geometry, but there can be unintended results when the surface is moving or deforming. This is because the object is moving without the projection node, which causes a texture sliding problem. To correct this, you can set up a non-deformed reference object to lock the texture on the geometry.

Tip: *Using texture reference objects is best when an object is deforming. Otherwise, it is easier to simply parent the projection node to the model itself.*

- Select a surface with a projected texture assigned to it.
- Under the **Rendering** menu set, select **Texturing → Create Texture Reference Object**.

An unselectable and unrenderable object duplicate will appear as wireframe in the viewport. This object is only selectable through the Outliner or the Hypergraph.

Note: *By converting a shading network to a texture, you do not require a projection and a reference object. The texture fits the geometry perfectly.*

Import a shading network

To map BigZ's medallion, you will import an existing texture into your scene and assign it to the surface. This is a good technique to know when you need to manage lots of objects, since you can build a library of shaders and simply import the required one without recreating it from scratch.

1   Scene file

- **Open** the scene *22-medallion_02.ma* from the last lesson.

This scene contains the final medallion geometry.

2   Prepare the UVs

Before you can import a shading network, you must ensure that the model has proper UVs. Mapping the UVs on a SubD model is a little more complex than for polygons. You must ensure that that you select every face on which you need to affect the UVs. Since the geometry has multiple levels, you must select all the components you need on each level.

- **RMB** on the *medallion* and select **UV**.
- Select every UV component on the model.
- Select **Subdiv Surfaces → Convert Selection to Faces.**

Doing so ensures that you have every face selected on every level.

- Select **Subdiv Surfaces** → **Texture** → **Planar Mapping** → ❑.
- In the option window, set **Mapping direction** to **Y-axis.**
- Click the **Project** button.

  The medallion now has proper UVs.

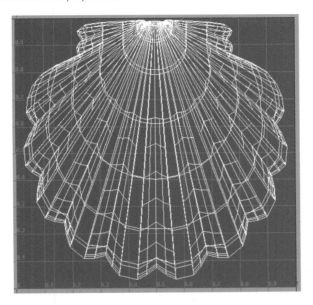

The SubD UVs

3   Import shading networks

Instead of creating the necklace shaders, you will now import shaders that were already saved in the *support_files*.

- From the Hypershade, select **File** → **Import...**
- In the browse window, select the file named *necklace.ma* from the folder *renderData\ shaders* from the current project's *support_files*.
- Click the **Import** button.

  The shaders from this scene file are now in your scene. There are two shaders—one for the medallion and one for the necklace's strap.

4   Assign the shaders

- Under the **Materials** tab in the Hypershade, **MMB+drag** the *medallionM* shader onto the *medallion* object in your scene.

  Doing so assigns the shader to the object.

- **Repeat** the previous step to assign the *strapM* shader to the necklace's *strap*.

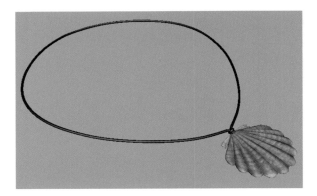

The necklace with shaders

5 Modify the texture

- Use the **3D Paint Tool** or a paint program to add the letter Z to BigZ's shell.

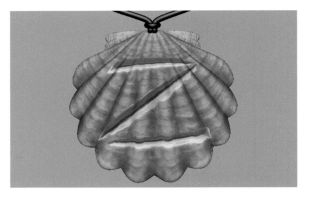

The added detail to the seashell

> **Note:** *Because the model uses a planar projection, any modification to the texture will also appear on the back of the shell.*

6 Exporting shading networks

If you want to export one or more of your shading networks, do the following:

- Open the Hypershade and select the topmost shader of your shading network. If you select more than one shader, then they will all get exported at the same time in the same file.

- Still in the Hypershade, select **File → Export Selected Network.**

- Choose a file name that reflects the selected shaders and click the **Export** button.

  The shaders are exported by themselves in a Maya file located in the renderData/shaders of the current project.

7   Delete the history

- Select **Edit → Delete All by Type → History.**

8   Save your work

- **Save** your scene as *23-medallionTxt_01.ma.*

Import a scene file

Now that the medallion is done, you must import it into BigZ's final scene file.

1   Scene file

- **Open** the scene *13-bigzRig_05.ma* from the second project.

  This scene contains the final character rig and is also the scene file referenced by other animated scene files. Changing and overwriting this scene will also update BigZ in all his other scene files.

2   Import the medallion

- Select **File → Import → ❑** from the main menu.

- In the option window, set the following:

  Use namespaces to **Off**;

  Resolve: All nodes with: this string to *necklace.*

- Click the **Import** button.

- In the browse window, choose the *23-medallionTxt_01.ma* scene file you have just created in project 4.

- Click the **Import** button.

  The necklace is now imported in the character scene file.

3   Place the necklace

- **Scale**, **move** and **rotate** the necklace to fit BigZ's neck.

- **Parent** the *necklace* group to the *geo* group.

- **Rename** the imported nodes to your liking.

- With the necklace group selected, select **Modify → Freeze Transformations**.

The necklace on BigZ

4   Deform the necklace strap

There are several techniques to bind a necklace to a character which can give you different levels of control over the animation of the necklace. This example will be quite simple and will have the necklace follow the body geometry without allowing you to animate the necklace on its own. You will do so by using a wrap deformer, which will ensure the necklace is moving as closely as possible to the skin.

- Select the *strap*, then **Shift-select** the *body* geometry.

   This selection order is important since the wrap deformer requires the object to deform to be selected first, followed by its influence.

- Select **Create Deformers → Wrap → ❑.**

- In the option window, set the following:

   Weight threshold to **1.0**;

   Use max distance to **On**;

   Max distance to **1.0**;

   Influence type to **Faces**.

- Click the **Create** button.

   If you rotate any joints in the character set-up, notice how the necklace perfectly follows.

5   Render stats

The wrap deformer changes the render stats of the deformer object so it is not renderable. Since this is not desirable, you will have to change back the render stats of the body object.

- Open the Attribute Editor for the *body* surface.

- Under the **Render Stats** section, set the following:

    Casts Shadows to **On**;

    Receive Shadows to **On**;

    Motion Blur to **On**;

    Primary Visibility to **On**;

    Visible In Reflections to **On**;

    Visible In Refractions to **On**;

6   Skin the medallion

To keep things simple, you will bind the medallion directly to the spine joint.

- Select the *medallion*, then **Shift-select** the *spine1* joint.

- Select **Skin → Bind Skin → Rigid Bind.**

The necklace perfectly following the character skin

7   Save your scene

- **Save** the scene as *23-bigzRig_01.ma.*

> **Note:** *If you want files referencing the character to be automatically updated with the necklace, simply save and overwrite the original file.*

Conclusion

In this lesson, you have learned how to manipulate UVs on SubDs and how to create shading networks in different ways. In the process you have also learned the basics of the wrap deformer. You should now feel comfortable texturing any type of geometry.

In the next lesson, you will create some more animation with the new models.

Lesson 23: SubD Texturing

Lesson 24
More Animation

Since you have created the surfboard model, you can now practice animation skills from a more artistic point of view. In this lesson, you will animate BigZ picking up his board next to his house. This time, rather than approaching animation from a mathematical standpoint, you will have to establish key poses based on artistic knowledge to generate the animation.

In this lesson, you will learn the following:

- How to update a reference
- How to establish key poses
- How to refine in-betweens
- How to playblast an animation
- How to fix the timing of your animation

References

When you first animated BigZ, you saw how to create a reference. You will now open that same animation file, but this time you will also reference the environment and the board. You will also update the character's reference to the one with the necklace created in the last lesson.

1   Scene file

* **Open** the scene file *20-lightsEffects_03.ma* from the last project's *scenes* directory.

2   Update a reference

* Select **File → Reference Editor.**

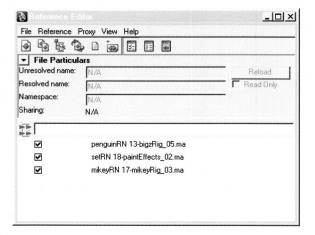

The Reference Editor

In the displayed window, you can see all the references currently in the scene. Notice how the scene file points to the older BigZ character scene. You will now correct this to reference the new set-up with the necklace.

* Highlight the *penguinRN* reference.

* Select **Reference → Replace Reference**.

* In the browse window, select the *23-bigzRig_01.ma* scene from the current project.

* Click the **Reference** button.

The character is now updated.

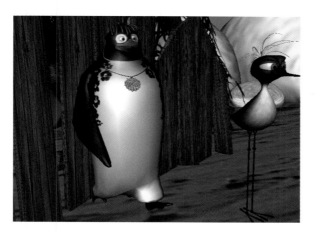

BigZ with his necklace

3 Create references

- Select **File** → **Create Reference** → ❑ from the main interface menu of the Reference Editor.

- Set **Resolve all nodes with this string:** *board.*

  This will prefix all the reference nodes with the string board.

- Click on the **Reference** button.

- In the browse dialog that appears, select the file *23-boardTxt_02.ma* from the fourth project, and then click **Reference**.

  The file will load into the current one.

> **Note:** *You may have to relink textures that are not automatically found. To do so, simply open the Hypershade, select the Texture tab and change the path of the texture through the Attribute Editor.*

4 Scaling

Looking at the elements in your scene; if there are scaling issues, correct the problem by scaling the geometry group either in this file or in the referenced file.

> **Tip:** *It is recommended to fix scaling issues in the referenced files so you will not have to fix the scaling everytime you reference the scene files together.*

- Use the board's *master* node to scale it and place it in front of the house.

The entire scene

> **Note:** *If the top node's scale attributes are non-keyable and unlocked, they will not show in the Channel Box, but the Scale Tool will still work. Alternatively, you can access the scale attributes in the Attribute Editor. If the scale attributes of the node are locked, you need to unlock them in the referenced file and then reopen the file.*

5 Save your work

- **Save** this scene to *24-moreAnimation_01.ma* in the current project's *scene* directory.

Picking the board up

Now that your scene is properly set up, you will animate BigZ picking up his surfboard. Once this is done, the new sequence will be saved as a Trax clip.

1 Penguin character

- In the **Active Character** menu next to the Range Slider, select the *penguin* character set.

2 Set the time range

- Set the **Start Time** and **Playback Start Time** to **1**.
- Set the **End Time** and **Playback End Time** to **50**.

3 Current time

- Move the current time indicator to frame **1**.

4   **Clear the Trax Editor**

As you may notice, BigZ is already animated in this scene. This is because the Trax Editor still contains the Trax walk cycle clip you create earlier. You will now clear the Trax Editor and start a new animation.

- Open the Trax Editor by selecting **Window → Animation Editors → Trax Editor**.

- If the walk clip is not visible, make sure to turn On the **List → Auto Load Selected Characters** options.

- Press **a** to frame all in the Trax Editor.

- Click on the *walk* clip to highlight it.

- Press **Delete** to remove it.

   The animation has now been removed, but the character has kept its initial step position which will be used as the starting pose of the new animation.

- Close the Trax Editor.

5   **Keyframe the start pose**

- Press the **s** hotkey to keyframe the entire *penguin* character.

- Enable the **Auto Key** button.

- **Translate** and **rotate** the penguin *master* so it is next to the door of the house.

The start pose

Tip: *Change the layer display to be **Reference**, to avoid picking other objects accidentally.*

6 Set keys for the picking up pose

- Go to frame **10**.

- Hold down the **w** hotkey then click in the view and choose **Object** from the marking menu.

  This changes the Move Tool's option.

- Bring the *rHeelControl* forward, next to the *lHeelControl*.

- Place the character as follows:

First pose

- Press the **s** key to set a key on the penguin character at this new position.

7 Set keys for the anticipation

- Go to frame **15**.

- Place the character as follows:

Anticipation pose

Tip: *Anticipation usually goes in the opposite direction of the actual motion.*

- Press the **s** key to set a key on the penguin character at this new position.

8 Constrain the board

Before you can make the character lift the object, you must first constrain the board to his hand. You will use the board's master for the constraint and any of the animation overrides to refine the board animation.

- Select the *rHandManip*, then **Shift-select** the board's *master*.
- Select **Constrain → Parent**.

   The board is now constrained to the hand for the entire animation range.

- Select the board's *parentConstraint1* node from the Outliner.
- **Keyframe** the **R Hand Manip Wo** attribute to **1** at frame **15**.
- **Keyframe** the **R Hand Manip Wo** attribute to **0** at frame **14**.

   The board is now constrained only starting at frame 15.

Tip: *Remember that if you move the timing of the animation, you will also have to move the constraint animation since it is not part of the character set.*

9 Set keys for the lifting pose

- Go to frame **20**.
- Place the character as follows with the board in mid air:

Lifting pose

- Press the **s** key to set a key on the penguin character at this new position.

10   Set keys to pose the board under the arm

- Go to frame **30**.
- Place the character as follows:

Grabbed pose

- Press the **s** key to set a key on the penguin character at this new position.

11   Set keys for the turning pose

- Go to frame **40**.
- Place the character spinning on his left foot, ready to take a step.

The turning pose

12 **Set keys for the next step pose**

- Go to frame **50**.

- Place the character bringing his right foot forward.

The final pose

Note: *It is a very difficult task to spin a character on himself and you might experience some problems when doing it. For instance, the set driven keys on the feet may no longer work correctly because there are no animation overrides allowing you to use both the set driven keys and the keyframe animation on the reverse foot se-tup. This is why much care must be taken at the rigging stage.*

13 **Tweak the animation**

- Scroll the timeline and tweak the poses to make the motion between them more fluid.

- Make sure you brought everything along when you moved the character.

- **Playback** the animation.

14   Playblast your animation

A playblast is a movie reflecting your scene animation. When making a playblast, Maya software generates the animation by grabbing the image directly from the active viewport, so make sure to display only what you want to see in your playblast.

- Frame the scene in the Perspective view to see it in its entirety.

- From the Show menu in the Perspective panel, hide object types that you do not want in your playblast such as **Grids**, **NURBS curves**, **Lights**, **Locators** and **Handles**.

- Press **6** if you want the textures to appear in your playblast.

- Select **Window** → **Playblast**.

  Maya software will render every frame, recording it into the playblast. Once the scene has been entirely played through, the playblast is displayed in your default movie player.

Note: *For more options on the playblast, select* **Window** → **Playblast** → ❏.

15   Animation refinement

Once you have seen the playblast and animation at its real speed, you can concentrate on correcting the motion and timing.

- Note areas that appear to be too fast or too slow in the playblast.

- To move a pose to a different frame, hold down **Shift** and click on a keyframe in the Time Slider.

- **Click+drag** the keyframe to the left to change the pose faster, and to the right to change the pose more slowly.

Note: *You might have to redo your playblast and perform some trial and error before finding the perfect animation speed.*

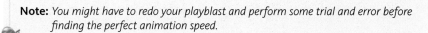

Tip: *Beginner animators tend to make everything slow motion when animating. Don't be afraid to have only 2 or 3 frames between your poses. An entire picking up motion should take about one second, which is only 24 frames.*

16   Save your work

- **Save** this scene to *24-moreAnimation_02.ma*.

Project 04

Create a Trax clip file

The animation is finished, so you will now create another Trax clip file.

1   Open the Trax Editor window

- Make sure that *penguin* is the current character set.

- Select **Window** → **Animation Editor** → **Trax Editor**.

2   Create a clip

- From the Trax Editor, select **Create** → **Animation Clip** → ❏.

- **In the Trax window, select Edit** → **Reset.**

- Set the following options:

   Name to *pickup;*

   Leave Keys in Timeline to **Off**;

   Clip to **Put Clip in Trax Editor and Visor**;

   Time Range to **Animation Curve**;

   Include Subcharacters in Clip to **Off**;

   Create Time Warp Curve to **Off**;

   Include Hierarchy to **On**.

- Click the **Create Clip** button.

- Press **a** in the Trax Editor to frame all.

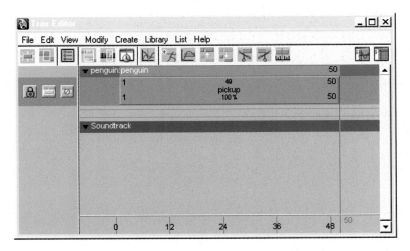

Pickup clip in Trax Editor

3   **Export the clip**

- Select **File → Visor...**
- Select the **Character Clips** tab to see the clip source.

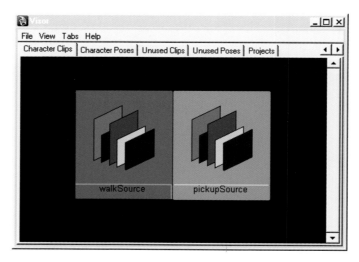

Pickup source clip in Visor

- Select the *pickupSource* clip.
- **RMB** on the clip and select **Export.**
- **Save** the clip as *BigZPickupExport*.
- **Close** the Visor.

> **Note:** *Since you are in a new project, you can either copy the other BigZWalkExport.ma file from the third project or export it again from here.*

4   **Save your work**

- **Save** this scene to *24-moreAnimation_03.ma*.

Conclusion

You have now completed a type of animation that requires much more artistic input. As you can see, a lot of practice is required to achieve good animation in an efficient manner and you might have to correct rigging problems as you work.

In the next lesson you will use the Trax Editor to combine the clips and create a new animated sequence.

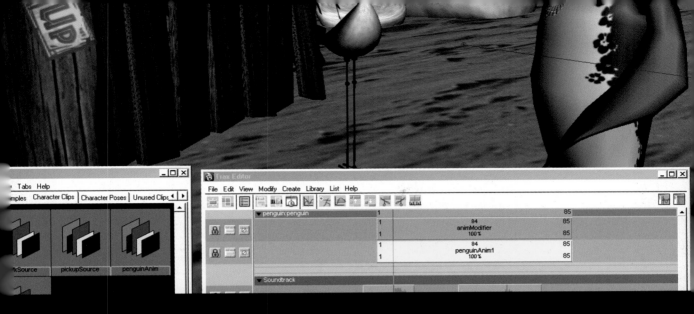

Lesson 25
Trax Editor

So far in this book, you have animated the penguin and created two Trax clips from the animated sequences. In this lesson, you will create a more complex motion by joining the walk clip with the pickup clip in the Trax Editor.

The advantage of working with Trax' non-linear animation lies in the ability to move, edit, connect and reuse multiple clips freely, without having to edit multiple time curves. You can also add sound files to the scene using Trax.

In this lesson, you will learn the following:

- How to work with relative and absolute clips
- How to clip, split, blend and merge clips
- How to use time wrap
- How to layer non-destructive keys over clips
- How to redirect animation
- How to use sound in Trax
- How to animate a two-node camera

Initial set-up

1   Scene file

- **Open** the file you saved at the end of the last lesson.

  OR

- **Open** the scene file *24-moreAnimation_03.ma.*

2   Set up the work area

- Set the **Playback Frame Range** to go from **1** to **200**.
- From the menus in any modeling window, select **Panels** → **Saved Layouts** → **Persp/Trax/Outliner**.

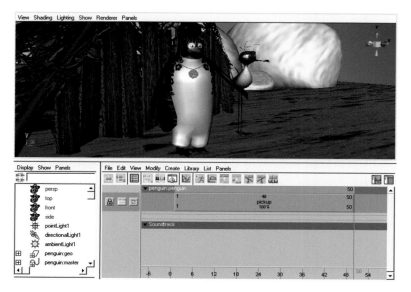

Persp/Trax/Outliner window layout

Generate the animation

The following exercise uses several Trax commands that will establish the animation of the penguin. The animation you want to achieve in the scene goes like this:

BigZ walks up to his house looking around. At the same time, Mikey looks at him, intrigued. BigZ picks up his board and swiftly turns around, getting ready to run toward the ocean.

1 **Load the first two clips**

- Select the *penguin* character from the **Current Character** menu at the bottom right of the interface.

  The Trax Editor will update, showing the pickup motion from the last lesson.

- Select **Library** → **Insert Clip** → **walkSource**.

  Both the walk and pickup clips are now in the Trax Editor.

- Press **a** to frame all.

- **Click+drag** each clip in the Trax Editor so that the *walk* clip starts at frame **1** and the *pickup* clip starts at frame **121**.

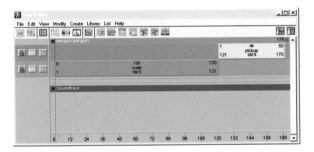

Walk and pickup clips

2 **Trim the walk clip**

- Scrub to frame **41** in the timeline.

  This is a good place to match the pickup clip, since it is a pose similar to the start pose.

- Select the *walk* clip.

- Select the **Trim After** icon from the Trax menu to **Trim** the clip after frame **41**.

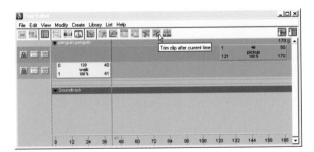

Trim the walk clip after frame 41

- **Move** the *pickup* clip to its new starting position at frame **41**.

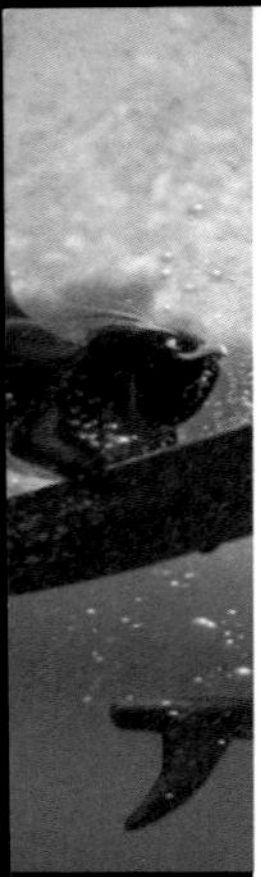

3   **View the clips with absolute offset**

- **Play** the animation by dragging the vertical time indicator in the Trax window.

    As the walk clip switches to the pickup clip during playback, you will see the penguin picks up the board back at its original keyframed position—or absolute offset.

4   **Change the pickup clip to relative offset**

- Select the *pickup* clip, then press **Ctrl+a** to open its Attribute Editor.

- Scroll to the **Channel Offsets** section and click the **All Relative** button.

- **Play** the animation.

    Now, as the walk clip switches to the pickup clip during playback, you will see that the penguin picks up the board from its new position at the end of the walk clip. This is because the clip's animation is relative to the end position of the clip preceding it.

5   **Ease out the walk clip**

At this point, you might notice a speed change between the end of the walk clip and the start of the pickup. The following steps will help smooth this.

- Select the *walk* clip.

- **RMB** on the clip and select **Create Time Wrap**.

    A time wrap is a curve that controls the speed of the clip animation. Using this, you will slow down the walk to have the penguin slow down before picking up the board.

- Click on the **Open Graph Editor** button located at the top right corner of the Trax Editor.

- Scroll down in the Graph Editor Outliner and highlight the **Time Wrap** attribute.

- Select the last keyframe and set its **Tangent** to **Flat**.

- With the keyframe still selected, select the left tangent manipulator.

- Press **w** to select the Move Tool, and then **MMB+drag** the tangent down a little, so it is not perfectly flat.

    If the tangent is perfectly flat, then the animation will gradually slow down in order to be a complete halt on its last frame. Moving the tangent down a little makes the animation slow down, but does not stop completely.

- Click on the **Open Trax Editor** button located at the top right corner of the Graph Editor.

- If you scrub in the animation, you will notice that the penguin is now slowing down before picking up the board.

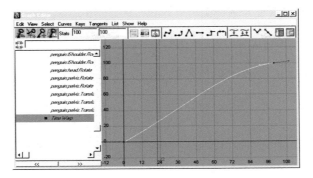

The time wrap curve

6 Blend between the two clips

- Select the *walk* clip, then **Shift-select** the *pickup* clip.

- Select **Create → Blend → ❑**.

- In the option window, set **Initial Weight Curve** to **Ease in out**.

- Click the **Create Blend** button.

- Select the *pickup* clip on its own and **drag** it so that it starts at frame **36**.

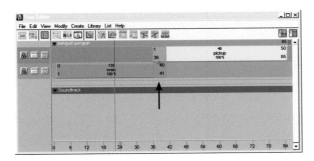

The newly created blend area

- **Playback** the animation. You will notice that the animation is now much more fluid.

Tip: *To frame the animation from the Trax Editor in the main Time Slider, **RMB** in the Time Slider and select **Set Range To → Enabled Clips**.*

Lesson 25: Trax Editor

7 Merge all the clips

- Select all the clips by **click+dragging** a selection box over the clips in the Trax Editor.

- Select **Edit** → **Merge** → ❑.

- In the Merge option window, set the following:

  Name to *penguinAnim*

  Merged Clip to **Add to Trax**

- Click the **Merge Clip** button.

  The newly merged clip is now in the Trax Editor, and has replaced all the previous clips.

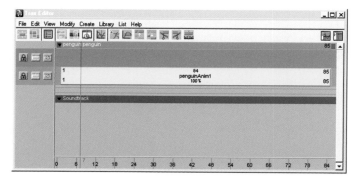

The new merged clip

Redirect the animation

Next, you will change BigZ's position so that he walks up to the board perfectly.

1 Change the animation orientation

- Select the penguin's *master* node.

- From the Animate menu set, select **Character** → **Redirect** → ❑.

- Select the **Translation** only option, then click the **Redirect** button.

  Doing so creates an override that allows you to move the animation to the proper place.

- Go to frame **50**.

  This is where the character picks up the board.

The redirect node

- Set the following:

    Translate X to **15**;

    Translate Y to **0**;

    Translate Z to **22**;

- Highlight all **translate** attributes in the Channel Box, then **RMB** and select **Key Selected**.

    Doing so will change the placement of the entire animation.

The correctly placed animation

2 Constraint timing

Since you moved the timing of the picking up motion, the parent constraint used to control the board animation is happening too early.

- Select the *parentConstraint1* node on the board's *master*.

- In the Graph Editor, **offset** the animation curve for the **R Hand Manip Wo** to happen from frame **50** to frame **51**.

    Doing so fixes the timing of the constraint switch. You will correct the position of the animation in the next exercise.

3 Save your work

- **Save** the scene as *25-trax_01.ma*.

Lesson 25: Trax Editor

Non-destructive keys

You have already experienced the flexibility of working with non-linear animation clips. To further refine the motion, you will add some non-destructive keys to the animation.

1 Add a start and end key on the head and eyes

When setting keyframes over a Trax clip, you need to set default keys before and after the region where you want to alter the animation. If you don't set those keys, the offset you keyframe will remain throughout the animation.

- Select the *neck1* joint.

- Go to frame **1**.

- Press **Shift+e** to keyframe this rotation.

- Go to frame **45**.

- Press **Shift+e** again to keyframe this rotation.

  You will notice some new keys being placed in the timeline.

2 Add keys to modify the head rotation

- Go to frame **10** and rotate the *head* joint so the penguin looks at Mikey.

- Press **Shift+e** to keyframe the head.

- Go to frame **20** and rotate the *head* joint so the penguin keeps looking Mikey.

- Press **Shift+e** to keyframe the head.

Note: *If Auto Key is On, you don't have to manually key the rotation after you have set a key once.*

- Select the keyframes at frames 10 and 20 in the Time Slider, then **RMB** and select **Tangents → Spline** to set the tangents of the selected keyframe.

- **Playback** the results.

  Now the penguin's head is deviating from his original clip-based animation.

3 Modify the lookAt

- **Repeat** the last steps in order to correctly animate where the penguin is looking throughout the animation.

The penguin now looks at Mikey

Note: *These keys are not altering the clips in any way. In fact, these keys can be deleted or moved around and the clip-based animation will remain intact. You could also create another clip from these new keyframes.*

4   Create a clip

- From the Trax Editor, select **Create → Animation Clip → □.**

- Set the following options:

  Name to *animModifier*;

  Leave Keys in Timeline to **Off**;

  Clip to **Put Clip in Trax Editor and Visor**;

  Time Range to **Animation Curve**;

  Subcharacters to **Off**;

  Time Wrap to **Off**;

  Include Hierarchy to **On**.

- Click on the **Create Clip** button.

  A new clip is added to the Trax Editor. The keyframes of this new clip are added to the existing animation clip.

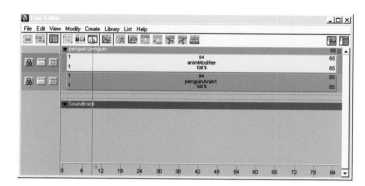

Animation modifier clip in Trax

5   Save your work

- **Save** the scene as *19-trax_02.ma.*

Adding sound to trax

The Trax Editor offers you the ability to import and sync sound files to your animation.

You can import **.wav** or **.aiff** sound files into Trax to synchronize motion and audio. More than one audio clip can be imported into the soundtrack, but you will be able to hear only one file at a time upon playback. The audio file at the top of the soundtrack display will take precedence over those below.

You will now import an existing sound file into your scene.

1   Set playback preferences

- Select **Window → Settings/ Preferences → Preferences**

- In the **Timeline** category under the **Playback** section, make sure **Playback speed** is set to **Real-time [24 fps].**

  If this option is not set to realtime, the sound might not be played.

2   Add a sound file

- From the Trax Editor, select **File → Import Audio...**

- From the *sound* directory, select *hop.wav.*

3   See and hear the sound file

- **RMB** in the Time Slider.

- From the pop-up menu select **Sound → Use Trax Sounds.**

  A green indicator bar will appear on the global timeline and the clips will display an audio waveform.

4 Move the clip

- Select the sound clip and **click+drag** it to frame **36**.

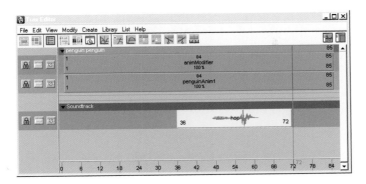

Sound clip in Trax

5 Import a second sound file

- Select **File → Import Audio...**

- From the *sound* directory, select *hey.wav*.

6 Sync the sound to the animation

- **Play** the animation with the sound.

  Notice that the top-most audio clip takes precedence as the scene is playing.

- **Click+drag** the sound clip so that it syncs up to when BigZ walks in front of Mikey.

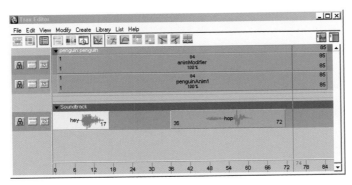

Two sound clips in Trax

Animating a camera

You will now add a new camera to the scene and animate it so that you can follow the penguin as he walks.

A camera can be created on its own or with additional nodes that provide control over the *aim point* and *up direction*. Most cameras only need one node that lets you key the camera's position and rotation. You will create a camera with aim to control both the *camera point* and the *view point*. Both these nodes can be keyed individually.

1   Set up your panel display

- Select a **Two Panes Stacked** view layout.
- In the *Perspective* view, make sure Show → Cameras and Show → Pivots are **On**.

  You will need to see these in order to work with the camera.

2   Create a two-node camera

- Select **Create** → **Cameras** → **Camera and Aim**.
- In the bottom pane, select **Panels** → **Perspective** → **camera1**.
- Press **6** to view the textures in the *camera1* view.
- In the *camera1* view, select **View** → **Camera Settings** → **Resolution Gate**.
- Still in the *camera1* view, select **View** → **Camera Attribute Editor**.
- Change **Fit Resolution Gate** to **Vertical**.

3   Frame the character

- Go to frame **1**.
- Select the **Show Manipulator Tool**.
- In the *Perspective* view, position the *camera* and *camera1_aim* handles like the image to the right.

Camera manipulator handles

> **Note:** *You can position the camera using either the Perspective or camera1 view.*

4   **Follow the action**

You will now set keys on the camera point to follow the character from frame 1 to 60.

- Set the current character to **None**.
- Go to frame **1**.
- Select the *camera1* and *camera1_aim* nodes.
- Press **Shift+w** to keyframe the current position.

  Doing so sets a keyframe for the current camera position.

- Go to frame **45**.

View at frame 45

- Move the *camera1_aim* node so that it is again looking at the character, framing both characters and the board.
- Select the *camera1* and *camera1_aim* nodes.
- Press **Shift+w** to keyframe the new view position.

5 Dolly around the board

The camera animation now frames the first portion of the animation correctly, but the second part of the animation could be better. You can set keys on the viewpoint node to fix this.

- Go to frame **85**.

- Move the *camera1* node from the *Perspective* view to the right of the scene.

- Select the *camera1* and *camera1_aim* nodes.

- Press **Shift+w** to keyframe the new view position.

View at frame 85

- If you don't like the framing in the in-between frames, you can reposition the camera and set new keys. **Repeat** this until you get the camera movement you want.

6 Playblast the animation

You can now playblast the scene to test the motion. This will give you the chance to confirm the camera animation.

Tip: *Make sure you maximize the camera view by tapping the spacebar and displaying only NURBS surfaces and polygons. You can also set the penguin's smoothness to be high resolution and set the NURBS smoothness to its finest setting.*

7 Save your work

• **Save** the scene as *25-trax_03.ma.*

Conclusion

In this lesson, you completed your first non-linear animation using Trax. You used some features available to you in the Trax Editor and you also animated on top of clips using non-destructive keyframes.

In the next lesson, you will learn about rigid bodies, which will allow you to create realistic animation using dynamics.

Lesson 25: Trax Editor

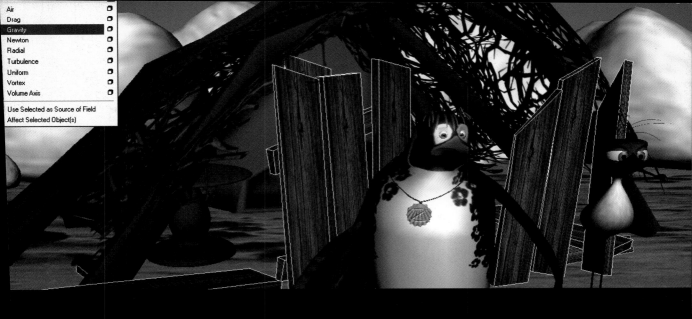

Lesson 26
Rigid Bodies

In animation, sometimes there are scenarios that just aren't worth spending the time to keyframe. Collisions between objects, for example, would be too complex to animate by hand. For this, it is better to use dynamic simulations.

In this lesson, you will experiment with the basics of rigid bodies, an example of dynamic simulations. Rigid bodies are polygonal or NURBS surfaces converted to unyielding shapes. Unlike conventional surfaces, rigid bodies collide rather than pass through each other during animation. To animate rigid body motion, you use fields, keys, expressions, rigid body constraints, or collisions with other rigid bodies or particles. In this example, the board will be colliding with the house and ground plane, all affected by a gravity field.

In this lesson you will learn the following:

- How to create a passive rigid body
- How to create an active rigid body
- How to add a gravity field to rigid bodies
- How to simulate your dynamics
- How to set rigid body attributes

Active and passive

Maya software has two kinds of rigid bodies—active and passive. An active rigid body reacts to dynamics—fields, collisions, and springs—not to keys. A passive rigid body can have active rigid bodies collide with it. You can key its translation and rotation attributes, but dynamics has no effect on it.

1   Test scene

- Select **File → New**.
- **Create** one polygonal cube and **scale** it so that it looks like a floor.
- **Rename** the cube to *floor*.
- **Create** a polygonal sphere and another polygonal cube and place them side by side above the floor.

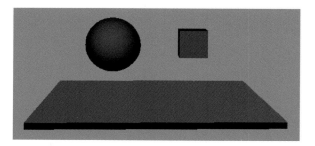

The test scene

2   Active rigid body

- Select the *sphere*.
- Press **F5** to display the **Dynamics** menu set.
- Select **Soft/Rigid Bodies → Create Active Rigid Body**.
- **Playback** the animation.

  Nothing is happening because there are no forces in the scene.

3   Playback the simulation

- Click the **Animation preferences** button found at the right side of the Range Slider.
- In the **Timeline** section, set the following:

  Playback Speed to **Play every frame**.

- Click the **Save** button.

Project 04

Note: *When working with rigid bodies or particles, it is **very important** that the playback speed is set to play every frame. Otherwise, your simulations may act unpredictably.*

4   Gravity field

- Select the *sphere.*

- Select **Fields → Gravity**.

- In the Attribute Editor, make sure the **Magnitude** is set to **9.8**.

  A magnitude of 9.8 mimics the earth's gravity.

- **Playback** the animation.

  The sphere falls straight down.

Note: *You may want to increase your playback range in the Time Slider.*

5   Passive rigid body

- Select the *floor.*

- Select **Soft/Rigid Bodies → Create Passive Rigid Body**.

- **Playback** the animation.

  The sphere falls and collides with the floor.

6   Rotate the floor

- Select the *floor* and **rotate** it sideways.

- **Playback** the animation.

  The sphere collides and rolls off the floor.

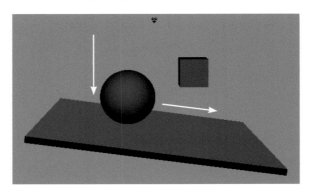

Rotate the floor

Note: *It is very important to rewind to frame 1 before playing a dynamic simulation to see accurate results. Also, you should not scrub in the timeline.*

7 **Set the cube as active**

- Select the *cube*.

- Select **Soft/Rigid Bodies → Create Active Rigid Body**.

- **Playback** the animation.

  The cube does not fall since it was not connected to the gravity field. Instead, the cube slowly spins and flies off.

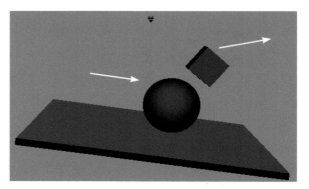

The cube collides without gravity

8 **Assign gravity**

- Select the *cube* and **Shift-select** the gravity field.

- Select **Fields → Affect Selected Object(s)**.

- **Playback** the animation.

  The cube falls on the floor like the sphere.

9 **Change dynamic attributes**

- Select the *cube*.

- In the Channel Box, highlight the *rigidBody* input connection.

- Set the following:

    Mass to **2**;

    Bounciness to **0.1**;

    Static Friction to **0.5**;

    Dynamic Friction to **0.5**.

Setting those attributes specifies that the cube is heavier and will react differently against other rigid bodies, that it doesn't bounce much, and that it has more friction against other rigid bodies.

- **Playback** the animation.

The cube falls and stops on the floor. This is because you have reduced attributes like bounciness and increased friction.

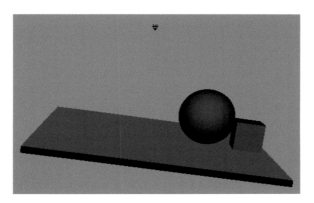

The cube stops the sphere

10 Center of mass

If you look closely at the rigid bodies, you will notice a small **x** which defines the rigid bodies' center of mass.

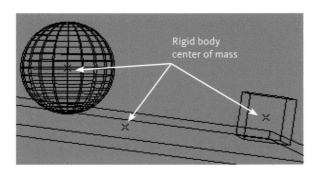

The center of mass

Objects don't usually have their center of mass exactly at their centers. For example, a clown's inflatable boxing bag stays straight even when it is pushed over because its center of mass is very low.

- Select the *sphere* to change its center of mass.

- In the Channel Box, highlight the *rigidBody* input connection.

- Set the **Center Of Mass Y** to **-1**.

  The center of mass icon moved to the bottom of the sphere.

- **Playback** the animation.

  The sphere falls and stops on the floor, bobbing from side to side.

The new center of mass

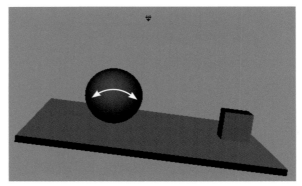

The sphere is bobbing in place

Simulation

With your knowledge, you can now add a rigid body simulation to your animated scene. You will first set the active and passive rigid bodies. You will then keyframe the rigid bodies from passive to active, which will allow them to maintain their position until they get hit by another object. Once the objects become active rigid bodies, they will crash onto the ground plane with gravity.

1 Scene file

- **Open** the file *25-trax_03.ma*.

2 Prepare the scene

Before adding dynamics to your scene, you will need to tweak the different objects to be involved in this lesson.

- Make sure that none of the *planks* interpenetrate with each other or the ground plane. If this happens, translate them to produce a small gap between the planks.

- Make sure that somewhere in your animation, the board touches the planks. For instance, contact could happen around frame **85**.

3   **Create ground rigid body**

- Select the *ground* surface.
- Press **F5** to select the **Dynamics** menu set.
- Select **Soft/Rigid Bodies** → **Create Passive Rigid Body**.

4   **Board stand-in**

The board geometry is quite complex to calculate dynamics for and is also made of subDs, which are not supported by the dynamic solver. A simple way to correct this is to place a large polygonal box over the entire board and use that stand-in geometry as a passive rigid body. Doing so will also speed up dynamic calculations since the model will be very simple.

- **Create** a primitive polygonal **cube**.
- **Tweak** the *cube* to be placed and shaped in a way similar to the board.

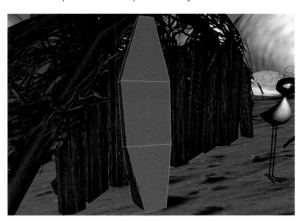

Board bounding box

- **Rename** the cube to *simpleBoard*.
- **Freeze Transformations** on the *simpleBoard* and **delete** its history.
- **Group** the *simpleBoard* to itself and **rename** it *simpleGroup*.

  You need to group the simplified board because both a parent constraint and a rigid body want to control the translation and rotation attributes of an object.

- **Parent constrain** the *simpleGroup* to the *board* node.

  The simple board should now be animated along with your earlier board and BigZ.

Lesson 26: Rigid Bodies

Tip: *If the board does not move, you have constrained the objects in the wrong order.*

5 Create the board rigid body

- Go to frame **1**.

  It is important to be at frame 1 when creating a passive rigid body on an animated object, or the dynamics might not simulate as expected.

- Select the *simpleBoard* box.

- Select **Soft/Rigid Bodies** → **Create Passive Rigid Body**.

- Press **Ctrl+h** to **hide** the *simpleBoard*.

6 Door stand-in

Alternatively, you can use stand-in geometry to drive a complex model. Here you will create a door stand-in and drive the door group from the stand-in dynamics.

- Select the *doorGroup*.

- Press **Ctrl+d** to **duplicate** it.

- Press **Shift+p** to **unparent** it.

- With the new group selected, select **Mesh** → **Combine**.

  You should now have the same door geometry, but in a single object.

- **Rename** the combined door to *simpleDoor*.

- **Freeze Transformations** on the *simpleDoor* and **delete** its history.

- **Parent constrain** the original *doorGroup* to the *simpleDoor* geometry.

  The original door should now properly follow your combined model.

7 Create the door rigid body

- Go to frame **1**.

- Select the *simpleDoor* model.

- Select **Soft/Rigid Bodies** → **Create Active Rigid Body**.

- Press **Ctrl+h** to **hide** the *simpleDoor*.

8 House planks

- Select all the *planks* from the house wall that are not part of the door.

- With all the *planks* selected, select **Soft/Rigid Bodies** → **Create Active Rigid Body**.

The active planks

9   **Test your scene**

* **Playblast** the animation.

    If your board collides with the planks, you will notice that they fly off.

The planks and the door flying off

Note: *During a dynamic simulation, if two objects intersect, a warning is displayed in the Command Feedback line and the objects are automatically selected.*

10   Assign gravity

- Select **Edit** → **Select All by Type** → **Rigid Bodies**.

- Select **Fields** → **Gravity**.

  A new gravity field with the default Earth gravity appears at the origin.

- **Playblast** the animation.

  Now all the rigid bodies react to the gravity and bounce on the floor as soon as the scene is played.

11   Active key

When you playback the animation, you will notice that the planks react immediately to the dynamics. What you really want here is for the dynamics to only start evaluating when the board comes into contact with them. The following will show you how to set active/passive keyframes on the rigid bodies.

- Select the *planks* and the *simpleDoor* geometry.

- Select **Soft/Rigid Bodies** → **Set Passive Key**.

  The objects are no longer affected by dynamics.

- Go to frame **82**, or anywhere else before the board comes into contact with the planks.

- With the geometry still selected, select **Soft/Rigid Bodies** → **Set Active Key**.

  The wall will now destroy itself as soon as the board collides with it.

> **Note:** *You can also set a dynamic initial state for the objects. An initial state tells the Maya software the position of the dynamics on the first animation frame. In order to set an initial state, playback your scene until you like the current position, then select* **Solvers** → **Initial State** → **Set for All Dynamic.**

12   Fine-tune the simulation

For a better simulation, the rigid bodies' attributes should be tweaked to give more realism to the scene. The following are some general steps that you should try, but the results may vary from scene to scene.

- For the *planks*, change the following:

    Change the **Mass** attribute to between **1.0** and **2.0,** depending on the size of the planks.

    Lower their **Bounciness** attribute to **0.2**.

    Increase their **Static Friction** and **Dynamic Friction** attributes to **0.5**.

- For the *simpleDoor*, change the following:

    Move down the **Center Of Mass Y** slightly.

    Change the **Mass** attribute to a larger value such as **5**.

    Lower the **Bounciness** attribute to **0.2**.

    Increase the **Static Friction** and **Dynamic Friction** attributes to **0.8**.

- For the *ground*, change the following:

    Lower the **Bounciness** attribute to **0.1**.

    Increase the **Static Friction** and **Dynamic Friction** attributes to **0.8**.

- For the *simpleBoard*, change the following:

    Lower its **Bounciness** attribute to **0.2**.

- **Create** more passive rigid bodies if needed so the planks don't interpenetrate with other objects.

The final simulation

13   Save your work

- **Save** your scene as *26-rigidBodies_01.ma*.

Simulation cache

When you simulate rigid body dynamics, the rigid body solver recalculates the simulation every time you play through the Time Slider. You can speed up the playback of your scene by saving a rigid body cache in memory. A cache stores the positions of all the rigid bodies at every frame, letting you quickly preview the results without having to create a playblast. This offers many benefits, including the ability to scrub back and forth in the Time Slider.

If you want to tweak the objects' attributes to alter the simulation, you will not see the results until you delete the cache so that the solver can recalculate a new simulation.

1 Enable the cache

- Select **Solvers → Rigid Body Solver Attributes.**

  This will open the Attribute Editor for the rigid body solver in the scene.

  Note: *It is possible to have multiple rigid body solvers in a scene. This is useful when you have distinct systems that don't interact together.*

- Scroll to the **Rigid Solver States** section in the Attribute Editor.
- Turn **On** the **Cache Data** checkbox.
- **Rewind** and **playback** the entire scene so that the solver can create the cache.

  When it finishes playing the scene and writing the cache to memory, you should see a difference in the playback speed since it does not recalculate the simulation.

  Note: *The rigid body cache is saved in the software's memory and is not written to disk.*

2 Tweak the simulation

- Select the planks and change some of their rigid body attributes.

  You should not see any difference when you playback your scene since no recalculation is done.

- Select **Solvers → Rigid Body Solver Attributes.**
- In the **Rigid Solver States** section, click the **Delete Cache** button.

  This will force the solver to recalculate the cache.

- **Rewind** your scene and **play** it so that the solver can create a new cache.
- If you want to disable the solver's cache, simply turn **Off** the **Cache Data** checkbox.

Conclusion

You have experienced the basics of the powerful dynamics tools found in Maya software. You learned how to create active and passive rigid bodies, as well as gravity fields. You also tweaked their attributes to add realism to your simulation.

In the next lesson, you will change scenes and animate BigZ surfing on an ocean wave using a motion path.

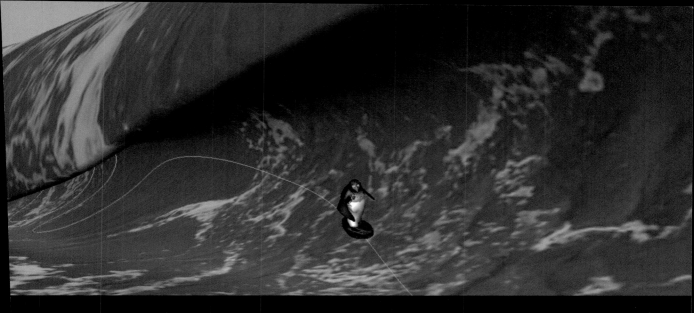

Lesson 27
Motion Path

In this lesson, you will animate BigZ on the board, surfing out in the ocean. To do so, you will use a motion path to determine the trajectory of the board, then keyframe some secondary animation to refine the motion.

In this lesson you will learn the following:

- How to make a surface live
- How to define a motion path
- How to shape the path to edit the animation
- How to update the path markers
- How to constrain the board to the normals of the ocean
- How to constrain the character to the board
- How to keyframe secondary animation

Path animation

Path animations are created by assigning an object or series of objects to a path. This creates a special *motionPath* node that allows you to key its motion along the path.

1   Scene file

- Start a **new scene**.
- **Reference** the scene file *19-waveAnim_01.ma* from the third project with the *ocean* prefix.
- **Reference** the scene file *23-bigzRig_01.ma* from this project with the *penguin* prefix.
- **Reference** the scene file *23-boardTxt_02.ma* from this project with the *board* prefix.
- Set the frame range to go from **1** to **500**.
- If needed, **scale** up the ocean *master* so the character looks tiny compared to the wave.
- **Save** your scene as *27-motionPath_01.ma*.

2   Make live

- Select the *ocean* surface.
- Select **Modify → Make Live**.

  When making a surface live, it is displayed in green wireframe. You can then draw a curve directly on the surface, which will create a curve that follows the shape of the ocean.

3   Draw a path animation curve

- Go to frame **1**.
- Select **Create → EP Curve Tool → ❑**.
- **Make sure to reset the options of the tool.**
- **Draw** a curve starting from the base of the wave, as follows:

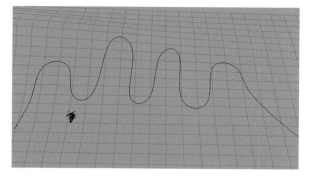

Path curve

> **Tip:** *Try to keep the curve points evenly spaced.*

- When you have finished, hit **Enter** to complete the curve.
- Select **Modify** → **Make Not Live** again to remove the live state of the ocean surface.

4 Animate the path

Because of construction history, you can animate the curve to stay at the same location on the wave.

- While in wireframe, select the path curve.
- Go to frame **1** and set a **keyframe** on the curve.
- Go to frame **500**.
- **Translate** the curve so that it stays in the barrel of the wave.

The translated path curve

> **Note:** *Notice that the move manipulator is bound by the curve's construction history.*

- Set a **keyframe** on the curve.
- **Playback** the scene and make sure the curve stays at a good location on the wave.

> **Tip:** *You may have to set a few more* **keyframes** *in order to keep the path in the barrel of the wave.*

5 Constrain BigZ

Before you go on with animating the board, you must set up BigZ to be perfectly synchronized with the board. The easiest way of doing this is to constrain BigZ's master to the board node.

Lesson 27: Motion Path

Project 04

- **Pose** BigZ on the surf board and **keyframe** the *penguin* character set.
- Select the *board* geometry, then **Shift-select** BigZ's *master* node.
- Select **Constrain** → **Parent** → ❏.
- In the **options**, make sure that **Maintain Offset** is set to **On.**
- Click the **Add** button.
- Test the constraint by moving the board's *master.*

  BigZ should follow the board perfectly.

6 Attach the board to the path

- Make sure the **Time Slider** range goes from **1** to **500** frames.
- Select the board *master* node using the Outliner, then **Shift-select** the path curve.

> **Note:** *In order to create a path animation, the path must be picked last. The last object picked is indicated in green.*

- Go to the **Animation** menu set.
- Select **Animate** → **Motion Paths** → **Attach to Motion Path** → ❏.
- Set the **Time Range** to **Time Slider.**
- Click the **Attach** button.
- **Playback** the results.

7 Edit the motion path input node

The board is moving down the path, but it is not aimed in the correct direction. You can change this using the *motionPath* input node.

- With the board *master* selected, open the Attribute Editor.
- Click the tab for *motionPath1* and set the following:

     Follow to **On**;

     Front Axis to **Z**;

     Up Axis to **Y.**

> **Tip:** *If the board does not face the right direction while moving down the path, change the **Front Axis** or turn **On** the **Inverse Front** checkbox.*

- **Playback** the results and notice how the board now points in the direction it is traveling.

Board attached to path

> **Note:** You can also use the **Bank** option to have the object automatically roll when following the path. In this example, you will use another technique involving constraints to have the board follow the surface's angle.

8   Edit the path's shape

Edit the shape of the path using the curve's control vertices and the object will follow the path.

- Select the path curve.
- **RMB** on the path curve and select **Control Vertices** from the context menu.
- **Move** the CVs in order to tweak how the board follows the wave.
- **Playback** the results.

9   Path timing

Notice the start and end markers on the path. They tell you the start and end frame of the animation along the path. You can insert new time keyframes and decide where the character should be on a certain frame.

- Go to frame **120**.
- Ensure that the **Auto Key** button is turned **On**.
- Select the path curve.
- In the Channel Box, click on the *motionPath1* input node.
- Still in the Channel Box, click on the **U Value** channel name to highlight it.

  Notice the two keyframes in the Time Slider at the first and last frame. Those keyframes are defining the animation of the motion path from start to end.

- Hold down **Ctrl** and **click+drag** the **MMB** to change the path value at the current frame.

  This specifies a new location where the board should be on the path at that frame.

- Use the virtual slider to move the board back on the path.

  *You have just set a key on the motionPath's **U** value. Moving the value lower basically slows down the animation before that frame.*

Updated path position

10 Manipulator

Instead of using the virtual slider, you can use the motion path manipulator.

- Go to frame **160**.

- With the *motionPath* still highlighted in the Channel Box, select the **Show Manipulator Tool** by pressing **t**.

  A manipulator appears with handles for positioning the object along the path. You will use the handle on the path to move the board forward, so that it speeds up as it goes down the wave.

- **Click+drag** on the center marker of the path manipulator handle to move the board down the wave.

  Another path marker is placed on the curve and a new key is set.

 Tip: It is always good to remember that input nodes may have manipulators that you can access using the Show Manipulator Tool.

New path marker

11 Edit the path marker's position

The position of the markers can be moved to edit the animation of the board.

- Click on the **Auto Key** button to turn it **Off**.

- Select the **Move Tool**.

- To select the path marker that is labeled as **160**, click on the number without touching other objects or the curve.

  This will select the marker on its own.

- **Click+drag** the marker to change the position of the board.

  The marker is constrained to the curve as you move it.

12 Edit the timing

Since the marker points are simply keys set on the U Value of the *motionPath* node, you can edit the timing of the keys in the Graph Editor.

- Select the *board master* using its selection handle, and then click on the *motionPath* input node in the Channel Box.

- Open the Graph Editor.

- Highlight the **U Value** attribute on the left of the Graph Editor.

- Press **a** to frame all in the window.

  The position of the attached object in the U direction of the curve is mapped against time. You can see that a key has been set for each of the path markers.

- Select the key at frame **160**.

- In the Graph Editor's **Stats** area, change the time from **160** to **150**.

- In the Graph Editor, select **Tangents** → **Spline**.

  You can edit the effect of the path keys' in-between frames using the same techniques as for normal keyframes.

- Select the last keyframe, then **Tangents** → **Linear**.

  You can see that the path marker is now labeled as **150** *in the view panel.*

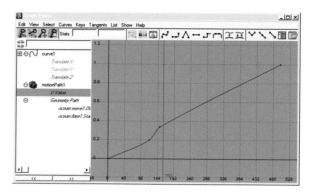

Edited path curve

Secondary animation

Now that you have a basic animation for your board, you can keyframe secondary animation on top of what you already have. Secondary animation usually adds life to an animation, making the scene more natural. For the board, you will create a normal constraint so it follows the ocean, and then keyframe some drifting.

1   Normal constraint

The normal constraint is a constraint that takes the normal from a surface and applies the associated rotation to a constrained object. Here, you will constrain the normal of the ocean to one of the board's animation override groups.

- Select the *ocean*, then **Shift-select** the board *transOverride*.
- Select **Constrain** → **Normal** → ❑.
- Set the options as follows:

  Aim Vector to **0, 1, 0**;

  Up Vector to **1, 0, 0**;

  World Up Type to **Object Up**;

  World Up Object to *board:master*.

You are setting the up object to be the board master since it already defines proper path rotation.

- Click the **Add** button.
- **Playback** the animation.

Notice how the board rolls sideways when on a slope.

The normal constraint effect

2   **Board animation**

- Make sure **Auto Key** is turned **On**.
- Go to frame **1**.
- With the *board* surface selected, press **Shift+w** and **Shift+e** to set a keyframe on translation and rotation.
- **Rotate** the board so its tail is in the water and so the front is sticking out of the water.
- Scrub in the Time Line to a place where you would like to change the board's position.
- **Translate** the board towards the outside of the curve and **rotate** it towards the path.

Doing so creates a drifting effect.

- When the board is up the wave, **rotate** the board so it gets less sideway banking.
- Bring the translation and rotation of the board back to **0** in all directions when you need to reset the board to its default position.

Project 04

Corrected position

3   Other animation

- Spend some time animating BigZ's reaction to his surfing.

  Doing so will add lots of realism to the actions, rather than having just a stiff character following the board.

4   Save your work

- **Save** your scene as *27-motionPath_02.ma*.

5   Playblast or render the animation

BigZ surfing render

Conclusion

You are now more familiar with animating using motion paths, constraining and keyframing secondary animation. As a result of your work, BigZ is now surfing waves out on the ocean.

You are now ready to delve into more advanced topics. In the next lesson, you will use dynamics along with particles.

Lesson 28
Particles

Particles are small object types that can be animated using dynamic forces in place of traditional keyframes. These effects are, in essence, simulations of physical effects such as water, smoke and mist.

To experiment with particle effects, you will add water particles to your scene. The mist will b generated using a modified version of the Maya default particle smoke effect. You will then create drops that will collide against the board and ocean.

In this lesson you will learn the following:

- How to add a smoke effect to an object
- How to change particle type and shading
- How to set the particles' initial state
- How to add an emitter
- How to define a particle attribute using a ramp
- How to collide particles against geometry
- How to add dynamic fields
- How to software render a particle animation
- How to hardware render a particle animation

Mist

Using one of the software's preset particle effects, you will add mist to your scene. The smoke preset will create everything needed to make the particles look and act like mist.

1   Scene file

- **Open** the scene file *28-particles_01.ma* from the *support_files*.

  This scene contains the same content from the last lesson, but with a simplified animation.

2   Create an emitter object

In order to have mist coming out from a good location on the board, you will create a curve to be used as an emitter.

- Use the **EP Curve Tool** to draw the following curve:

The emitter curve

Notice how the curve outlines the area of the board that disturbs the water.

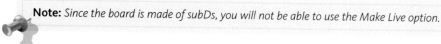

Note: *Since the board is made of subDs, you will not be able to use the Make Live option.*

- **Parent** the curve to the *board* and **rename** it to *smokeLocation*.

3   Adding smoke

- Press **F5** or hold down **h** and click in the viewport to select the **Dynamics** menu set.
- Select the *smokeLocation* object.
- Select **Effects → Create Smoke → ❑.**

- Set the following:

  Sprite image name to *Smoke.o;*

  Start and **End Image** to **0.**

  You will be modifying the particles later on so the texture is not important at this stage.

- Click the **Create** button.

  The smoke effect is the result of a particle object that is controlled by dynamic fields—in this case, turbulence. The smoke preset adds these elements to your scene and lets you easily control them.

- **Rewind** to frame **1** and **playback** the simulation.

Default smoke particles

> **Note:** *When working with dynamics, it's important that you always use the rewind button to move to the beginning of your simulation and ensure that the scene playback is set to **Play every frame** in the general preferences. Never scrub through a scene that has dynamics in it unless you cache the particles to disk. Otherwise, you might get unpredictable results.*

4 Changing the emitter type

At this time, the particle are only emitting from the curve CVs. You will change this behavior so the particles emit from the entire curve length.

- In the Outliner, select the *SmokeEmitter* which is child of the *smokeLocation* curve.

- In the Channel Box, set the following:

  Emitter Type to **Curve;**

  Rate to **25.**

- **Rewind** and **playback** the simulation to see the difference.

5   Editing the smoke attributes

You will now tweak the smoke effect to create mist-like particles.

- Select the *SmokeParticles*.
- In the Attribute Editor, make sure that the *SmokeParticleShape1* tab is selected.
- Scroll to the **Lifespan Attributes** section.

This is where you can change the particle general behaviour.

- Set the following attributes:

  Lifespan to **0.5**;

  Lifespan Random to **0.4**.

This changes the number of frames the smoke lives before disappearing.

- Scroll down to the **Render Attributes** section.
- Set the **Particle Render Type** to **Cloud**.

Cloud particles are a type of particle renderable with the software renderer.

- Click the **Current Render Type** button for more attributes related to this type of particle, such as **Radius**.

6   Changing the particle shader

Software particles need to have a shader assigned to them in order to be rendered properly. You will now assign the default particle shader to the smoke.

- Select the *SmokeParticles*.
- Under the **Rendering** menu set, select **Lighting/Shading** → **Assign Existing Material** → **particleCloud1**.

The particleCloud1 is now assigned and makes the particles renderable.

7   Add wind

At this time, the particles emit and move up a little. It would be much more realistic to see them being dragged by wind toward the back. You will now add a new dynamic field.

- Select the *SmokeParticles*.
- Select **Fields** → **Air.**

A default air field is created, which will affect your particles.

- In the Channel Box, set the following:

  Magnitude to **50;**

  Use Max Distance to **Off;**

  Direction X, Y, Z to **-1, 0** and **0.**

• **Playback** the simulation to see the effect of the field on the particles.

8 Setting the initial state

One thing you may notice with the simulation is that there are no particles when the animation starts. If you want the mist to be visible right from the beginning, you must set the particles' initial state.

• Select the particles.

• In the Channel Box, set the **Start Frame** attribute to **-30**.

  Doing so tells the particles to start emitting at frame **-30**.

• **Playback** the scene, then **stop** it and **rewind**.

  Particles are emitted correctly.

• With the particles still selected, select **Solvers** → **Initial State** → **Set for Selected**.

• In the Channel Box, set the **Start Frame** attribute back to **1**.

• Go back to frame **1** and **playback** the simulation.

  By setting the initial state for the particles, you can see that by frame 1, the particles are already created.

9 Test render the particles

• Press **F6** to go to the **Rendering** menu set.

• From the **Render** menu, select **Render current frame...**

  The scene is now rendered with the mist particles included. Some particles can be rendered using the software renderer, which allows them to be automatically integrated into the scene.

Software rendering

Lesson 28: Particles

Note: *If you don't need the mist to cast shadows, simply open the Attribute Editor for the particles, and disable* **Casts Shadows** *in the* **Render Stats** *section.*

Tip: *For a faster rendering, lower the anti-aliasing setting in the* **Preview quality** *preset in the Render Settings.*

10   Save your work

- **Save** your scene as *28-particles_02.ma*.

Water drops

As an added effect, you will set up more particles that will represent sprayed drops from the board. To create particles that look like drops, you need to adjust various particle attributes. In this case, you will create streaks particles that will die fairly quickly after being emitted. Their color will start out white, and then turn to blue. You will also set up the drops to collide with the surrounding geometry.

1   Add an emitter

In order to have new particles in your scene, you must first create a particle emitter.

- Select the mist particles and press **Ctrl+h** to hide them.
- Press **F5** to go back to the **Dynamics** menu set, then from the **Particles** menu, select **Create Emitter**.

An emitter will appear at the origin.

- Select the new emitter, then **Shift-select** the *board*.
- Press **p** to **parent** the emitter to the *board*.
- Place the emitter on top and at the back of the board.
- **Playback** your scene to see the new default particles being emitted.

2   Change render type to streak

Particles can have their render type set from a list of possible looks. You can switch between the different types until you get one that suits your needs.

- Select the new particles.
- **Rename** them *drops*.
- In the Attribute Editor, go to the **Render Attributes** section of the *dropsShape* node.

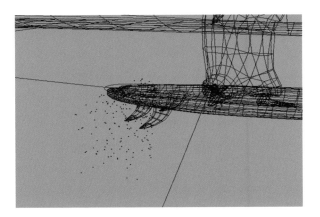

Default particles

- Set **Particle Render Type** to **Streak**.

  This render type is designed to work with hardware rendering. This means that later, you will have to composite the final hardware rendered particles with software rendered scenes.

3   Add and edit render attributes

- Click on the **Current Render Type** button.

- Set the **Render Attributes** as follows:

      Line Width to **4**;

      Tail Fade to **0**;

      Tail Size to **5**.

  This gives the drops a much stronger presence. The higher tail size value lengthens the drops.

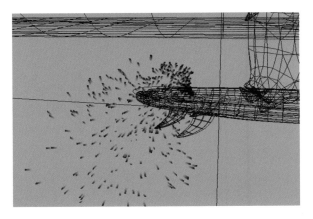

Streak particles

Lesson 28: Particles

4   Add color per particle

The particle node has the ability to have new attributes added to it as needed. This lets you add complexity to a particle node when necessary.

You can use this technique to add color to the particles individually (per particle or PP), instead of as an entire group.

- In the **Add Dynamic Attributes** section of the Attribute Editor, click on the **Color** button.

- From the Particle color window, select **Add Per Particle Attribute,** then click the **Add Attribute** button.

  This adds an rgbPP line to the **Per Particle (Array) Attributes** *section.*

- Click on the **rgbPP** field with your **RMB** and select **Create Ramp**.

- Click again on the **rgbPP** field with your **RMB** and select **<-arrayMapper.outColorPP** → **Edit Ramp**.

  In the Ramp window, you will find three markers, each with a square and a circular icon.

- Click on the circle icon at the bottom of the ramp, then click on the color swatch next to **Selected Color**.

- Change the color to **white**.

- **Delete** the center marker, then set the top marker to be a **light blue**.

- Press **6** to go in hardware texturing mode.

5   Particle lifespan and randomness

The **Lifespan** attribute lets you determine how long the particle will remain in the scene before it disappears or dies. You will add a slight randomness to the lifespan of the particles.

- With *drops* selected, go to the **Lifespan Attributes** section in the Attribute Editor.

- Change **Lifespan Mode** to **Random range**.

- Change the **Lifespan** to **1.5**.

- Change the **Lifespan Random** to **0.5.**

  The lifespan is uniformly distributed with **Lifespan** *as the mean and* **Lifespan Random** *as the width of the distribution.*

  The particles in this case have a lifespan between **1** *and* **2**. *This gives the drops a more random look.*

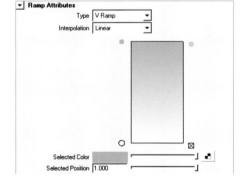

Particle color ramp

6 Change the settings of the emitter

Some attributes on the emitter should be changed to get better drop simulation. The rate at which the emitter creates particles should be decreased and the emitting speed should be increased.

- Select the *emitter* from the Outliner.

- In the Channel Box, set the following:

  Emitter Type to **Volume**;

  Rate (Particles/Sec) to **50**;

  Direction X, Y, Z to **0**, **1** and **0**;

  Speed Random to **5**;

  Random Direction to **5**;

  Directional Speed to **10**.

- **Scale** the *emitter* volume so the area from which the particles emit covers the tail of the board.

- **Playback** the simulation.

The particles emit straight up

Fine tuning the drops

The current particles don't quite move like real drops. They should react to gravity and collide with the surrounding surfaces.

1 Add gravity to the particles

- Select *drops*.
- From the **Fields** menu, select **Gravity**.

   A gravity field appears at the origin.

- Select the *drops*, then **Shift-select** the air field created earlier.
- Select the **Fields → Affect Selected Object(s)**.
- **Playback** the simulation.

   Now the particles react like real drops.

2 Set up particle collisions

To make the particles collide with the ocean to create a splash, you must define them as colliding objects.

- Select the *drops* particles.
- Press the **Shift** key and **select** the *ocean*.

Note: *The ocean should be selected last.*

- From the **Particles** menu, select **Make Collide**.
- Playback your scene.

   The particles now bounce off the ocean surface.

Particle collision

3 **Adding friction**

As you playback the scene, the drops seem to bounce off the ocean object. To fix this, you must change the resilience and friction attributes for the *geoConnector* node.

- Select the *drops* particles.

- At the top of the Attribute Editor, click on the *geoConnector* tab.

  The geoConnector object has been created for the collision object and specifies how it should affect the dynamics.

- Set the following attributes:

  Resilience to **0**;

  Friction to **1**.

- **Playback** the simulation.

  Now the drops react more realistically when colliding with the ocean by going with the flow. Resilience is used to calculate the bounciness of a surface and friction is used to slow down the particles when they touch a surface.

4 **Create a particle event**

Use the **Collision Event Tool** to emit a new smoke particle upon collision.

- Select the *drops*.

- From the **Particles** menu, select **Particle Collision Event Editor**.

- In the Particle Collision Event Editor, go to the **Event Type** section and set the following:

  Type to **Emit** enabled;

  Num particles to **5**;

  Spread to **1**;

  Target particles to *SmokeParticle1*;

  Inherit velocity to **1**;

  Original particle dies to **On**.

- Click **Create Event** and close the window.

  The options used tell the solver to emit five smoke particles per collision with inherited velocity, and kills the drop particles after the collision.

- **Unhide** the *CloudParticles*.

- **Playback** the simulation.

  Several cloud particles are emitted after the drops collide.

Particle collision event

5   Initial state

Use what you have learned earlier to set the initial state for both the smoke and drop particles.

6   Save your work

- **Save** the scene as *28-particles_03.ma.*

Rendering particles

It was mentioned earlier that the drops used a particle type that can only be rendered using hardware rendering, while the mist smoke used software rendering. The question, therefore, is— how do you bring hardware rendered particles together with a software rendered scene?

The answer is to render them separately, and then bring them together using a compositing package such as Autodesk® Combustion® software.

To composite the drop particles with the rest of the scene, you will need to render the top layer (in this case, the drops) with a matte, or *mask.*

The mask is a grayscale channel that defines which areas of the color image are going to be transparent when brought into a compositing package. In this scene, the background contains all the scene's geometry.

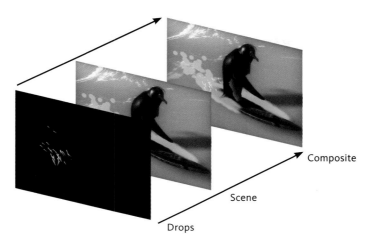

Diagram of compositing layers

Software rendering

The mist created using the smoke effect can be rendered using software rendering. This means creating another batch rendering of your scene. This will represent the first render pass that can be later composited together with the drops.

1   Change your motion blur type

Since the 2D motion blur used so far doesn't render well with the smoke particles, you will switch to the 3D motion blur type.

- Select **Window → Rendering Editors → Render Settings.**

- Open the **Motion Blur** section and change the **Motion Blur Type** to **3D**.

   This type of motion blur renders more slowly, but is more accurate and works better with software rendered particles.

2   Fix the smoke shadows

Earlier it was noted that the shadows generated from the particles didn't look correct. The depth map shadows cannot recognize the subtleties of the volumetric shader used by the particles. Raytrace shadows are needed.

- Select the directional light that is casting shadows in the scene.

- In the Attribute Editor, open the **Shadows** section, scroll down to **Raytrace Shadow Attributes** and set **Use Ray Trace Shadows** to **On**.

- Set the **Ray Depth Limit** to **2**.

   This sets up the light, but to use raytraced shadows you will need to turn on raytracing itself.

Lesson 28: Particles

- Open the **Render Settings**.
- Open the **Raytracing Quality** section and turn **Raytracing** to **On**.
- If you turned Off the **Casts Shadows** option for the *smokeParticles*, turn it back **On**.

Note: *Maya software uses a selective raytracer and only objects that require reflections, refractions or raytraced shadows will use this technique.*

3 Limiting the reflections

When raytracing is turned on, any shader that has a reflectivity value will render with reflections. If the object is not required to be reflective, then it's a good idea to turn Reflectivity off.

- Go into the material node and set its **Reflectivity** to **0**.
- **Repeat** for each material in the scene that has a shader with unwanted **Reflectivity**.

  OR
- Select the geometry that you don't want to be involved in raytracing.
- Under its **Render Stats** section, turn **Visible in Reflections Off**.

  When you do this, the object will not reflect and won't be calculated in the raytrace.
- **Repeat** for each object in the scene that has a shader with the **Reflectivity** attribute.

Note: *Lambert shaders do not have a reflectivity attribute.*

4 Render settings

- Open the **Render Settings**.
- Change the **Common** attributes so you can render from frame **1** to **100**.
- Change the **File name prefix** to *background*.
- Change the **Quality** preset to **Production quality**.

5 Batch render the scene

- Select **File → Save Scene as...**
- Enter the file name *28-background_01.ma* and click **Save**.
- Press **F6** to change to the **Rendering** menu set and select **Render → Batch Render**.

  This will create a render pass that includes the geometry and software particles. You will now render the drops using hardware rendering.

The software render

Tip: *From now until the end of this lesson, do not move the rendered camera, or the software and hardware renders won't match. You can use the **[** and **]** keys to undo and redo camera moves.*

Hardware rendering

You have been using hardware rendering in the Perspective view panel to help preview the scene. You can also use hardware rendering to render the drop particles so that they match the rendered scene.

1 Set the hardware render attributes

- Select **Window** → **Rendering Editors** → **Render Settings.**
- Select **Render using** the **Maya Hardware** renderer.
- Change the **File name prefix** to *drops*.
- Under the **Maya Hardware** tab, change the **Enable Geometry Mask** to **On**.

  This will use the geometry as mask objects to hide particles falling behind them. An alpha channel, also known as a matte channel, is important for layering images in a compositing package.

- Change the **Motion blur** to **On**.

2 Batch render the scene

You can now render an entire animation. Compared to software rendering, the Maya Hardware renderer lets you use the speed of hardware rendering to generate animations quickly.

- Select **File → Save Scene as...**
- Enter the file name *28-drops_01.ma* and click **Save**.
- Press **F6** to change to the **Rendering** menu set and select **Render → Batch Render**.

  This will create a render pass that includes only the hardware particles.

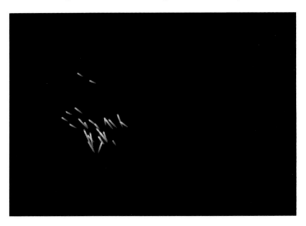

The hardware render

3 Preview the resulting animation

Once the rendering is finished, you can use the fcheck utility to play the rendered animation.

4 Composite rendered animations

You currently have a software rendered animation of mist, and a hardware rendered sequence of drops with an embedded alpha channel. You can now use your compositing software to layer these elements together.

There are several advantages to compositing your layers instead of rendering all of them into one scene:

- By separating background and foreground elements and rendering them individually, rendering times can be greatly reduced.
- By rendering different elements on different layers, it is easier to make revisions to one layer later without having to re-render the whole scene.
- By compositing hardware and software rendered particles, you can achieve interesting effects.
- By using different layers, your compositing software can adjust the color for one particular layer without affecting other layers.

Final composite

Conclusion

You now have a better understanding of Maya hardware and software particles. You created and modified the preset smoke effect and added your own effect by customizing the emitter and particle attributes. The lesson also covered some of the most important aspects of particle simulations, including per particle attributes, gravity, collisions and collision events.

In the next lesson you will experiment with MEL scripting.

Lesson 29
MEL Scripting

In this lesson, you will set keys on the blink attribute that you created on the *lookAt* node in the character rig from project 2. To help with this task, you will create a MEL (Maya Embedded Language) script that will help you animate the blink.

MEL is a powerful scripting language that can be used by both technical directors and animators to add to the software's capability. Animators can take advantage of simple macro-like scripts to enhance their workflows, while technical directors can use more advanced MEL commands to rig up characters, add special visual effects or set up customized controls.

If you know nothing about programming and scripts, this lesson will, at first, seem foreign to your world of graphics and animation. While you can certainly be successful with Maya software without relying on the use of MEL, this lesson offers a good chance to get your feet wet and see the possibilities. If you do learn how to use MEL, you might be quite surprised how a simple script can be used to enhance your work.

In this lesson you will learn the following:

- How to recognize and enter MEL commands
- How to create a MEL script procedure
- How to use this procedure within the existing Maya UI
- How to build a custom UI element for the procedure
- How to animate the creature's blinking using the procedure

New scene

Rather than working in the character scene file, you will practice using MEL in a new scene. Once your scripts have been written and saved, you will return to the character scene and use the custom UI tools in context.

1 **Start a new file**

• Select **File → New Scene**.

• Set up a single *Perspective* view panel.

• Make sure the Command line, the Help line and the Channel Box are all visible. If not, you can make them visible in the **Display → UI Elements** menu.

What is MEL?

MEL stands for Maya Embedded Language. It is built on top of the Maya software's base architecture and is used to execute commands used to build scenes and create user interface elements. In fact, every time you click on a tool, you are executing one or more MEL commands.

Note: *This book will not cover Python™ scripting.*

A MEL command is a text string that tells the software to complete a particular action. As a user, it is possible to ignore the graphical user interface and use these commands directly. Generally, animators will choose the user interface instead—but it is still a good idea to know what MEL can do at a command level.

The Command Line

You will now use the Command line to create and edit some primitive objects. The goal at this point is to explore how simple commands work.

1 **Create a cone using the Command line**

• Click in the Command line to make it active.

The Command line can be found at the bottom left of the interface, just above the Help line.

• Make sure the Command line is set to accept **MEL** commands by clicking on the button on the left of the Command line until **MEL** is shown.

- Enter the following:

Entering a MEL command

- After you finish, press the **Enter** key on the numeric keypad section of your keyboard.

Tip: *The keyboard has two **Enter** keys that each work a little differently with the Command line. The **Enter** key associated with the numeric keypad keeps your focus on the Command line, while the **Enter** key associated with the alpha-numeric keyboard switches your focus back to the view panels.*

2   Rotate and move the cone with commands

The next step is to transform the cone using MEL commands.

- Enter the following:

```
rotate 0 0 90 < Enter >

move 5 0 0 < Enter >
```

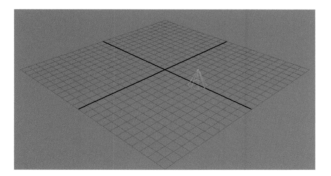

Perspective view of cone

You now have a cone sitting on the ground surface, five units along the X-axis. You first entered the command, then you added the desired values.

Lesson 29: MEL Scripting

3 Rename the cone

You can also rename objects from the
Command line.

- Enter the following:

    ```
    rename nurbsCone1 myCone
    ```
    < Enter >

    *Look in the Channel Box to confirm that
    the object has been renamed.*

Channels Object		
myCone		
	Translate X	5
	Translate Y	0
	Translate Z	0

Channel Box with cone's name

4 Execute three commands at once

If you want to quickly enter more than one command without pressing the Enter key along
the way, you can place a semicolon between the commands.

- Enter the following:

    ```
    sphere; move 0 0 6; scale 4 1 1 < Enter >
    ```

    *Using the semicolon(;), you executed three commands in a row. First, you created a sphere,
    then you moved it, then you scaled it. The semicolon will become more important later
    when you write scripts.*

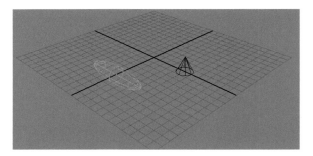

Perspective view of new sphere

5 Execute a command on an unselected object

If you want to execute a command on an object that is not selected, you simply add the
name of the node that you want to affect. The node will follow the command without
requiring the object to be selected.

- Enter the following:

    ```
    move -5 0 0 mycone < Enter >
    ```

    Oops! You got an error message saying that the Maya software cannot find the **mycone**
    *object. This is because the object name has a capital C for the word "Cone." MEL is case
    sensitive, which means you should be especially aware of how you spell and capitalize any
    names or commands.*

- Enter the following:

```
move -5 0 0 myCone < Enter >

scale 5 1 1 myCone < Enter >
```

Always remember the importance of spelling the commands correctly. Just like the semicolon, correct spelling will be essential later when you write scripts.

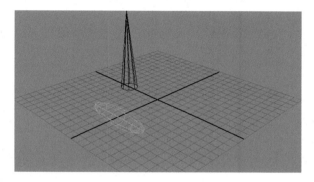

Perspective view of edited cone

6 Use command flags

Another important MEL capability is the command flag. You can use these flags to be more specific about how you want the commands to be executed. The command flags can have short or long names. Flags are indicated with a hyphen in your script. Shown below are examples of both kinds of flags.

- Enter the following using long names for flags:

```
cylinder -name bar -axis 0 1 0 -pivot 0 0 -3 < Enter >
```

- Enter the following using short names for flags:

```
cylinder -n bar2 -ax 0 1 0 -p 0 0 -6 -hr 10 < Enter >
```

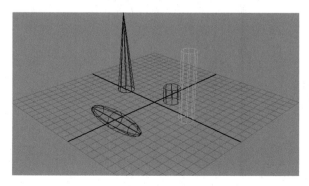

Perspective view of cylinders

Project 04

The short flag names represent the following:

-n	**name**
-ax	**axis**
-p	**pivot**
-hr	**height ratio**

Tip: You will notice that long flag names can create a command that is easy to read but hard to type in. Short names are harder to decipher but easy to type. Generally, the Command line is a good place for entering short flags, while long flags should be used in scripts to aid in readability.

7   Delete all objects

- Enter the following:

```
select -all; delete < Enter >
```

The Script Editor window

You may have noticed that the Command line is a small space to work in and only has one line of feedback. The Script Editor is a special user interface element that will make entering commands easier.

Up until now, you have been entering random commands in order to learn about their syntax and how they work. You will now use the Script Editor to build a sphere and a locator that will mimic the *eyeballs/lookAt* relationship that you created in the character rig from this book. The ultimate goal is to set up a blink attribute that will control the blinking of your character's eyes.

1   Open the Script Editor window

- Click on the Script Editor button in the lower right of the workspace, or select **Window → General Editors → Script Editor**.

  The window opens to show all of the commands you just entered.

  The upper part of this window contains the commands already executed (the history), while the bottom portion is the input section where you enter commands.

- From the Script Editor, select **Edit → Clear History**.

2   Create a primitive sphere

- Select **Create → Polygon Primitives → Sphere**.

  In the Script Editor, you can see the MEL command that was used to create the sphere. Also included are the flags, with default settings presented in their short form.

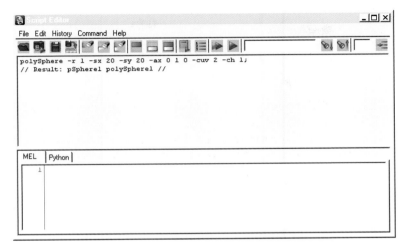

Script Editor

- In the lower portion of the Script Editor, type the following:

```
delete;
```

- Press the numeric keypad **Enter** key to execute the command.

Tip: *In the Script Editor, the numeric keypad's **Enter** key executes an action while the alpha-numeric keypad's **Enter** key returns to the next line.*

---

3 Copy and edit the sphere commands

Now that the sphere command is in the Script Editor's history, you can use this command as a starting point for writing your own command.

- In the Script Editor, select the part of the command with the **-r 1** flag.
- **Copy** the text into the lower portion of the Script Editor.

  *You can do this by highlighting the text and selecting **Edit → Copy** from the Script Editor window, or by pressing **Ctrl+c**. Then, click in the input section and select **Edit → Paste** or press **Ctrl+v**. You could also use your **MMB** (LMB on Macintosh) to drag and drop the script*

- Edit the first part of the command to read as follows:

```
polySphere -r 2 -ax 1 0 0 -name eyeball
```

- Press the **Enter** key on your numeric keypad.

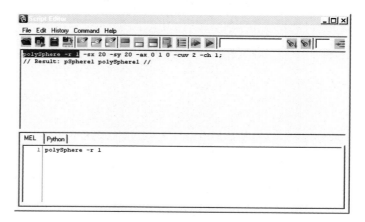

Copied script in the Script Editor

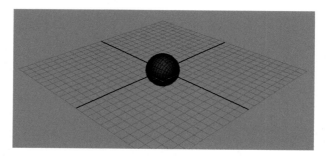

The eyeball

4   Create a locator

- Select **Create → Locator**.

In the Script Editor, you will see a corresponding MEL command.

- Enter **undo** to go back one step.

5   Echo all commands

- In the Script Editor, select **History → Echo All Commands**.

- Select **Create → Locator**.

In the Script Editor, you can now see a MEL command that you can use to create a locator:

```
createPrimitive nullObject;
```

- In the Script Editor, select **History → Echo All Commands** to turn this option **Off**.

> **Note:** *This command is surrounded by other commands that belong to Maya software. You only need to focus on the locator command.*

6 Rename and move the locator

You will now name the locator as *lookAt*. This object will be used as a substitute for the control node you built earlier in the character scene.

- Enter the following:

```
rename locator1 lookAt;

move 10 0 0 lookAt < Enter >
```

7 Add an attribute to the locator

You will now add a Blink attribute. This command is the same as using **Modify** → **Add Attribute** from the UI.

- Enter the following:

```
addAttr -ln blink -at "float" -min 0.1 -max 1 -dv 1 lookAt < Enter >
```

The short flag names represent the following;

-ln	**long name of the new attribute**
-at	**attribute type**
-min/max	**minimum/maximum values for the attribute**
-dv	**default value for the attribute**

8 Make the attribute keyable on the Blink attribute

At this time, the attribute has been added to the node, but is visible only in the Attribute Editor and not in the Channel Box until you set it to keyable. The following will solve this issue.

- Enter the following:

```
setAttr -keyable true lookAt.blink < Enter >
```

9 Set up your Perspective view panel

- Set up your view panel to see the eyeball object and locator.
- Press **5** to turn on hardware shading.
- Select **Display** → **Grid** to turn **Off** the grid.
- Select **Shading** → **Wireframe on Shaded**.

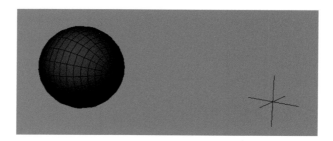

Eyeball and locator

Learning more about commands

You now know how to use a few of the many Maya software commands. To learn more about the commands, refer to the online documentation where you will find a complete list of all the commands available in MEL. Each command is listed with descriptions of the various flags.

Expressions

When you write an expression in the Expression Editor, it can be written as a MEL script. You can also use MEL to create the expressions from within the Script Editor.

You will create an expression to control the *scale Y* of the *eyeball* node. In your character rigs, you used a different set-up involving connections, but for the sake of this lesson, it will be simpler to mimic the blink by animating the scaling of the sphere. You can thus compare the use of expressions and connections.

1 Add an expression to the eyeball

This expression will ensure that the Blink attribute scales the eyeball on the Y-axis.

- Enter the following:

```
expression -n blinkExpression -s "eyeball.sy = lookAt.blink"
< Enter >
```

2 Test the Blink attribute

- Enter the following:

```
setAttr "lookAt.blink" 0.1 < Enter >
```

3 **Set keys on the Blink attribute**

  • Enter the following:

```
setKeyframe -at blink -t 1 -v 1 lookAt;

setKeyframe -at blink -t 5 -v 0.1 lookAt;

setKeyframe -at blink -t 10 -v 1 lookAt < Enter >
```

  The short flag names represent the following:

  -at   **attribute that is being keyed**

  -t   **time at which you want the key set**

  -v   **value of the attribute you want to key**

  • **Playback** the results.

  Keys have been set on three frames so the eye is closing and opening.

Building a blink procedure

You are now going to create a blink procedure that you will save as a MEL script. The next few steps outline every part of the MEL script, with some tips on how to enter and execute it. At the end of this lesson, you will find the script without descriptive text. You can enter the script later, in case you want to read over this section first.

Writing the script

You will write the blink procedure, not in the Script Editor, but in a Text Editor. A Text Editor is an application that lets you work quickly with text and then save in a generic text format.

1 **Open a Text Editor**

  • Open a Text Editor such as *WordPad* or *TextEdit*.

> **Tip:**   *The output document needs to be a simple text file without any formating.*

2 **Type comments to create header information**

  Every script should start with a header that contains important information for other people who might read your script later. Below is an example header. The // placed in front of these lines indicates that they are comments and therefore will be ignored when you later execute the script.

Lesson 29: MEL Scripting

- Type the following:

```
//

//          Creation Date:                    Today's date

//          Author:                           Your name here

//

//          Description:


//              Learning Maya tutorial script

//              This script builds a procedure for animating

//              the character's lookAt.blink attribute

//
```

Tip: *Don't underestimate the importance of commenting on your scripts. Down the line, someone will need to read what you have done and the comments are much easier to follow than the actual script.*

3   Declare the procedure

The first thing you enter is designed to declare the procedure. This line loads the procedure into the Maya software's memory so that it can be executed later.

- Type the following:

```
global proc blink (float $blinkDelay){
```

This line defines a procedure named *blink*. The required argument resides within the parentheses. This tells Maya what the script requires to execute. In this case, the length of the blink action is required. This is defined as a floating value called **$blinkDelay**. Because this value is not yet determined, it is known as a variable. The $ sign defines it as a variable. The open bracket—the { symbol—is added to the end of the declaration to let you start inputting MEL statements.

4   Set up variables

Within your script, you will use variables to represent values that may need to change later. At the beginning of the script, you need to set up the variables and set their value. In some cases, you may set their value with an actual number. But for this script, you will use attribute names and values instead.

- Type the following:

```
// Set up variables that will be used in the script

string $blink = "lookAt.blink";

float $time = `currentTime -query`;

float $blinkCurrent = `getAttr $blink`;
```

The first variable set defines *$blink* as the *blink* attribute found on the *lookAt* node. The second variable queries Maya for the current time. The third attribute gets the actual value of the *lookAt.blink* at the queried time.

Note: *To generate the quotation marks for the float $time and float $blinkCurrent in the above lines, use the ` quotation mark located to the left of the number 1 key on most keyboards.*

5 **Set keys on the blinking**

Next, you want to set keys on the Blink attribute at the beginning, middle and end of the blink. The length of the blink will be defined by the *blinkDelay* variable that was set as the main argument of the procedure. Notice that while other variables were set at the beginning of the script, the *blinkDelay* is used as an argument so that you can set it when the script is executed later. As you enter the keyframe commands, notice how you use the normal set-up of command/flag/node name.

- Type the following:

```
// set key for the blink attribute at the current time

setKeyframe    -value $blinkCurrent

                              -time $time

                              -attribute $blink

                              $blink;
```

Lesson 29: MEL Scripting

```
// set key for a blink of 0 half way through the blink
    setKeyframe      -value 0
                              -time ($time + $blinkDelay/2)
                              -attribute $blink
                              $blink;


// set key for the original blink value at the end of the blink
    setKeyframe      -value $blinkCurrent
                                        -time ($time + $blinkDelay)
                                        -attribute $blink
                                        $blink;


    }
```

In this part of the script, you have set keys using the *setKeyframe* command. The keys set at the beginning and end of the blink use the queried value of the Blink attribute, while the key set in the middle uses a value of zero. At the end, a closed bracket—the } symbol—is used to declare the statement complete.

6   Save your script

You can now save your script into your *Maya* scripts directory. This will ensure that the procedure is easily available any time you need it.

• In your Text Editor, save the script using the following path:

```
\[user profile]\maya\scripts\blink.mel
```

Note: *Because the procedure is named blink, you should save the file as "blink.mel." Though this is not required, Maya software will automatically source the script when MEL calls "blink."*

7   Loading the script

Because you named the file *blink.mel* and placed it in your *maya/scripts* directory, the script will be loaded automatically the next time you launch the Maya software. For now, you need to load the script manually.

- In the Script Editor, select **File** → **Source Script**...
- **Browse** for the script you saved in the last step.

  The script is loaded and you now have access to it.

8   Testing the script

If you enter **blink** with a value for the blink delay, Maya software will look in the scripts directory for a procedure called *blink.mel*.

- Set the Time Slider to frame **40**.
- Enter the following:

      blink 10 **< Enter >**

- Scrub in the Time Slider to test the results.

  If this works, you can congratulate yourself on completing your first MEL script and move on to the next section.

  If it doesn't, you must have typed something incorrectly. Open the Script Editor to review its feedback to find your mistake.

9   Debugging your script

To debug your script, you need to find out which line is causing the error, and then go back and check your spelling and syntax. Did you use the correct symbols? Did you name your nodes correctly? Is your capitalization correct?

- To display line numbers in the Script Editor, enable **History** → **Line numbers in errors**.

Adding the function to the UI

Now that you have created your own function, you will want to have easy access to it. Below are three methods for adding your function to the default UI, which you can easily set up using interactive methods.

1   Creating a shelf button

- In the Script Editor, select the text **blink 10**.
- Click on the selected text with the **MMB** (**LMB** on Macintosh) and drag it up to the shelf.
- Select MEL when you are asked if your script is MEL or Python.

  It is placed on the shelf with a MEL icon. You can now move the Time Slider to a new position and test it. You could also drag up different blinkDelay settings to offer different blink options. Or, you could set up a marking menu as outlined below.

2   Creating a blink marking menu set

- Select **Window** → **Settings/Preferences** → **Marking Menu Editor**.
- Click on the **Create Marking Menu** button.
- Click on the top middle square with your **RMB** and select **Edit Menu item...** from the pop-up menu.
- In the Edit North window, type *Blink 10* in the **Label** field.
- In the **Command(s):** field, type `blink 10.`
- Click **Save** and **Close**.
- **Repeat** for the other quadrants to set up blink commands that use a *blinkDelay* of **20**, **30**, and **40**.
- In the **Menu name** field, enter: `blinking`.
- Click the **Save** button, then **Close**.

3   Prepare the blink marking menu for a hotkey

The blink marking menu now needs to be set up.

- In the **Marking Menus** window, set the following:

   Use marking menu in to **Hotkey Editor**.

   Now the marking menu can be set up in the Hotkey Editor so that it can be accessed using a hotkey.

- Click the **Apply Settings** button, then **Close**.

4   Assign the blink marking menu to a hotkey

- Select **Window** → **Settings/Preferences** → **Hotkey Editor**.
- Scroll to the bottom of the **Categories** list and click on the **User Marking Menus** category.
- In the **Commands** window, click on the **blinking_Press** listing.
- In the **Assign New HotKey** section, set the following;

   Key to **9**;

   Direction to **Press**.

   A message will appear stating whether or not a particular key has been assigned or not. In this case, 9 is not assigned.

- Press the **Assign** key.

   A message should appear stating that the hotkey will not work properly unless the release is also set. The Maya software will ask if you want the release key set for you.

- Click **Yes**.
- Click on **Save** in the **Hotkey Editor** window and then **Close**.

5 Use the new marking menu

- Go to frame **80**.
- Press and hold the **9** hotkey, **LMB+click**, then pick one of the blinking options from the marking menu.

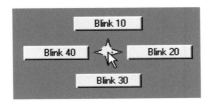

Blink marking menu

Building a custom UI script

In the next section, you will write a second script that will build a custom user interface window that includes a slider for the *blinkDelay* variable and a button that executes the blink procedure you scripted earlier. In the Maya software, you have the ability to use MEL to build custom user interface elements.

Custom user interface window

1 Start a new text file

2 Adding the opening comments

Start the script with a commented header that helps others read your work. While this was mentioned earlier, it should be emphasized again.

- Type the following:

```
//
// Creation Date:          Today's date
// Author:                 Your name here
//
```

```
// Description:

//                    Learning Maya tutorial script

//                    This script builds a custom user interface

//                    for executing the blink procedure

//                    and for setting the blink delay

//
```

3   Declare a get info procedure

You are now going to create a procedure called *blinkGetInfo* that will be used to get the *blinkDelay* value from a slider, which you will build later in the script. Since the value set in the slider is meant to be the chosen value for the blink, this procedure queries the slider to set the *blinkDelay*, and then adds that value next to the blink command.

- Type the following:

```
global proc blinkGetInfo() {


    // get necessary information from the Maya software


    float $blinkDelay = `intSliderGrp

    -query -value blinkWindow|columnLayout|delaySlider`;


    blink $blinkDelay;

}
```

4   Declare a second user interface procedure

You are now going to declare a procedure that will build a floating window. This window will look and act like any other window in Maya, but will be designed to help you keyframe a blink to any of your character rigs.

- Type the following:

```
global proc blinkWindow() {
```

5   Remove any existing blink windows

As you start a user interface script, it is a good idea to check if the same UI element already exists in the scene and, if so, to delete it. This ensures that your new element is the only one recognized by Maya software at any one time.

- Type the following:

```
// clean up any existing blinkWindows

if ( (`window -ex blinkWindow`) == true ) deleteUI blinkWindow;
```

6   Build the window called blinkWindow

The next part of the script is designed to build a window that is 400 pixels wide and 75 pixels tall. You will call it Blink Control in its title bar, but the software will know it as *blinkWindow*.

- Type the following:

```
window

        -width 400

        -height 100

        -title "Blink Control"

blinkWindow;
```

7   Form a column layout

Within the window, you need to organize your user interface elements. One method of organization is a *columnLayout*. This sets up a column with a particular spacing in relation to the window.

- Type the following:

```
columnLayout

        -columnAttach "right" 5

        -rowSpacing 10

        -columnWidth 375

columnLayout;
```

8   Create a slider group

Within the layout, you want to build a slider that lets you set the *blinkDelay* value. MEL offers you preset *kits* using special group commands that build several UI types in one go. The *intSliderGrp* builds a slider along with a field for seeing the resulting value and for entering the value yourself. This slider is set to integer values, since frames are generally set in whole numbers. The flags let you set the various values for the minimum and maximum settings of the slider.

- Type the following:

```
intSliderGrp

        -label "Blink Delay"

        -field true

        -minValue 2

        -maxValue 30

        -fieldMinValue 0

        -fieldMaxValue 100

        -value 10

delaySlider;
```

9   Create a button

The next part of the script builds a button that you will be using to execute the *blinkGetInfo* procedure, which in turn uses the *blinkDelay* value from the slider to execute the *blink* command. At the end, you will enter *setparent* to link the button to the *columnlayout*.

- Type the following:

```
button

        -label "Blink"

        -width 70

        -command "blinkGetInfo"

button;

        setParent ..;
```

10 **Show the window**

You are almost finished! Now you must tell Maya to show the window.

- Type the following:

```
showWindow blinkWindow;
```

11 **Finish the script**

Finally, you must complete the procedure and make one final declaration of the *blinkWindow* procedure name.

- Type the following:

```
}

blinkWindow;
```

12 **Saving the script**

You can now save your script into your *Maya* scripts directory.

- In your Text Editor, save the script using the following path:

```
\[user profile]\maya\scripts\blinkWindow.mel
```

13 **Test your script**

- In the Script Editor, select **File** → **Source Script** and browse to the script you just saved.
- In the Command line or the Script Editor, type the following:

```
blinkWindow < Enter >
```

The window should open. You can now set the Time Slider to a new time, and then set the blink delay using the slider. Pressing the button will key the blink.

Keyframing the blink

Congratulations! You now have your own custom user interface element built and ready to go. You can open your character file, such as *13-bigzRig_05.ma,* and use this script to make the character blink.

This will only work if you named your *lookAt* node correctly and created a **Blink** attributes outlined.

Note: *If your character has been referenced, chances are that it has been prefixed with a certain string. You might have to change your scripts to reflect this name in order to have your script work.*

The scripts

Here are the two scripts listed in their entirety for you to review:

Tip: *These scripts can be found in the MEL folder of the project4 support files.*

blink.mel

```
//
// Creation Date: Today's date
// Author:         Your name here
//
// Description:
//                 Learning Maya tutorial script
//                 This script builds a procedure for animating
//                 the character's lookAt.blink attribute
//
global proc blink (float $blinkDelay){

// Set up variables that will be used in the script
    string $blink = "lookAt.blink";
    float $time = `currentTime -query`;
    float $blinkCurrent = `getAttr $blink`;

// set key for the blink attribute at the current time
    setKeyframe    -value $blinkCurrent
```

```
            -time $time

            -attribute $blink

            $blink;


    // set key for a blink of 0 half way through the blink

        setKeyframe    -value 0

                       -time ($time + $blinkDelay/2)

                       -attribute $blink

                       $blink;


    // set key for the original blink value at the end of the blink

        setKeyframe    -value $blinkCurrent

                       -time ($time + $blinkDelay)

                       -attribute $blink

                       $blink;


    }
```

blinkWindow.mel

```
    //

    // Creation Date: Today's date

    // Author:        Your name here

    //

    // Description:

    //              Learning Maya tutorial script


    //              This script builds a custom user interface

    //              for executing the blink procedure

    //              and for setting the blink delay
```

```
//


global proc blinkGetInfo() {


    // get necessary information from Maya


    float $blinkDelay = `intSliderGrp -query -value blinkWindow|colu
mnLayout|delaySlider`;


    blink $blinkDelay;

}


global proc blinkWindow() {
    // clean up any existing blinkWindows
    if ( (`window -ex blinkWindow`) == true ) deleteUI blinkWindow;
    window

            -width 400

            -height 100

            -title "Blink Control"

    blinkWindow;


    columnLayout

            -columnAttach "right" 5

            -rowSpacing 10

            -columnWidth 375

    columnLayout;


    intSliderGrp

            -label "Blink Delay"
```

```
            -field true

            -minValue 2

            -maxValue 30

            -fieldMinValue 0

            -fieldMaxValue 100

            -value 10

    delaySlider;


    button

            -label "Blink"

            -width 70

            -command "blinkGetInfo"

    button;


            setParent ..;


    showWindow blinkWindow;


}


    blinkWindow;
```

Conclusion

By setting keys on the blink attribute and using MEL to animate the blink, you took the next step toward advancing your workflow. Understanding MEL scripts and commands and how they fit into your current user interface will allow you to build custom UI elements.

Project 05

In this project, you will use Autodesk® Combustion® software for compositing. You will first learn how to render using render layers. Once that is completed, you will learn the basics of the Combustion software interface and from there you will jump into compositing frames from the support files. After this project, you should feel comfortable rendering and compositing your creations.

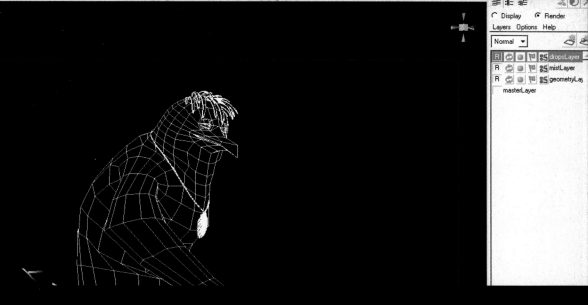

Lesson 30
Render Layers

Compositing is the process of merging layers of image information into one image to create a
final look. In order to create layers to composite together, you can use render layers, which allows
you to separate different objects and Render Settings within the same scene. In this lesson, you

Rendering Considerations

Before rendering, you should consider which is the best renderer for your needs, as well as setting attributes on the surfaces themselves and in the Render Settings. Listed below is a checklist of some of the considerations you should keep in mind when rendering.

OBJECT ISSUES

Some render attributes need to be set for your objects' shape nodes. You can set these attributes in the Rendering Flags window, in the shape node's Render section in the Attribute Editor, or in the Attribute Spread Sheet window. Below are some of the attributes you should consider when you render.

Surface tessellation

Set a NURBS surface tessellation that is appropriate to the scene. Larger and more prominent objects will require a larger tessellation than background elements.

It is important that you do not over-tessellate, otherwise you will slow down your renders.

You can also use the default tessellation settings, or choose **Explicit Tessellation** and refine even further.

Motion blur

When you turn on motion blur in the Render Settings, you can decide which objects will or will not use motion blur. If you have objects that are motionless or barely moving, turn motion blur off to speed up rendering.

You must also choose between 2D and 3D motion blur. The 2D motion blur is faster.

Lights and shadows

Limit the number of lights casting shadows in your scene. If possible, use depth map shadows, which are a little faster. If you want to add a lot of lights to a scene, consider linking some of the lights to only those objects that need the illumination.

RENDER ISSUES

Frame range

If you want to render an animation, you must choose a **Frame/Animation Ext.** in the **Render Settings** that supports animation. It is very easy to forget this and send off what you think is a long night of rendering frames, only to come in the next day to see just a single frame.

Renderable camera

Do you have the right camera set up for rendering? By default, only the Perspective camera will be used when rendering. Do not leave the default *persp* camera as *renderable* when you want to render another camera.

Masks and depth masks

If you plan to composite your renderings later, you may want to use these settings to create a matte layer (mask) or a Z-depth layer (depth mask) to assist in the compositing process.

Render resolution

What is the render size that you want? Be sure that if you change the pixel size, you use the *resolution gate* in your view panel to make sure that the framing of your scene is preserved.

Raytracing

Do you want to raytrace some of your objects? Remember that the Autodesk® Maya® software has a selective raytracer and only objects that require reflections, refractions or raytraced shadows will be raytraced.

Therefore, if you limit your reflective and refractive materials to key objects, you can raytrace them knowing that other objects in the scene are using the A-buffer.

If you are raytracing, try to limit the number of reflections set in the render settings. A setting of 1 will look good in most animations unless, for example, you have a chrome character looking into a mirror.

Render quality

You may want the *Anti-aliasing Quality presets* dropdown menu to suggest render quality options until you are familiar with the individual settings.

OTHER RENDERING CONSIDERATIONS

Test render, test render, test render

Do not start a major rendering unless you have test rendered at various levels. You should consider rendering the entire animation at a low resolution with low quality settings and frame steps to test your scene. Render random full-size single frames to confirm that materials, lights, and objects are rendering properly.

The more you test render, the less time you spend redoing renderings that didn't work out the way you wanted.

Command line rendering

You have learned how to batch render from within the Maya software. You can also render from a command prompt. Here is the basic workflow for a Maya command line render for Windows:

- Set up your Render Settings.
- **Save** your scene file.
- **Open** a command prompt.

  Windows users, select **Start** → **Run**. In the Run prompt, type cmd and press **Enter**.

  Macintosh users, **open** the **Terminal** utility. At the prompt type cd /Applications/ Autodesk/[maya version]/Maya.app/Contents/bin/ and press **Enter**.

> **Note:** *[maya version] corresponds to the folder of your current Maya Software installation.*

- Type Render -help for a list of all the command line options.
- Type chdir or cd into the directory with your file.
- Enter the Render command along with any flags, such as the start and end frames for the rendering, followed by the file name as shown in the following:

```
Render -s 1 -e 150 -b 1 walkTest.mb
```

Compositing advantages

A common misconception is that compositing is for large productions with many artists. However, smaller production facilities and individual artists can also benefit from the opportunities and advantages offered by compositing. For example, with compositing you can:

- Have the flexibility to re-render or color correct individual elements without having to re-render the whole scene.
- Increase creative potential and achieve effects with a 2D compositing package that are not possible with the renderer.
- Take advantage of effects that are faster and more flexible in 2D, such as depth of field and glow, rather than rendering them in 3D.
- Combine different looks from different renderers, such as hardware and software particle effects.
- Combine 3D rendered elements with 2D live action footage.
- Save time when rendering scenes where the camera does not move—you only need to render one frame of the background to be used behind the whole animation sequence.
- Successfully render large complex scenes in layers so that you don't exceed your hardware and software memory capabilities.

Render for compositing

Rendering in layers refers to the process of separating scene elements so that different objects or sets of objects can be rendered as separate images. The first step is to determine how to divide the scene into layers. This may be very simple or incredibly complex, depending entirely on your needs for any given project. Once you have decided how you want to separate your scene elements, you can set up render layers to suit your needs.

Render layers

A typical approach to separating your scene elements is to use *render layers*. You can assign objects to render layers using the same workflow as you would when working with display layers.

Render layers allow you to organize the objects in your scene specifically to meet your rendering needs. The most basic approach would be to separate objects into foreground, mid-ground and background layers. Or, you may decide to divide the scene elements by specific objects or sets of objects.

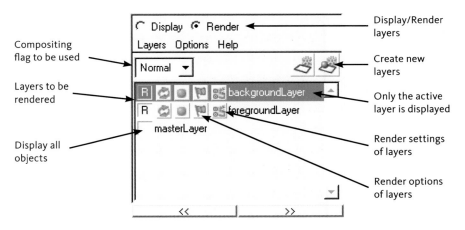

Render Layer Editor

Render passes

If you need to have very precise control over the color of your rendered objects separate from the shadows on them, you can further breakdown your scene by rendering separate passes within any render layer. The term *render passes* generally refers to the process of rendering various attributes separately, such as beauty, shadow, specular, color and diffuse. The Render Layer Editor allows you to set this up.

The following image shows BigZ rendered with two different render passes—specular highlights and diffuse. The image to the right shows the resulting composite image.

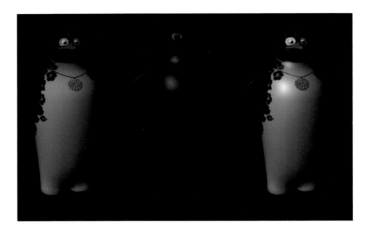

Diffuse and specular render passes along with composite image

Mist example

In order to experiment with render layers, you will render the mist that was created in
Lesson 28: Particles in three distinct passes. The first layer will be for geometry, the second for
the mist software particles and the third for the drops hardware particles.

1 Scene file

- Set your current project to the *project5* folder.

- **Open** the scene file *30-surfRender_01.ma*.

  This scene is the same scene as the particle scene from the last project.

2 Render layers

- In the Layer Editor located at the bottom of the Channel Box, select the **Render**
  radio button.

- Select **Layers → Create Empty Layer**.

  A new layer is created along with a masterLayer.

- Click on the new *layer1* to highlight it.

  Notice that all objects in your scene disappear. This is because this render layer is empty.

- Click on the *masterLayer* to highlight it.

  The masterLayer contains all the objects in your scene, so everything in the scene is displayed.

3 **Assign objects**

- **Double-click** on the *layer1* and **rename** it to *geometryLayer*.

- Click on the *masterLayer* in order to see the content of your scene.

- Select **Edit → Select All by Type → Polygon Geometry**.

- **RMB** on the *geometryLayer* and select **Add Selected Objects**.

- **Repeat** the last two steps to add all **NURBS Surfaces** to the *geometryLayer*.

- **Repeat** again the last steps to add all **Subdiv Geometry** to the *geometryLayer*.

4 **Assign lights**

By default, the renderer will render a scene that has no lights using default lighting. The same occurs when rendering render layers. In order to get your scene to render properly, you must add your lights to the render layer.

- Select **Edit → Select All by Type → Lights**.

- **RMB** on the *geometryLayer* and select **Add Selected Objects**.

The geometry layer content

5 **Render layer settings**

By default, all layers use the same Render Settings, so if you change something in the Render Settings window, all the layers will be updated accordingly. Fortunately, you can create layer overrides that are layer dependent. Each render layer can then have its own Render Settings. You will now specify specific Render Settings for the geometry layer.

- Click on the **Render Settings** button located to the right in the *geometryLayer* item in the Layer Editor.

  Doing so brings up the Render Settings specific to this render layer.

- Set **Render Using** to **Maya Software**.

Lesson 30: Render Layers

- **RMB** on the **Render Using** attribute's name in the Render Settings window to pop up a contextual menu.
- Select **Create Layer Override** to override this attribute for the selected layer.

  Notice the overridden attribute's name is now displayed in orange.

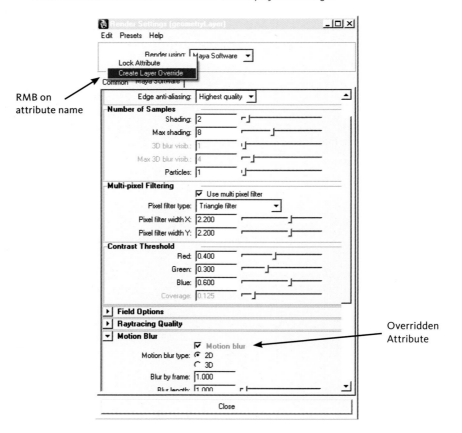

Overridden attributes in the Render Settings

- Set the different attributes to your liking, with motion blur, high anti-aliasing, etc., making sure to always **Create Layer Override** for each modified attribute.

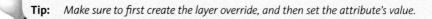

Tip: *Make sure to first create the layer override, and then set the attribute's value.*

- **Create** a layer override on the **File name prefix** from the **Common** tab and set it to *geometry*.

Tip: *Macintosh users may have to* **Ctrl-RMB** *on the* **File name prefix** *in order to create a layer override.*

Note: *By clicking the Render button at the top of the Maya interface or when selecting* **Render → Render Current Frame**, *only the selected render layer will be rendered.*

6 Mist render layer

- Select the *masterLayer*.
- Select the *smoke* particles.
- To create the new render layer, click on the **Create new layer and assign selected objects** button in the Layer Editor.
- **Rename** the layer to *mistLayer*.
- **RMB** on the *geometryLayer* and select **Select Objects**.
- **RMB** on the *mistLayer* and select **Add Selected Objects**.
- With the *mistLayer* still highlighted and the geometry objects still selected, go to the **Rendering** menu set and select **Lighting/Shading → Assign New Material → Surface Shader**.

  This assigns a black surface shader material to the selected objects only for the selected render layer. The Attribute Editor is shown to let you customize the new material.

Note: *Make sure all the visible objects in the layer are properly assigned to the new surface shader. If some objects are not* **properly** *assigned, simply select them and assign the new material again from the Hypershade.*

- Set the **Out Matte Opacity** of the *surfaceShader* to be completely **black**.

  Doing so ensures that the surface objects render with a black alpha channel, leaving only the front particles with a proper alpha channel to be composited later on.

- Set the proper rendering attributes to your liking for this layer.

The mist layer content

Lesson 30: Render Layers

- **Create** a layer override on the **File name prefix** from the **Common** tab and set it to *mist*.

7 Drops render layer

The drops layer is different from the mistLayer only because it will be using the hardware renderer rather than the software renderer.

- Highlight the mistLayer.

- From the Layer Editor, select **Layers** → **Copy Layer** → ❑.

- In the option window, make sure to select the **Copy layer mode: With membership and overrides**.

- Click the **Apply and Close** button.

- **Rename** the new layer to *dropsLayer*.

- Select the *smoke* particles, then **RMB** on the *dropsLayer* and select **Remove Selected Objects**.

- Select the *drops* particles from the *masterLayer*, and then **add** them to the *dropsLayer*.

  You now have a layer similar to the mistLayer, but with only the drops visible.

- Click the **Render Settings** button for the *dropsLayer*.

- Change **Render Using** to **Maya Hardware**.

- Under the **Render Options** tab in the **Maya Hardware** tab, turn **On** the **Enable**

The drops layer content

- **Create** a layer override on the **File name prefix** from the **Common** tab and set it to *drops*.

Batch render

You now have three render layers in place, ready to be rendered. You will now launch the renders with a single command once the final touches are brought to the scene.

1 Renderable camera

It is important to define the proper camera to render your scene from. By default, only the Perspective camera's **Renderable** option is turned **on**. If you keep more than one camera renderable, Maya software will be rendering all of them when batch rendering.

- Open the Hypershade and select the **Cameras** tab.
- In the Attribute Editor for each camera, make sure only the desired camera, such as the Perspective, is made **Renderable** under the **Output Settings** section.

2 Object attribute override

Just like for the Render Settings, it is possible to add render layer overrides to an object's attributes. Here you will set the sky as blue for the geometryLayer, but black for the other particle layers.

- With the *perspShape* camera displayed in the Attribute Editor, open the **Environment** section.
- With the *geometryLayer* highlighted, **RMB** on the **Background Color** attribute and select **Create Layer Override**.
- Set the **Background Color** to be a light blue.
- **Repeat** the previous steps to set the **Background Color** to **black** for the *mist* and *drops* layers.

3 Place the camera properly

- Make sure to frame the scene properly.

> **Tip:** *Display the camera's* **Resolution Gate** *if you want to clearly see what will be rendered.*

4 Common Render Settings

It is also very important to set the proper frames to render in the Common tab of the Render Settings.

- Select the *masterLayer* in the Render Editor.
- Click on the **Render Settings** button at the top of the Maya interface.

- Under the **Common** tab, make sure to set the following:

    Frame/Animation ext to **name.#.ext**;

    Start Frame to **150**;

    End Frame to **250**;

    By Frame to **1**;

    Image format to **Tiff [tif]**.

Tip: *For testing purposes, you might want to set a much smaller frame range.*

5 **Test render the layers**

- In the Layer Editor, select **Options → Render All Layers → ❑.**

    *When **Render All Layers** is enabled, this option window allows you to choose from three basic options for previewing your composite image in the Render view. The first one, **Composite layers**, will render all the layers and then composite the frames together. The second option, **Composite and keep layers**, will allow you to display all layers plus the composite images in the Render view. The third option, **Keep layers**, will only show you the individual layers.*

Note: *The order of the layers will determine the order of compositing. The bottom layer is furthest from camera and the top layer is closest to the camera.*

*When **Render All Layers** is disabled, only the current layer will be previewed in the Render view.*

Tip: *You can specify for each render layer how you would like to blend the layers together by selecting a **Blend Mode** from the dropdown menu at the top of the Layer Editor.*

- Set the **Keep Layers** option, and then click the **Apply and Close** button.
- In the Layer Editor, select **Options → Render All Layers** to enable it.
- If you do not want to render a specific layer, simply toggle the **R** located on the left of the render layer item in the Layer Editor.

6 **Save your work**

- **Save** your scene as *30-surfRender_02.ma*.

7 Batch render

The time has come to launch a batch render and take a well-earned coffee break. The following shows how to launch a batch render.

- From the **Rendering** menu set, select **Render** → **Batch Render** → ❑.

- If your computer has multiple processors, you may profit from the **Use all available processors** option.

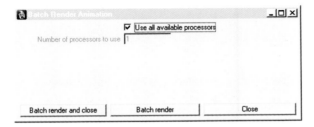

The batch render options

- **Click the Batch render and close button.**

  The batch render will launch and you can read the feedback messages in the Command Feedback line at the bottom of the interface.

Note: *Once the batch render has started, you can close the software and the batch render will still be executed.*

8 Look at rendered images

- You can look in the current project's *images* folder for the output images that are placed in a folder named after each render layer.

  The rendered images will be composited together in Lesson 32.

Conclusion

In this lesson, you have learned the basics of render layers. You should now have several rendered images ready to be composited together.

In the next lesson, you will learn about the Combustion compositing software. With your knowledge of Combustion techniques, you will be able to finalize your scene render and even implement additional effects.

Lesson 31
Combustion

This lesson is intended to provide a basic understanding of how to operate the Combustion software, Autodesk's powerful desktop solution for creating stunning visual effects. It is a resolution-independent, vector paint, animation, editing and 2D/3D compositing software application for multi-platform work—from the Web to video and HDTV to feature film.

Whether you are a motion graphics designer, animator, visual effects artist or Web designer, the Combustion software empowers you with the tools you need to create outstanding visual effects for your projects. You will now learn the basics of this compositing package.

In this lesson you will learn the following:

- About the Combustion terminology
- How to build a workspace
- About the Combustion interface
- How to navigate in the workspace
- How to use operators
- How to create particle effects

Terminology

With Combustion software, you create workspaces that contain composites, paint projects and other effects projects. Each of these contains footage items (movie clips or images) that you process to achieve the results you want to render.

Interface

The interface is defined by multiple viewports that allow you to simultaneously see the results of different operators. The workspace can be configured to support up to four independent monitors.

Operators

Operators define the different actions taken in your compositing tasks in order to get to the final composite image.

Branch

When an operator is applied to the output of another operator, it creates a flow of image data. Each separate image flow, or stream, is called a branch.

Process tree

The process tree is the collection of all the branches in the workspace. There is only one process tree in each workspace file.

Workspace

A workspace contains all the work you have done within the same process tree. You can save your work as a workspace file (a file with the .cws file extension).

Clips

Sequence of consecutive images that are part of the same animation.

Composite

A composite is made up of layers. Layers are 2D objects that you can move in 2D or 3D space. Combustion software offers powerful 3D compositing and optimized 2D compositing when the Z-axis, camera and lights are not needed. The engine also supports OpenGL hardware, so a composite can be modified, played and rendered quickly.

Particles

The software contains powerful 2D particle systems along with a library of predefined emitters. Those particles and emitters give you full control over their properties so that you can customize their look for your needs.

Create a workspace

Next, you will learn how to build a workspace in the Combustion software. Since this is only intended to allow you to experience the various features of the software, you will open single images and manipulate them throughout this lesson.

1   Install Combustion software

A link to a trial version of the Combustion software can be found on the DVD accompanying this book. Before continuing with this project, you will need to install this package.

2   Launch Combustion software

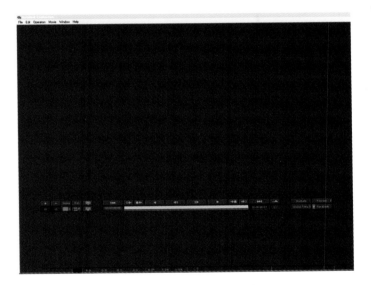

Combustion interface without workspace

3   Import footage

As you can see, when you launch the Combustion software, the viewport is empty because a workspace has not been created yet. All you see is the viewport options, the playback controls, and the animation and display quality options.

To start a workspace, you either create a workspace and then import footage into the workspace, or import footage and then choose the type of workspace you want to import the footage into.

- Select **File → Open** or press **Ctrl+o**.

Doing so brings up the Open dialog in which you can select the footage you want to import.

Open dialog

- You can see the files as **Thumbnails** or in **List View** by clicking on the button in the upper-right corner of the dialog. You can also choose to collapse image sequences with consecutive frame numbers.

- Select the *cody_render.jpg* and *wave_render.jpg* images from the *project5/image* directory of the support files.

Tip: *You can select more than one file in the same folder by holding down **Ctrl** or **Shift**.*

- Click the **OK** button.

  *The **Open Footage** dialog appears. This is where you choose what you are going to do with the selected footage. For this lesson you are going to create a **2D Composite** branch.*

- Select **2D Composite**, then click on the **OK** button.

  A 2D composite branch containing the footage you just imported is created. The cody_render image appears in the viewport since it is the footage you selected to import first, before the wave_render image.

Tip: *You can customize the appearance of the interface by selecting **File → Preferences**.*

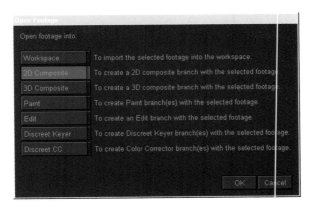

The Open Footage window

• Select **Window → Fit in Window.**

Doing so will enable you to see the entire image in the viewport.

The current workspace

4   Save the workspace

In order to be able to close the program and later come back to the workspace you just created, you will need to save your work.

- Select **File → Save Workspace**.

  A browser is displayed, allowing you to save your workspace on your drive.

- Give the workspace a proper name, such as *myFirstWorkspace,* and then click the **OK** button.

  A file called myFirstWorkspace.cws will be saved at the chosen location.

Note: *When using a trial version of Combustion software, the Save Workspace option is disabled.*

Interface overview

You are now going to review the Combustion interface. Once you have gone through this, you should be able to navigate the interface and locate the various key components.

Viewport

Viewport Options

Toolbar & Workspace Panel

Info

Animation and Display Quality Options

Timeline. Operators & Operators Controls Panel

Combustion workspace

Viewport

The *Viewport* shows the current composite at any point in the process tree. It also provides preview playback as you work on projects and updates dynamically as you make changes to your work. You can also use the viewport to select, transform and animate objects and layers.

Tip: *You can toggle* **On** *and* **Off** *the* **Show Viewports Only** *by pressing* **F11.**

Viewport options

The *viewport options* enable you to organize the viewport layout and to zoom and pan. You can switch between five multiple-viewport layouts or use the single-viewport layout. It also gives you the ability to switch to a schematic view.

Playback controls

Combustion software provides realtime playback for your composites. Use the *Playback Controls* to preview your work by playing or scrubbing through the clip.

The viewport options

The playback controls

> **Tip:** Upon display, rendered frames are kept in memory and can be later played back in realtime.

Display Quality options

The *Display Quality* options enable you to control the amount of image detail displayed in the viewport(s). The higher the image quality setting, the more time is required to update the viewport(s). Enable the Feedback option to redraw objects in the viewport(s) as you modify them.

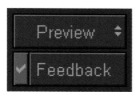

The Display Quality options

Toolbar

The *Toolbar* shows the tools that you use as you work with operators.

The toolbar

> **Note:** The toolbar is context sensitive. It shows the tools for the current operator.

Lesson 31: Combustion

Workspace panel

The *Workspace panel* is shown as a hierarchy tree view. Use it to select layers, access operator controls and choose what is displayed in the viewport. You can also use it to organize the operators, the order of operator branches, or the layers to control your final output.

Note: *You will learn more about operators in the section* **Working with operators** *later in this lesson.*

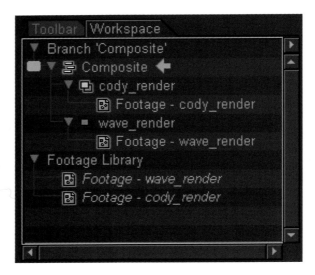

The workspace panel

Tip: *To expand the workspace panel you can press* **Shift-F10** *to dock the workspace panel on the left side of the interface.*

Timeline

The *Timeline* provides an overall view of all animated objects and channels in the workspace. Use it to view and edit the keyframes, or to create and modify expressions. The timeline can be viewed in two different modes:

- The **Overview** mode displays the duration of a layer, an object, or an operator in the composite.

Project 05

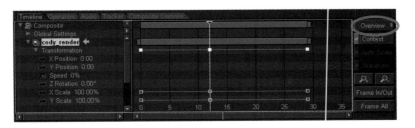

The timeline in Overview mode

- The **Graph** mode shows the value of a category's channel over time.

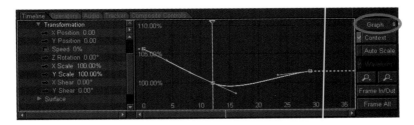

The timeline in Graph mode

Tip: *To increase your timeline's view, press* **Shift-F11** *to expand as a toggle mode.*

Operators panel

Use the *Operators panel* to quickly add operators to the process tree. The operator panel includes a list of operator categories on the left, and a list of operator buttons in the selected category on the right.

The Operators panel

Lesson 31: Combustion

Operator Controls panel

The *Operator Controls* panel is context sensitive. Only the controls that apply to the selected operator are displayed. When you select an operator in the workspace panel, its controls appear and the name of the panel changes to that of the selected operator.

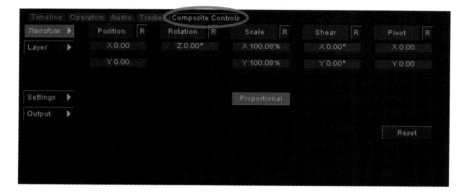

The Composite Controls panel

Info Palette

The *Info Palette* is located across the bottom of the interface and displays information about the cursor position, current tool, workspace name, cache and memory.

The Info Palette

Note: *You can choose which elements to display on the Info Palette by right-clicking on it.*

Customization

You can hide or show each one of the interface panels by accessing the **Window** → **Palettes** menu. You will be able to customize your Combustion interface as you like it.

Navigating the workspace

Perhaps the most useful panel to work with is the workspace panel. You use the workspace panel to select layers, access operator controls and choose what is displayed in the viewport. More importantly, you can use it to organize the order of operator branches, operators or layers to control your final composited image.

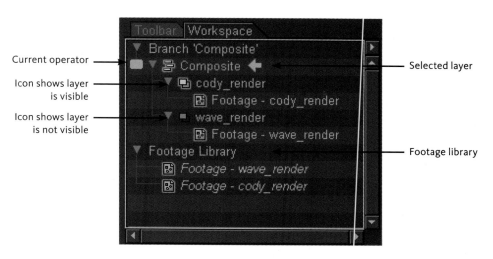

Current operator

Icon shows layer is visible

Icon shows layer is not visible

Selected layer

Footage library

The Workspace panel

Current operator

To display an operator in the viewport, **double-click t**he operator's name in the workspace panel. The viewport icon shown next to the operator indicates it is the current operator.

Selected operator

To select an operator in the workspace panel, simply click on its name. An arrow will appear to the right and the information in the timeline and Operator Controls panel is updated.

Active and inactive layers and operators

To activate or deactivate a layer or operator in the workspace panel, simply click the layer's or operator's icon. The icon is highlighted when activated.

Layer and operator order

You can use the workspace panel to organize the order of the layers and operators in your composite by **click+dragging** the layer or operator to another location in the workspace panel.

Nested layers and operators

Nesting means taking selected layers or operators and grouping them. The following shows how to nest layers.

- Highlight a layer, and then hold down **Ctrl** to select additional layer(s).
- **RMB** on any of the selected layers and select **Nesting...** from the context menu or select **Object → Nest.**
- Click **Selected Layers** from the **Nesting Options** window.

Lesson 31: Combustion

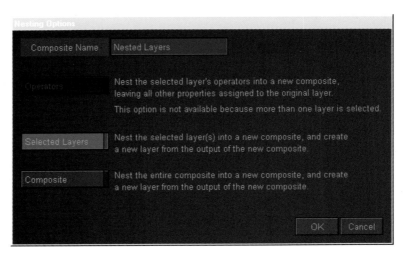

The Nesting Option window

- Click the **OK** button.

  The layers you selected are now nested.

Footage Library

The list of all footage used in the workspace appears in the Footage Library, located at the bottom of the workspace panel.

Renaming layers

To quickly recognize each element that is part of your workspace, it is recommended that you rename the elements. You can rename layers, operators and any operator objects. Do so by **right-clicking** on the element in the workspace panel and choosing **Rename** from the context menu.

Working with operators

An *operator* is an operation that modifies a layer or a composite. It can be as simple as a blur or as complex as painted tracked animation. Operators are processed one after another in the process tree. The result of one operator serves as the input for the next. You can apply an operator to a single layer or to an entire branch.

You will now work with operators with basic examples.

1 Workspace

- **Open** your last saved workspace named *myFirstWorkspace.cws*.

- Double-click the *wave_render* layer in the workspace panel to make it current.

- Select the **Operators** panel.

  All the available operators are listed.

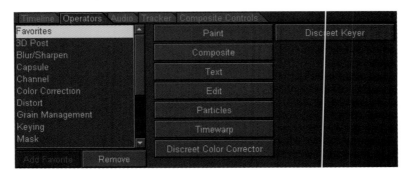

The Operators panel

2 Apply new operator

You will now experiment with the Discreet® Color Corrector operator.

- Select the **Color Correction** category on the left side of the **Operators** panel.

  The list of operators from this category is displayed.

- Click the **Discreet Color Corrector** operator.

  The Discreet Color Corrector is added to the wave_render layer in the workspace panel.

Operator added
to a layer

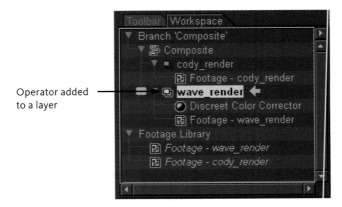

The Operators panel

> **Tip:** *When creating an operator, hold down* **Ctrl** *at the same time as clicking the operator button to automatically display the operator's* **control panel.**

3   Modifying operators

- Select the **Color Correction Controls** panel.

The Color Correction Controls panel

- **Tweak** the operator's properties and watch the results as the viewport gets updated.

> **Tip:** *For a faster preview of the operator, you can temporarily decrease the viewport display quality by changing the Display Quality options located to the right under the viewport.*

4   Storing operator settings

You can use the storage buttons to store up to five versions of your operator setting and then quickly switch between the different settings to compare the results.

Storage buttons

The Operator storage settings

- At the bottom right corner of the **Color Correction Controls** panel, **enable** the **Store** option.

  The current operator setting is stored in the first storage button.

- Select the store button **2** to create a new setting.

- **Tweak** the operator's properties.

- You can now switch from **store 1** to **store 2** to compare the different settings.

Project 05

5 Copying operators

Operators can be copied to get the same effect on another layer.

- In the workspace panel, **RMB** the *Discreet Color Corrector* operator and select **Copy** from the context menu.

- In the workspace panel, **RMB** the *cody_render* layer and select **Paste** from the context menu.

  A Discreet Color Corrector operator with the same settings is copied and applied to the cody_render layer.

Tip: *You can also use* **Ctrl+c** *and* **Ctrl+v** *to copy and paste operators.*

Operator examples

Now that you know how to apply an operator to a layer, you can experiment with other types of operators to see their effects. The following are some popular operators and filters that you might end up using in your work.

Blur/sharpen

Use a blur operator to create a blurring effect or a sharpen operator to make an image appear sharper. The following are some simple examples of these operators.

- **Box blur**

  Use a box blur filter as a quick and effective method for creating a blurring effect. It is fairly close to the look achieved using Gaussian blur, but renders much faster.

The result of a box blur effect

- **Pan blur**

  Use a pan blur operator to simulate a directional blur created by fast-moving objects.

The result of a pan blur effect

- **Dolly blur**

  Use a dolly blur operator to create a radial blur that increases outwards from a defined center point.

The result of a dolly blur effect

- **Sharpen**

  Use a sharpen operator to increase the clarity and sharpness of an image.

The result of a sharpen effect

Color correction

There are several operators in the Color Correction category, but Discreet Color Corrector is perhaps the most versatile operator. This operator contains many functions that will alter footage to reach the desired custom look.

- **Discreet Color Corrector**

  Use the Discreet Color Corrector when you need a high level of control and precision to perform color adjustment on your images.

The result of a Discreet Color Corrector operator

Distort

Use a distort operator to distort the shapes and contours of your images.

> **Note:** *Distort filters have no effect on color values.*

- **Mirror**

  Use a mirror operator to have one side of your image reflected to the other side.

The result of a mirror effect

- **Pinch**

  Use a pinch operator to make your image appear squeezed either inward or outward from the defined center point.

The result of a pinch effect

Noise

You can use noise operators to break flat computed generated images, or to simulate film grain.

- **Add noise**

  Use an add noise operator to give your image a grittier, more textured look. This operator adds random pixels to your images.

The result of an add noise effect

- **Turbulence**

  Turbulence is like a texture generator since it generates an effect over your layers. You can use a turbulence operator to simulate fog in a scene.

The result of a turbulence effect

Stylize

The stylize operators use the colors in a layer to generate creative effects.

- **Glow**

  Use a glow operator to generate subtle gradations of light in your image.

The result of a glow effect

- **Lens flare**

  Use a lens flare operator to create an effect similar to when a camera lens is hit directly by the sun or another bright light source.

The result of a lens flare effect

Note: *You should experiment with the operators and filters mentioned above to familiarize yourself with the operators. Try tweaking the properties of the different operators to obtain different results. You can also enable multiple operators at the same time and change their order.*

The result of combined operators

Particle effects

The particles operator creates particles on 2D layers, giving the illusion of 3D without the time and set-up required by 3D simulation.

In this exercise, you will use the particles operator to add smoke emitting from the surfboard.

1   **Load workspace**

  • **Load** the workspace called *myFirstWorkspace.cws* created at the beginning of this lesson.

  • Turn **Off** the *cody_render* layer to show only the *wave_render* layer.

2   **Particle layer**

  Particles can be applied as an operator to any layer or as a layer on its own. In most cases, it is better to create particles as an independent layer to have more control over the final result. By doing so, you will automatically get layer opacity and transfer mode, which would not be accessible with an operator.

  • Select the **Composite** operator from the **Favorites** operator category.

- Highlight the **Composite** operator in the workspace window.
- Select **Object** → **New Layer**.

  This brings up an options window.
- In the **Type** option, make sure **Particles** is selected.
- Give your new layer a name for easier identification in the **Name** field, such as *mist*.
- In the **Format Options** menu, choose the **Custom** preset.
- Set the following to match your current workspace:

  Set **Width** to **1280**;

  Set **Height** to **771**;

  Set **Pixel Aspect Ratio** to **1**;

  Set **Frame Rate** to **24**;

  Set **Fields** to **No Fields**;

  Set the **Transparent** option to **On** to add the alpha channel to the layer.

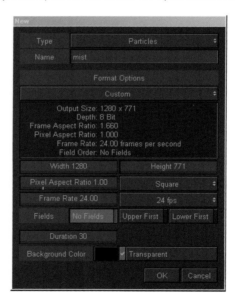

New layer window

- Select **OK** to create the particles layer.

  Once created, the particles layer becomes the current layer shown in the viewport. The viewport icon can be seen next to the layer name in the workspace panel.

3   Smoke library

Now that the particles layer is added to your composite, you can define the type of particle effect you want by choosing an emitter from the default particles library. You can also load additional particle presets.

- In the **Particle Controls** panel, click the **Load Library** button.
- Select the *Smoke.elc* file from the Load Emitter Library window.

The Load Emitter Library option window

- Select **OK** to load the smoke library.

  Several smoke emitter presets are now available.

- Scroll down in the smoke library and double-click **Smoke Jet** from the **Impulse Smoke** folder.

- In the preview panel to the right, make sure **Preview** is enabled.

  A preview of Smoke Jet is rendered.

The Smoke Jet preset

Lesson 31: Combustion

> **Tip:** *You can **click+drag** in the particle preview window to interact with the emitter's position.*

4 Add smoke particles

- Select the **Toolbar** panel to access the particle tools.
- Make sure the **Point Emitter Tool** is selected.

The Point Emitter Tool from the Toolbar

> **Tip:** *Double-click an emitter in the library to automatically select its default Particle Tool.*

- Click in the viewport where the mist is supposed to raise behind the board.

  The Smoke Jet emitter is added to the workspace.

> **Note:** Emitters will start emitting particles from the frame in which the emitter is added to the clip**.**

- **Double-click** the *Composite* operator to see its output in the viewport.

5 Emitter settings

Now that the emitter is created, you can tweak its settings.

At this time, the mist is not visible because the particle system starts its first particle on frame 1. To make the mist directly visible on the first frame, you must preload the particle.

- Highlight the *Smoke Jet* operator.
- Click the **Emitter** button from the **Particles Control** panel.
- Change the **Emission Angle** to **180** degrees.
- Set **Preload Frame** to **100**.

  This will give time to emit some mist particles before the first frame of your sequence.

- Set **Life** to **20%**.

  This will reduce the particles' lifespan.

- If required, click the **Transform** button in the **Particle Controls** panel and set the **Position X** and **Y** of the emitter manually.

- Highlight the *Particle – mist* layer from the workspace panel.
- Click the **Surface** button from the **Composite Controls** panel.
- Change the **Transfer Mode** from **Normal** to **Add** to have the particles blend with the background image.
- **Tweak** the properties of the *Smoke Jet* preset to create your own custom effect.

The final result showing smoke particles

6   Other particle emitters

As you can see, there are several particle emitter presets available within different libraries that you can load or even download from the Internet. Try some of the particle emitters from the Combustion particle library to familiarize yourself with the different particle emitters available within the software.

7   Save your work

- The saved workspaces from this exercise can be found in the *support_files* as *smokeWorkspace.cws*.

8   Close workspace

- Select **File → Close Workspace**.

Conclusion

You have now learned the basics of the Combustion software! You first learned the terminology and the interface of the software, and then you experimented with different operators, layers and particles to create a composite image to your liking.

Using what you have learned so far, you can now experiment on your own rendered sequences. In the next lesson, you will composite the layers you rendered in Lesson 30.

Lesson 31: Combustion

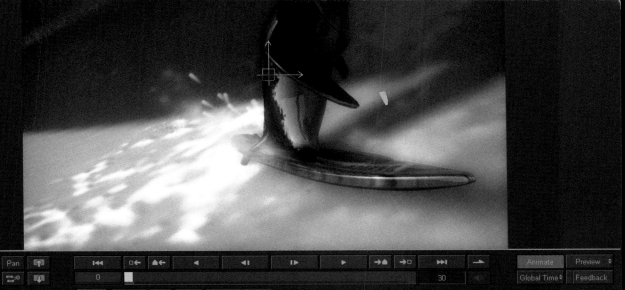

Pan ☐◄ ▲◄ ◄ ◄I I► ► →▲ →☐ ►►I →

0 30

Animate   Preview
Global Time   Feedback

Lesson 32
Compositing

In this lesson, you will assemble the different render layers created previously from the scenes
in this book. Doing so will allow you to practice with Combustion software, using real examples.
By the end of this lesson, you should be able to composite simple sequences and use additional
2D effects.

Building your first project

Now that you know Combustion software better, you will try to generate final images from the sequences you rendered in Lesson 30.

1   Footages

- In an empty workspace, select **File → Open**.

> **Note:** *Make sure Collapse is enabled in the Open dialog to collapse image sequences in one file, with the [#] symbol replacing the frame number.*

- Locate your own rendered sequences.

    OR

- Locate the rendered sequences from the *project5/images* of the *support_files*.

2   Select rendered layers

- Add the file *drops.[#].tif* from the *project5/images/dropsLayer* directory.
- Add the file *mist.[#].tif* from the *project5/images/mistLayer* directory.
- Add the file *geometry.[#].tif* from the *project5/images/geometryLayer* directory.

> **Tip:**   *The order in which you select the files will be the same order in which the layers are ordered. However, you can always reorder the layers in the workspace panel at any given time.*

The selected footage to be opened

> **Tip:** *You can **click+drag to the left or right** on a thumbnail in the Import Footage window to preview a clip.*

- Click the **OK** button.
- In the **Open Footage** window, select **2D Composite,** then click on the **OK** button.

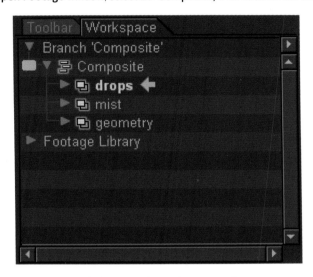

The layers in the workspace panel

Your now have a 2D composite branch comprised of the footage you imported.

- Press the **spacebar** to play the sequences.

  When a sequence is rendered, it is kept in memory and you can playback the computed frames in realtime.

> **Tip:** **RMB** *in the Info Palette and select* **Cache Meter** *to see the memory usage.*

3 Display time in frame numbers

By default, the Combustion software displays time in *timecode*. Since you are used to working with frames in the Maya software, it will be easier for you to set display time as frames instead of timecode.

- Select **File → Preferences** or press **Ctrl+;**.
- In the **Host → General** category, change the **Display Time As:** to **Frame (From 1)**.

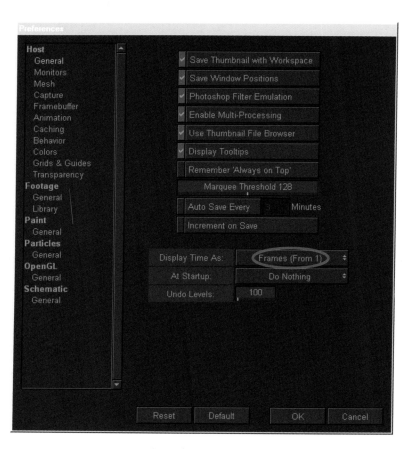

The Preferences window

- Click the **OK** button.

Tip: *To change the time display, you can also click the **Duration** field in the Playback Controls to toggle between **timecode** and **frames.***

Setting layer properties

1 Premultiplied color channel

The layers using an alpha channel have a black transition where the alpha is revealed. There is an option called **Premultiplied Color Channel,** which combines the color information with the alpha channel information by using a specific color as a base. You can enable this option to get a better alpha result on the layers that have an alpha channel.

- **Expand** the *mist* layer in the workspace panel and select the *Footage- mist[###]*

The Footage operator is highlighted

- In the **Footage Controls** panel, enable the **Premultiplied with** option.
- Make sure the color box next to the **Premultiplied with** option is set to **black**.

  Depending on this option, the application will calculate the alpha differently for a layer. The color channels combine the color information with the alpha channel information.

The Footage Controls panel

Note: *Try different settings for the* **Premultiplied with** *option to better see the difference in how the alpha is calculated.*

- **Repeat** this step for the *drops* layer if required.

2   **Change layer properties**

Layers have surface properties that determine how they appear in the composite and how they react to light. You can change the way a layer's surface is blended with the layers behind it by changing its **Transfer** mode. You can also change the **Opacity** of a layer to set a transparency. In this step, you will change some of the properties on each layer to get a better composite image.

Currently, the *mist* layer is on top of the *geometry* layer, hiding the board. You will now change the layer's transfer mode to reveal the board behind the mist.

- Select the *mist* layer.

- Click the **Layer** controls in the **Composite Controls** panel.

- Change the **Transfer Mode** to **Screen.**

  Notice how the mist layer blends with the geometry layer.

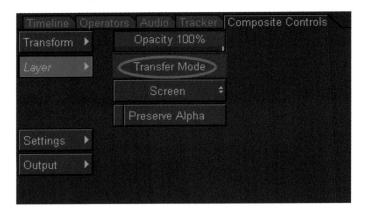

The Transfer Mode in the Layer controls

Note: *Try the other transfer modes to see how they react with the geometry layer.*

- **Repeat** the previous steps for the *drops* layer.

3   **Layer opacity**

As you are looking at your composite image, you may notice that the drops layer is a little too opaque. This can be fixed by changing the layer's opacity to make it more subtle.

- Select the *drops* layer.

- Click the **Layer** controls in the **Composite Controls** panel.
- Change the **Opacity** to **60%**.

4   Save the workspace
  - Select **File** → **Save Workspace**.
  - Give the workspace a name, such as *surfWorkspace_01*.
  - Click the **OK** button.

Working with operators

Now that you have a complete workspace set up with all your layers and good animation, it's time to refine the look of your 2D composite by applying some operators to the layers.

1   Add a glow
  The mist layer still doesn't look well integrated into the geometry layer at this time. To improve the look of the mist, you can add some operators to the layer.

  - Select the *mist* layer.
  - Add a **Glow** operator from the **Stylize** category in the Operators panel.
  - Select the **Operator Controls** panel to access the new operator's options.
  - Set the **Radius** value to **10.0**.
  - Set the **Strength** value to **2.0**.

2   Color correction
  As a final touch to the mist layer, you will change the color of the mist.

  - Select the *mist* layer.
  - **Add** a **Discreet Color Corrector** operator from the **Color Correction Category** of the **Operators** panel.
  - Select the **Operator Controls** panel.
  - Click the **Basics** button.
  - Set the **Gain** value of **RGB** to **200**.

  The mist is now improved.

The mist layer with operator on it

3 Turbulence

The mist layer is missing some detail, since it was created from default Maya particles. The following will add details to the layer without any need to render the sequence again in Maya software.

- Select the *mist* layer.

- Add a **Turbulence** operator from the **Noise** category of the Operator panel.

- Select the **Operator Control** panel to access the new operator's options.

- Set the following:

    Amount to **50%**;

    Octaves to **10**;

    Horizontal Scale to **5%**;

    Vertical Scale to **5%**.

*The mist is now less flat and homogeneous, but if you play the animation, the turbulence doesn't move. You need to animate the **Time Slice** value over the whole animation to correct this.*

- Go to the beginning of the clip at frame **1** by clicking the **Go to Start** button in the Playback Controls.

- Activate the **Animate** mode by pressing the **A** key.

Doing so enables keyframing and sets a keyframe with the current value at the current frame.

- Go to the end of the clip at frame **160** by clicking the **Go to End** button in the

Playback Controls.

- In the **Turbulence Controls** panel, set the **Time Slice** value to **1**.

Doing so sets a second keyframe at frame 160.

- Disable the **Animate** mode by pressing the **A** key again.

If you look in the Timeline panel, you will notice two new keyframes on the Time Slice channel.

The keyframes in the Timeline panel

4   Operator order

At this time, the Turbulence operator gets evaluated after the previously created Discreet Color Corrector. As a result, the mist seems darker. You will now reorder the operators so the turbulence gets evaluated before the other operators.

- **Click+drag** the **Turbulence** operator in the Workspace panel below the **Glow** operator.

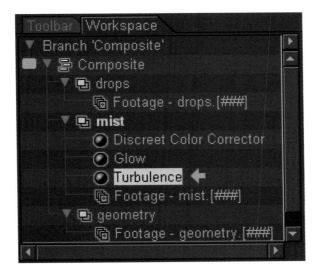

The reordered operators

Lesson 32: Compositing

5   **Drops glow**

- Select the *drops* layer.
- **Add** a **Glow** operator from the **Stylize** category of the **Operators** panel.
- Select the **Operator Controls** panel to access the **Glow** options.
- Set the **Radius** value to **1.5**.
- Set the **Strength** value to **2.0**.

The new drops color

6   **Apply operator on composite**

Until now, you have added operators on individual layers, but you can also add operators on the composite.

- Select the *Composite* layer.
- Add an **Add Noise** operator from the **Noise** category of the **Operators** panel.
- **Double-click** on the new **Add Noise** operator from the workspace panel to make it the current operator.

  A viewport icon shown next to the operator in the workspace panel indicates the Add Noise operator is the current operator.

- Select the **Operator Control** panel to access the **Add Noise** options.
- Set **Amount** to **4**.

  A small noise effect is added to the entire composite. This gives the image a grainy look similar to film grain. This effect usually increases the realism of computer graphic renders.

Project 05

The final composite

7 Continue to tweak the final composite

You can now spend some time exploring different ways to improve your composite. For instance, try adding a Glow operator to the Composite before the noise you have just added.

8 Save the workspace

- Select **File → Save Workspace As**.

- Give the workspace a name, such as *surfWorkspace_02*.

- Click the **OK** button.

Render your composite

Now that you are happy with the look of the final composite, it is time to render it out to disk. Rendering a composite in Combustion software is quite simple, but can sometimes take several minutes to complete.

- Select **File → Render**...

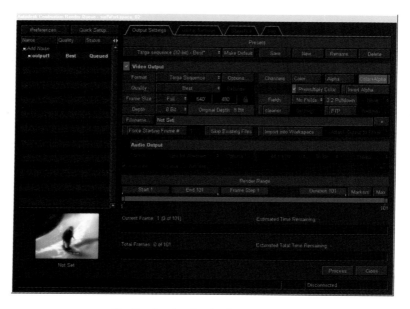

The Combustion Render Queue options

- Change the **Format** option to **Tiff Sequence** at the top of the window.
- Click the **Filename** button to choose a location for saving your final image sequence on your disk.

Tip: *If required, create a new folder to contain your new image sequence.*

- Enter a name, such as *composite.[#].tif*, in the **Filename** field at the bottom of the window.
- Click the **Process** button at the bottom of the Combustion Render Queue window.

  Doing so will start rendering the sequence output, giving each frame the name you have entered, followed by the frame number and file format extension.

- Once the sequence finishes rendering, click the **Close** button to close the Render Queue window.
- **Review** the output of your final composite images for the rendered project using an image sequence player such as the *fcheck* utility.

Note: *You can load the final rendered composite with fcheck from the project5/images/composite folder. You can also open the final workspace named surfWorkspace_02.cws.*

Conclusion

You have now completed a project using Combustion software with Maya renders. You have managed to tweak the layers without any need to render your sequences again with Maya software, thus saving lots of time.

It is now time to look back at everything you have achieved thus far with this book and see how your knowledge has grown. The real test is learning how to apply this knowledge in your day-to-day 3D tasks. This book has been designed to allow you to extrapolate what you have learned here and relate it to your specific project needs. Good luck with your future work!

Index

Notes

Revolutionary Visual Computing Solutions
The definition of performance. The standard for quality.

As a DCC professional, your workflow demands graphics solutions that keep up with your abilities. With NVIDIA Quadro® graphics solutions at your side, you can accelerate your projects all the way through the end of production.

For more information on NVIDIA solutions, please visit **www.nvidia.com**

THE MAGAZINE FOR 3D ARTISTS

If you're serious about 3D, you need 3D World. Each issue of this high-quality magazine comes packed with news, inspiration and practical advice for leading software packages, including 3ds Max, Maya, LightWave 3D, Cinema 4D and XSI

View the latest subscription offers online at:
www.myfavouritemagazines.co.uk

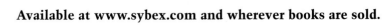